Making a Voice

Making a Voice

African Resistance to Segregation in South Africa

Joyce F. Kirk

WestviewPress

A Division of HarperCollins*Publishers*

African Modernization and Development Series

Copyright © 1998 by Westview Press, A Division of HarperCollins Publishers, Inc.

Published in 1998 in the United States of America by Westview Press, 5500 Central Avenue, Boulder, Colorado 80301-2877, and in the United Kingdom by Westview Press, 12 Hid's Copse Road, Cumnor Hill, Oxford OX2 9JJ

Library of Congress Cataloging-in-Publication Data
Kirk, Joyce F.
  Making a voice : African resistance to segregation in South Africa
/ Joyce F. Kirk
     p.   cm. — (African modernization and development)
  Includes bibliographical references (p.   ) and index.
  ISBN 0-8133-2769-5 (hardcover)
   1. Apartheid—South Africa—Port Elizabeth.   2. Port Elizabeth
(South Africa)—Race relations.   3. Social conflict—South Africa—
Port Elizabeth—History—20th century.   4. South Africa—Race
relations.   I. Title.   2. Series: African modernization and
development series.
DT2405.P68K57   1998
305.8'009687'52—dc21

                                                                    97-30476
                                                                       CIP

10   9   8   7   6   5   4   3   2   1

This book is dedicated to my mother,
and to my ancestors

Contents

Illustrations and Maps

Abbreviations

AAWMU	African and American Working Men's Union
AMEC	African Methodist Episcopal Church
ANC	African National Congress
AZM	American Board Zulu Mission
BBNA	Blue Book on Native Affairs
CAD	Cape Archives Depot
CO	Colonial Office
CT	Cape Times
EPH	Eastern Province Herald
ICU	Industrial and Commercial Workers' Union
Iliso Lomzi	Vigilance Association
Imbumuba	Imbumba Yama Nyama African Political Association
Imvo	Imvo Zabantsundu (Native Opinion)
KVMB	Korsten Village Management Board
LMS	London Missionary Society
MOH	Medical Officer of Health
MLA	Minister of Legislative Assembly
NAD	Native Affairs Department
PAD	Pretoria Archives
REVD	Reverend
SAP	South African Party
SNAD	Secretary of Native Affairs Department
SANNC	South African Native National Congress
UNIA	Universal Negro Improvement Association
VOC	Dutch East India Company

Acknowledgments

My first acknowledgement must go to my Mom for instilling in me the belief that I could accomplish my goals and insisting that education was the key to success. Next, I must thank my family, brothers, sisters, nieces, and nephews for being supportive through all the years it has taken me to complete this book. I must also thank the following: undergraduate teachers, Cathern Davis, and Erlie Burton at Malcolm X College, Chicago, Illinois. Sterling Plumpp, University of Illinois—Chicago Circle, for inspiring me with African literature and talk of the Limpopo river that germinated a burning desire to study African history and do research in South Africa. In graduate school the friendship of my sisters in spirit, Keletso Atkins, Lynda Day, Susan Grabler, Rene Tantala and Hazel Symonette and brothers in spirit, David Anthony, Jim Giblin, David Newbury, Jacob Mohlamme, and Mbudzeni Sibara. And other supportive friends: Carolyn McVeigh, Cheryl Johnson, Carline Edie, Helen May, Blandina Giblin, Fabu Carter, Donna Jones, Robert Dale, Robert Baum, Robert Rinfrow, Vincent Smith, Kweku Embil, members of the Zito Dance Troupe, and many others.

The three American professors that influenced me most were Steven Feierman, Jan Vansina, and Tom Shick (passed on). I thank you. The six months I stayed at Jan's house saved me financially and helped me to complete a considerable amount of microform reading. Steven Feierman exhibited great patience and fortitude in sending me taped comments to make corrections on the dissertation and being available exactly when I needed him most.

I want to thank Patrick Harries and Christopher Saunders for their hospitality each time I was in Cape Town, and Helen Bradford in both Johannesburg and Cape Town. Thanks to Gary Baines for helpful correspondence and deeds over the years. A special thanks and appreciation to my South African sister in spirit, Lindiwe Mzo, and also to Nenzi Plaatjes, Magala Ngatane, Poppy Huna, Puci Headbush, Teboho Moja, and Zola Vakalisa. And to my South African brothers in spirit Jeff Peires, Zweklakhe Tshandu, Trevor Mdaka and family, Moses Molapo (passed on), Wilmot James, Motepele Malebana, Ivan Evans, Nenzi and all the families in the eastern Cape, in particular, members of the Headbush family. In the Cape thanks to Celiwe and Celika, the sisters who helped me enormously with research and housing. A thousand thanks to Nozipho, my interpreter in Port Elizabeth, for introductions and interviews each time I did research in Port Elizabeth and for generous hospitality in the Cape, the Headbushes, the Mzoboshes, and the Evans. In the Transvaal, Andries and Gaby, Makgala Ngatane, Thapelo, Jackie, and most of all to Trevor Mdaka and family for helping me to settle in and conduct interviews in the Cape and Transvaal. In the U.S. thanks to Fred Cooper and Jane Burbank for their hospitality while I was on a fellowship at the University of Michigan in 1989. I apologize to any friends I failed to mention and ask their forgiveness.

I was affiliated with the African Studies Institute (now known as the Institute for Social and Economic Research) at the University of the Witwatersrand when doing field research in 1981–1983, 1987, and 1993. I appreciate assistance from Tim Couzens, Charles Van Onselen, Alan Mabin, and especially Phil Bonner. Many people at the University of Cape Town, University of Western Cape and Rhodes University offered assistance. A special thanks to Colin Bundy for assistance in Oxford and Cape Town and his offers of hospitality. And thanks to Stanley Trapido for hospitality during my first visit to Oxford. Thanks to Shula Marks, Saul Dubow and others who read my work for the *Journal of Southern African Studies.* I greatly appreciate the assistance of the staff of the libraries and archives, especially the South African library, Queen Victoria Street, Cape Town, Cape Archives, (the old and new locations), and University of the Witwatersrand.

For financial assistance towards completion of this project I acknowledge Title VI language fellowship 1981; Fulbright Hays, 1982; Ohio State University, Small Grant, 1985; Dubois, Mandela, Rodney fellowship, 1989; and Institute on Race and Ethnicity fellowship, 1990.

I want to thank all of my colleagues at the University of Wisconsin-Milwaukee, Department of Africology for the enormous support in providing a nurturing and pleasant work environment and moral support in completing my book manuscript. They are the best colleagues around the academy.

I acknowledge the following for permission to reprint portions of Chapter 2, 4 and 6. Parts of Ch. 2 of the present work appeared in a slightly different version as "Race, Class, Liberalism and Conflict: Resistance to Segregation in Port Elizabeth, 1880–1884," in *International Journal of African Historical Studies* 24 (1991): 293–321 by Boston University Press, Boston, MA.; Parts of Ch. 4 of the present work appeared as "Africans and Black Americans in Pan-Economic Cooperation in Nineteenth Century South Africa," in *Paths Toward the Past*, edited by Joseph Miller, David Newbury, by African Studies Association Press, 1994, pp. 325–344,

Atlanta, GA.;Parts of Ch. 6 appeared in a different version as "A 'Native' Free State at Korsten: Challenges to Segregation in Port Elizabeth, 1901–1905," in *Journal of Southern African Studies* 17 (1991): 309–336. Journal of Southern African Studies, Carfax Publishing Limited PO Box 25, Abingdon Oxfordshire OX14 3UE UK

Preface

This book emerged from my dissertation topic, not at the beginning of field research that began in October, 1981 but almost at the end of a year in South Africa. The topic evolved when, in order to better understand the history of the Industrial and Commercial Worker's Union (ICU) in the Eastern Cape and the Transvaal, my original research focus, I felt I should know more about the period prior to its formation. Consequently, I began to read about the conditions of life in Port Elizabeth, where Masabalala had led the 1920 ICU strike. In doing so, I realized that Africans in Port Elizabeth, especially the western-educated leadership, had been struggling a long time for basic civil and political rights that did not specifically touch the wage struggle, which was the initial focus of the ICU.

I soon found myself drawn toward a study of the struggle between the black population in Port Elizabeth and the white local and central government over African ownership of land and housing and residential segregation in the town. It became increasingly clear that this struggle was much more than a conflict between the government and Africans over the geographical location of black workers. Rather, there were fundamental questions at issue not only about control of the workforce but also about who would determine where and under what conditions Africans would live; who would pay for the reproduction of the black labor force in Port Elizabeth—the employers, the local government or the workers themselves; and to what extent Africans would be incorporated into the colonial economy, as equals or as exploited labor. A major obstacle to the government resolving these questions was the existence of an emerging black middle class that was in the forefront of resistance to the erosion of their political, economic, and civil rights, especially land rights, in the urban areas. In their protest against exploitation they invariably prevented blanket exploitation of the black working class.

Secondly personal reasons also influenced my decision to focus on the struggle over residential segregation. During the time I was in South Africa doing my field research, from October 1, 1981 to January 23, 1983, I travelled through all four of the provinces, as they were at that time, (Transvaal, Orange Free State, Natal and The Cape) and lived in the Transvaal and the Cape for periods of three to six months. Because I am an African American, and I share many features of many black South African women, e.g. skin color, cheekbones, body build, and height (I also wear my hair in a short, natural hairstyle), I faced, at least initially, until they heard my "American" accent, racial discrimination from many whites.

A continuous and crucial problem for me was housing, because the laws of South Africa sanctioned racial discrimination and residential segregation. Although these laws, for example the Population Registration Act and the Group Areas Act, have since been abolished, de facto discrimination continues, albeit much more covertly). Even though I often stayed in the black areas, situated between 15 and 30 kilometers from the towns, there were times when I needed to be closer to the archives and library. This was nearly an impossible feat, and when it was possible it required that I and others whom I resided with, including coloreds (designation for mixed race people in South Africa) and whites continuously break the laws of the land.

As a result, I was made vividly aware of the extreme importance of everyday, basic amenities, such as where one eats and sleeps and performs personal hygiene and with whom one interacts. I had realized intellectually the effects of racial segregation and apartheid and that where one lives is closely related to much broader subjects associated with class, race, power, finances, use of space, and reproduction of labor. Yet the personal experience and pain of the effects of insults while searching, sometimes frantically, for housing, enhanced my understanding and made me want to examine more closely the rise of racial laws and practices sanctioning residential segregation and racial discrimination.

I found that many larger questions needed consideration, questions that few had focused on, about the late nineteenth and early twentieth century, particularly the role of Africans and their impact on the process of establishing and enforcing discriminatory laws in the Cape. Port Elizabeth evolved as the focus because of the wealth of sources and because of the hospitality that met me there. As I interviewed men and women about the ICU, I sensed that behind the establishment of the union lay a rich story of how the black population emerged in Port Elizabeth, of how the class and ethnic differences evolved and how a base for the rise of the ICU was laid in the struggle over the "place" Africans would occupy in the town. Prior to the establishment of the New Brighton township, a long and established black community had emerged at Strangers' location in the nineteenth century and it was this factor that led me to examine the social relations among and between the "races" as they struggled over residential segregation.

In 1987 I successfully defended my dissertation and the next summer, I returned to South Africa as an assistant professor, rather than a graduate student, to do more research. I again confronted the usual difficulties of finding housing in a segregated society. Perhaps if I relate an episode I had with an English woman in Cape Town, who was willing to rent an apartment over the telephone to an American visitor, but not to a black American in person, the point will hit home. I had called to inquire about the apartment, and we set a time to meet. Upon seeing me, Mrs. Smith, said "Oh, you sounded so American." I responded: "I am American!" It is interesting that if I were in the United States, I probably would never have uttered these words so emphatically, given the treatment of African Americans in this country. We viewed the apartment, which was in a white area not far from the Cape archives and agreed that I would take it. We arranged to meet the next morning and make final financial arrangements.

A few hours later she called to say that a man who was interested in the apartment wanted the place for an extended period and she felt that he must supersede me since I was staying a shorter period, unless I could pay for the entire month. I agreed to pay a month's rent, but I must admit that the chip on my shoulder began to throb when I heard her voice on the phone. However, I was pleased that she only wanted to change the arrangements. When I returned to the living room my "colored" friends were waiting to hear what Mrs. Smith had said. I had already told them that I had found a place to live and the circumstances, when Mrs. Smith called, so they were anticipating a negative message. We were all relieved we admitted that she had not called to cancel out.

Mrs. Smith called back 45 minutes later. She said in a very nervous voice that she had talked to her husband about my staying in the apartment and they felt that it was just not something they could do because the other tenants might complain, and so on. She said, "If it were up to me, it would be fine. I'm not a racist." She apologized several times and said to me, "I do hope that you understand." I said, "Yes, of course, but you shouldn't have agreed if you were going to change your mind." We hung up. I was furious, hurt, and disgusted, and I complained bitterly to my friends about the apartheid system of racial segregation. They viewed my predicament with sympathy but were not at all surprised that Mrs. Smith had backed out. I cannot honestly say that I was surprised either, only that I had hoped that the situation had changed since 1983 so that I could obtain housing closer to the archives. Eventually, I located satisfactory housing on the University of Cape Town campus, at the medical school dorms for two weeks, and then at the guest faculty housing for a month. I resolved to put the apartment episode behind me.

However, every time someone asks me about "honorary" white status for foreign blacks in South Africa, (during the time of official apartheid, when I was doing my research), I think of Mrs. Smith and others who continually treated me as a non-person, as they did most black people in South Africa.

Thus academic and personal reasons influenced my decision to study African resistance to residential segregation in South Africa. My personal experiences in South Africa, good and bad, have sustained me when I felt at times that the project was too unwieldy and unending. My primary objective was to show how African resistance always influenced the government schemes and legislation to impose segregation in the urban area and sometimes dramatically reshaped the envisioned policy and even prevented implementation.

A note on terminology in this book. The terminology for the most part is explained in the Introduction. When I use the term "black" it applies to black South Africans, unless otherwise noted, since during most of the period of the study some separation existed between the coloreds and black South Africans. I use black and African interchangeably. I have used the word "kafir" in parentheses since, it was in general an insulting term applied to the Xhosas and later to all Africans. The term "colored" first appears in parentheses with an explanation and thereafter without. "King Williams Town" appears on Map 1.1. as three words, but in the text is written as one word, "Kingwilliamstown", since this is the common usage in South Africa.

1

Introduction: Segregation, Labor, Ideology, and the Emergence of African Working and Middle Classes in Port Elizabeth

Introduction

This book is concerned with the resistance of Africans to the appropriation of their land, labor, and power as the process of urban residential segregation unfolded during the colonial years in South Africa. African resistance to government policies to impose racial segregation and discrimination has a long history in Southern Africa. An early site of African protest, Port Elizabeth, is a town in the eastern Cape, an area that includes the Ciskei and Transkei, located about 700 miles from Cape Town. In 1820, Port Elizabeth was given its name by Sir Rufane Donkin, the Acting Governor of the Cape, in honor of his beloved and deceased wife.[1] That same year, five thousand British settlers arrived, assisted by Donkin and other colonial administrators to become stockfarmers on land won in the Cape-Xhosa wars in the eastern Cape. Many of the settlers, unsuccessful as farmers, moved to the small towns such as Port Elizabeth *(eBhayi)*.[2] It was a British-controlled town that had passed segregationist legislation before the second half of the nineteenth century to formally separate Africans from whites.

Critics of the apartheid (racial and territorial separation) government that took power in 1949 have often cited the strategies used by the Afrikaners (mainly the descendants of Dutch speakers) against the African population to maintain white supremacy in the twentieth century. These strategies included forced removals, relocations, and resettlements to ensure territorial segregation in both rural and urban areas. But in the nineteenth century—and long before the apartheid state and the entrenchment of Afrikaner nationalism—these strategies were part of local government initiatives to impose residential segregation in the

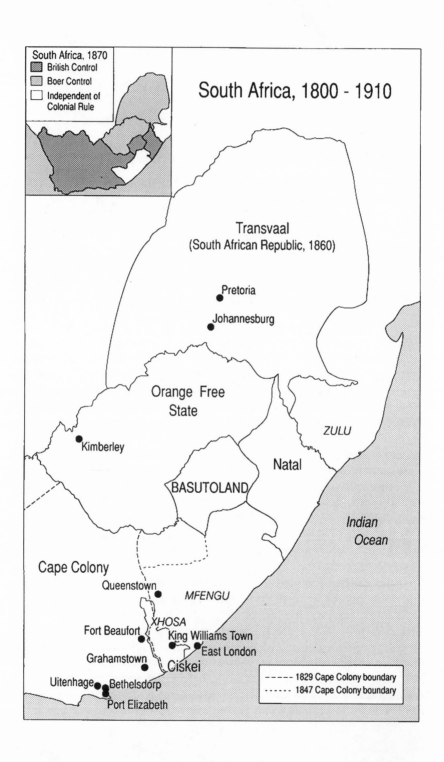

South Africa, 1870
British Control
Boer Control
Independent of
Colonial Rule

South Africa, 1800 - 1910

Transvaal
(South African Republic, 1860)

● Pretoria
● Johannesburg

Orange Free
State

ZULU

● Kimberley

Natal

BASUTOLAND

Indian
Ocean

Cape Colony

Queenstown
● MFENGU

XHOSA
Fort Beaufort ●
King Williams Town ●
● East London

Grahamstown ●
Ciskei

Uitenhage ● ● Bethelsdorp
● Port Elizabeth

----- 1829 Cape Colony boundary
······ 1847 Cape Colony boundary

towns of the British-controlled Cape colony. It is to these small towns that we must look for the beginnings of urban segregationist policies. It is in areas like Port Elizabeth that the tradition of resistance to segregation emerged. Sadly, the history of this struggle has been neglected and this book serves to begin to fill that gap.

Residential Segregation, Racial Discrimination, Exploitation, and African Agency

This book presents the first in-depth study of African resistance to residential segregation in Port Elizabeth that aimed to deprive them of their land, labor, and power as the process of establishing racial segregation unfolded during the years 1855–1910. Just as local governments developed segregationist policies that would be repeated in other places in South Africa, so, too, did African men and women develop strategies and tactics of resistance to combat racial discrimination and segregation. Time and time again, African protest thwarted and reshaped the political, economic and social schemes of the colonial government that sought to establish white domination, which included imposing residential segregation. To combat these attempts to control their rights to land, property, housing, and free movement, Africans used a variety of methods. They made use of petitions, deputations (selected representatives sent to government officials to present grievances), strikes, voting, alliances with white liberals, alliances with African Americans, and the establishment of their own organizations and businesses. Furthermore, the tactics used by Africans at Port Elizabeth set a precedent for similar types of resistance to segregation and apartheid that were employed elsewhere in a later period.[3]

Residential segregation is a crucial stage in the process of establishing institutional racial discrimination. In fact, residential segregation frequently lays the groundwork to ensure other types of systematic exploitation in the socioeconomic and political arenas. Often the physical separation of a population is part of an interlocking process that is accompanied by restrictions on ownership of land and property, political rights and power, occupational and educational choices, business opportunities, use of public transportation, recreation, and other social practices. Thus, residential segregation plays an enabling role in allowing other forms of racial oppression. "Residential segregation is the institutional apparatus that supports other racially discriminatory processes and binds them together into a coherent and uniquely effective system of racial subordination."[4]

From the beginning of the conflict two major issues provided the basis for a continuing struggle between the government and the African population in urban areas. These were (1) whether Africans would be permitted to own land and (2) to what extent the government would shape and control the material and social lives of black workers. Residential segregation and rights to own land and property, including housing, were closely linked in creating an exploited and subordinate black population on the one hand and a wealthier and dominant white one on the other. So, almost from the start, the efforts of the white governmental authorities to residentially segregate Africans was aimed not only at restricting and controlling living spaces, but also depriving blacks of rights to land and property ownership in the urban area, and dictating their working conditions. Consequently, African protest against residential segregation was often accompanied by demands for land and property rights, sanitary living conditions, and working class actions such as strikes and boycotts to gain higher salaries and an improved working environment.

In understanding the concerted resistance by the African population at Port Elizabeth I will try to analyze African agency[5] (actions), and the forms it took during these crucial years; the goal is to increase our understanding of the importance of this period in creating a tradition of African resistance. By African agency I mean examining the events by asking about African perspectives and standards of that time based on pre-colonial African customs among the Xhosa, prior to interaction with the Dutch, beginning around the 1770s in the eastern Cape. Xhosa speakers were the largest African presence in Port Elizabeth during this period 1855–1910, primarily because the "frontier" was geographically close to the town.

Of course, the writer realizes that no society is stagnant and that the descriptions of Xhosa customs may freeze them in place and thus be imperfect yet they provide us with a ground base of African experiences. Moreover, the aim is to examine the complexity of African responses and actions and what influences, for example, associated with age, gender, religion, kinship, culture, and hierarchy led black men and women at particular times to take actions that slowed the process of residential segregation and the interconnected oppressions. At times we hear in the sources the "voice" of African men and women as they tried to make sense of the assaults on their lifestyle, by the white colonists in general and government officials in particular.

What happened in Port Elizabeth is important not only because of its reputation as a center of protest but also because similar struggles between the black population and the local government were unfolding over racially discriminatory legislation in disparate parts of South Africa. As one of the largest towns in the Cape colony prior to the mineral discoveries—diamonds in 1867 and gold in 1886—the segregationist practices initiated by the white local government were representative of a pattern of racial practices and discrimination that emerged in other towns in the nineteenth and twentieth centuries to create the racial segregationist patterns for which South Africa has become infamous. Thus, the passage of laws to curb African movement and residence, occupations, transportation, education, business opportunities, recreation, land ownership, and political rights, were part of a process that emerged in Port Elizabeth by the last half of the nineteenth century. Consequently, by the time the four colonies of the Cape, Natal, the Orange Free State and the Transvaal (later changed to the South African Republic), merged in 1910 into the Union of South Africa much of the segregationist rhetoric and practices had been tried at Port Elizabeth. The architects of segregation and later apartheid therefore had a partial blueprint drawn from local laws and practices experimented with in Cape colonial towns like Port Elizabeth. Thus, the findings here hold a much deeper resonance.

Port Elizabeth's Reputation for Resisting Segregation in the Twentieth Century

The city of Port Elizabeth has long had a reputation as a stronghold of African resistance to government policies as well as that of a liberal town where Africans faced fewer government restrictions. However, most studies that explore the events that contributed to that reputation focus on the period after 1910. Among the activities examined have been those of the tenacious Port Elizabeth branch of the first black trade union formed in 1918, the Industrial and Commercial Workers' Union (ICU); the establishment in the 1940s of several trade unions and the strikes and bus boycott that followed; and the role of the Port Elizabeth branch of the African National Congress in the 1950s Defiance Campaign, which was an organized protest against apartheid laws.[6] More recently, Port Elizabeth was the focus of a video entitled *Changing This Country* that depicts the trade union movement in the 1980s and African protest against apartheid.

It is also noteworthy that historians have offered a number of explanations for the propensity of Africans at Port Elizabeth to resist segregation. These include the ethnic homogeneity of the black population, the majority of whom speak Xhosa; the sizeable working population who lived with their families, and the relatively large number of female residents; family housing as opposed to compounds for single migrant workers; the conversion of a good number of blacks to Christianity; the more relaxed legal environment, in particular the absence of influx control (restraints on Africans entering the towns); Cape liberalism (this concept will be explained later in this chapter); and finally, "the deep historical roots of modern political culture."[7]

"The deep historical roots of modern political culture" is perhaps the key phrase underscoring all of the other reasons, but to my knowledge it has yet to be adequately explored. I propose that only by analyzing the seeds of these deep historical roots and their relationship to residential segregation that were nurtured in the initial period of African resistance in Port Elizabeth can we determine just how important the various factors were or were not in producing a political culture. While scholars have recently begun to address the struggle between the black population and the local government over residential segregation, most of the work has focused on the twentieth century.[8] Also, even if the past studies do focus on the growth of segregation during the nineteenth century, they tend to discuss the outcome as a given—as if a policy of segregation were easily implemented. So although we have data that examine how urban residential segregation emerged prior to the formation of the Union of South Africa in 1910, we know little about how African agency or actions shaped that process.

The timing of urban residential segregation was influenced by the particular historical circumstances of white and African interaction, economic development, geographical region, population size, and African and white settlement. Before the discovery of minerals, Port Elizabeth, Cape Town, and East London (all port towns) were among the few large commercial areas with populations in excess of 10,000. Places such as these where initial attempts occurred to formally segregate the black labor force in "locations" or (reserves) were the first to experience the changes in the economy: from pre-colonial primarily subsistence production to colonial commercial production; the growth of commercial capitalism; and the beginnings of urbanization.

It is noteworthy that at first, locations referred to the land in the frontier or rural areas that the colonial government designated as separate and segregated areas for Africans. These locations were established at different times in both the Cape and Natal colonies, often as a result of wars between Europeans and Africans. As different African groups began to lose these wars more often than they won them, their lands were demarcated, and they were increasingly forced to live in limited reserves. Established over time in both rural and urban areas, these locations became labor pools for the South African government but provided only an economically marginal living for their occupants. Meanwhile, the colonial government allowed white settlers and land speculators to make large and virtually unrestricted land claims. In the urban areas, the term "locations" was used by colonial government officials in reference to residential settlements occupied by Africans, although for a time other groups were allowed to trade and sometimes live in these areas on a restricted basis. Eventually, as residential segregation evolved, the term "African

Township" began to be substituted or used interchangeably with locations to designate segregated residential areas for blacks (and in some cases "Coloreds" [mixed-race], hereafter Coloreds, and Indians).[9]

It was in these areas, such as Port Elizabeth, where the first generation of an African working class and African middle class began to emerge that urban locations were initially set up by the colonial government. These towns were also among the first to experience conflict over African settlements and segregated housing. Just as the formation of a black working class began early in these colonial towns, so, too, did the class struggle between workers and the state over the use and control of urban space, land and property rights, constraints on the movement of the labor force, problems of overcrowding, and the unhealthy living and housing conditions. Although the evidence for organized African resistance in urban areas points to the period beginning around 1880, the earliest efforts by British officials to impose segregation must be examined to set the stage for the later period. Thus, it is necessary to provide a brief backdrop.

Early Settlement and Segregation Initiatives

Port Elizabeth was laid out in 1815, and, not surprisingly, the arrival in 1820 of the British settlers in the eastern Cape led to an increased population. Established as a port town, it functioned to handle and later process the goods and materials passing through the harbor and to meet the market needs of the hinterland. The settlement grew as a result of the expansion of trade, particularly the development of pastoral (livestock raising, especially cattle and sheep) activities in the interior of South Africa after the 1840s and then mining in the 1870s and 1880s. (See Map 1.1)

By 1855 the population of Port Elizabeth was approximately 3,509 Europeans and 1,284 Coloreds (Africans). Although the population was small, Port Elizabeth was one of the largest commercial towns in the Cape colony. For example, the town was the major port for exporting wool, which was the hinterland's premier agricultural crop. In 1868 the port reached its commercial peak, exporting over 17 million kilograms, or 82 percent, of the Cape's products. In fact, Port Elizabeth was considered the "Liverpool of the Cape."[10]

As Port Elizabeth grew in size and population a municipal body was formed and a Board of Commissioners or Town Councillors was elected in 1847. This all-male, all-white body, drawn primarily from the mercantile elite, issued the first formal regulation, in 1848, to separate the African population from the European townspeople.[11] For a range of reasons, the location was not established until seven years later; it was designated to

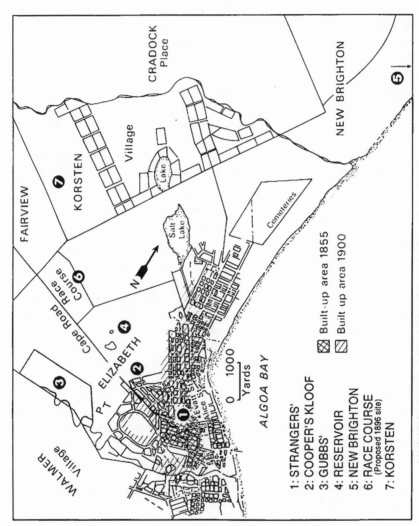

MUNICIPAL AND PRIVATE LOCATIONS · 1855-1905

1: STRANGERS'
2: COOPER'S KLOOF
3: GUBBS'
4: RESERVOIR
5: NEW BRIGHTON
6: RACE COURSE (Proposed 1896 site)
7: KORSTEN

Built-up area 1855
Built up area 1900

Table 1.1 Population of Port Elizabeth 1855–1911[a]

Year	Africans	Coloreds[b]	Whites	Total
1855		1,284	3,509	4,793
1865	1,716	2,117	6,940	10,733
1875	1,867	2,454	8,728	13,049
1891	4,258	6,481	13,785	23,266
1904	9,750	9,432	22,336	42,063
1911	8,058	12,746	18,973	39,777

Notes: a. The Asian population was usually included in some other group and was approximately 2,000.

b. Both Coloreds and Africans were grouped together for the 1855 count.

Source: Cape of Good Hope Parliamentary Papers, Census reports (1857, 1866, 1876, 1892, 1905a); Union of South Africa Parliamentary Papers, U. G. 32-1912; Following Gary Baines, "New Brighton, Port Elizabeth c 1903–1953: A History of an Urban African Community" (Ph.D. diss., University of Cape Town, 1994), p. 14, Table 2.1 the 1904 and 1911 figures have been adjusted to include Korsten and New Brighton since the African populations in these areas were excluded from the official census.

be upon land that the Cape colonial government granted to the Municipality. During the time between the first initiative and the establishment in 1855 of the Strangers' location, as the black settlement was called, it is possible to trace how local issues including land, housing, military, labor, and social control drove the officials' decision to try to impose residential segregation.[12]

When the Board of Commissioners attempted to segregate the Africans from the whites, the primary consideration was controlling the widespread practice of Africans squatting (settling on empty land) on town commonage and private property and erecting their houses. This practice brought white complaints about the right of Africans to live in different areas in an unrestricted manner. In fact, many whites were clearly worried about the African population rising beyond the acceptable ratio, or "crucial number" as whites termed it.[13] It is likely that whites also worried that property values would decline if too many blacks lived near them.

Other white fears were fed by the fact that Port Elizabeth was geographically situated near the frontier where independent African territories existed. Therefore, it was plausible that the town could be overrun by the "Kafirs," the term used by whites to refer to the Xhosas, as had occurred in the 1834–35 war when the Xhosa had attacked the settler towns. Thus, also influencing this attempt to impose residential segregation in 1848 was the whites' anxiety about defending the town. Apparently safety from "Kafirs" beyond the town's boundaries continued to preoccupy white townspeople since, according to Redgrave, a census of the population was taken on April 11, 1846, to determine "what amount of manpower could be mustered in case of a sudden attack on the town by hostile Kafirs."[14] Moreover, these fears were not groundless, since military conflict between the Europeans and Africans continued in the Ciskei, although several hundred miles away.

Another white complaint related to the "sanitation syndrome," a metaphor for racial discrimination that Maynard Swanson has discussed for the turn-of-the-century Cape colony.[15] Indirect evidence that ideas about sanitation and race provided fodder for the formal segregation of the Africans is discernable from the topics discussed by the white townspeople prior to the formation of the first Board of Commissioners in 1846. Included was talk about cleaning up the town, carting away household refuse and "putting order in what was chaos," and establishing a municipality and a police force to deal especially with the "unruly element" including the Colored community, whose number were rapidly increasing.[16] That unsanitary conditions were not unusual in these early towns such as Port Elizabeth is made clear by Redgrave's statement that "Little Bess (Port Elizabeth) was shamefully but correctly described in the (eighteen) forties as an unkempt and dirty fishing village and that she was styled as being nothing more than a large piggery."[17] Neither was the conclusion that it was the poor, and especially those of darker-skinned color, who were more to blame than anyone else. Not surprisingly, less than a year after the establishment of the location in 1855, Port Elizabeth passed its first Health Act. Thus, from the beginning Africans, control and sanitation were linked in Port Elizabeth with the establishment of legislation to create wider powers for the whites and to create a segregated location aimed at curbing the power of blacks.

Yet another reason underlying the segregationist initiative that assumed urgency in the 1850s was the question of exerting some type of control over the independence of the African labor force. Three strikes, by the African port workers illustrated the problem; one in 1846, the other in 1852 and yet other in 1854. Since Port Elizabeth had no harbor, the town was almost completely dependent upon these workers. Produce had to be unloaded from ships anchored in the bay and shipped in lighters (small boats) to the open beach. Without the port workers ships and passengers could neither be loaded or unloaded. The labor was arduous and intensive, and the "workers demanded higher wages once they realized their bargaining power."[18] On the surface white ability to dictate the place and conditions under which Africans should live, had little to do with containing the port worker strikes. On second glance, however, it could relate to the production of a colonial culture that required establishing the legitimacy of the local government and curbing the power of the workers. The idea of exerting power, control, and discipline, of creating a certain type of dependency, a dispossession, and respect for the law among Africans, was important to the idea and practice of white dominance and superiority. Thus, whites sought to establish colonial laws in the urban areas, much as they had done in the rural areas, to exert control over the black population through legislation.

By the 1840s the black work force was made up primarily of the Mfengu (Fingo), the first large group of Africans to take up wage labor in Port Elizabeth. Their total number was perhaps 444 men, women and children, mostly men.[19] The Mfengu were viewed and treated as allies of the Europeans, since they had taken sides against the Xhosa in the 1846 war, between the British and the Xhosas. It is worth noting that the Cape-Xhosa wars were seldom simply black versus white; rather the Khoikhoi and Xhosa had been allies of the Europeans in all previous wars, but Switzer correctly states that it was the Mfengu who became the prime allies and greatly aided the British in all subsequent wars after 1834. Significantly, the Mfengu were rewarded with Xhosa land in the eastern Cape and also were exempted from the colonial law requiring "natives" to carry passes to enter the colony.[20]

The larger Mfengu population in Port Elizabeth helps to explain why the municipal authorities envisioned removing the informal "Fingo" village, one of four sites where Africans resided in self-constructed huts in the 1840s, to a new site.[21] The authorities surveyed 144 plots and decided to allow the erection of "Fingo-style" huts. The Board of Commissioners hoped to contain all the Africans in one settlement, including new arrivals entering Port Elizabeth to work, as well as to restrict those already squatting on the town commonage and on private properties.

Between 1846 and 1855 the African population increased from approximately 595 to 1,284 adding to the number that would require segregation. The 1855 census does not include a breakdown by ethnic group, so we cannot be sure how much the 1846 numbers were supplemented by the Xhosa wage-earners rather than the Mfengu. Yet clearly the increased number of Africans in the town was related to the loss of land as a result of wars between and among whites and blacks. As the African work-seekers entered the Cape colony, including Port Elizabeth, many of them settled on the outskirts of town.

Playing into the whites' fears for their safety were the popularly accepted images of Africans as dark-skinned "savages." The evidence from Port Elizabeth is sketchy on popular images, but it is clear that whites were critical of the lifestyle of some of the Africans in the town. J. J. Redgrave discloses that in the 1840s in Port Elizabeth whites complained about the lack of clothing worn by Africans. This was a frequent refrain, since port workers were often naked. Whites also lamented about the "faction" (fighting between Africans, not necessarily but often by ethnic groups) fights, drunkenness, and crime.[22]

Invariably, then and later, the government justified attempts to segregate the workers by stating that it was for the benefit of Africans because their housing and living conditions would be improved. The government did build a model cottage at the site with the idea that Africans would build their structures along this line. But the government did not provide houses, building equipment, or sanitation at the settlement, so "improved living conditions" was a dubious claim.

The Creation of Strangers' Location

The initial regulation the Board issued in 1848 included a stipulation with regard to the site where "native huts" or housing could be erected. That same year the Board also made use of a colonial government proclamation authorizing "native" locations within one or two miles of the town center or village, to create a separate site where Africans would be required to reside.[23] The local colonial authorities encouraged Africans to move to the site called the "Native Strangers' Location" (hereafter Strangers') situated at the edge of town.[24] (Map 1.2) Although the law did not actually compel Africans to live there, they could be forcefully evicted and their dwellings torn down if they did not move. Newspaper reports indicate that plots were offered for lease, and within three months most were taken.[25] Despite these newspaper reports it is also apparent that many Africans responded to the regulation with studied inactivity and refused to move until they were coerced. In a sense it was the first forced removal of Africans, since police moved some of them to the area.

Plots at Strangers' were offered on a 21-year lease rather than on freehold (individual ownership of land), suggesting that the local government officials were ambivalent about freehold for Africans near the town. The stipulation that the land be leased rather than owned also indicates that as "strangers," the Africans were considered to be temporary workers rather than permanent workers who would return to their homes and land in the countryside. In other words, the whites viewed the Africans as strangers' who were in the white controlled colony to work temporarily and as such were not entitled to landrights in the town nor did they require landrights since their permanent place was in the countryside.

The twofold response by Africans, some taking up the plots while others refused to move to Strangers' signifies that already in the town views were split on accepting formal residential segregation in return for land sites and improved housing. Some Africans, especially longer-term Christian residents, might have welcomed the resettlement. Other Africans who were temporary target workers, and uninterested in land

and improved housing in the town, would not. This dichotomy between the African population was a recurring theme. Also, the voluntary and involuntary movement by Africans into Strangers' probably stems from the seven year lapse in the proposal for segregation by the Port Elizabeth Board of Commissioners and the actual establishment of Strangers' Location. In any case, the Board's aim to house all Africans at Strangers' location could not be realized since, by the time the regulations were enforced, the black population had increased beyond the capacity of the site. A problem with government delays in implementing legislation to racially segregate Africans from the whites and trying to force blacks to occupy overcrowded locations would also become a reoccurring problem.

The creation of Stranger's in 1855 represented the beginnings of formal urban residential segregation in the Cape. Similarly, as pointed out by A. J. Christopher, African locations were established or enlarged in the eastern Cape towns of Grahamstown, Cradock, and Graaff-Reinet in 1855.[26] This was no coincidence, but resulted from changes in the political economy.

The Wider Colonial Initiatives Influencing Segregation

During the seven-year lapse there were several important political changes in the wider colonial society that affected segregation initiatives. Among others, the Cape British colony attained representative government in 1853, the Ciskei Xhosa were militarily conquered in the eighth Cape-Xhosa war in 1852–1853, and the power of their chiefs was undermined. In the eastern cape among the conquered Xhosa, locations and reserves were set up. The new administrative entity of British Kaffaria consisting of territories that had been claimed by the Xhosa in the Ciskei beyond the Fish River set the stage for the white penetration and entrenchment to take root in towns like Port Elizabeth. The Xhosa territories were broken up, and British administration through indirect rule, was established. British officials, called Magistrates or Commissioners, were brought in to administer the Ciskei and Transkei territories, now British Kaffaria. The chiefs were awarded salaries, thus owing their position to the British officials. Not surprisingly, these changes began to erode the position of the chiefs in Xhosa society and to enhance the authority of the British. These alterations were the brainchild of Sir George Grey, the new Governor of the Cape colony, and his policy was called "civilization." The goals were twofold. First to provide a plentiful, docile and cheap labor force for the whites and second, to undermine the Xhosa social institutions in which the chief was the pivotal authority.[27] But since the political, economic, and social were so closely intertwined in Xhosa society, Grey's plan of "civilization" aimed to destroy these institutions which were the basis of pre-colonial Xhosa society.

"Civilization" entailed the establishment of alternative institutions for the Xhosa and required new ways of thinking. Grey believed that this could be accomplished through mission education. To this end, Grey offered grants of money and land to the missionaries, and several mission schools were established in the eastern cape and opened to boys and girls. Western customs accompanied missionary teachings, and the Africans were encouraged by the whites to reject the African lifestyle and replace it with the western. Thousands did so, many seeking spiritual explanations for their defeat and decline in colonial society. It is noteworthy that it would be from among these mission-educated Africans that the leaders would emerge to lead the protest against racial discrimination and exploitation.

Colonial legislation that facilitated the establishment of Strangers' location at Port Elizabeth, the role of the state that is so crucial in determining time and degree of exploitation of particular politically subordinate groups was enhanced with the "civilization" policy. The Church, bible, civilizing policies and western practices lined up against the Xhosa to undermine their ideological and cosmological beliefs and sought to replace them with a new version of European civilization.

The attempts by government to establish residential segregation were influenced by several factors including: regional diversity in initial contact between the whites and the Africans, differences in the conditions of black settlements in the town, the size and permanency of the African population, and the degree of urbanization as well as shifts in the South African economy. Despite variations in these factors there were two fundamental questions that had to be answered by the colonial government. First, what would be the status of Africans in the towns in the social, economic, and political arena? That is, would they be incorporated into the colonial economy and colonial life or isolated from the whites? Second, how could the movement of African "strangers" into, within, and out of the towns be controlled so that the workforce would be put to optimal use?

Answers to the foregoing questions changed over time and depended upon the nature of the local economy. Nevertheless, during the nineteenth century the local authority's usual response to these questions with regard to the status and control of Africans was to try to restrict the movement of labor by legislating segregated housing for Africans in the form of locations at Port Elizabeth and compounds (single-sex, barrack-like housing) at Kimberley.[28]

Despite the regional interests and concerns that gave rise to segregation in these two different towns, both types of housing were meant to control the movement and labor of Africans by containing them within stipulated boundaries. In neither case did rigid segregation occur, but the groundwork was laid for further formal separation of the races.

The significant point here is that prior to large-scale industrialization, mineral discoveries, and the use of racial science to justify segregation, the British local government at Port Elizabeth tried to formally segregate African workers. Thus, earlier studies that implied that white racist attitudes and the decision to segregate Africans coincided with the mineral discoveries come up short.[29] Similarly, a more complex explanation is needed than the recent conclusion that residential segregation began with the establishment of the closed housing compounds at Kimberley in 1886, "well before the officially designed and regulated townships."[30] On firmer ground is a more recent general review of urban apartheid in South Africa that points out that the reasons for segregationist initiatives were not necessarily tied to industrialization and developed manufacturing but rather could be tied to "social considerations."[31]

In fact, scholars such as Richard Elphick and Hermann Giliomee have argued that for South Africa "the racial order [w]as largely in place by the end of the eighteenth century," and that it originated in the legal status groups that the Dutch East India Company (VOC) imposed on the Cape in the first ten years after their arrival in 1652.[32] In this legal status system, race, class and color were closely correlated with the European landholders being at the top of the social ladder and almost everyone else being at the bottom as low-paid unskilled laborers. This included the indigenous KhoiSan, who were primarily cattleherders, and an enslaved population (slaves were first introduced to the Cape in 1658, six years after the Dutch arrived). The enslaved were brought from Mozambique, Madagascar, and Java, and also included some recaptives from West Africa. Some white ex-sailors also provided unskilled labor. However, initial social interaction between racial groups were slowly overtime, restricted, and taboos against intermarriage imposed a racial and class hierarchy.

Also, a recent study by Clifton Crais on white supremacy and black resistance in the eastern Cape in pre-industrial South Africa concludes that the social relations established between the Dutch and the enslaved as well as independent Africans helped to establish an ideology of white superiority, and in practice, a relationship where the white foreigners dominated. Inferiority of race and culture was collapsed into views about the dark-skinned enslaved population, the indigenous KhoiSan, other Africans, and their cultural practices.

The Dutch were the first to encounter the indigenous KhoiSan, many of whom died as a result of wars and foreign diseases, especially smallpox. Scholars agree that slavery at the Cape produced ideology and practices about race and color that substantiated beliefs in white superiority and black inferiority. In particular, there developed a racial division of labor and the association of manual work with slavery. Whites' use of enslaved dark skinned laborers was the accepted norm although most whites at the Cape, as in the southern United States during the period of slavery, did not own slaves. Nonetheless, the lifestyle of the slavemaster and slavemistress was the ideal and thus the aspiration for many whites of different classes. Slavery was abolished by the British in 1834 but the attitudes inculcated during slavery continued.

Several factors facilitated the establishment of this status system. These factors included European ethnocentrism, cultural chauvinism, and the "somatic norm image or a collectively held picture of ideal human appearance" so that one prefers one's own group and people that look like them, and economic and political considerations. Elphick and Giliomee concluded that by the eighteenth century in Cape colonial society, an ideology of racism was evolving, and racially discriminatory practices were common, including in "domicile and movement" (i.e., residential segregation).[33] The conclusions of these researchers emphasize the considerable depth of racial thinking and racial discriminatory practices at the Cape even before the arrival of the British, the establishment of Port Elizabeth, and the influence of mineral discoveries. Also, Elphick and Giliomee illustrate the need to study the different phases of the evolution of racial thinking and segregationist practices in conjunction with the changing political economy at specific times and in specific regions to understand their long and complex history.

British Notions about Superiority, Segregation, and Civilization

Having said this, it is important to note that beginning in 1806, during the second British occupation, the old social order was undergoing change. That is, a different layering of ideas was applied with the new British administration and the arrival of the missionaries. Among these new ideologies were liberalism (freeing of labor) and humanitarianism (moral equality). Legislation, such as Ordinance 50 in 1828, reflected these new ideas; it made KhoiSan and free blacks equal with Europeans before the law prior to the abolition of slavery in 1834. Perhaps, however, these laws had less to do with challenging the social order and more to do with restructuring labor relations. Notwithstanding the new legislation and the onset of British administration, the status quo remained fundamentally constant: The ideology of European supremacy was widespread, and the British and other immigrants "easily assimilated to the privileges of the long-resident Dutch-speaking Europeans."[34]

Meanwhile, as previously mentioned, around 1820, Port Elizabeth was established as a British colonial port, with the first settlers drawn from the five thousand English immigrants to the eastern Cape that same year.[35] Their arrival, which was facilitated by the British military victory over the Xhosa in the eastern territories in the war of 1811, personified belief in British imperialism and superiority. Nonetheless, since Port Elizabeth was administered by British officials influenced by liberal and humanitarian ideology as well as beliefs about British imperialism and superiority we might expect a more benevolent attitude toward Africans.

However, the past history of the British in relationship to colonial segregation must be kept in mind. For example, Christopher traces colonial urban segregation back to the English colonization of Wales and Ireland in the thirteenth century. Similarly, Ronald Takaki using Shakespeare's play *The Tempest* as metaphor to explain the roots of racism in America, discusses the English invasion of Ireland in the sixteenth century and the way in which ideas about "civilization," "savagery," and the "wild Irish" were intertwined to justify British brutality, colonization, and settlement of Irish lands. He tell us that "like Caliban, the Irish [and native Americans] were viewed as "savages," a people living outside of "civilization."[36] The British certainly had centuries of practice in applying these ideals, so it would not be surprising that the English settlers and officials at Port Elizabeth supported racial residential segregation. To understand how residential segregation evolved at Port Elizabeth, the political and socioeconomic relations between the Africans and the settlers—and the new beliefs and ideologies competing with the old order—must be examined in conjunction with the practices of racial discrimination and segregation.

Added to British notions about "savages" and "civilization" were ideas about the concept of "black" and "white," or color prejudice. Several scholars have illustrated that negative associations about the color "black" existed among Europeans and Asians for centuries prior to contact with Africans.[37] By the time both the Dutch and the British occupied the Cape colony, the trade in black slaves was widespread, as was the association of slavery, inferiority, and blackness with Africans. David Brion Davis cautions that despite color symbolism and the association of blackness with "death, danger, evil, and grief that has been common to many cultures, it is simplistic to assume that such symbolism accounts for the growing Muslim and Christian conviction that black Africans were in some way "made" to be slaves . . . He concludes that color symbolism . . . provided additional justification for new patterns of enslavement. . . ."[38] Certainly European enslavement of Africans had an effect on ideology, practices and the religious justifications based on race and color that whites offered for the exploitation of black people. In fact, at the same time justifications based on skin color and race were emerging so too was the ideology of white skin color as a basis for unity, white supremacy and declarations of white superiority. That is white racism and white superiority were opposites sides of the coin of black inferiority. Whether or not color prejudice in Port Elizabeth was greatly differentiated from race or class will also be analyzed.

The data indicates that the reasons for urban segregation were not simply economic; rather, they emanated from a variety of contexts including "social considerations." Clearly, we need to more closely evaluate the forces influencing the government's attempts to segregate the Africans who lived and worked in the towns during the early period of mercantile and industrial capitalism.

Constant Factors Throughout the Study

Throughout the time period under study (1880–1910), several factors remained constant with regard to the status and movement of blacks in Port Elizabeth that had a significant influence on the struggle over racial segregation and discrimination between blacks and whites. These were as follows: (1) the existence of a large number of African workers who resided permanently in town and who lived in a family situation; (2) an emergent African middle class drawn from the permanent working sector that was anxious to own land and property; (3) the large number of Africans who were Christian, Western educated, registered voters, and supporters of the Cape "liberal tradition" (exemplified by the political alliance between the African voters and liberal white politicians); (4) the growth of an ideology of segregation designed to subordinate Africans to white control as a counterpoint to the decline of the inclusionist strategy of liberalism that had aimed to uplift the "civilized" and western educated Africans; (5) the structural weaknesses of the local and central governments, exhibited by their inability to enforce racially discriminatory legislation—partly because of the lack of police power; and (6) the divisions among the white population about how to address the "native" problem.

These constant factors and their relationship to the two major issues mentioned earlier, rights to land and property in urban areas and control of the material and social lives of the black workers, form the backbone of this study. Until recently most studies discussed the establishment of urban residential segregation policies in late nineteenth and early twentieth century South African towns as if they were easily imposed.[39] African resistance to segregation has been largely ignored. This book will show that at least in one South African town, resistance, both formal and informal, from a variety of actors, including liberal whites, an emerging

African middle class, and working class, both males and females, dampened official hopes of implementing a strategy that would ultimately shape and control the economic and social lives of black workers.

The Emergence of an African Middle Class in South Africa

Another major concern of this book is to analyze the emergence of an African middle class and its role in leading the resistance against segregation. Here the term "middle class" means a group of Africans who owned property, shared a common ideology influenced by Christianity and Western education, and had the right, although limited, to accumulate capital. The men and women in this class, many of whom had attended mission schools, were often second and third-generation Christians. They strived hard to put into practice the Christian principles they had learned from the missionaries and to take part in the colonial society according to the liberal principles associated with free trade, free speech, and equality before the law.

"Middle class" also has another meaning. In terms of the socioeconomic relationship to the means of production in the capitalist social system, middle class refers to those occupying an intermediate position between the bourgeoisie and the working class. Among the black middle class in South Africa were teachers, clerks, interpreters, seamstresses, clergy, artisans, and small businessmen. Race divided the emerging classes, and a black middle class evolved—separated from the white capitalist bourgeoisie and the white working class. This black middle class was highly cognizant of the changing economic forces associated with industrial capitalism undermining their already precarious position and upward mobility in the colonial-capitalist society. Their insecurity mounted with the passage of legislation that decreased their position of relative privilege in the colonial society. Their privileges included the right to qualified franchise, Western classical education, property ownership in urban areas, and exemption from some of the colonial laws affecting "natives." Toward the end of the nineteenth century, racially discriminatory legislation increasingly eroded the "privileged standing" of this group. It may seem strange to talk about the privileged standing of a group of Africans in a society where, numerically speaking, they were the majority. Yet by 1880 the Xhosas, the largest African group in the Cape, were militarily conquered, the power of their chiefs in colonial society was minimal, and they were governed by legislation that discriminated against them by race and color. Consequently, to enter into the boundaries of the British-controlled Cape colony, Africans had to show a pass; they were not to be served in taverns; they were segregated on public transportation, colonial and intercolonial; and they faced numerous obstacles in pursuit of becoming successful capitalists.[40]

It has been problematic for scholars to categorize and name the African middle class that began to emerge in the late nineteenth century. In South Africa the black middle class has been called by a variety of terms, including the educated elite, aspirant petty bourgeoisie, petty bourgeoisie, communicators, or *amakholwa* (the believers), or *amaphakathi* (people-in-the middle, or people close to the king), and the high ones.[41] The confusion has emerged in large measure from the work of scholars who were uncertain whether they could effectively use Marxist analysis to discuss Africans in a colonial situation that seemed to have much more to do with race than with class.

Scholars were also influenced by the fact that, for a long time, the liberal analysis, which tended to focus primarily on race, was paramount in most studies about Africans and urban segregation. Liberal historiography reflected the success of segregation and apartheid based on racial ideology and, concomitantly, an absorption with such themes as multiracial relations, liberalism, black nationalism, and racial oppression, which, for the most part, ignored class analysis.[42]

In the 1970s Marxist scholars began to sharply criticize this liberal analysis for failing to scrutinize a range of critical problems and issues that pertained to class relations. Although the Marxists did not deny the importance of race and ethnicity, they sought to bring into the equation questions regarding the interrelationship of class, the structural relations of capitalist production, capitalist accumulation and development, and the struggle between labor and capital.[43] Through their focus on the political aspects of the economy, class struggle, worker and class consciousness, and popular culture, these revisionist studies have significantly added to our knowledge about Africans and "history from below" in both rural and urban areas.[44] For instance, in terms of recognizing and defining an African working class and middle class, Andre Proctor's important study centered on the early history of a permanent urban black population, rather than on migrant laborers, who lived in African townships between 1905–40. He analyzed the forces that influenced the formation of a black working class and middle class as well as the various factors—including class—that affected their methods and willingness to contest residential segregation.[45]

Andre Odendaal has documented the history of the emergence of a politically conscious, educated African elite in the late nineteenth and early twentieth centuries in South Africa and their establishment of political organizations to represent their interests.[46] Odendaal's data was reinforced by Brian Willan's examination of the ideological and cultural base of an African petty bourgeoisie at Kimberley before the turn of the century. A common element of these studies was the attempt to explain "the reasons for the willingness or unwillingness of the black middle class to act in concert with the black masses."[47] Philip Bonner's study emphasized the importance of the ideological influences on the leadership of a "stunted and evolving" urban African petty bourgeoisie and the possibilities for upward or downward identification with the black working class in 1918–20 Johannesburg.[48]

In her well-documented analysis of the organic intellectual leadership of the ICU, Helen Bradford observes that it is not unusual for another social group or class to provide the leadership for the working class.[49] Her study, especially because of the inclusion of oral African testimonies, illustrates the complexity and flexibility of the African leadership. She also cautions that it is unwise to attempt to place that leadership in rigid class categories and to move leaders around as if their actions are predictable. Alan Cobley made similar observations concerning class consciousness and leadership in his informative analysis of the development of the black petty bourgeoisie in South Africa from 1924–1950.[50]

Although the above-mentioned studies have contributed to our ability to define and to understand the growth of an African middle class, they began primarily after the 1920s. Thus, for the nineteenth and early twentieth centuries, our knowledge remains limited about the permanently urbanized African population. It is the period between 1880 and 1910—when the African working and middle classes were emerging—that needs to be examined more closely. By doing so, we can begin to better understand the complex interactions of resistance and ideology between and among the different groups that so strongly affected government policies prior to 1910.

Ideological influences and African Resistance to Segregation

The emphasis on the role of the black middle class in leading the organized struggle against the colonial governments' passage and implementation of racially discriminatory laws is not intended to diminish the value of other types of leadership among working-class Africans or "traditional" leaders (traditional political, economic and social leadership or authority according to traditions and customs among the Ciskei Xhosa rested with the male king (paramount chief), chiefs, royal clan members, and senior males of the homestead (*umzi*), of each commoner family and was hereditary).[51] However, detailed aspects of the lives of western-educated and Christian Africans are more readily available for this period for several reasons. First, their complaints were in English, which was the language of the dominant political group in the Cape. Thus, such sources as letters to the newspapers and testimony to government commissions were printed. Second, some Africans held the franchise, so their opinions, expressed at local political meetings and through appeals and representations to the Town Council and the Cape Parliament, were reported. Third, white politicians discussed African voters in their correspondence and at parliamentary meetings. Finally, the African newspapers such as *Imvo Zabantsundu* and *Izwi Labantu* reveal African opinion, in both English and *isiXhosa*.

Despite the lack of information on the state of the African working-class leaders in Port Elizabeth, data about their lifestyles, social practices, work habits, recreational activities, and resistance to proletarianization (dependence on wages as a way of life) can be pieced together through local newspapers, commission reports, magistrate's reports, and the vernacular press. Also, oral testimony collected in the 1980s from Africans from different class backgrounds in Port Elizabeth about township life in the first decade of the twentieth century provides supplementary information. Therefore, we are able to show that as proletarianization proceeded, the actions of the emerging African working class profoundly affected the shaping of residential segregation. Sometimes the documents offer us resounding silence on just the issue we are analyzing. Nonetheless, whenever I was able to hear the "voice" of Africans through the sources mostly interpreted by whites I tried to refilter it through an African centered lens to gain a different perspective.

In their representations to colonial officials, members of the emerging African middle class claimed that they represented not only their own interests but also those of the other Africans in town. Usually these claims were legitimate. This was particularly true in situations like those existing in Port Elizabeth, where racial discrimination limited the upward mobility and the political expression of Africans, as well as their access to land, housing, and public transportation. Under these circumstances the actions of the black middle class could influence all Africans and foster cross-class unity.

It is worth reiterating that in a society where race is used to establish privileges for one group although restricting the rights of the other, ideological considerations may have even more resonance among a middle class.[52] At critical points in time common experiences of racial discrimination in many different areas of life could act to create a climate of resistance that affected the responses of both the black working class and the black middle class. As these experiences accumulated, at times the language of nationalism and resistance served to provoke "imagined communities" among Africans and transcended ethnic, class, religious, and gender differences.[53]

It is significant to note that the schism developing between the emerging African working class and middle class was not yet too wide to bridge, especially because colonial segregationist legislation continually pushed the aspirant black middle class back toward the class from which they were trying to escape. As Cobley commented about the black petty bourgeoisie in South Africa, this class "does not simply appear full grown, defined and self-conscious,"[54] but is shaped by experiences.

The Cape Liberal Tradition

The Cape liberal tradition was a major factor that influenced the ideology and consciousness of the African middle class.[55] This tradition has been primarily linked to the non-racial qualified franchise or vote that was introduced in the Cape colony in 1853 when the white Dutch and British settlers were granted their first constitution by the British government, which included representative government with their own parliament. At the time the debate about whether or not the voting qualifications should be high or low were given more attention than whether to exclude men by race. This was because the number of African and Colored men who could qualify to vote was so small it was seen as irrelevant. Eventually it was agreed that the qualifications for the franchise would require that a man had to own £25 worth of property or earn an annual income of £50.[56] It was not until the 1880s that the number of black men qualified to vote rose high enough to influence the outcome of the elections; this is when the first voting restrictions were introduced by the all-white Parliament. All of the districts where the African vote was significant were in the eastern Cape and included towns with a relatively stable black population, like Port Elizabeth.

Many of the black men who eventually held the right to vote were among the emergent middle class, and they believed in the liberal alliance. The liberal alliance in the Cape Colony was based upon the Victorian liberalism originating in Britain in the nineteenth century during the transition from mercantile capitalism to industrial capitalism. The liberal ideals of the British middle and upper classes, such as the right to private property and to free speech, freedom of religion and of individual conscience, and a free press were voiced by the Protestant missionaries, all of them male, that first arrived in the eastern Cape. It was during the nineteenth century that several missionaries from numerous denominations arrived in South Africa and also in many other parts of Africa to establish permanent mission stations and to compete for black souls. Included among the denominations that set up mission stations in the Cape colony between the 1820s and 1850s were the Wesleyans in the 1820s, the Scots Presbyterians (Glasgow Missionary Society) in 1820, the Congregationalists, the Lutherans (Berlin Missionary Society) and the Anglicans. The missionaries concentrated on the Ciskei, where the majority of Africans resided. Their arrival followed soon after the British agitation for an end to the trans-atlantic slave trade, abolished by Britain in 1807, and increased agitation for an end to slavery in the British possessions, including the Cape colony. There were also calls from critics of slavery for "legitimate" trade and the civilization of the less civilized and nonchristian peoples.

Thus, along with Christianity, the missionaries also transmitted Western customs, education, language, and liberal beliefs which promised that those Africans who became "civilized" enough would be accorded the same rights as British citizens. Of course, whites decided who was civilized, based upon certain criteria such as the Africans' acceptance of Western culture, education, religion, and occupations. Once Africans were deemed to have attained a "civilized" status, they could be incorporated and allowed to compete equally with whites, because Cape liberalism was modeled on mid-Victorian liberalism, which theoretically viewed society in terms of class. Many Christian Africans strongly supported this incorporationist perspective that pervaded the liberal tradition of the Cape.

Although the Cape liberal tradition was associated with ideas of freedom, justice, and the franchise as well as rights in land and property for the individual, it did not advocate an equal social and economic position for all members of the society. Rather, coterminous with the incorporationist strategy was the liberal belief in white superiority, especially of the British who felt their opinion was nondebatable. In fact, they considered it to be their preordained duty to guide the less fortunate and less civilized. Because beliefs about racial and class differences were similar among many British colonizers, white liberals in the Cape colony saw no contradiction in the pursuit of liberalism and white supremacy. As Phyllis Lewsen notes, "Liberalism was not in the nineteenth century identical with democracy."[57] Rather, a relationship of deference and dominance between the upper and lower classes was common.[58] Yet the possibility existed that liberalism could be undermined by its own limitations with regard to democracy, race, class, and power.

Between 1880 and 1910 several changes in the political economy threatened the alliance between black liberals and white liberals in the Cape colony. For example, the discovery of minerals drastically altered the direction of the economy and, concomitantly, heightened the need for a large labor force. As these wider colonial changes and British imperialism created incentives to discriminate, the urgency for segregation became apparent. The growth of the town's labor force influenced local governments to increase their efforts to formally segregate Africans. Moreover, the opposition to liberalism increased as the rural basis for the initial economic coalition between white liberals and Africans that supported the growth of an African peasantry and the expansion of commercial capital-ism began to be undermined.[59] Also, as independent African territories were conquered, the incorporation of many more Africans into the colo-nial boundaries coincided with the discovery of minerals. Many white settlers clamored for Africans to be brought under control, disarmed, de-prived of land, and used as a cheap labor force. In short, these white set-tlers sought to dominate and to exploit the Africans. Consequently, local governments—such as that of Port Elizabeth in the Cape Colony—re-sponded with increased legislation to try to segregate the blacks from the whites and to ensure land and labor control in the urban areas.

African Women

African women played an important role in the struggle against segrega-tion in Port Elizabeth. As mentioned earlier, many Africans working in that town lived in a family setting, and both men and women were af-fected by the socioeconomic and political changes discussed earlier. The changes occurring in the colonial society meant that women who entered the urban areas had to adjust to a different world from their pre-colonial rural existence. Information on the role of African women in early or pre-industrial Xhosa society remains controversial and scarce.[60] Nonetheless, it is clear that Western notions that draw clearcut and sharp boundaries between the roles of men and women in the political, economic and so-cial arenas, and scholars who apply white feminist theories without re-gard for cultural practices and beliefs have fallen short of the mark. The old ideas held for example by some European missionaries that African men used African women as beasts of burden while they rested under the trees do not stand up to scrutiny.

Rather, drawing on primarily anthropological sources from the nine-teenth century describing the Xhosa lifestyle and from inferences derived from other relevant data focused on women in Africa, it is possible to reach a clearer understanding of the complimentary relationship between African men and women that was family and communal oriented. This is not to deny a degree of subordination and stratification in African society that was gender based but rather to suggest that men and women were provided a series of ideological and practical roles that were kinship de-rived and valued within Nguni society.[61] These roles were influenced not only by gender but also by age, geography, lineage, clan and hierarchy. Not surprisingly, their pre-colonial lifestyles would affect their new sta-tus as black female workers in the British towns.

Significantly, African women also began to take up wage labor in the nineteenth century towns primarily as domestic workers. Thus, this book would be incomplete without attempting to understand the influence of

African women on the process of urban residential segregation and African resistance to segregation. This is a difficult undertaking, because the studies of African women in urban areas begin almost invariably in the twentieth century, and they focus on such topics as black, Christian-educated women and their resistance to the pass laws, the *manyano* (women's unions) in the Christian churches, the deprivation of the migrant labor system on women and their families, exploitation of domestic workers, and resistance to state initiatives to control beer brewing.[62] A small number of studies examine women living in the South African countryside and their resistance to state structures aimed at restricting their livelihood.[63] There is virtually nothing written that analyzes African women in towns during this early period of movement into industrial capitalism, although we do know that some women migrants worked periodically for white settlers in the nineteenth century.

Yet on particular occasions, African women in Port Elizabeth played key roles in resisting residential segregation and altering the direction of the struggle. Chapters 5 and 6 explore that information. The available data gives us a new perspective on African women in towns prior to the entrenchment of the migrant labor system. That data also sheds light on the contentious application of the numerous restrictions imposed by the colonial government to facilitate exploitation and control of the black work force.

Looking Ahead

Throughout this study the formation of the African middle class is discernible in terms not only of its economic position but also its social and political position with relation to the black working class. As the story unfolds, it becomes possible to recognize the structural position of the middle class as well as to identify their changing perspectives on political, economic, and social issues as they take action to ensure their middle class position and also respond to government initiatives to prevent their upward mobility. Underlying the process of urban residential segregation at the local level were broader patterns of economic and political development at the regional and national levels, such as British imperialism, white settler sub-imperialism, the discovery of minerals, and the struggle between the Dutch and the British for control of the colonies and the mineral resources. These patterns motivated government initiatives over the 30-year period (1880–1910) under study.

These formative years were perhaps one of the most propitious for some members of the emerging black middle class to act as "organic intellectuals."[64] Nevertheless, many social distinctions could and did create divisions among blacks. Among these divisions were class, Western education, political rights, housing, occupations, social rights, and status. Nonetheless, at crucial times, the actions of the black working class propelled the educated Africans into leadership stances, and the latter were called upon to represent diverse interests. In order to promote disunity across class lines, the government offered land and property concessions to the emergent black middle class.

Fragmentation of the opposition became an acknowledged governmental tactic, but with unpredictable results. Some African leaders capitulated to concessions that appealed to their individual class interests, such as freehold land rights and the right to rent a business site if they moved into the segregated locations. Still others adamantly refused concessions that would undermine a given community of interests. Factors that affected their choices varied according to the class interests of different segments of the emergent middle class, which were, in turn, influenced by education, occupation, and status. Despite the cleavages that occurred among African leaders, government officials learned to be wary of introducing racially discriminatory legislation, since they could expect it to be carefully scrutinized and resisted.

As mentioned, in South Africa changes in the political economy in the late nineteenth and early twentieth centuries also influenced the crystallization of an ideology of segregation. Because of its ambiguities, this ideology could attract all kinds of supporters, since the messages received about segregation depended upon the recipient's needs. White businessmen, merchants, housewives, workers, and governmental officials made various demands that, in theory, the ideology of segregation had to meet. Merchants and businessmen wanted a controlled and cheap labor force, workers wanted to limit competition, household employers wanted laborers close by and on call and governmental officials wanted whites to be safe and happy. Thus, residential segregation seemed to be a good solution for all.

Still, when the Port Elizabeth Town Council tried to segregate Africans by residence, members of the various white interest groups applied for exemptions for their black employees. Indeed, it was they, as well as the Africans, who refused to abide by the segregation laws. Although many whites preferred segregation in theory, in practice they actually wanted an uninterrupted labor flow and easy access to African labor. In fact, whites wanted black workers at their beck and call, especially their domestic servants, and they did not want them separated into faraway townships.

The desire of white employers for cheap and accessible black labor, despite preferring not to live in close proximity to blacks, has characterized the contradiction of social and economic relations between Africans and whites. Such a tendency was palpable in 1903 when the Native Reserve

Locations Act was passed, and officials sought to implement it. And so, the lack of unanimity among local whites with regard to the removal and segregation of Africans was another important factor that often hindered successful implementation of legislation that had been enacted.

This study examines how and why the emergent black middle class in Port Elizabeth challenged or complied with racially discriminatory legislation passed by the local and central government. Organized African resistance—led by an emergent black middle class and influenced by liberal whites, African women, and the emergent black working class—significantly altered governmental plans to create a strategy that would ultimately shape and control the material and social lives of black people. Various social structures and traditions that culminated in the materialization of cross-class community consciousness, as exhibited by popular political participation, continues to influence South African history to this day.

In Chapter 2 we examine how, in 1883, the Port Elizabeth Town Council attempted to remove Africans from Strangers' location to a segregated area because it was now situated near the town's center and its expansion was blocked. The debate over the removal indicated that whites' beliefs and language were motivated by pseudo-scientific racism.

However, members of the emergent African middle class strenuously objected to any erosion of their privileges. Moreover, their beliefs and language were swayed by liberal white promises and African beliefs about justice. African resistance prevented the implementation of residential segregation as envisioned by the white officials and thus shaped the perimeters of the contestation over land, labor, and social control.

The types of legal and illegal protest actions taken by Port Elizabeth Africans against racial discrimination and segregation were repeated in other places in the twentieth century. As Shula Marks and Stanley Trapido pointed out, "Whatever the controlling purpose and ambiguities of the incorporationist strategy, for the emerging black petty bourgeoisie it opened up unintended political opportunity and real material benefits."[65] Also Colin Bundy has aptly demonstrated, the material benefits of this incorporationist strategy were evident in the rise of the African peasantry.[66] Yet as the peasantry declined, Africans in the growing towns tried to ensure their rights to land and property and to decent living conditions in the black settlements where many of them lived.

In Chapter 3 we analyze the backdrop to an important compromise between Africans and the local officials in 1896 to ensure freehold land and house building rights if Africans agreed to move into a segregated black settlement. The African leaders were prompted to negotiate with the local authorities by the passage of legislation, in 1887 and 1892, that deprived them of the franchise. The debates and passage of the Glen Grey Act introduced to that district, among other things, individual tenure and a limited advisory role for Africans in local government; the Act also influenced the changing relations between the white colonials and the African population at Port Elizabeth. To subordinate Africans living in the towns and the rural areas, the government was trying to establish a "native" policy. On the one hand, with the 1896 agreement the government's aim to use land and property concessions to co-opt the African middle class and distance them from the working class became more viable. On the other hand, and from the African perspective, that agreement ensured African property ownership and the establishment of a native advisory board, which was an unprecedented concession to blacks living in urban areas.

Although the Christian Africans were negotiating the 1896 agreement, they also sought unity, protection, and strength by forming their own political, economic, and social organizations. As will be discussed in Chapter 4, one such economic organization was the African American Working Men's Union (AAWMU), a relatively successful business venture established in alliance with black Americans who lived in Port Elizabeth in the 1890s.[67] More importantly, however, the alliance accentuates an aspect of the nationalist and pan-Africanist connection between and among black South Africans and black Americans hitherto neglected by researchers.

Many scholars have focused on the Ethiopian, or separatist church, movement and on the educational linkages with black American colleges between 1890–1910.[68] Also, a few general studies, such as the one by Clements Keto, have discussed African Americans in South Africa during this period. Still other works have touched on various historical, cultural, and political linkages.[69] Nevertheless, these sources have been largely silent with regard to the African and African American connection as related to segregation and economics.

Some of the aforementioned studies also have discussed the historical aspects of white supremacy and segregation in the United States and South Africa. Furthermore, the studies showed the commonalities that black people experienced in racial discrimination. Understandably, racial empathy was a magnet that drew Africans and African Americans together. Thus, the formation of the AAWMU within South Africa in this early period of urbanization substantiates the influence of pan-Africanism.[70] Nevertheless, black South African nationalism was tempered by the reality of the onslaught of segregationist policies that required decisions that would have long-term implications for the status of Africans in urban areas. The attempt to establish economic independence in conjunction with African Americans was one strategy to combat segregation. Another strategy was to work out compromises with the white officials who were demanding that all Africans be segregated by race.

In Chapter 5 an analysis of the background to the African general strike in June 1901 indicates that compromises were sometimes not possible until concerted action was taken. Moreover, this general strike was unprecedented in South Africa, since it was the first strike that included African female domestic workers. The strike was precipitated when the government tried to impose racially discriminatory health legislation against the entire African population. In addition, the government used the Public Health Act to close African settlements in order to achieve residential segregation. Eventually, the Native [Urban] Reserve Locations Act of 1902 established segregated black settlements in the towns. That act was a precursor to the passage and implementation of the 1923 Native Urban Areas Act, which sought to establish national segregation. The 1902 legislation also authorized the building of the first formal government-constructed segregated township (New Brighton) in Port Elizabeth.

As discussed in Chapter 6, this initiative was only partly successful, primarily because of the growth of Korsten, a housing area located outside the municipal boundaries. Thousands of Africans voted with their feet by avoiding New Brighton, leading to what one official called the "native free state at Korsten." Korsten was a settlement located outside of the government's jurisdiction and thus unaffected by the 1902 Act. The small but significant number of African voters used their political power in 1903 to elect liberal white parliamentary representatives who agreed to support the establishment of a Korsten Village Management Board (KVMB). The aim of the voters was to try to assure their rights to land and housing in the urban area. The KVMB was an indication of the strength of the liberal alliance and the power of the black vote. But the KVMB was soon disbanded, and the precariousness of the black middle class position, their lack of power, and the decline of the liberal alliance was clear.

My analysis of these early years at Korsten underscores that the African middle class, emerging from the black working class between 1880 and 1910, was not monolithic. Rather, it was based on experiences of its members, who occupied different positions in their upward climb. Yet the body of issues that sometimes sparked alliances among different classes of Africans was clearly illustrated in their concentrated efforts to oppose residential segregation.

In the final chapter, I analyze the continuing struggle over land, housing, local government, and control as the old conflict takes on new life as it is influenced by Africans living at New Brighton and also by those living outside its boundaries. A new influence seldom discussed in conjunction with the struggle over residential segregation in urban areas is the "Ethiopian" movement, or the establishment of African independent churches among blacks in both rural and urban areas. The data informs us that, for a brief moment, Reverend James Dwane of the African Methodist Episcopal Church (AMEC) in the mid-1900s became an important actor in the struggle for land and housing at Port Elizabeth.

Chapter 7 also examines why New Brighton, the first segregated African location in Port Elizabeth to be administered by the central government rather than by the local government, failed to meet the expectations of either the government or the Africans. I briefly review the activities of the New Brighton Advisory Board that began to function by 1906. Also, an analysis of the similarities between the 1903 and 1923 Native Urban Areas Acts illustrates that the types of issues underlying the conflict between the government and Africans forced to live in black urban locations similar to New Brighton later radiated out to the rest of South Africa. Yet once a segment of the African population was coerced or enticed into New Brighton, protest and criticism of government policy continued, since only the site of struggle was altered.

More often, however, resistance to segregation gave way to resistance against exploitation and freedom from government control within the African location. Religion, recreation, and lifestyle were constantly negotiated terrain between the government and the New Brighton residents. The chapter ends with an assessment of the effects of the role of the black middle class on the shaping of segregation in Port Elizabeth. Ultimately it is important to realize that their structurally ambiguous position meant that some members of this class remained closely identified with the working class, even as community struggle entered a new phase in the resistance to racial segregation and another generation of Africans workers and leaders emerged. Consequently, residential segregation at New Brighton was never to occur without ambiguity and resistance.

Notes

1. A. J. Christopher, "Formal Segregation and population distribution in Port Elizabeth," *Contree* 24 (September 1988): 5–12. Port Elizabeth was established as a military station known as Fort Frederick in 1799 and became a township in 1815; J. J. Redgrave, *Port Elizabeth in Bygone Days* (Wynberg, Cape: Rustica Press, 1947), pp. 17, 56, relates that Donkin's wife died in India in 1818. He was enroute to England and travelled by way of the Cape, where he was appointed Acting Governor of the Cape Colony. Also British officials encouraged the settlers to produce merino sheep wool for the market and to improve the land.

2. They also moved to such towns in the eastern Cape as Uitenhage *(Tinara)*, Grahamstown *(Rina)*, Graaf-Reinet *(Rafu)*, and Kingwilliamstown *(eQonce)* that began to emerge in the first half of the nineteenth century. The Xhosa names for the towns are courtesy of Mrs. Sisisi N. Tolashe of Queenstown, South Africa. These towns are mentioned to illustrate the language difference that would also affect the world view of English and Xhosa as expressed in naming places; In a

recent study Les Switzer, *Power and Resistance in An African Society: The Ciskei Xhosa and the Making of South Africa* (Madison: University of Wisconsin Press, 1993), Part 1, "The Precolonial Past," pp. 17–42 says there were nine Cape-Xhosa wars between the Europeans (Dutch and later British) and the Xhosa over the hundred year period, 1779–1879. The Xhosa language is often referred to as a southern Nguni language, while northern Nguni is Zulu and Swazi. Nguni is a linguistic term used to describe the Bantu languages spoken between the geographical region of the Cape and the Transvaal. Nguni speakers shared common economic, political, linguistic and cultural practices with some regional variations. The language of the southern Nguni is Xhosa and this is also the name of one of the main southern Nguni ethnic groups. Two of the main Xhosa clans, the *Rharhabe* and the *Gcaleka* are discussed in J. B. Peires, *The House of Phalo: A History of the Xhosa People in the Days of their Independence* (Johannesburg: Ravan Press, 1981); Much of this study is focused on Xhosa speaking men and women who occupied the eastern Cape and became the largest group of workers in Port Elizabeth.

3. Numerous studies support this assertion. For example, Philip Bonner, et al., eds., *Holding Their Ground: Class, Locality and Culture in 19th and 20th Century South Africa* (Johannesburg: Ravan Press, 1989); Tom Lodge, *Black Politics in South Africa since 1945* (New York: Longman, 1983).

4. For a more recent argument about this process focused on African Americans, see Douglas S. Massey and Nancy A. Denton, *American Apartheid: Segregation and the Making of the Underclass* (Cambridge: Harvard University Press, 1993), p. 8.

5. E. P. Thompson, *The Poverty of Theory and Other Essays* (New York: Monthly Review Press, 1978), pp. 1–210; P. Anderson, *Arguments Within English Marxism* (London: Redwood Burn Ltd., 1980, distributed in the U.S. by Schocken Books, New York), pp. 21–23.

6. Helen Bradford, *A Taste of Freedom: The ICU in Rural South Africa, 1924–1930* (New Haven: Yale University Press, 1987); Gary Baines, "From Populism to Unionism: The Emergence and nature of Port Elizabeth's Industrial and Commercial Workers' Union, 1918–1920," *Journal of Southern African Studies* 17 (1991): 679–716; Robin Bloch, "The High Cost of Living: The Port Elizabeth Disturbances of October 1920," *Africa Perspective* 19 (1981): 39–59; Lodge, *Black Politics in South Africa Since 1945*.

7. Lodge, *Black Politics in South Africa Since 1945*. Lodge notes that, with the exception of ethnic homogeneity, similar factors existed on the Rand (where the gold mines are). Nevertheless, little evidence suggests that ethnic or linguistic differences among Africans or between Indians and Africans inhibited political response in the Transvaal. But there is evidence that ethnic differences affected responses in Natal, where the Indian population was significantly larger and viewed as the exploiters of African consumers in Bonner, *Holding Their Ground*, see Iain Edwards, "Swing the Assegai Peacefully?" pp. 59–103; Also, for the period under study, similar reasons for protest existed in several eastern Cape towns, such as East London and Kingwilliamstown, but obviously the specific historical circumstances need elucidation before any comparisons can be made.

8. See Andre Proctor, "Class Struggle, Segregation and the City: A History of Sophiatown," in Belinda Bozzoli, compiler, *Labor, Townships and Protest: Studies in the Social History of the Witwatersrand* (Johannesburg: Ravan Press, 1979), pp. 49–89; Bonner, *Holding Their Ground*; An exception is Clifton C. Crais, *White Supremacy and Black Resistance in Pre-Industrial South Africa* (New York: Cambridge, 1992).

9. See T. R. H. Davenport and K. S. Hunt, eds., *The Right to the Land* (Cape Town: David Philip, 1974); David Welsh, *The Roots of Segregation: Native Policy in Colonial Natal, 1845–1910* (Cape Town; New York: Oxford University Press, 1971). For example, at Durban, Natal, Sir Theophilus Shepstone established a system of land reserves, administered through a British official by means of chiefs and indirect rule, see Monica Wilson and Leonard Thompson, eds., The *Oxford History of South Africa* (New York; Oxford: Oxford University Press, 1969, 1971), 2 vols, 1:376–379; Also see Shula Marks and Stanley Trapido, *The Politics of Race, Class and Nationalism in Twentieth Century South Africa* (New York: Longman, 1987), pp. 26–32, for more on the term "Coloreds," (hereafter Colored) the Dutch called them *"Kleuring,"* and how the term and culture evolved from the eighteenth to the twentieth century to refer to the offspring of many people including the Dutch, Africans (Khoisan, Xhosa and others), and enslaved people. Culturally, the Coloreds were closest to the Dutch including in speaking what developed into the Afrikaans language. Similarly for a discussion of the arrival of Indian indentured servants in Natal, South Africa and their structural position see pp. 32–36.

10. A. J. Christopher, "Race and Residence in Colonial Port Elizabeth," *South African Geographical Journal* 69 (1987): 5. At this time Colored referred to all people of color including Africans.

11. *Cape of Good Hope Government Gazette,* 18 November 1847 (Section 27 of the Municipal Regulations of Port Elizabeth). Strictly speaking, as pointed out by Gary Baines, "The Control and Administration of Port Elizabeth's African Population, c. 1834–1923," *Contree* 26 (1989): 13, the principle of segregated locations for indigenous people was first established by the London Missionary Society (LMS) as a "Hottentot Location" for Khoikhoi and other colored people who were members of the LMS Mission Church, in Port Elizabeth in 1834. However, the LMS as a religious body establishing a mission station is quite different from a formal government regulation backed by legalized violence.

12. Gary Baines, "The colonial origins of segregation: The case of Port Elizabeth's Native Strangers' Location," (Unpublished paper presented to the Eleventh Biennial Conference of the South African Historical Society, University of Stellenbosch, 20–23 January 1987); Significantly, in 1841, similar reasons were voiced by the Natal colony officials in pursuit of establishing a native reserve, including the statement that "on further complaints that the Kafirs begin to multiply amongst us, and that depredations are not only increasing, but that they make locations on inhabited places, erect numerous *kraals* (Dutch word for Xhosa settlements), and may become dangerous to our inhabitants . . ." Davenport, *The Right to the Land,* p. 13.

13. R. J. Johnston, *Residential Segregation, the State and Constitutional Conflict in American Urban Areas* (New York and London: Academic Press, 1984), Depart-

ment of Geography, University of Sheffield, Institute of British Geographers, Special Publication, 17, pp. 8–9, discusses crucial numbers and perceptions of blacks as undesirable neighbors in the United States and conflict over the social and built environment.

14. On white fears of being "swamped" and also on the "frontier" wars between the Xhosa and the British see Wilson and Thompson, *Oxford History*, vol. 1: 367–68 and Chap. 6; Redgrave, *Port Elizabeth in Bygone Days*, p. 367 states that the unofficial census determined that there was a total of 2,405, all "races." The Coloreds (including Africans) totaled 118 men, 72 women and 117 children.

15. Maynard Swanson, "The Sanitation Syndrome: Bubonic Plague and Urban Native Policy in the Cape Colony, 1900–1909," *Journal of African History* 18 (1977): 387–410.

16. Redgrave, *Port Elizabeth in Bygone Days*, p. 368.

17. Ibid.

18. In 1846, the Mfengu workers demanded higher wages; in 1852 the Mfengu struck work against a municipal ordinance requiring them to work clothed; in 1854 they struck work for higher wages and disagreements with management over the time to stop work on Saturday, see E. J. Inggs, "Mfengu Beach Labor and Port Elizabeth Harbor Development, 1835–1870," *Contree* 21 (1987): 9–10.

19. The Mfengu replaced the KhoiKhoi as beach laborers, J. Inggs, "Liverpool of the Cape: Port Elizabeth Trade 1820–1870," *The South African Journal of Economic History* 1 (1986): 77–98; For history of Mfengu see R. A. Moyer, "Some Current Manifestations of Mfengu History," University of London, *Institute of Commonwealth Studies*, Collected Seminar Papers on the Societies of Southern Africa in the 19th and 20th Centuries (October 1971–June 1972): 16:3. The total figure for the Mfengu is based on data from a Wesleyan missionary report, and an unofficial census taken on April 11, 1846 "done by a few gentlemen." R. A. Moyer, "A History of the Mfengu of the Eastern Cape, 1835–1870" (Ph.D. diss., London University, 1976), p. 290; Redgrave, *Port Elizabeth in Bygone Days* for census figures, p. 367; For recent debate on the Mfengu (Fingo) see A. C. Webster, "Land expropriation and labor extraction under Cape colonial rule: The war of 1835 and the 'emancipation' of the Fingo," (master's thesis, Rhodes University), 1991, 72 (fn.2) cited in Switzer, *Power and Resistance*, p. 375 (n.13); Peires, *House of Phalo* pp. 86–111; Julian Cobbing, "The *Mfecane* as Alibi: Thoughts on *Dithakong* and *Mbolompo*," *Journal of African History* 29 (1988): 487–519; The Mfengu spoke Xhosa or southern Nguni.

20. Switzer, *Power and Resistance*, pp. 139, 60. He relates that nine Cape-Xhosa wars were fought between 1779 and 1878, p. 52; Also see Wilson and Thompson, *Oxford History*, 1:240.

21. Cited in Baines, "The Control and Administration of Port Elizabeth's African population," Among the several areas that Africans lived were "on the hillside above the town center; near the landing beach; and in two villages, each fifteen minutes walk in opposite directions from the center of the town." p. 13.

22. Redgrave, *Port Elizabeth in Bygone Days*, p. 369.

23. *Cape of Good Hope Government Gazette*, 18 November 1847.

24. The name the white colonists chose for the African settlement denotes both their views about the alienation of Africans as "Strangers'" from the area demar-

cated as the Cape colony, and the place of Africans in the town as strangers or foreigners, there to work temporarily for the whites. Some African locations in other colonies were also called "Strangers"; See Map 2 for Port Elizabeth African locations in the nineteenth and early twentieth centuries.

25. "Town Council," *EPH*, 4 September 1855, 2 October 1855.

26. Christopher, "Race and Residence," p. 7; E. L. Nel, "Racial Segregation in East London, 1836–1948," *South African Geographical Journal* 73 (1991): 60–61, notes that similar to Port Elizabeth, at East London, a government notice was issued in 1849 requiring "Fingoes and other colored natives" to live in "locations."

27. James Rutherford, *Sir George Grey* (London: Cassell and Company Ltd., 1961). Grey's design for the Cape colony was similar in most features to his civilization policy in New Zealand, p. 304.

28. Rob Turrell, "Kimberley: Labor and Compounds, 1871–1888," in Shula Marks and Richard Rathbone, eds., *Industrialization and Social Change in South Africa: African class formation, culture and consciousness 1870–1930* (New York: Longman, 1982), pp. 1–44; After diamonds were found in the 1860s, the town of Kimberley developed and by the 1880s the closed compounds were built to house the Africans migrating to the town to work at the diamond mines. The "closed" (restrictions on workers going and coming into the area) compounds were single-sex barrack like structures first established in 1885 and functioned to control and subordinate the black working class and to enforce racial segregation between the white and black workers since the white workers were not housed in compounds but could live where they chose; J. Rex, "The Compound, Reserve and Urban Locations—essential institutions of Southern African Labor Exploitation," *South African Labor Bulletin* 1 (1974): 4–17; Joyce F. Kirk, "Race, Class, Liberalism and Segregation: The 1883 Native Strangers' Location Bill in Port Elizabeth, South Africa," *International Journal of African Historical Studies* 24 (1991): 293–321.

29. For example Martin Legassick's study of "The Making of South African 'Native Policy', 1903–1923, The Origins of Segregation," University of London, *Institute of Commonwealth Studies*, Collected Seminar Papers, The Societies of Southern Africa in the 19th and 20th Centuries, vol. 3 (1971–1972).

30. Alan Mabin, "Labor, Capital, Class Struggle and the Origins of Residential Segregation in Kimberley, 1880–1920," *Journal of Historical Geography* 12 (1986): 5.

31. Paul Maylam, "The Rise and Decline of Urban Apartheid in South Africa," *African Affairs 89* (1990): 54, 58. However, Maylam says nothing about Port Elizabeth or African initiative in influencing the segregation process.

32. Richard Elphick and Hermann Giliomee, eds., *The Shaping of South African Society, 1652–1840* (Middletown, Connecticut: Wesleyan University Press, 1989), pp. 522–527. Also see Editor's Introduction, in Jeffrey Butler, Richard Elphick, and David Welsh, eds., *Democratic Liberalism in South Africa* (Claremont, South Africa: David Philip, Distributed by Harper and Row: Scranton, 1987), p. 9.

33. Elphick and Giliomee, *Shaping of South African Society*. They state that: "colonial officials and colonial courts discriminated among the four status groups in many areas of daily life, such as domicile, right of marriage, right of movement, taxation, militia service, land ownership and so on." p. 529, see esp. 522–529.

34. Ibid., say the abolition of slavery began in 1834 and concluded by 1838, see pp. 549–553.

35. E. Morse Jones, *Role of the British Settlers in South Africa* (Cape Town: 1820 Settlers Monument Committee, 1971).

36. A. J. Christopher, "From Flint to Soweto: Reflections on the Colonial Origins of the Apartheid City," *Area* 15 (1983): 145; Ronald Takaki, *A Different Mirror: A History of Multicultural America* (Boston: Little, Brown and Co., 1993), pp. 26–28; Winthrop Jordan, *White Over Black: American Attitudes Toward the Negro 1550–1812* (Baltimore: Penguin Books, 1969), Chap. 1; and George Frederickson, *White Supremacy: A Comparative Study in American and South African History* (New York: Oxford University Press, 1981), pp. 13–17, calls British colonization in Ireland and Indonesia rehearsals for America and South Africa.

37. David Brion Davis, *Slavery and Human Progress* (New York: Oxford University Press, 1984), pp. 37–38; Alden T. Vaughn, *Roots of American Racism* (New York: Oxford University Press, 1995), p. 54; Paul Gordon Lauren, *Power and Prejudice: The Politics and Diplomacy of Racial Discrimination* (Boulder: Westview Press, 1995), says early patterns of color prejudice and association of skin color with negative and positive attributes existed among Hindus and Japanese but race had not assumed a moral reason or been attached to specific peoples. Rather, he states these cultures exhibited what has been called "an impulse to inequality," pp. 6–8.

38. David Brion Davis, *Slavery and Human Progress,* p. 38

39. T. R. H. Davenport, "African Townsmen? South African Natives (Urban Areas) Legislation Through the Years," *African Affairs* 68 (1969): 95–109; Christopher, "Race and Residence."

40. See Ch. 4 of this book. Also, Brian Willan, "An African in Kimberley: Sol T. Plaatje, 1894–1898," in Marks and Rathbone, *Industrialization and Social Change,* pp. 238–258.

41. Leo Kuper, *An African Bourgeoisie—Race, Class and Politics in South Africa* (New Haven and London: Yale University Press 1965); Norman Etherington, *Preachers, Peasants and Politics in Southeast Africa, 1835–1889: African Christian Communities in Natal, Pondoland and Zululand* (London: Royal Historical Society, 1978); Andre Odendaal, "African Political Mobilization in the Eastern Cape, 1880–1910" (Ph.D. diss., University of Cambridge, 1983); Helen Bradford, *Taste of Freedom* (New Haven: Yale University Press, 1987); Alan Cobley, *Class and Consciousness: The Black Petty Bourgeoisie in South Africa, 1924–1950* (New York; London: Greenwood Press, 1990).

42. Wilson and Thompson, *Oxford History of South Africa,* 2 vols.

43. Shula Marks and Anthony Atmore, eds., *Economy and Society in Pre-Industrial South Africa* (London: Longman, 1980); Marks and Rathbone, *Industrialization and Social Change;* Belinda Bozzoli, compiler, *Labor, Townships and Protest* (Johannesburg: Ravan Press, 1979); Frederick Cooper, *Struggle for the City: Migrant Labor, Capital, and the State in Urban Africa* (Beverley Hills and London: Sage Publications, 1983), p. 9.

44. Most were welcome additions, although initially a few scholars were unable to move beyond economic determinism. For example, see Merle Lipton, *Cap-*

italism and Apartheid: South Africa 1910–84 (Aldershot: Gower/Maurice Temple Smith, 1985).

45. Other studies on urban Africans focused on a later period. These include *Langa* by Monica Wilson and the three volume study of the Xhosa in East London in the mid-1950s, D. H. Reader, *The Black Man's Portion* (1961) vol. 1; Philip Mayer, *Townsmen or Tribesmen* (1961) vol. 2; B. A. Pauw, *The Second Generation* vol. 3 (1963) (Cape Town: Oxford University Press).

46. Andre Odendaal, *Black Protest Politics in South Africa to 1912* (New Jersey: Barnes and Noble, 1984).

47. Also see Thomas Nyguist, *African Middle Class Elite* (Grahamstown: Rhodes University, Institute of Social And Economic Research, Occasional Papers, 28, 1983), who dismissed the black middle class in the eastern Cape town of Grahamstown as marginal to community leadership.

48. Philip Bonner, "The Transvaal Native Congress 1917–1920: The radicalization of the black petty bourgeoisie on the Rand," in Marks and Rathbone, *Industrialization and Social Change*, pp. 270–313; For a later period see Lodge, *Black Politics in South Africa since 1945*.

49. Bradford, *A Taste of Freedom*.

50. Cobley, *Class and Consciousness*.

51. Peires, *The House of Phalo*, Chaps 1,2; Crais, *White Supremacy and Black Resistance*, pp. 18–20.

52. Nicos Poulantzas, *Classes in Contemporary Capitalism* (London: NLB, 1975) pp. 290–97.

53. Benedict Anderson, *Imagined Communities: Reflections on the Origin and Spread of Nationalism* (London: Verso Press, 1983), p. 15.

54. Cobley, *Class and Consciousness*, p. 3.

55. Stanley Trapido, "The Friends of the 'Natives': Merchants, Peasants and The Political and Ideological Structure of Liberalism in the Cape, 1854–1910," in Marks and Atmore, *Economy and Society*, pp. 247–274.

56. According to Wilson and Thompson, *Oxford History*, 1:322–323. The aim was to prevent the wealthy white men and businessmen, who were mostly English from excluding the farmers who belonged more to the middle class and the poor and were Dutch.

57. Phyllis Lewsen, "The Cape Liberal Tradition-Myth or Reality?" University of London, *Institute of Commonwealth Studies*, Collected Seminar Papers on the Societies of Southern Africa in the 19th and 20th Centuries, 1 (1969–70): 77.

58. Douglas A. Lorimer, *Color, Class and the Victorians: English attitudes to the Negro in the mid-nineteenth century* (Leicester: Leicester University Press, 1978), pp. 92–107.

59. Colin Bundy, *The Rise and Decline of the South African Peasantry* (Berkeley: University of California Press, 1979).

60. For example on the authority of African women in precolonial times we often hear simply that women were subordinate in a patriarchal society, e.g., Clifton Crais, *White Supremacy and Black Resistance* in his 1992 study of the Ciskei Xhosa simply relates that women were subordinate. A refreshing alternative to this refrain is that of Keletso Atkins, *The Moon is Dead! Give Us Our Money! The*

Cultural Origins of an African Work Ethic, Natal, South Africa, 1843–1900 (Portsmouth, New Jersey: Heinemann, 1993). She states that women were central to en-
hancing the authority of the household, and cleverly illustrates that in Zulu society women had rights in garden land, and the fruits of their labor that could be
used to enhance the position of the wife and the position of the husband. p. 42.

61. Rosalyn Terborg-Penn, Sharon Harley and Andrea Benton Rushing, eds.,
Women in Africa and the African Diaspora (Washington: Howard University Press,
1987); I. Schapera, *The Bantu-Speaking Tribes of South Africa, an Ethnographical Survey* (London: Routledge and Kegan Paul Ltd., 5th Impression, 1956).

62. Cherryl Walker, *Women and Resistance in South Africa* (London: Onyx Press,
1982); Deborah Gaitskell, "Wailing for Purity: Prayer Union, African Mothers and
Adolescent Daughters, 1912–40," in Marks and Rathbone, *Industrialization and So-
cial Change*, pp. 338–357; D. Gaitskell, "Housewives, Maids or Mothers? Some
Contradictions of Domesticity for christian Women in Johannesburg, 1903–1939,"
Journal of African History 24 (1983): 241–256.

63. See Part Six "African Resistance: Perspectives on Class and Gender," in
Bozzoli, *Class, Community and Conflict*; William Beinart, "Amafelandawonye (the
Die-Hards): Popular Protest and Women's Movements in Herschel District in the
1920s," in William Beinart and Colin Bundy, *Hidden Struggle in Rural South Africa*
(London: James Currey, 1987), pp. 222–269.

64. I use the term here in a broad sense much like David Moore in his "Review
Article: The Zimbabwean 'Organic Intellectuals' in Transition," *Journal of Southern
African Studies* 15 (1988): 96–105 in which he abbreviates Antonio Gramsci's concept, *Selections from the Prison Notebooks*, ed. and tr. Quinton Hoare and Geoffrey
Nowell Smith (New York: International Publishers, 1971). Moore notes that 'intellectuals' are not "those strata commonly described by this term, but in general
the entire social stratum which exercises an organizational function in the wider
sense—whether in the field of production, or in that of culture, or in that of political administration." p. 98; Similarly, for South Africa, Bradford, *A Taste of Freedom*, in a discussion of the branch organizers of the Industrial and Commercial
Workers' Union (ICU), declares that those drawn from the "less prestigious sectors of the middle strata, . . . were much more likely than senior officials to act as
organic intellectuals of their constituencies," p. 15.

65. See Introduction in Marks and Trapido, *The Politics of Race, Class and Nationalism*, p. 6.

66. Colin Bundy, *The Rise and Fall of the South African Peasantry.*

67. Andre Odendaal, "African Political Mobilization in the Eastern Cape,
1880–1910."

68. Peter Walshe, *The Rise of African Nationalism in South Africa* (Berkeley and
Los Angeles: University of California Press 1971); W. Manning Marable, "Booker
T. Washington and African Nationalism," *Phylon* (December 1974): 398–406; R.
Hunt Davis, Jr., "The Black American Education Component in African Re-
sponses to Colonialism in South Africa: (ca. 1890–1914)," *Journal of Southern
African Affairs* 3 (1978): 65–83; J. M. Chirenje, *Ethiopianism and Afro-Americans in
Southern Africa, 1883–1916* (Baton Rouge and London: Louisiana State University
Press, 1987).

69. Harry Dean, *The Pedro Gorino: The Adventures of a Negro Sea Captain in Africa and on the Seven Seas in His Attempt to Found an Ethiopian Empire* (New York: Houghton and Mifflin, 1929); John S. Burger, "Captain Harry Dean: Pan Negro Nationalist in South Africa," *International Journal of African Historical Studies* 11 (1979): 83–89; Clements Keto, "Black Americans and South Africa, 1890–1910," *A Current Bibliography on African Affairs* 5 (July, 1972): 383–406; Richard Ralston, "Africa, Africans, and Afro-Americans: Cultural and Political Exchange," *African Directions* (Spring, 1978): 48–58; E. De Waal, "American Black Residents and Visitors in the S.A.R. before 1899," *South African Historical Journal* 6 (1974): 52–55; Veit Erlmann, "A Feeling of Prejudice: Orpheus M. McAdoo and the Virginia Jubilee Singers in South Africa 1890–1898," *Journal of Southern African Studies* 14 (April, 1988): 331–350; David B. Coplan, *In Township Tonight* (London and New York: Longman, 1985); Cell, *White Supremacy*.

70. P. O. Esedebe, *Pan-Africanism: The Idea and Movement, 1776–1963* (Washington: Howard University Press, 1982); Immanuel Geiss, *The Pan-African Movement* (New York: Africana Publishing Co., 1974); Colin Legum, *Pan-Africanism: A short political guide* (Westport, Connecticut: Greenwood Press, 1962); Odendaal, *Black Politics in South Africa to 1912*; Walshe, *The Rise of African Nationalism*.

2

Race, Class, Segregation, and the 1883 Struggle Over the Removal of the "Native" Strangers' Location

Introduction

In 1883, the Port Elizabeth Town Council attempted to pass and implement the Native Strangers' Location Act.[1] The purpose of this Act was to force the black population to move from the "native" Strangers' location to Reservoir, a new site that was further away from town. Africans understood that the forced move to Reservoir would drastically alter their status, specifically with regard to the customary rights to land at Strangers'. In the broader housing and property dispute between the Town Council and the African population, this was of major consequence. By the 1880s, because of its central location, the Strangers' settlement had become particularly important. Whereas Strangers' had originally been on the outskirts, now, as a result of urban growth, it blocked the expansion of the white business and residential districts.

During the 1880s, the Cape liberal tradition, the large permanent black population, and the emergent middle class, along with the evolution of the ideology of segregation, were factors that interacted to influence the struggle between the government and the black population. Ultimately these factors forced the government to alter its plans for relocation. Resistance slowed the process of segregation and contributed to a relative freedom from restrictive regulations for the black working and middle class. So although the Act was passed in 1883, it was never used to remove and segregate the black population because of the concerted resistance by black and white Cape liberals. This resistance led to the addition of two amendments that effectively crippled the legislation.

Labor and Class Formation

In the mid-nineteenth century, Port Elizabeth was second only to Cape Town in population and trade. Port Elizabeth was paramount in the import/export trade because of its proximity to the agricultural producers in the hinterland who used the port facilities. Wool—the leading export—rose from 98,000 kilograms in 1835 to 16.9 million by 1870; in 1868 it accounted for 82 percent of colonial produce exported.[2] By the turn of the century, established industries included tanneries, wool washeries, and factories that made footwear, soap, explosives, and cigarettes.

In 1882, the total population was approximately 16,000, including 10,000 Europeans, mostly of British heritage, and 4,000 Africans of Mfengu, Xhosa, Sotho, and Zulu origin, as well as Coloreds, Chinese, and Indians.[3] The Mfengu continued to be the largest group of Africans to take up wage labor in Port Elizabeth, followed by the Xhosa, who were forced onto the market by the aftereffects of the disastrous cattle-killing (April 1856 to June 1857). Jeff Peires has analyzed the beliefs held by many Xhosa that led 85 percent of Xhosa adult men to destroy their cattle, corn and other goods to obey Nongqawuse's prophecy. He concludes that the Xhosa actions were not simply the reaction of a pagan people to colonial onslaught but rather linked to the lungsickness cattle disease that in 1854 began to decimate their stock. The main prophet was Nongqawuse, a fifteen year old girl. She, and several other prophets, claimed that the cattle and goods were contaminated and prophesied that the Xhosa people must kill their cattle, destroy their crops and wait for the millennial rise of the ancestors who would replenish the cattle herds and provide food and lands for all those who obeyed. While about 15 percent of the 70,000 Xhosa did not comply, thousands did but the promised visit of the ancestors failed to materialize and the believers found themselves destitute.

Over the thirteen months of the cattle-killing 400,000 cattle were slaughtered, about 40,000 people died, and over 150,000 were displaced from their homes.[4] Then about 33,000 Xhosa entered the Cape colony, destitute and facing starvation. At first they turned to the government for food, then remained as laborers. The employers in the towns were delighted at the unexpected supply of labor. One government official confirmed that: "All the Kafirs sent here for service have been greedily engaged at fair wages and there is a great demand for more. Public companies at Port Elizabeth want 130 at 3/6 to 3/- per day, you may send as many as fast as you like. . . . You need be in no fear of overdoing it. The last two batches of a hundred each were taken up on the day of their arrival."[5]

Other Africans entered Port Elizabeth to work, prompted by the loss of land to white encroachment, the need for money to pay tax (or *lobola*), or to satisfy new wants and aspirations stimulated by traders and mission education.

The skilled labor force in Port Elizabeth was generally made up of white immigrants from Britain and other countries; Africans filled most of the unskilled jobs. This division of labor by race was the result of discriminatory practices that had occurred over the years of interaction among Europeans, Africans, and Coloreds. By the 1880s, the black working population included both migrant and permanent workers. African men were paid lower wages than the whites in colonial society; the reason generally offered by whites was that the work was unskilled.

The temporary or migrant labor force, whose period of contracted service was generally three months to a year, was largely unskilled. The men worked in stores, in private homes or hotels, at sanitation work, in building operations, or on the railroad. Others were employed at the boating companies, where their duties were extremely arduous because of the inefficient port facilities.[6] For the most part, African women were employed in domestic service as cooks, laundresses, and housekeepers. Some vended foodstuffs; others brewed and sold beer (illegally by municipal law) to supplement their income. A few mission educated women worked as seamstresses and teachers. The skilled workers earned from £1 to £3 a week. (At this time the currency was British pound sterling coins and paper; the English £ pound was the equivalent in U.S. $ dollars of about five pounds for one dollar.) In 1884, wages for unskilled men averaged about 3/- (three shillings) a day; and the average wage for females was 20/- to 30/- per month.[7]

African women first began working for the white colonists in the rural areas, primarily on the farms. Jacklyn Cock relates that the women were paid lower wages than men, which whites justified by claiming that domestic work was unskilled labor, and the cost for board and lodging was substantial; in the rural areas female servants lived on the premises. As African women took up employment in Port Elizabeth, their wages remained lower although initially most lived in the black settlements with their own families, not on their employees' premises.[8]

Affected in the nineteenth century by European biases about race, class and gender, African women were restricted for the most part to domestic service. Mostly hostile and critical of African culture, the missionaries misinterpreted the important agricultural role of women in "traditional" society. They believed that African women were subordinate and treated as slaves so the missionaries preached that it was the men who should labor in the fields, and the women who should labor in the household. The upper class Western gender roles, modeled on Victorian Britain, that separated the spheres of work of men and women to internal (household for women) and external (outside the household for men) was offered to

Africans as the appropriate division. Underlying these roles was the belief that men were superior to women and women were to be perpetually subordinate. Jacklyn Cock relates that "these views were rooted in a class bias, that wanted to educate working girls to run their own homes as housewives eventually but first to be the servants of the middle class."[9] First applied to the British working classes they were imported to the colonies and applied to the Africans and added to this was a race and color prejudice. At Lovedale missionary school, opened in 1841 by the United Free Church Mission of Scotland, the first and most prominent educational institution that trained whites and blacks, girls were trained in the industrial department as domestic servants or seamstresses. The chief subjects, until 1873 were housekeeping, cooking, sewing and laundry work. "By 1887 three main occupations were offered, domestic servants, teachers or housewives. . . . The missionaries helped to link an ideology of domesticity that was rooted in European gender roles to an ideology of domestication generated by the problems of controlling a colonized people."[10]

The missionaries and settlers almost totally misunderstood or ignored the roles of women in southern Nguni African society. The work of African women included tending to their gardens, a major source of food for the family, fetching water, child care and the myriad responsibilities associated with contributing to the family's labor and prestige. But the woman's place in society devolved not only from her economic role but was intertwined with the social and political life of the kinship groups with which she lived. In the communal society, each individual had certain rights and responsibilities to the whole influenced among other things by gender, kinship, rank, and age. The dependency role that the missionaries applied to African women was an aberration. In Chapter 5, in conjunction with the actions of African women during the 1901 general strike, I will further discuss and explain in more detail their position in African society.

It is noteworthy that many of those among the approximately 2,150 Africans in the permanent workforce, defined by one government official as "having consistent employment in town," had lived in Port Elizabeth for fifteen or twenty years. They filled all levels of occupations, from the unskilled to the professional.[11] Reports from the Superintendent of Locations and the Resident Magistrate in Port Elizabeth indicate that most of the permanent workers lived in a family setting.[12] For a great number of these individuals, the overriding ambition was to accumulate enough capital to establish their own businesses and to become landowners.

By the 1870s, an aspirant African middle class was emerging from among these permanent workers. With discernible economic, political, and social interests, this group was comprised mostly of Christians who had adopted Western habits and customs. Their number totalled about 1800, and they were drawn from among the different ethnic groups. Some were mission educated and had in common their experience at one of the ten mission schools opened by missionaries and situated primarily in the eastern Cape. Among them was Lovedale missionary school. By the 1870s, "Lovedale included a teacher training school, a theological school and several industrial departments, together with boarding facilities for over 250 students."[13] Other mission schools included St. Matthew's, an Anglican foundation (1855), Healdtown, a Wesleyan church school (1857), and Blythswood, a United Free Church school in the Transkei (1877) and Amanzimtoti, the American Board Zulu Mission school in Natal (1853). Acculturation and rejection of African customs was encouraged at the mission schools and although only a small number of Africans could acquire a mission education, status, prestige, and economic rewards awaited them. Some of these western educated Africans worked as teachers, ministers, court interpreters, and clerks. Still others operated small businesses as butchers, bakers, or shopkeepers. Their training in these categories of employment essentially provided the basis for the growth of an "occupational elite" serving as they did as a yardstick for evaluating class position (much as rights of property and income do) and also separated this elite from other categories of workers.[14]

Yet, the economic separation between and among the emerging working and middle class was still quite fluid. Often members of the latter had initially been laborers; through Western education, they were able to enter professional occupations or to accumulate enough capital to open a business. Sometimes individuals balanced precariously between the two categories, holding multiple jobs either concurrently or consecutively to maintain a livelihood. Frank Makwena, for example, an alumnus of the Lovedale missionary school, worked as a clerk, a real estate broker, and a store proprietor over a period of fifteen years.[15]

Many members of the African working class, especially the Christian element, identified ideologically with the small black middle class and aspired to join their ranks. Although the Africans came from diverse ethnic backgrounds and religious denominations, they held common beliefs. These beliefs were shaped by disparate components, including missionary teachings, christian practices, acceptance of the western lifestyle, and a belief in Cape liberalism as preached by liberal whites. Many in this group of the aspirant black middle class considered themselves to be British citizens entitled to justice under the colonial law. Furthermore, they accepted that the road to upward mobility and assimilation into colonial society was through ownership of property, Western education and the franchise. However, increasingly racially discriminatory legislation was passed by the colonial government as changes in the economy such as the discovery of diamonds and gold added significantly to the need for cheap labor to work at the mines and in the emerging towns. Similarly, the imposition of new tax laws that Africans were encouraged to pay in cash required more men to go out and labor for the whites. Political changes followed, such as new voting regulations in 1887, aimed at limiting the number of black voters in the towns and countryside.

Despite the fact that some members of this emergent African middle class considered themselves to be British citizens many did not completely discontinue their African cultural practices. For example, in both the countryside and urban areas, Christian and western educated Africans continued to observe the custom of offering *lobola* (bridewealth) whereby negotiations between the families of the bride and groom resulted in an agreement that the groom's family would pay the bride's family a stipulated amount of wealth, which at the time was usually a certain number of cattle or an amount of British currency, an adaptation of the practice to foreign influence. But to avoid offending the missionaries most of whom thought that *lobola* was buying women and most certainly un-christian, the Africans said that *lobola* was simply a practice of exchanging gifts between families. Still other Africans, such as John Tengo Jabavu, the most important black leader of the era, were critical of this sentiment. Jabavu, apparently supporting the foreign ideas about *lobola,* proposed by the missionaries, strenuously opposed the practice and declared that Africans "should be ashamed for continuing the *lobola* custom."[16]

In the meantime—and as a result of so-called "class" legislation, that is, legislation that was biased against blacks—a noticeable philosophical shift was occurring among members of the emerging African middle class. It is noteworthy that at this time problems between the British and Dutch speaking populations, were often characterized as racial problems. This was because of the history of the conflict between the two white groups, beginning in 1795 in the Cape colony. As a result, when racially discriminatory legislation was first passed against Africans in the nineteenth century it was called "class" rather than "race" legislation. Whether characterized as race or class legislation the imprecise labelling left no doubt that the government's aim to subordinate Africans was partially driven by ideas about race, color, class and the inferiority of Africans compared to the whites.[17] As a result, the response of many mission educated Africans was to lean toward promoting racial and black unity in order to protect their limited privileges. Consequently, Africans began to form their own local and regional organizations, including the Native Educational Association (NEA) and the *Imbumba Yama Nyama* (Native Improvement Association), which held its founding meeting at Port Elizabeth in September 1882. The *Imbumba* was significant in that it

was organized by mission-educated Africans and was the first black political organization. In general, it sought to promote solidarity and, according to Isaac Wauchope, the secretary, to represent and unite "all
kinds of people—Xhosa, Fingo, Tshaka (Zulu), and Sotho." Furthermore,
Imbumba was formed as a regional organization partly as a response to
the creation of the Afrikaner Bond.[18]

At the local level, the *Imbumba's* leaders sent written appeals or representatives to the Town Council on many issues that affected the life of
Africans living in the municipal locations. For example, when there was
a threatened outbreak of smallpox, Wauchope sent a letter suggesting
that a committee be formed of "natives" at Strangers' and Cooper's Kloof
(an off-shoot of Strangers' location). Apparently his letter was ignored,
probably because a smallpox committee had already been established,
with Reverend John W. Gawler as the African representative. In any case,
the threat of smallpox had subsided.[19]

Often Christian-educated Africans provided the leadership necessary
in the urban environment. Because they had the knowledge of English,
and when convenient, were accepted by whites, they were perceived as
speaking for all blacks. In many ways, Isaac Wauchope, a well-known
leader who worked as an interpreter at the Magistrate's Court in 1882, ex-
emplifies some of the characteristics found among this group.[20] Born in
1852 at Door Hoek, near Uitenhage, Wauchope was the son of an elder at
the Union Chapel Church. He first attended school and worked as a
woolwasher, then moved to Port Elizabeth, where he was employed as a
storeman. In 1874, he entered Lovedale mission school and later passed
the teacher's exam. After doing mission work in Central Africa and teaching in Uitenhage, he relocated to Port Elizabeth in 1880 and began
working as a clerk and interpreter. Wauchope was also a Sunday school
teacher, temperance lecturer, and lay preacher. He subsequently married
Ntame Lukalo, a Lovedale alumna (as were her two sisters); it is believed
that she taught at the Wesleyan school in Stranger's location. In 1885, at
least fourteen of Lovedale's female African alumna were living in Port
Elizabeth, and five of them were employed.[21]

The Wauchope marriage was typical of the practice among educated
Africans to marry similarly schooled Christian partners. Men wanted
mates who, according to Reverend Elijah Makiwane, had "imbibed the
same ideas of progress which we suppose the young men to have received."[22] The head of the Native Educational Association formed in
1879, Makiwane practiced what he preached. In fact, he married a
Lovedale alumna and saw to it that his children were all well-educated.[23]

Another vehicle that united the black community was the *Isigidimi
Samaxhosa* (Christian Express) newspaper to which many Africans sub-
scribed and contributed articles. Through the newspaper columns, edu-

cated Africans voiced their opinions especially on religion and education. They also conducted debates and discussed strategies to facilitate sharing political power with the whites. The realization that the old methods of waging armed war must give way to a different method of combat was captured in one of the earliest Xhosa poems. Using the pseudonym I.W.W. Citashe, Isaac Wauchope wrote the poem and published it in *Isigidimi Samaxhosa.*

> *Go rescue them! Go rescue them!*
> *Leave the breechloader alone*
> *And turn to the pen.*
> *Take pen and ink.*
> *For that is your shield.*
> *Your rights are going.*
> *So pick up your pen.*
> *Load it, load it with ink.*
> *Sit on a chair.*
> *Repair not to HoHo,**
> *But fire with your pen.*[24]

It is noteworthy that in the 1870s, *Isigidimi's* largest readership (over 100) was at Port Elizabeth. First published in 1870, the newspaper had a circulation of 800 by the end of the year; and at least 500 subscribers were African. A few years later, the *Imvo Zabantsundu,* edited by John Tengo Jabavu, became a widespread political voice for Africans.[25]

Wauchope, and Africans like him, was a beneficiary of the Cape liberal tradition whose main principle was the non-racial qualified franchise. This meant that to be eligible to vote, one had to be a male, twenty-one years old, earning £50 per annum or £25 with free room and board or occupying any property worth £25. With the establishment of the Cape constitution the non-racial franchise was introduced. As previously mentioned, in 1853, the white settlers at the Cape had been granted representative government with their own Parliament. At this time, there was little thought that Coloreds and Africans would be in a position to meet the franchise qualifications. Initially, few Africans qualified, but by the 1870s increasing numbers of people were voting. In Port Elizabeth in 1883, most of the approximately 250 registered African voters, out of a total of 2,800, qualified through wages rather than through property ownership.[26]

---

*Hoho was a forest stronghold in the mountains where the *Ngqika* chief, Sandile, was killed in June 1878.

"The white political allies of Cape African voters stemmed from" among other things, the "politicians elected to the Cape Parliament after the granting of responsible government in 1872." In the 1884 election, there is evidence that black voters in the southeastern district, which included Port Elizabeth and Uitenhage, generally supported the re-election of liberal John McKay, the Minister of the Legislative Assembly (M.L.A.), for the Uitenhage seat. Nonetheless, he lost. However, the candidates for the two Port Elizabeth seats, known to be unsympathetic to African grievances, were unopposed. That may have led the black voters to concede the election, since the local newspaper commented on the unusual lack of election participation by the Colored voters.[27]

Another factor that influenced the reputation of the Cape as liberal were the alliances formed between white liberals drawn from "merchants, lawyers, newspaper editors, and missionaries, who served as the mission-educated community's secular and spiritual councillors, and as mediators at various levels in the eastern Cape, in Cape Town and in London."[28] The message of these individuals was strongly assimilationist and their aims to "civilize" Christian Africans and draw them into economic production fit in well with the expanding economy and received the support of mission educated and Christian blacks. Yet as Trapido has shown, the altruism associated with the Cape liberal tradition and the amount of support for it by white liberals was shaped by changing social, economic and political imperatives that constantly refashioned liberalism.[29] The Cape liberal tradition was linked with ideas of individualism, the right to liberty and justice, education, free trade, private property and a non-racial qualified franchise. However, as one scholar has noted: "Liberalism was not in the nineteenth century identical with democracy . . . it . . . accepted as axiomatic that the civilization of the West was superior to all others, that its creed of hard work and duty was inseparable from its values, that morally and technically its advantages were indisputable, and its duty to backward and lesser peoples was to guide, uplift them, and teach them its ways."[30] Although the makeup of the liberal camp shifted, for most of the nineteenth century there was always a small core of white intellectuals and political leaders who helped maintain the liberal tradition. These leaders included Saul Solomon, J. W. Sauer, W. P. Schreiner, and John X. Merriman.

Between the 1860s and 1880s, several changes occurred in the political economy that threatened the alliance between black and white Cape liberals. In particular, the discovery of diamonds in 1867 drastically altered the direction of the economy and concomitantly heightened the need for a labor force. People were needed to work in the mines, build the infrastructure, and supply the goods and services for an expanding population and economy. As Trapido points out, this shift in the economy helped to undermine the rural basis of the liberal alliance between the African peasantry and the white liberals.[31] Still another factor was Lord Carnarvon's pursuit of British expansionism and federation with the other three colonies in 1867, which required a change in the Cape's liberal "native" policy as compared to that of the other colonies. For example, the Orange Free State and the Transvaal colonies controlled by the Afrikaners were adamantly opposed to Africans owning land and exercising the franchise. Similarly, in Natal, the other British colony, a reserve/locations land scheme had been established in the mid 1840s by Theophilus Shepstone, the Diplomatic Agent in Natal to contain Africans in specific settlements. Shepstone has been credited by some scholars with establishing the system of segregation in Natal and in fact the reserves predated Grey's scheme. Ineffective because of government refusal to allocate funds, white officials on the spot, but especially Theopolis Shepstone administered the locations. This system of indirect rule closely resembled the one set up in British Kaffaria (the Ciskei) by Sir George Grey and later by Sir Frederick Lugard in other parts of Africa. Although theoretically Africans in Natal were allowed the franchise, obstacles erected by the colonial authorities ensured that few were able to vote. In the political sphere, the Cape colony was granted responsible government by Britain in 1872 which meant the white settlers were in a stronger position to pass and implement discriminatory legislation in their own interests.[32]

Several laws were passed to facilitate colonial administrative control and promote "native" labor. For example, the Cape Colony passed Location Acts in 1869 and 1876 (amended in 1884) to exercise more control over "natives" living on Crown and privately owned land. The former required Africans living on Crown land to pay a 10 shilling house tax; the latter imposed a tax on both the private landowner and squatters. All squatters in the "bona fide" employment of the landowner were exempt.

The intent was to reduce land use options for "natives" such as labor tenancy, share-farming, and renting, which had facilitated the rise of an African peasantry. Also, to force men out to labor the government required that the tax had to be paid in cash. The general effect was to increase the supply of labor either for the landowner or to push labor onto the market. At first, the number of farm laborers rose as squatters signed on to avoid the tax. Similarly, a Cape 1879 Vagrancy Law led an increased number of Africans to seek work in the colony.[33]

During the 1880s, this type of legislation was largely ineffective. Moreover, the labor shortage continued, since it was primarily created by employers who were unwilling or unable to pay competitive wages. Another factor that promoted a change in the liberal policy was the last frontier war in 1877–78 between the Xhosa and the white settlers. Subjection of the African chiefdoms and kingdoms was also proceeding apace in the other colonies. This significantly increased the number of Africans under colonial jurisdiction emphasizing the need for control. Many whites felt that the conquered Africans should be available for use as a cheap reserve labor force. Complaints about the "uncivilized and back-ward" Africans mounted as whites questioned why the majority of the black population continued to reject religious conversion and Western ideals, clinging instead to their cultural practices. Also, resentment from the white settlers surfaced against political and economic competition from the educated Africans and the black peasantry that threatened the growing white dominance. These sentiments were evident under the Sprigg government that passed discriminatory legislation such as the Peace Preservation Act in 1878 (also known as the Disarmament Act) to disarm the "natives." As a result of the Act, war occurred in 1880–81 be-tween the Cape colony and the Sotho. Also, it is noteworthy that the 1870s witnessed the growth of Afrikaner nationalism, which culminated in the formation of the provincial Afrikaner Bond at the Cape in May 1883.[34] Moreover, this put stress on the liberal alliance, since Bond mem-bers favored withdrawing "privileges" from Africans, including voting rights, and establishing an overall "native" policy without regard for class differences.

In the meantime, the liberal alliance was expressed in the real rela-tionships between whites and Africans. Although the actions of the whites were often ambiguous and paternalistic nonetheless the link be-tween these two groups was maintained.[35] The "small" liberal tradition, i.e., the coalition between whites and blacks in the towns such as Port Elizabeth, was exhibited by the interactions among missionaries, politi-cians, and Christian Africans. For instance, whites attended black so-cials, such as tea meetings and concerts, and worked in temperance and self-help organizations. Thus, the Mayor, several town councillors, and other leading whites were present at a special ballad concert conducted by Paul Xiniwe, who was a well-known figure among educated blacks during this period.[36]

Attendance by the Mayor and his cohorts was not accidental. In fact, such gatherings were a symbol of acculturation as well as a way to act out the paternalism that undergirded these relationships. Whites also acted in a paternalistic manner by working closely with African organi-zations and supervising three of the four "native" societies.[37] Often a fea-ture of colonial relations, and slave societies, paternalism is a mixed metaphor for many types of relations that include a dominant and dom-inated group threaded throughout with a veneer of politeness tinged with violence.

The church was also a place where some whites actively participated, and it was a focal point for Christian Africans. The Wesleyan was the

largest and most active of the four "native" churches. In 1882, a new
church was built to seat 650 people at a cost of £2,250, and by the opening, almost £1,000 had been paid. Because it was often difficult for
African families to survive even when there were two incomes, this was
no small matter. It is likely that in a typical Christian family, which had
four or five children and in which both husband and wife worked, the
total income was £60 a year. Since their expenditures for rent, taxes,
church contributions, clothing, food, and school fees averaged £60, nothing was·left over at the end of the year. As one African remarked, "To live
in towns like Port Elizabeth, where there is no chance of farming, hardly
pays."[38]

At both the local and regional level, sports such as lawn tennis, cro-
quet, and cricket were important social activities that drew the Christians
together. For the most part, whites tolerated these activities, although
newspaper reports often ridiculed the "dark" sportsmen and women.
Whites believed that the Western-type leisure activities were evidence of
acculturation and represented a degree of control over Africans outside
the workplace. Nevertheless, other social activities practiced by the black
population were viewed with less tolerance and were strongly criticized.
These included dancing, gambling, fist fighting, fighting with knobkerries (a stick with a knob at the top used for hunting, walking, and fighting), drinking "kafir" beer, and congregating at *shebeens* (a place where illegal liquor is sold). From the whites' perspective, the most ubiquitous
problem was making, drinking, and selling alcohol in the locations,
which was prohibited by municipal regulations.

The trade in liquor by Africans was a burning issue because it had important political, social, and economic connotations linked with control
and power and the development of the black working class.[39] For both
African men and women, regardless of class, making and selling alcohol
could provide a way to avoid wage labor or to supplement an income. A
lucrative income, and possibly a fortune, could be made in the liquor
trade. The risks were high, but so, too, were the returns. In 1882, a good-
sized cask of beer was worth about £10, and it was said that "the natives
who successfully carry on the business [are] living in laziness and comparative luxury."[40] In other words, these Africans had found a way to
avoid working for the whites. That same year, the Town Council tried to
curtail beer brewing by prohibiting beer consumption in the houses at
Strangers'.

Superintendent John MacPherson made numerous arrests under the
new liquor regulations, and the magistrate imposed heavy fines of £2 to
£5 or three months' in jail. Some Africans accused of private beer brewing tried to evade the law by arguing their own interpretation in court.
Thus, an African from Strangers' accused of making "kafir" beer told the

Magistrate, "I am not guilty. Where is my home? You have to prove it is my house."[41] Apparently the accused thought he had found a loophole in the law and that ownership, rather than occupancy of the house, had to be proved in order to convict. The magistrate dispelled this notion by sending the man to jail. Moreover, the magistrate's interpretation may have been unfairly influenced by his concern for upholding colonial law against Africans, thereby entrenching white civil administration.

Sometimes when African women were arrested for illegally brewing beer, they claimed they were trying to earn money to pay their housing site rent and to support their children. For example, an African woman named Ilatywa, charged in the magistrate's court in November 1882 with illegally brewing beer, claimed that she needed the money to support her children.[42] As mentioned earlier, race, class and gender discrimination limited job options of the African women and two salaries were often insufficient to make ends meet. Thus, it is not unusual that many women sold beer to secure supplemental income. Usually, the lucrative returns for brewing "illegal" beer allowed them to pay for both fines and site rent. So, for some, brewing and selling beer from their homes allowed them to work at home and if necessary to care for their children without having to go out to work for a master or mistress.

Many of the arrests for selling and brewing alcohol resulted from police raids and the use of "traps." The traps were African informers used to entrap illegal liquor brewers and dealers. For example, a trap would enter an establishment, order liquor, and pay for it with marked money.[43] Later the trap would return with the police, the marked money would be recovered, and the dealer or brewer would be arrested. Not surprisingly, liquor dealers, brewers, and location residents shared an animosity against the trap system.

For many Africans, the trap undoubtedly represented the ultimate collaborator because he assisted the authorities in invading African housing and space that, more often than not, was at the center of the struggle over the use of the urban environment. It is not surprising that traps both on and off duty were often attacked in the location. To preserve a trap's anonymity, Africans were barred from the courtroom when cases of illegal liquor selling were heard. Nevertheless, it became difficult "to procure good boys as traps because they soon become known [and] their lives are endangered."[44] In contrast to how Africans viewed the traps, black liquor dealers were held in high regard. This is evident from the case of Joseph Nyusela who, as he attacked and stabbed a trap, uttered, "You are the man who trapped Dungwa." (Daniel Dungwa was a notorious liquor dealer who had been arrested three times in six months and fined a total of £100.)[45] Even the magistrate disliked using traps to capture the liquor dealers; sometimes they gave lighter sentences to the dealers while scolding the police about the distastefulness of the system. Apparently entrapment offended the notions of liberal whites about fair play and justice.

In comparison, and ironically, it was suitable to restrict the liquor trade at Strangers' while allowing licensed white proprietors to operate liquor canteens near the settlement. As Parry has commented, however, it is necessary to differentiate between colonial laws applied only to Africans and laws applied to private property that affected everyone.[46] In fact, the trapping system related to laws of private property and applied to all races. It is noteworthy that by restricting the liquor trade at Strangers' the government could administer a "legitimate" liquor trade that disallowed black competition and provided revenue in licensing board fees for the Municipality.[47] This arbitrary application of the colonial law was doubtless highly questionable and caused resentment and disrespect for the law among Africans.

The social and cultural differences between Christian and non-Christian Africans as a result of Western influences was never absolute. This was readily apparent in the variety of attitudes about alcohol consumption and the liquor trade. It seems that some Christian Africans were involved in the beer trade; when their minister censored them, they set up a church known locally as the "Hop Beer Church."[48] These same Christian beer-brewers formed a mutual protection association that probably had several functions, including providing burial insurance, bribing the police, and paying the high fines of those arrested. Brewing beer for home use was a practice that some educated Africans viewed as a right. As early as 1878, they petitioned the Town Council to exempt them from the prohibition, emphasizing that it was an "age-old custom." The entire situation was a dilemma, as other educated Christians were totally opposed to alcohol consumption and supported temperance organizations and petitions to the licensing board against liquor canteens near the location.[49]

The incessant attempts by the authorities to control illegal liquor indicates that the moral habits of the workers were only one concern. Other concerns were the socialization of the workforce to acceptable recreational behavior outside the workplace and the legitimization of the wage labor system. Liquor dealing provided Africans with an alternative avenue for earning an income, thus promoting independence and undermining the legitimacy of the wage labor system. Social functions viewed as disreputable by most whites and some Christian Africans also challenged the system and illustrated the lack of official control over the labor force. Government harassment of "illegal" liquor dealers and moral condemnation by whites and blacks, of other types of activities associated with the "uncontrolled element" were aimed at encouraging the "legitimate" activities practiced by the dominant whites and "civilized" Africans.

Land and Housing

Despite the emerging class distinctions, Africans lived intermixed in municipal and private locations by the early 1880s. Some resided in dwellings erected on their employer's premises, and many rented rooms throughout the town, all within walking distance of work. Only the two municipal locations, Strangers' and Cooper's Kloof, were administered by the Town Council, which was advised by a Locations Committee. The Superintendent of Locations, whose duties included maintaining order, appointed two African men to assist him. Although they were designated as "headmen," they acted more in the capacity of policemen. An indication of their allegiance was their willingness, as they expressed it, "in rooting out the curse of the location—Kafir beer."[50] They also testified against beer brewers in court.

Strangers' was the oldest and largest municipal location and in 1882, between 1,500 and 3,000 people resided there, including "Mfengu, Kafirs (Xhosas), Basutos, Zulus and Hottentots (KhoiSan)."[51] As early as 1841, an inter-ethnic population lived in Fingo City, the section first settled by the Mfengu. Although kinship, ethnicity, friendships, and time of arrival influenced residence, this pattern continued. Established in 1877, Cooper's Kloof, housed about 300 to 500 people who were also to be removed. Most of the permanent residents at Strangers' and Cooper's Kloof were regular churchgoers and sent their children to the various denominational schools.

Gubbs' was the largest location on privately owned land. Apparently around 1857, some Africans living at Strangers' approached Mr. Gubbs, a leading resident and member of the Town Council, "to ask him to allow them to live on his farm . . ." Despite complaints from whites, he consented, "provided they paid site rent."[52] Once this was allowed, other Africans moved there, and by 1881, Gubbs's population had grown to 1800. Residents included many "traditional" or "raw" Africans, so described because as new arrivals they were ignorant of town life or because they wore blankets and adhered to their African beliefs and practices and for the most part rejected Western culture.

As stipulated in the 1855 land grant, the landholding system at Strangers' was based on a twenty-one-year leasehold whereby the tenants built their own housing and leased the site, renewable annually, for a rent of 30/- per year. Even though the land was not owned individually in the Western sense, the Africans had lived on the property for so long they had attained "tenure through occupancy," i.e., common law rights.

According to the mayor of Port Elizabeth, the "residents have built houses and the property is like their own and we cannot deal with it satisfactorily."[53] Moreover, since the land was inhabited by many Christian Africans who had long been encouraged by liberal whites to take up individual land tenure in comparison to communal ownership of land by the family or corporate group, concepts such as liberalism, paternalism, and the Victorian ethic were bound up with the issue of the land. Further, the grant contained a memorial statement indicating that the land should be held in perpetuity for the "natives" and should only be used as a "Strangers' location" and that if "the natives ... chose to become purchasers, they would have that liberty."[54] Under these circumstances, the right to freehold tenure (ownership of the land) was a crucial element in the struggle when removal of Strangers' was attempted. Often, the liberal whites believed that Africans were incapable of individual ownership of the land so landgrants were held by the missionaries or the mission society; a paternal aspect of colonialism.

Given the unprincipled way the Municipality treated the Africans who had voluntarily moved from Strangers' to Cooper's Kloof, the foregoing was an especially hotly contested issue. The move was prompted by the fact that as the population at Strangers' had become overcrowded, some of the Christian blacks who wanted to build new cottages but who were prevented from making housing improvements by a Council regulation, agreed to move into Cooper's Kloof. They knew that Strangers' might be closed and were induced by the opportunity for a plot and building rights in a less crowded area.

Once the Africans complied, however, the Municipality enforced by-laws that reduced the twenty-one-year leasehold to three years and "retain[ed] the right of removal from any site at any time within the terms of the lease."[55] Africans complained that the new lease left them in an insecure position, but those complaints went unanswered. Consequently, the outcome of their agreement to move was a significant change in their structural position, from long-term tenants with occupancy tenure to the precarious state of short-term tenants subject to eviction. Having carefully followed this development, the remaining residents of Strangers' location stiffened their resolve to resist any threats by the Municipality to remove them.

Although the Africans resisted moving to another site, they found that given the arbitrary location regulations, living at Strangers' had its drawbacks. For example, the Council's restriction on housing improvements—for fear of increasing the compensation when the Africans were moved—was, not surprisingly, a sore issue between the black population and the authorities. This regulation was especially irritating, because many residents were accustomed to treating the property as their own. In fact, they often erected buildings without bothering to get permission from Mr. MacPherson, the Superintendent of Locations. Also, in order to supplement their incomes, many rented out rooms and allowed others to build on their plots. The new law tended to cripple such initiatives.

The Strangers' Location Committee submitted a petition to the Council protesting the regulation and requesting that it be withdrawn, since the restriction on building rendered their structures dilapidated and contributed to unsanitary conditions.[56] Nevertheless, the Council refused to withdraw the regulation. Ignoring the prohibition, one exasperated resident, Mr. Majiba, went ahead and built a wooden house. But he was prosecuted for building without permission and for threatening to kill MacPherson, who had ordered the structure torn down.[57] Many people circumvented such regulations, and blacks coalesced around their common grievances.

In the various housing settlements, many Africans complained about overcrowding. At Strangers', the average occupancy was six people to one house. In some cases, however, twenty-five people occupied one site. Consequently, unsanitary and unhealthy conditions prevailed. Both black and white critics blamed the Municipality since, in administering the locations, the practice was to subdivide and lease individual sites rather than limit the number of people to a site. Moreover, almost no sanitary facilities were provided. In fact, stand-pipes for water were few; Africans had to use rain or river water for cooking, bathing, and washing. These inadequacies were probably felt most acutely by the Africans who resided permanently in Port Elizabeth and who were anxious for their homes to meet European standards. Other irritating features of location life included routine liquor raids by the police, often at early morning hours, and frequent harassment for loitering, walking on the sidewalks, and committing a nuisance.

The Council had decided to close only the municipal town locations undoubtedly because they lacked the financial and police power to enforce the segregation of all Africans. Also, as in London, removing the scourge from the town to an outlying area provided a way to temporarily clean up the "slum" rather than building decent housing for the workers.[58] Further, these removals were a way to promote an orderly and controlled labor force without commitment of resources for a more permanent solution to the much discussed health problem. The economic depression in the early 1880s left many houses empty. This meant that landlords who rented to Africans would be unlikely to support a total removal for fear their profits would decline. Also, objections would probably ensue from the employers of live-in labor who wanted their servants readily available.

The white townspeople wanted to determine where and under what circumstances the black workforce would reside. And as happens elsewhere, most whites were unwilling to have large numbers of Africans living close to them. Thus, in 1881, when Christian Africans took advantage of the opportunity to move into alternative housing, whites strongly opposed the move. Reverend Rayner, the Wesleyan minister for the black congregation at Edward's Memorial Church, purchased land adjacent to Strangers' on which he built and subsequently rented cottages to his church members. In a memorial to the Council, whites in the area objected to "natives" living in their neighborhood. In fact, they demanded that the Town Council solicit legal counsel to determine if a law existed that "would cause the removal of the . . . structure."[59] Some whites went so far as to threaten to burn the place down. Since Rayner had not broken any laws, however, the Africans moved in, and the area became known as Rayner's Barracks.

Problems of Municipal Control

White animosity toward Africans living near them escalated when a "faction fight" (often used to refer to fighting between Africans that has an ethnic base) between Xhosa from Gubbs' and Mfengu from Strangers' thoroughly panicked the town. Fighting began on Sunday night, October 1, 1881, and lasted five days. Over 800 men took part; at least four men died, and several were injured.[60]

During the disturbances, work was almost completely disrupted, much to the displeasure of white employers who were almost totally dependent on African labor to run homes and businesses. To prevent a complete breakdown in unloading the ships, on "the day of the great location fight . . . the supervisors had to pitch in to maintain operations."[61] Perhaps the magnitude of the turmoil can be grasped by the fact that not only local Africans but also those from surrounding areas such as Uitenhage and Humansdorp took part in the fighting. The absence of the participation of black Christians is noteworthy. In fact, only a few were involved, and it was reported that some of them asked the government through their missionary for protection "for fear of being attacked."[62]

Although knowledge of socio-political practices among African workers in the nineteenth century towns is limited, it is known that certain African men, labeled headmen in newspaper reports, exerted a powerful influence on many of the workers. The majority of the men who took part in the disturbances were southern Nguni and among them the headmen's functions were acting as representative for the homestead, leading battles, and settling disputes.[63] Thus, during the commotion, a number of headmen, and not those appointed by the Superintendent, exhorted their followers to fight and led the charges. Moreover, at one meeting, the Mfengu and Xhosa leaders negotiated a place for the confrontation (also a common practice during disputes). At another meeting, the resident Magistrate discussed with designated spokesmen, apparently chosen by each side, how to end the fighting.

During the combat, military discipline was displayed, and scouts were sent out "to observe the movements of the enemy and . . . the men sang war songs and used the Zulu horn formation."[64] It seems likely that it was these headmen in charge of the ranks, rather than the colonial authorities and educated Africans, who were expected to settle the disputes in the location. This supposition is supported by the fact that at the court trials, a code of silence hampered the court proceedings. Consequently, all the men accused of taking part in the "faction fight" were equally silent. Not one was willing to reveal why the violence erupted or to identify anyone involved. In fact, the testimony was primarily from black Christians and Superintendent MacPherson.

White officials and colonists offered two main reasons for the fighting. The first and most frequently voiced was that the "faction fights" erupted because of "intertribal feuds fomented by beer drinking."[65] Many white colonists shared this assumption, since it was accepted that the old enmity between the Mfengu and the Xhosa had been transferred to the urban area. This animosity between the groups was rooted in the earlier colonial period and their relationship with the white settlers. The Mfengu people had migrated into Xhosa territory as refugees from the *mfecane* (wars) in Natal. Not all Mfengu were fully incorporated into Xhosa society when some of them became allies of the white colonists in wars against the Xhosa. That is, they aided the whites "in the last four wars [with the Xhosa] of 1834, 1846, 1850 and 1877."[66] The government awarded the loyal Mfengu land that belonged to the Xhosa and issued certificates of citizenship that exempted the Mfengu from colonial laws restricting the movement of "natives" into and out of the colony.[67]

By 1879, however, some white officials in the countryside reported a narrowing of the cleavage between the Xhosa and Mfengu. These officials cited colonial legislation such as the Disarmament Act of 1878, which discriminated against Africans regardless of ethnic background. The Act required even the Mfengu to turn in their guns. In consequence, the Civil Commissioner at Queenstown in the eastern Cape reported that the policy of disarmament was "causing much and deep rooted dissatisfaction among the natives. . . ." Most Africans in his district were Mfengu, and they especially felt that being "deprived of their arms is a mark of degradation" because of their past loyalty. They also felt "their manhood has been taken from them."[68]

The second and less frequently voiced reason offered for the "faction fight" came from the Civil Commissioner of Port Elizabeth, Alfred Wylde. He maintained that "kafir beer may have invited [the fighting] but the true cause was a struggle between the Fingoes with Zulus against Xhosa (Kafirs) for the beach work."[69] His statement bears close examination, especially in light of Van Onselen and Phimister's seminal analysis of the 1929 "faction fight," also called the "knobkerrie war," in Bulawayo. They point out that citing ethnic differences as an explanation for violence in urban areas is insufficient to understand a complex process.[70] Rather, the various contributing factors should be examined. These include economic changes brought by colonial rule and the effects and pace of proletarianization on the specific groups involved. The authors conclude that: "The fights can be interpreted as intra-working class eruptions which occur in colonial urban ghettos when there is restructuring of a labor market in which employment, to differing degrees, is 'ethnically' defined by employers and/or by workers. Violence is most likely in recessions or depressions when intra-working class competition for jobs is intense . . . "[71]

Their conclusions, the two reasons offered for the violence, and the conditions operating at Port Elizabeth indicate the need to carefully assess the backdrop to the "faction fight." For example, what was the importance of the fixed ethnic categories such as Mfengu and Xhosa that officials used to describe African interaction in relationship to specific changes in the political economy? Also how important was ethnic consciousness in day-to-day relationships between and among African workers, in Port Elizabeth. And, what other factors operated to promote unity or conflict among the African workers, since ethnicity does not operate in isolation from other influences on consciousness such as culture and class. Moreover, as Epstein demonstrated long ago in his study of protest among African workers in the Copper Belt, ethnic boundaries and divisions become primary depending on the "situation."[72]

In Port Elizabeth, ethnic identification was apparent but not rigidly practiced. In fact, some degree of cross-ethnic interaction commonly occurred in the home, at work and in the recreational arena. For example, as noted previously, different groups of Africans lived intermixed in the various locations, although it seems that the majority of Mfengu lived at Strangers' location. Also, the different ethnic groups usually congregated at Gubbs' to drink beer because it was located on privately owned land. Thus, unlike the situation in Municipal locations, Gubbs' was not subject to regulations against beer brewing. An indication that cooperation was the norm was the fact that for fifteen years there had been no "faction fights."[73]

The boating companies employed the largest number of Africans in Port Elizabeth, and the probability for ethnic conflict, about work related issues, was highest among the beach workers. This was partly because the absence of a suitable harbor—"everything had to be landed or shipped from the open beach"—increased the companies' dependence on the laborers.[74] Inggs has described the extraordinary strike power of the Mfengu beach workers as a result of the shortage of labor in the 1850s and that it began to decline when the Xhosa arrived to work.[75] Nonetheless, beach workers' strikes had occurred in June 1872, August 1876, and July 1877. All three involved Mfengu, and in the 1877 strike for higher wages, "all five 'ringleaders' arrested were Mfengu."[76] The data suggests that prior to the 1881 "faction fights," many of the Mfengu and the Xhosas disagreed about which group should work at the beach and whether or not to strike. Although the Mfengu beach workers wanted to strike, the Xhosa refused.

Several noteworthy factors probably prompted the call for a strike and the Xhosa's refusal to participate. First, the Xhosa population in 1881 was increasing in relation to that of the Mfengu population. The location reports indicate that although the Mfengu remained the majority African population, the Xhosa grew from "600 in 1865 to 1,800 in the early 1880's."[77] One reason for the increase was the last military war in 1877–78 between the Xhosa and the white settlers. In the conquered territories, the men were encouraged to work in the towns and on the farms, and many migrated to Port Elizabeth. Another reason for the growing African population was drought conditions in the countryside. Official Cape Blue Book reports for 1879 through 1881 indicate that both Mfengu and Xhosa responded by requesting passes to leave the territories, many for railway work, others for towns such as Port Elizabeth. The larger number of Xhosa beach workers could increasingly undercut the bargaining power of the Mfengu workers.

Yet another factor that could undercut the bargaining power of the Mfengu was "the construction of jetties from the 1870s that reduced the boating companies' reliance on one landing method," and thus on the beach workers.[78] Also, workers at the boat jetties and those unloading trucks were paid less than were beach laborers, since the work was deemed less demanding by the employers. It seems feasible that conflict arose over the difference in pay scale and the allocation of higher and lower paying jobs. It is uncertain if jobs were allocated by ethnic group, although it seems likely that seniority was probably an important influence. Consequently, since the Mfengu were the longer-term workers, they probably demanded the higher-paying jobs. Moreover, the need for fewer workers on the jetties probably increased competition for jobs. In this respect, Mabin has determined that the Cape Colony was entering an economic downturn and it is feasible that this too affected the overall labor market, since there was an increasing competition for jobs in the smaller towns and also fewer jobs at Kimberley. Supporting this supposition is the occurrence of "faction fights" around this time in other eastern Cape towns, including Grahamstown, East London, and Papendorp, where the Mfengu had been the primary laborers. The abovementioned factors could have affected the Xhosa's ability to resist the Mfengu leaders who usually called the strikes suggesting that the conflict may have been work related.[79]

Apparently after the Mfengu called for a strike and the Xhosa refused, animosity had been brewing for about a week. The first confrontation seems to have erupted when one Fallani, a Mfengu, was at Gubbs' having a drink at the house of a Xhosa. Fallani stated that, "We saw some men coming towards us with kerries, and they commenced to beat the other Kafir who was with me. . . ." The two men ran, and when cut off by the chasers, Fallani asked "what they wanted." They responded "Don't you ask anything for you have killed our chief."[80] This was doubtless a reference to the recent 1877–78 war between the Cape colony and Xhosa during which the Xhosa chief Sandile was killed. His death was blamed on the Mfengu who had fought for the colony. After this verbal exchange, the men commenced beating Fallani, and he landed in the hospital.

Forthwith, the Mfengu and Xhosa armed themselves with knobkerries, and the fighting began. Much of the fighting involved the Mfengu, sometimes supported by the Zulu, attacking the Xhosa at Gubbs' location. Because of their larger numbers, the Mfengu could overwhelm the Xhosa and force many out of Gubbs'. The houses of the Xhosa were also targeted, and they "were ransacked by the Fingoes and poultry, dogs, and every living thing destroyed."[81] Whether intentional or not, the fighting prevented many men from going to work. Countercharges issued from both sides. For example, one Xhosa man, when asked why he was going to fight, complained that "the Fingoes would not let the Kafirs go to work." On the other hand, a Zulu man charged that the Xhosa were preventing them from going to work. Both sides also spoke about protecting their children and preventing their houses from being burned down. Thus, Mahili, a Zulu, testified that, "We were afraid the Kafirs would come into our location [Strangers'] and kill our women and children, so we thought it safer to go out and drive them back."[82]

John MacPherson, the Superintendent of Locations, was the only white man attacked and beaten. As he tried to help a wounded Mfengu man and also counsel the men not to fight, two Xhosa beat and stabbed him, then took his watch and gun. He survived.[83] Several people tried to solve the puzzle of why MacPherson was the only one who was attacked. One commentator thought perhaps the reason was the crackdown on beer brewing and the removal of rubbish at Strangers'. Enforcement of both "affected the living arrangements" of Africans, which could mean a number of things, including that some were forced to move to a less crowded site, to stop selling beer, or to pay fines. Also, the fact that MacPherson had a gun that he fired in the air may have inspired the Africans to attack him. Or it could have simply been as Malingi, a Basuto, said, "I think they must have known he was the Superintendent of the Location."[84]

Explanations for the Disturbances
and the Taint of Racial Science

Whatever the reasons, it quickly became apparent that the police could not control the disturbances. The inefficiency and capriciousness of the police were the butt of jokes, even at Town Council meetings. Moreover, the police themselves were irresponsible, for in several court cases, they were charged with being drunk or sleeping while on duty. The opinion of Mr. Alfred Marks, a Town Councillor, represented one view about their incapacity to regulate the black population. Although he praised the Divisional Police for a job well done, he insisted that if they "had shot a Kafir, they [the Africans] would no doubt have had their revenge by setting fire to some of the stores in town. As to supplying the men [police] with their toy revolvers, that was absurd. Had they fired their playthings they would have been taken from them by the Kafirs."[85]

Mayor Henry William Pearson also spoke passionately about the lack of control and the required supervision at Gubbs'. "If it was necessary to have 5,000 natives for the labor of the town, they should be paid the same attention as 5,000 horses would be if they employed them and be taken care of just the same. If they had natives to make profits out of then they should provide police for them."[86]

The Mayor's words reflect two intertwined factors, both increasingly important in the struggle over segregation, that were expressed in the comments that whites made about the disturbances. These were (1) the need to control the workforce and (2) an almost unconscious reference by whites to commonly held, negative, racial stereotypes about Africans that illustrated how older racial prejudices were influenced by the rise of racial science in the nineteenth century.[87] The latter factor requires some clarification, since racial science was an important, although subtle, influence on colonial policy.

A few scholars have discussed the rise of racial science (also called pseudo-scientific racism) and its effects on the establishment of segregation prior to the establishment of the Union of South Africa in 1910.[88] However, the scholarly debate has focused on the beginning of the ideology of segregation, when the word, segregation, was used by whites in South Africa, and the lack of a coherent theory of racism until the twentieth century.[89] It is almost as if since the racially based actions of nineteenth-century colonial officials were not given a name by the perpetrators, then their actions did not warrant being called an ideology, which is exactly what John Cell argues. Cell states that even though color discrimination was practiced before the twentieth century, not until the early 1900s does the "conception of segregation as something more than the physical separation of peoples enter the English language . . . and become conscious thought."[90]

However, even if theories of racial difference did not crystallize into an ideology of white supremacy in the nineteenth century, it is possible to analyze the words, images and metaphors from that period to provide the context and to suggest connections within which segregationist initiatives emerged. As George Frederickson explains with regard to distinguishing between the: "academic and popular meanings of racism, one way is to differentiate between the explicit and rationalized racism that can be discerned in nineteenth—and early twentieth-century thought and ideology and the implicit or societal racism that can be inferred from actual social relationships. If one racial group acts as if another is inherently inferior, this is racism in the second sense, even if the group may not have developed or preserved a conscious and consistent rationale for its behavior."[91] The implicit actions of local and central government officials were building blocks toward white supremacy because a belief in white superiority and black inferiority underlay these actions. "The very notion of white progress, of white superiority, of whiteness as a privileged place in the evolutionary ladder of humankind" was implicit in language and actions of many nineteenth-century whites.[92]

It is noteworthy that the preconditions for racial segregation existed prior to the nineteenth century. The European prejudices against Africans had their origin in the sixteenth century and earlier. Based on the differences between Africans and Europeans in color, features, culture, and religion, these prejudices led the British to view Africans as objects of contempt. Thus, for centuries Africans were mythologised as brutish, evil, satanic, lecherous, savage, and beast-like. Much of this was related to the concept of blackness in England, which was equated with dirty, soiled, foul, wicked, evil, dangerous, deadly, repulsive, malignant, ugliness, and devilish. The opposite was white, denoting purity, virginity, virtue, beneficence, God, and beauty. When complemented by red, white denoted "the color of perfect human beauty, especially female beauty."[93]

This negative labelling of differences between blacks and whites, explains Dona Richards, provided the groundwork for the ideology of European dominance. Furthermore, Richards states that the "Western European ethos appears to thrive on the perception that those who are culturally and radically different are inferior. It relates to other cultures as superior or inferior, as powerful or weak, as 'civilized' or 'primitive.'"[94]

This helps to explain the western European concept of the Great Chain of Being. The idea of the Great Chain of being goes as far back as "Aristotle's *'scala naturae'* in which it was imagined that nature produced living things in a great and continuous ladder, each rung of the ladder being separated from the next by almost imperceptible differences," [95] those at the bottom were physically stronger. At the top were humans, at the bottom, animate nature passed by gradual steps into inanimate matter.

The Chain also embodied the idea of naturalism. As one passed up the scale, the characters of each being merged . . . into the next, so that higher organisms shared to some degree the nature of lower animals. Also, the scientific study of primates, the animals nearest to humans on the great chain, strengthened the association between man and animals.

By 1800 "the Great Chain was now used to suggest that a racial hierarchy, as well as other social hierarchies, were real aspects of nature's order."[96] The British had encountered Africans and the great apes at the same times in Africa, compared the two and further concluded that Africans were the same species or cousins of the apes. Thus Africans were the closest to the savage beasts that in appearance most resembled humans. Moreover the Europeans speculated, influenced by earlier traditions about beasts and venery that Africans shared not only aspects of appearance, and color but also the characteristics especially the venerous nature of apes. This comparison became one of the most popular in human history.[97] Racial stereotypes were popularized and became fixed by the printing press, restricting the way Europeans "saw" and understood real Africans."[98] In the eighteenth century such comparisons became commonplace and were often made by scientists as well as ordinary men and women. For example, in 1799, the Manchester physician, Charles White, in his book titled *An Account of the Regular Gradation of Man,* used the concept of the Chain to suggest the lowly position, ape-like nature, and independent biological existence of the Negro.[99] Slowly the idea of the Great Chain was applied to race. Not surprisingly those at the top were western Europeans, while those deemed least capable, the Africans remained at the bottom.

Over time, then, popular ideas about racial types associated blacks with the lower social orders and an inferior status. In the eighteenth century says Nancy Stepan "the idea of the Great Chain of Being was revived by a number of natural scientists, and . . . it was only too easy to apply the Great Chain to the problem of race."[100] The biological sciences in particular were of great importance in this process. Biology, writes Greta Jones, helped to "create the kind of moral universe in which nature reflected society and vice versa." Old ideas comparing Africans to the great apes of Africa and placing them at the bottom rung on the Great Chain, with Europeans occupying the top, were accepted as general knowledge. By the

1860s some social scientists influenced by deeply embedded racist and evolutionist assumptions applied Darwin's theories about the biological doctrine of natural selection in natural organic life and the theory of evolution, mixed in Herbert Spencer's conclusions about the "survival of the fittest" and Social Darwinism was born.[101]

To support the idea of the Great Chain of Being, a number of theories were offered by white scientists concerning the origins of humans and their separation into unequal races. In the nineteenth century new scientific disciplines emerged, including comparative anatomy, physiology, histology, paleontology, psychology, anthropology, and sociology, to shape the study of human races.[102] All were supposed to be based on scientific objectivity but many searched for "truth" that would verify white superiority and black inferiority. It is noteworthy that the use of the concept of the Great Chain for racialist purposes was not typical of racial science in the late eighteenth century and the early nineteenth century.[103] Several respected scientists in defending the idea of monogenism, or the belief that man emerged from one source (rather than from several, or polytheism), attacked and rejected the Great Chain as a true principle of nature. Despite their attacks, the concept of the Great Chain was accepted as the cornerstone of nineteenth-century racial science and twentieth-century Social Darwinism and eugenism. According to Dubow, "The language of Social Darwinism was thoroughly impregnated with biological metaphors. Examples include 'adaptation', 'segregation', 'degeneration', 'hygienic', 'fitness', 'hybridization', 'stock', and so on."[104]

The concept of the Chain of Being confirmed the British belief, in the words of, Dr. James Hunt, in the first presidential address to the Anthropological Society of London in 1865, "that the Negro race can only be humanized and civilized by Europeans."[105] Hunt shared the principal characteristics of many social scientists, scientists and historians who pronounced general laws, and universal theories, invariably reflecting the time and place in which they wrote. Their data seemed to justify the political and economic exploitation of the people they considered inhuman and uncivilized.

One of the most influential studies in the nineteenth century was *The Races of Men* by Robert Knox, published in 1852, in which he "sought to prove that 'race is everything literature, science, art—in a word, civilization depends on it" and that human character, both national and individual, is traceable solely to the nature of that race to which the individual or nation belongs." Knox was barred from practicing medicine when two men who supplied him with human dead bodies through illegitimate means by murdering them were convicted. Knox began to write for a new audience, the common man, and presented his conclusions "without qualification, without question, and without solid evidence." It is significant that Knox had an intimate relationship with the eastern Cape of South Africa, having spent three years there as an army surgeon from 1817–1820. Moreover, in his study Knox drew heavily on South African examples and "many of his reflections on the physical and mental characteristics of the 'Bosjeman', [the San, pejorative Bushmen] the 'Hottentot', [KhoiKhoi] and the 'Caffre', [the Xhosa, pejorative Kafir] as well as the questions he posed about their racial origins, were taken up in earnest by scientists some fifty years later."[106] It may not be too farfetched to propose that even though most ordinary people did not read intellectual studies by scientists like Knox, conclusions that "race is everything" circulated as a popular stereotype.

To return to the analysis of Mayor Pearson's remarks, the implicit comparison of "natives" as equivalent to horses on the Chain of Being reveals the perhaps unconscious racial assumptions that distorted the lens through which many whites viewed Africans. Almost in the same breath, however, the Mayor voiced his fear that the Municipality "would be called upon to pay for a good deal of the losses sustained" during the rioting to both white and "native" claimants for property damages.[107] These seemingly contradictory attitudes towards the "natives"—as, on the one hand, animals and, on the other, as humans with property rights—were not uncommon. The latter reflects nineteenth-century ideological influences, those of mid-Victorian liberalism, humanitarianism, and other ideas about class, "progress" and the "rights of man," including the right to own property. The Mayor's remarks also reflected the debate about evolution and the possibility that Africans could rise on the human scale as they became more civilized. It was just such ambiguities that created problems when attempts were made to segregate Africans based only on race.

But racially prejudiced beliefs ran deep. Expressing a view about the need to supervise the black laborers, an irate white citizen asked, "How long [was] this sort of behavior . . . to be put up with, and how long [did] the inhabitants of the town, with its vaunted civilization, intend to allow the quiet of their homes to be disturbed at all hours of the night by a horde of naked, yelling barbarians . . . ?"[108] Again, this was a reference to racial stereotypes, of civilized whites compared to black barbarians. In a milder tone the editor of the local newspaper suggested that stringent discipline, vigilant control, and surveillance of the Africans was necessary. It is likely that these attitudes provided a fertile bed for the growth of the ideology of segregation that contrasted sharply with mid-Victorian liberal ideas.

The Removal of Strangers' Location

Prodded by these trenchant white reactions to the "faction fight," the Town Council stepped up its plans to close Strangers' location. Although a move had been discussed for several years before 1880, a location removal committee to choose a new site was not formed until mid-1881. The Town Councillors advanced several reasons for removing Strangers'. Some of them were similar to those cited in 1855 when Strangers' was established. They included statements such as, "it was necessary to alleviate the overcrowded conditions which created a health hazard for the Africans as well as the white townspeople, a high crime rate existed, it was an eyesore, and it was too close to the white residents who were forced to view the "indecent habits of the uncivilized people."[109] As in 1855 it was argued that the removal would benefit both blacks and whites.

Undoubtedly some of the reasons were legitimate. In fact, the locations were overcrowded and unsanitary, and they represented a health hazard. Nevertheless, many parts of the town where whites lived were unhealthy as well, lacking a sufficient water supply and a proper drainage system. Although the white areas were receiving attention from the local authorities (a drainage system was being built), the African areas were not. As for the high crime rate (as defined by whites), the numbers at Strangers' were low in relationship to the total population. Moreover, the offenses seemed mainly to involve brewing beer, drinking liquor, gambling, and walking on sidewalks—scarcely public dangers. Clearly the definition of crime was determined in an atmosphere that was hardly racially neutral.

But the concern about the public danger alluded to more than committing crime against property. Rather, the common thread woven throughout the complaints was dissatisfaction with the unlawful social activities in which some Africans engaged in defiance of local regulations. To some whites it probably seemed that some blacks living in the town continually disrespected or mocked the power, or lack of it, of the colonial authorities by refusing to observe the laws and, thus, exhibiting a certain amount of independence. Notions about the public danger of the working class in itself were not unusual. In fact, studies about the emergence of the working class show government attempts to create controls on the space and work habits of the laborers in England, France, and the United States.[110] However, these notions about public danger were influenced by negative beliefs about other ethnic groups who had a different skin color and were further compounded by a colonial situation. This combination created in the minds of whites the fear that they would be overrun by uncontrollable, wild, and barbaric Africans. Put another way, by the 1870s many whites held a racist and white supremacist world view that was influenced by popular notions about Africans as well as Social Darwinism and racial science. It is clear that deeply embedded in the psyche of both scientists of the day and in white public opinion was belief in the superiority of white Europeans and the inferiority of black Africans.[111]

Under these circumstances whites found it easy to believe that the African presence was inherently a public danger and a threat and that containment was the remedy. Such beliefs were evident in a letter from an Englishman to the editor of the local newspaper in Port Elizabeth. The man queried, "Who does this Colony belong to?" Then he explained that having traveled around the Eastern Cape, he was in a fog because "Anyone can't walk the pavements now, but what he is sure to knock up against a nigger, who manfully asserts his rights, and being a nigger, makes the best use of his privilege [sic]."[112] This colonist's statements were related to a popular belief that Africans should not be entitled to share the sidewalks with whites, especially white women, and should walk in the streets or move off the sidewalk when approaching a white person. Obviously inferior black beings were to give way and show the proper deference to superior white beings.[113] Just as obviously there were Africans who did not feel compelled to submit to these expectations.

There is additional evidence that the old racial stereotypes and the new racial science were in the minds of other whites in Port Elizabeth when discussing location removal. For example, one Town Councillor said he was afraid that if Africans were allowed to live in town rather than in separate locations, "a part of the white class would be reduced to a lower state . . ." because "the blacks were *strong* . . . and every time they [the whites] put themselves on a level with the natives they lowered themselves."[114] The belief in the physical *strength* of Africans in comparison to their *weak* intellect indicates the Councillor's awareness of evolutionary ideas about cultural inferiority and moral degeneration. Whites expressed fears about racial "degeneration" as black (who were said by whites to be morally degenerate) and white (who whites said belonged to a superior race) workers interacted in the towns and cities. It was believed by many whites that too close an association between whites and blacks could bring about racial degeneration thus the fear expressed by the councillor. Saul Dubow has observed that moral degeneration was one of the three important areas of political debate found in the "imagery of Social Darwinism." The other two were speculation about the relative intelligence of blacks and whites . . . and the almost universally expressed horror of miscegenation. Also evident was the influence of the biological debates on eugenics or the "science of racial stocks" that permeated nineteenth century British thought and disputed the notion of evolutionary progress.[115] Among members of the working class and intellectuals alike these ideas were attaining popular acceptance in South Africa and were being used to challenge mid-Victorian liberalism and to justify exploiting Africans, who outnumbered the whites.

The reality of the lived experiences, or what actually occurred between black and white, did not fit the dogma about the "civilized whites" and the "African barbarians." An example that illustrates this point, as well as shows the diversity among the population, was the reaction of some whites during the "faction fight." The sources tell us that although Prince Alfred Volunteer Guards tried to prevent the fighting, other white men committed unlawful acts. For instance, it was reported that some Europeans and Coloreds looted the homes of the Xhosa and Mfengu and took souvenirs while the latter groups were away fighting. Moreover, it is clear that some whites viewed the battles as though they were observers at a sports arena. Consequently, when the authorities tried to intervene, "The white people set the Fingoes on again and desire[d] them not to be afraid of the few white policemen who were there."[116] These reactions did not emanate only from the white poor or criminal element. In fact, among those encouraging the confrontation were young "gentlemen" who apparently had no qualms about actively provoking ethnic rivalry between the Xhosa and the Mfengu.

One of the primary reasons for the removal of Strangers' was that changes in the economy had led to a growing number of black laborers in Port Elizabeth living in close proximity to whites. But the most significant reason was that the value of the land on which Strangers' was located was rapidly rising. This was because when Strangers' location was originally established, it had been on the outskirts of town. Now, however, it was situated near the town center, close to the best residences and the most valuable property. As the Resident Magistrate stated in reference to Strangers', "There is no doubt . . . that the land in this vicinity is rapidly rising in value . . . squalid barbarism . . . is in the midst of the best part of the town."[117] In short, the settlement blocked white expansion. Not only would the land be targeted for capitalist enterprises once Strangers' was removed, but also the African landlords would be deprived of rental income—their means to upward mobility.

Many merchants supported the removal of Strangers', doubtless viewing segregation as a way to facilitate control of the undisciplined native workers who had caused them so many problems in the past. Gaining control of the valuable town land for specific or speculative capitalist ventures was probably another concern. The opinion of A. J. Mosenthal, a well-known big businessman and a member of a mining syndicate, was probably representative. In the early 1870s, the syndicate had purchased the farmland, Vooruitzicht, where Kimberley and DeBeers (the two richest diamond producing mines) were situated. Mosenthal clearly sanctioned the removal. Thus, his was the main signature on a petition signed by over 267 whites ratepayers from Ward 5. They claimed that removal of Strangers' would ensure the health and safety of the white population and also "greatly benefit the natives."[118] The six other wards—there was a total of seven—submitted similar petitions, with over 1800 signatures.

It is noteworthy that during this same period the closed compound system was being created to house African workers at the Kimberley diamond mines where H. Mosenthal, a relative of A. J. Mosenthal, was a director of both the DeBeers Company and the London and South African Exploration Company. These companies were formed in 1870 to explore and develop mines. Many industrial merchants in Kimberley and Port Elizabeth advocated the segregation of Africans to facilitate control and to prevent "black political dominance in the future."[119] Moreover, in 1882, thousands of Africans passed through Port Elizabeth enroute to work at Kimberley and other places. During that year, 1,845 Africans arrived and 5,472 departed, the majority listing Kimberley as their destination.[120] The Town Council, made up primarily of merchants who were anxious to regulate the movement of black workers, viewed housing segregation as one way to control "vagrancy" while encouraging migration to other work centers.

For the emergent African middle class and their liberal supporters, the most potent issue in the struggle over the removal of Strangers' was the ownership of land. Beginning in the mid-nineteenth century, Africans were landholders in the Cape under both indigenous and various forms of European tenure. In the strictest sense of the law, Africans in Port Elizabeth were not landowners. Nevertheless, they were technically recognized as such. And, clearly, Africans who aspired to the middle class wanted to secure their occupational rights. As Isaac Wauchope explained: "The quiet, law-abiding and well-disposed Africans who worked permanently in the town want freedom for self-improvement and land from the government which they can hold for an *unlimited* time (his emphasis) where they can build substantial and respectable houses. . . . for the Kafir beer-brewing portion at Strangers', who have shown no signs of ameliorating from their state or of trying to improve their social conditions, a move to another site where substantial cottages were set up for rental would be a gain."[121] Obviously, Wauchope was making a distinction between the African population: one section to be land owners, the other to be renters. Nonetheless, it is important to note that he was attempting to speak for both sections.

But the government considered no such divisions between Africans, and the Native Strangers' Location Bill called for the removal of all residents at Strangers' regardless of social or class differences. And here we have the crux of the matter. For Africans who aspired to the middle class, passage of the Bill would impose a more rigid type of segregation; deny them property ownership, including land; and close off investment opportunities in the urban areas, thus impeding their advancement.

With regard to the African freehold question, the opinions of whites were mixed. Again, this reflects the ambivalence about the right of the "civilized" to property ownership and land. Thus, the Mayor maintained that most Council members and the public supported closing Strangers', removing the residents to the Reservoir site and refusing freehold rights at the new site, although in future freehold might be possible on another grant of land. The Mayor, who was also one of the two M.L.A.'s for Port Elizabeth, differentiated between the "large number of very respectable coloured people . . . [in] the location" and "the influx of a large number of pure savages, who come in large droves [to Strangers' location]." But J. A. Holland, the M.L.A. in earlier years for Port Elizabeth, met with Strangers' residents three years before removal had first been broached and told them that he would insist "upon their being fully compensated for any damage." Also, he said that "those people who had valuable houses of brick or stone . . . might be given a piece of ground in freehold . . . "[122] However, the majority of whites were swayed by their interest in acquiring the best land in the center of town rather than supporting the African christians to "progress" by providing attractive housing and land and property rights.

Nevertheless, the local administration refused to include freehold rights in the original Bill. Moreover, if the Bill were passed and implemented as written, the authorities would be able to dismiss any claims for land rights. Also, new lease agreements could be imposed to redefine the space that Africans could occupy and to determine the landlord/tenant relationship. As a member of the opposition noted, if Africans moved to Reservoir, they would all become tenants who could be treated like "mere footballs, to be shoved about from point to point, to suit the convenience of the European."[123] In short, overall control of the emergent black working class and middle class would become feasible.

This is not to say that all whites held these views. In fact, some members of the white working class (of which we know little for this period) lived intermixed with Africans, and their opinions may have differed from that of the "gentlemen" and the government officials. Nonetheless, as early as 1855 when Strangers' was established, it was clear that the ruling elite believed that blacks should live in a separate residential area and that Africans were in the urban area simply to serve the labor needs of whites. As the black population grew and the economy changed, white adherents of residential segregation increased. Moreover, the foregoing occurred long before the passage of legislation such as the Cape 1902 Native Locations Act or the national 1923 Native [Urban] Areas Act.[124]

During the latter part of 1881, the Port Elizabeth Town Council sent an inquiry to the central government in Cape Town to determine if the 1878 Locations Act could be used to remove the Strangers' settlement. In May

1882, the colonial government responded that: "no authority existed under the 1855 grant" since the land was set aside for use only as a Strangers' location. Consequently, an Act of Parliament would be necessary. Undaunted, the Council had its lawyers draw up the Native Strangers' Location Bill. Although most of the white leaders agreed that Africans should be in their own area away from the town, the need for legislation was cause for alarm. In fact, in prior attempts the "friends of the natives" on the Council such as John McKay, a merchant and businessman, refused their support until they were satisfied the "natives" would receive just treatment.[125]

Opposition to the Removal

Within the context of Cape colonial politics, the proposed statute was an attack on the alliance among liberal politicians, their supporters, and their views on the process of "civilizing" and "uplifting" blacks. In a moral sense, Victorian liberalism and the Christian faith were being tested. If law-abiding Christians could be unjustly exploited because of racial prejudice, how could the alliance maintain its credibility and their loyalty and respect? Moreover, the right to own property, particularly individual freehold, was an important element of the liberal tradition.

Both whites and blacks used letters and petitions as their primary means to oppose the proposed legislation. Within these appeals, the common thread was the focus on the injustice and hardship that the removal of Strangers' location would mean for the Christians, or the "respectable" and "civilized" people, rather than the effect it would have on all of the black population. For example, Reverend John Walton, the Governing Superintendent of the Wesleyan missions, wrote a heated letter to the Town Council. In the letter, he objected to the removal because the black Christians would be deprived of their churches and schools. In particular, Walton expressed outrage, because before he had approved the construction of the new Wesleyan church at Strangers' at a cost of £3,000, the Council had assured him there were no plans to remove the location. But now the Council was unjustly trying to force the church members to move.[126]

Other white supporters appealed for fair treatment for the Africans. One man pointed out the improvements made on the houses at Strangers' in the last twelve months and argued that middle class blacks "should be given a little consideration, and guidance to convert the Location into a very different place to what it is now."[127] Clearly, these statements were within the liberal tradition that promised to include Africans as they attained the proper accoutrements of the "civilized" population. It is significant that most whites objected not to the principle of segregation but to how it was to be accomplished. At the same time, they wanted to appear to be just and to exempt "respectable" Africans.

It is even more noteworthy that during the debate the newly formed *Imbumba* held several meetings in Port Elizabeth. Among the ten main objectives of the *Imbumba's* constitution were to protect the rights of all Africans in South Africa with regard to land and to monitor the actions of the Municipality.[128] At a regional conference at Port Elizabeth in January 1883, the delegates, many of them recognized leaders among the mission educated, discussed the registration of voters, township grievances and education.[129] They probably also conferred about the Council's attempt to remove Strangers' and the best defense strategy. Of particular significance is the timing of *Imbumba's* formation and the stated attempt to unite and to protect the interests of all Africans. This was a concrete expression of nationalism and evidence of the changing perspective of the educated blacks about the need to promote and protect black interests and the role they would play apart from the liberal alliance. It is uncertain what effect these changes might have on their decisions about retaining rights to housing and land.

It may be possible to determine that effect by examining the comments of the Africans from Strangers' who submitted a petition opposed to removal to the Select Committee that was established to review the Bill. The petitioners (there were over seventy signatures) blamed the Council and Superintendent of Locations for the overcrowding. They focused on the unjust effect the removal would have on the black Christians who had worked for many years in the town, were law abiding, and provided the needed labor. The petitioners pointed out that as the laboring class or servants of the town, they were entitled to have a fixed place of residence near their work or master's premises and that the new site was too far from the business center. Also, they emphasized their respect for the law by exhibiting their willingness to cooperate with the local administration to prevent nuisances, such as beer-brewing, and to impede the spread of smallpox. Finally, they argued that considerable funds have been expended in erecting substantial wooden and iron cottages . . . and churches and schools at Strangers' and it would be extremely inconvenient to get to these facilities from the new site, and "further we consider our residence in proximity to Europeans as calculated to raise us in the scale of civilization."[130]

Clearly the petitioners aspired to European civilization and viewed themselves as separate from the other Africans, whether the non-Christians, the lawless elements, or the migrant laborers. The emphasis on providing the needed labor, being law-abiding, and being "civilized" by living in cottages and attending Western-type churches and schools illustrates that they recognized the need to assure the whites of the Christian Africans' willingness to act as a reliable, law-abiding labor force. Also, it may indicate that there was a contradiction between the *Imbumba's* expressed nationalism and the specific interests of the petitioners in their move toward middle class status. Nevertheless, it is important to remember that their definition of nationalism was in the making, as was their middle class status. It is also apparent that these African petitioners were aware of the racial science rhetoric since they spoke of the "scale of civilization." Seemingly, a stock phrase for the time, its definition was connected to the liberal ideology that Africans although culturally different were not innately inferior because of race but rather they were capable of becoming good British citizens under the British Empire.

For example, Alfred Wylde, the civil commissioner for Port Elizabeth used this phrase in the 1882 annual report in his description of christian Africans who continued to dress in a red blanket and relish the taste of kafir beer.

> Nature is not so quickly changed as some good men fancy. The common-sense way of raising them [Africans], on the "scale of civilization," is by fair municipal regulations, separation into families, and where it is practicable allotments with commonage under the same civil and criminal laws as other colonists. It is doubtful if the present sufficient brain power exists in them that would justify generally the same scholastic training as for European. If a hunting race be at once educated as the purely civilized, they perish in the ordeal. Unfortunately the native during his time on earth until he be pushed off by the *stronger* races seems fated to be the shuttlecock of party prejudice, and the debris of each failing policy is visible, as European civilization is advanced.[131]

Commissioner Wylde's statement seems on the one hand to be sympathetic to the integration of christian Africans and fair treatment on a footing with the whites [based on the old evangelical, humanitarian attitudes toward alien and heathen peoples]. Yet as he continued we soon recognize words used in the racial science debate to purport white superiority and black inferiority such as "stronger races," and "insufficient brain power," but in contrast to the earlier discussion of the word *stronger* the meaning seems to be the reverse. That is, rather than the blacks being *stronger* it is the whites who are said to be *stronger*. Wylde is defining the *stronger* according to the popular idea that was also propagated by racial scientists in the nineteenth century which predicted that the weaker races, all of them "colored" would die out as part of the universal evolutionary process as they came into contact and were conquered by the Europeans.[132] Different and even contradictory definitions, interpretations and conclusions were offered by various "scientists" for the same words. Yet as long as the interpretations fit with the Europeans preconceived notions and understanding of race the data could somehow be made consistent with beliefs that supported and explained white supremacy.

It is worth mentioning that the African petitioners' failure to discuss black unity may reflect an agreed-upon strategy influenced by the liberal whites. Comments from John McKay to the select committee on behalf of the "civilized natives" indicate that white and black liberals had conferred on a strategy to follow in protesting against the removal. He testified that the people the Town Council wanted to move were "churchgoers, law-abiding, and their houses were kept clean." Further, McKay stated that "it was another element, the roughs who were the main problem." He said that it was not the fault of the Africans that the "whites had built to its [Strangers'] borders and wanted to move the natives because their skin was black . . . and [this] would not be attempted with any Europeans."[133] McKay was correct. In fact, the Mayor admitted as much when questioned about why Africans were being moved, even though similar conditions existed in Alice and Emmett Streets where a low quarter of Europeans lived. Moreover, he had candidly responded that a low quarter of Europeans and a low quarter of natives have to be dealt with in different ways.[134]

During his testimony, McKay emphasized several times that the "respectable" permanent black residents who had been working in Port Elizabeth for a long period of time should be allowed to remain at Strangers'. In contrast, the newly arrived residents at Strangers' and also those people living there temporarily should be moved to the site at Reservoir. As a compromise, he suggested that the disorderly temporary workers should be moved to Reservoir, while the "respectable" and permanent workers should be allowed to live at Strangers' and become landowners. McKay stated that this would reduce the overcrowding and allow the respectable blacks an opportunity to improve their dwellings and occupy their own plots. At the same time, he believed it would bring the unruly element of the working class under control. McKay's views were congruent with the 1883 Cape Native Laws Commission, which had concluded that individual tenure for Africans should be pursued as a future policy. His views were also similar to those of J. W. Sauer, the staunch liberal who was the Secretary of Native Affairs and Chairman of the Select Committee that was reviewing the Native Strangers' Location Bill.[135] Both men supported African freehold rights in the urban areas, which was a continuation of the incorporation policy that was being influenced by economic and political realities. From an economic standpoint, white townspeople in Port Elizabeth desired a stable, permanent, and law-abiding working class. Moreover, it was to their advantage to encourage retention of the "civilized" Africans to serve this purpose. And because the liberals depended on the African vote for electoral victory, the idea of a buffer to mediate conflict between whites and blacks was still important in the growing towns.

In addition to McKay's testimony, several letters to the Select Committee from the white clergy in Port Elizabeth supported the African complaint regarding the churches and schools. These letters stated that the churches and schools would lose their support if the Africans were moved. To prevent a complete loss, the clergy requested that if the Bill were passed, compensation should be included that allowed churches and schools to be built in the new location.[136]

Despite the concerted opposition by both blacks and whites, the Native Strangers' Location Bill was passed and became law in 1883. But the Act was never properly administered, and only about fifty families moved from Strangers' into Reservoir.[137] Christopher states that between 1883 and 1884, Strangers' population declined from 3,000 to 1,700. He maintains that this decrease was not solely because of resettlement but also because of the introduction of steam cranes that replaced labor. Although Strangers' population fell drastically, it was not because Africans entered Reservoir Location, since only fifty families moved from Strangers' to Reservoir between 1883 and 1891. The other Reservoir residents were new arrivals in town, having moved there after 1884. Thus, an estimated total of 300 people (six in each household) relocated because of the legislation, not 1300. The other 1,000 may have left town because of job scarcity or entered another type of living arrangement. Since the permanent population at Strangers' was approximately 1,500–2,150, the decrease did not radically affect this group.

Thus, although the opposition failed to prevent passage of the Bill, they encouraged the Select Committee to add two amendments that effectively sabotaged the Act. The first amendment stipulated that the churches and schools in the Strangers' location could claim compensation from the Municipality if the move was forced rather than voluntary. The second amendment awarded freehold title to each family head who had been a resident at Strangers' for at least three years (including those at Cooper's Kloof) whenever they moved to the new site.

These amendments were total anathema to the Town Council because their plan had been to force the Africans to move with as little expenditure as possible. But now in order to acquire the revenue necessary to compensate the churches, the Council would have to approach the white ratepayers. Of course, this was an unattractive proposition, especially since the white ratepayers were notorious for demanding improvements and then refusing to pay for them.

Most important, however, was the threat of freehold titles for Africans, because if it became necessary in the future to remove the location, it would be even more difficult to force landowners to move. The legislation would affect at least 1500 people whose family heads would become landowners in a town where many of the whites favored segregation and believed that no compensation should be paid to the Africans for moving. In fact, the whites regarded the Strangers' residents as squatters who had no right to compensation, let alone a freehold plot.

Freehold tenure for Africans implied that it was acceptable for them to be viewed as permanent residents rather than as temporary "strangers," and this issue was by no means settled. Also, the specter of creating a substantial number of property owners who might qualify as voters was raised. All in all, the costs of removing Strangers' location were extremely high. At this point, the Town Council attempted to persuade the occupants to move voluntarily. Since compensation to the churches and schools was required only if the Africans were *forced* to move, this would eliminate some of the financial burden.

For the most part, however, the black population, refused to participate in the government's segregation scheme. The positive aspect of obtaining title to a site was superseded by the negative, for if Africans moved to the Reservoir, they accepted the principle of racial segregation and second class citizenship. It may be that not all the occupants perceived the location removal by the government as a plan to segregate and discriminate against them. Also, other considerations must have come into play. These included the longer distance they would have to travel, since Reservoir was further away from the town; the attachment to their homes; and the familiarity of the area and neighbors. Eventually the Reservoir location was occupied more by new arrivals than by Strangers' residents. This situation compounded the problem when the government next attempted to close the municipal locations in the mid-1890s.

Conclusion

In 1883, the alliance between the white liberals and the aspirant black middle class clearly prevented the implementation of the Native Strangers' Location Act. The success of this alliance influenced all the African residents, since under the legislation no one was forced to move from Strangers'. Nevertheless, the victory revealed the ambiguity and inherent contradiction of the liberal alliance. Ultimately, it was a relationship of dependence in which the Africans were subordinate. In spite of upholding the right to the land for this aspirant middle class, the amendment set a limit on the number of people able to become property holders. At the same time, it supported the segregation and control of the "uncivilized" members of the working class. Further, the liberal whites and Christian blacks had argued for the division of the African working class in order to protect their own class interests. This was in contradiction to the nationalist dialogue and the call for ethnic and denominational unity expressed at the *Imbumba* meetings. Yet the fact that Africans were forming their own organizations suggests not only that they wanted to protect their interests, but that they realized the limits of the liberal alliance. This raised the possibility of a different choice at a future date.

Still, the two amendments profoundly affected future resistance as well as government tactics to implement segregationist legislation, since any subsequent removal would have to include compensation and address the question of freehold title. In fact, however, the local government's unwillingness to pay the costs of segregation was a reoccurring obstacle.

The response of liberal whites must be viewed as a strategy to maintain and strengthen the alliance between whites and Christian Africans. Moreover, it represented an assertion of paternalistic control and leadership to combat the growth of a nationalist minded black group educated in Western ways that urged cross-ethnic racial cohesion among the working class and aspirant middle class. Undoubtedly, the liberals feared that if the Bill passed without amendments, it would accelerate the decline of policies aimed at incorporating Africans as colonial citizens with the same rights as the whites and illustrate that the coalition between whites and blacks was unable to prevent class legislation. As racially discriminatory laws continued to be passed to facilitate exploitation of Africans in Port Elizabeth, the decline of Cape liberalism was evident. Still, the alliance retained some of its viability, as middle class blacks continued to agitate to protect their rights to land. For the time being, white liberals and the black middle class alliance were able to slow the process of racial residential segregation.

Notes

1. Joyce F. Kirk, "Race, Class, Liberalism, and Segregation: The 1883 Native Strangers' Location Bill in Port Elizabeth, South Africa," *International Journal of African Historical Studies* 24 (1991): 293–321.

2. Alan Mabin, "The Rise and Decline of Port Elizabeth, 1850–1900," *International Journal of African Historical Studies* 19 (1986): 276.

3. *Eastern Province Herald* (hereafter EPH), These figures are based on data from Superintendent of Location Reports to the Town Council on 1 March 1882 and 15, 18 January 1883.

4. J. B. Peires, "The Central Beliefs of the Xhosa Cattle-Killing," *Journal of African History* 28,1 (1987):43–64; James Rutherford, *Sir George Grey* (London: Cassell and Co., 1961), p. 368; Also see J. B. Peires, *The Dead Will Arise: Nongqawuse and the Great Xhosa Cattle-Killing Movement of 1856–1857* (Johannesburg, Ravan Press; Bloomington, Indiana University Press, 1989).

5. Rutherford, *Sir George Grey*, p. 367.

6. Sheila Van der Horst, *Native Labor in South Africa* (London: Oxford University Press, 1942), p. 97.

7. Ibid., p. 94.

8. Jacklyn Cock, "Domestic Service and Education for Domesticity: The incorporation of Xhosa women into colonial society," in Cherryl Walker, *Women and Gender in Southern Africa to 1945* (Cape Town: David Philip, 1990), pp. 79–80.

9. Ibid., p. 89.

10. Ibid., pp. 85–90.

11. "Town Council," *EPH*, 15, 18 January 1886.

12. Ibid.

13. James Stewart, *Lovedale: Past and Present: A Register of Two Thousand Names* (Lovedale: Lovedale Press, 1887), pp. 533–34.

14. James Stewart, *Lovedale: Past and Present*, Intro. pp. 9–13; Cape Archives Depot (CAD), CCP 11/1/21, Cape of Good Hope, 1887 List of Persons residing in the electoral division of Port Elizabeth; Also see Alan Cobley, *Class and Consciousness: The Black Petty Bourgeoisie in South Africa, 1924–1950* (Westport, Connecticut; New York; London: Greenwood Press, 1990), for discussion of an "occupational elite" for the period, 1924–1950 whose range now extended to trained nurses, lawyers, medical doctors, and social workers, p. 38.

15. Stewart, *Lovedale*, p. 177; "Cricket," *Imvo Zabantsundu* (hereafter *Imvo*), 30 March 1885; "Town Council," *EPH*, 24 May 1895.

16. "A Great Mistake," *Imvo*, 15 December 1892. The *lobola* custom was an important institution for African men and women of different backgrounds. Although the context within which it operates has changed, the practice continues; Jeff Guy, "Gender oppression in Southern Africa's precapitalist societies," in Walker, *Women and Gender*, pp. 1–33; Ellen Kuzwayo, *Call Me Woman* (London: The Women's Press, 1985).

17. Michael D. Biddiss, ed., *Images of Race* (New York: Holmes and Meier Publishers, Inc., 1979). Biddiss states that Victorians used the term "race" no less readily and confusingly than their twentieth-century successors, Intro., p. 11. For example, race of man, race of birds and so the term remained imprecise; The same point for "class" legislation such as the Masters and Servants Act of 1856 passed in Cape colony that was influenced by "ethnological denunciations begun by settlers during the 1820s against Africans," see Clifton Crais, *White Supremacy and Black Resistance Resistance in Pre-Industrial South Africa* (Cambridge: Cambridge University Press, 1992), p. 140.

18. "*Imbumba yomfo kaGaba*," *Isigidimi Samaxhosa*, 1 November 1882, translated from the original by Monde Ntwasa; also see T. R. H. Davenport, *The Afrikaner Bond* (Cape Town: Oxford University Press, 1966).

19. "Town Council," *EPH*, 22 December 1882.

20. Stewart, *Lovedale*, p. 438. Wauchope returned to Lovedale to study the ministry and in 1892 was posted to Fort Beaufort. The ministry was one of the most fertile and highly regarded fields open to educated Africans. Moreover, it was the ministers who often acted as liaison between municipal authorities and the African population. For more information on the role of African ministers, see R. Hunt-Davis, Jr. "School vs. Blanket and Settler: Elijah Makiwane

and the Leadership of the Cape School Community," *African Affairs* 78 (January 1979): 15.

21. Stewart, *Lovedale*, twenty-seven female African alumna who were born or had lived in Port Elizabeth were listed.

22. "Educated Natives," *Imvo*, 9 February 1885; on Makiwane, see Hunt-Davis "School vs. Blanket."

23. Both Wauchope and Makiwane were among the small number of Africans who were able to obtain a classical education at Lovedale. During the 1880s, a debate about the efficiency of a classical education for Africans led to a change in the direction toward an industrial or vocational education that would presumably better suit Africans for their role in society. For the debate, see Richard Davis, "Nineteenth Century African Education in the Cape Colony: A Historical Analysis" (Ph.D. diss., University of Wisconsin, Madison, 1969).

24. Albert S. Gerard, *Four African Literatures* (Berkeley: University of California Press, 1971), p. 41. Although this poem was published under the name Citashe, Wauchope seldom used it for his writings; in all of his letters to *Imvo*, for example, he used the surname Wauchope. Also see Les Switzer, *Power and Resistance in an African Society: The Ciskei Xhosa and the Making of South Africa* (University of Wisconsin Press, 1993). He says that Sandile was killed in May, 1878 in a skirmish near Kingwilliamstown with the British army in the last Cape/Xhosa war, p. 74.

25. D. D. T. Jabavu, *Life of John Tengo Jabavu, editor of Imvo Zabantsundu, 1884–1910* (Lovedale: Lovedale Mission Press, 1922).

26. CAD, CCP 11/1/15, 1883 Voter's List, based on an estimated count from the names since race was not designated and comparison with other data, including later voter's list.

27. "Editorial," *EPH*, 11 February 1884.

28. Switzer, *Power and Resistance*, p. 137.

29. Stanley Trapido, "The Friends of the 'Natives': Merchants, Peasants and the Political and Ideological Structure of Liberalism in the Cape, 1854–1910," in Shula Marks and Anthony Atmore, *Economy and Society in Pre-Industrial South Africa* (London: Longman, 1980), pp. 247–74.

30. Phyllis Lewsen, "The Cape Liberal Tradition-Myth or Reality?" University of London, *Institute of Commonwealth Studies*, Collected Seminar Papers, on the Societies of Southern Africa in the 19th and 20th Centuries, 1 (1969–1970): 77.

31. Trapido, "Friends of the 'Natives,'"; Colin Bundy, *The Rise and Fall of a South African Peasantry* (Berkeley: University of California Press, 1979).

32. Monica Wilson and Leonard Thompson, The *Oxford History of South Africa* (New York; Oxford: Oxford University Press, 1969), 1:374–379. Recommendations were made that the Natal locations should be "supervised by a Resident Agent with assistants, and a police force with white officers and Africans in other ranks." p. 375; Shepstone grew up on mission stations in the eastern Cape among the southern Nguni and was viewed among the whites as an authority. He was described as extremely paternalistic, with a belief in British superiority; On Lord Carnarvon and British imperialism in South Africa see Anthony Atmore and Shula Marks, "The Imperial Factor in South Africa in the Nineteenth Century Toward a Reassessment," *Journal of Imperial and Commonwealth History* 3 (October,

1974): 123–25; On the significance of responsible government see J. L. McCracken, *The Cape Parliament* (Oxford: Clarendon Press, 1967), p. 24.

33. Van der Horst, *Native Labor*, pp. 114–16; Christopher Saunders, "The New African Elite in the Eastern Cape and Some Late Nineteenth Century Origins of African Nationalism," University of London, *Institute of Commonwealth Studies*, Collected Seminar Papers (1969–1970): 44–49, discusses attacks on the privileges of educated Africans and their responses.

34. Davenport, *The Afrikaner Bond*, pp. 54–69.

35. For a good case study, see Neville Hogan, "The Posthumous Vindication of Zachariah Gqishela: Reflections on the Politics of Dependence at the Cape in the Nineteenth Century," in Marks and Atmore, *Economy and Society*, pp. 275–293.

36. "Concert," *EPH*, 8 September 1882. Sung by a thirty-member chorus, the concert celebrated the South African Exhibition held at Port Elizabeth in 1886. Prior to this occasion, the African choir had performed several numbers at a church concert in 1885, including solos of "Rocked in the Cradle of the Deep" and "Wings." This rendition was followed by a lecture from Isaac Wauchope on "The Christianization of the Natives" and a poetry reading by Paul Xiniwe, who was to later direct an African choir that travelled abroad. The choir was modeled along the lines of the McAdoo Singers says Veit Erlmann, "A Feeling of Prejudice: Orpheus M. McAdoo and the Virginia Jubilee Singers in South Africa 1890–1898," *Journal of Southern African Studies* 14 (April 1988): 331–350.

37. Cape of Good Hope, Blue Book on Native Affairs (BBNA) (G8-1883) p. 69. The four societies were the True Templar's Lodge, the Band of Hope, the St. Cyprian's Benefit Society, and the Native Improvement Association (also called the African Improvement Association).

38. "Natives in Town," *Imvo*, 19 July 1888.

39. See David Coplan, "The Emergence of an African Working Class Culture," in Shula Marks and Richard Rathbone, *Industrialization and Social Change in South Africa: African class formation, culture and consciousness 1870–1930* (New York: Longman 1982), pp. 356–75; For an excellent analysis of alcohol, capitalism and workers, see Charles van Onselen, *Studies in the Social and Economic History of the Witwatersrand, 1886–1914*, vol. 1, New Babylon (Johannesburg: Ravan Press, 1982), pp. 44–102; Also, for the relationship of alcohol to protest, see Paul la Hausse, *Brewers, Beerhalls, and Boycotts* (Johannesburg: Ravan Press, 1988).

40. "Town Council," *EPH*, 12 July 1882.

41. "Magistrate's Court," *EPH*, 16 June 1882.

42. "Magistrate's Court," *EPH*, 24 November 1882; Also see "Magistrate's Court," *EPH*, 23 January 1895 where an African woman testified that she needed the money to pay rent; in both cases the women paid their fines.

43. "Magistrate's Court," *EPH*, 27 November 1882.

44. "Magistrate's Court," *EPH*, 17 January 1883.

45. "Magistrate's Court," *EPH*, 14,15 July 1903.

46. Richard Parry, "Birds on a Flat Rock: Black Workers and the Limits of Colonial Power in Salisbury, Rhodesia, 1890–1939" (Ph.D. diss., Queen's University, Kingston, Ontario, 1988), esp. Chap. 3.

47. "Licensing Board," *EPH*, 5 March 1884 and *Imvo*, 8 December 1882.

48. "Hop-Beer Church," *Imvo*, 10 August 1887.

49. "Hop-Beer Church," *Imvo*, 10 August, 1887; For African support of beer brewing, see Cape Archives Depot (CAD) NA478, Petition from Strangers' Location, September 25, 1878; for temperance support, "Licensing Board," *EPH*, 5 March 1884.

50. "Town Council," *EPH*, 23 June 1882.

51. The population figures for Strangers' conflict; however in 1881, it was approximately 2,500–3,000, Cape of Good Hope, Select Committee on the Port Elizabeth Native Strangers' Location Bill (A10-1883), 4,9 (hereafter 1883 Select Committee Report); *EPH*, "Town Council," 3 March 1882 and 15 January 1886; BBNA (G8-1883), pp. 67–69.

52. CAD, NA734,B1334, "A Short Story of Gubbs' Location," 11 May 1903.

53. 1883 Select Committee Report, p. 6.

54. Ibid., p. 25.

55. Ibid., p. 7.

56. "Town Council," EPH, 18 August 1881.

57. "Magistrate's Court," *EPH*, 9 October 1881 and 18 September 1882.

58. G. S. Jones, *Outcast London* (London: Oxford University Press, 1971), p. 161.

59. "Town Council," 28 July and "Location Riot," 11 October 1881, *EPH*.

60. "Location Riot," *EPH*, 7 October 1881.

61. "Work at the Harbor Board-Location Fight," *EPH*, 11 October 1881.

62. "Location Fight," *EPH*, 11 October 1881.

63. Cape of Good Hope, Report on the Native Laws and Customs, G4-1883 (Cape Town: Government Printers, 1968).

64. See *EPH*, "Location Riot," 1 October; "Location Fight," 11 October; "The Late Fight at the Location," 14 October; "Magistrate's Court," 18 October 1881; and see D. H. Reader, *The Black Man's Portion* (Cape Town: Oxford University Press, 1961) on customary practices of Xhosa in town for a later period.

65. "Editorial," *EPH*, 11 October 1881.

66. Richard A. Moyer, "The Mfengu, Self-Defense and the Cape Frontier Wars," in Christopher Saunders and Robin Derricourt, eds., *Beyond the Cape Frontier* (London: Longman, 1984), p. 123.

67. The system of certificates was open to abuse since Mfengu were not readily identifiable, not all were loyal to the government and no specific rules for issuance were observed. The Acting Civil Commissioner for Victoria East, W. M. Fleischer, claimed in December 1878—during the last Xhosa war—that the "certificate of citizenship system proved itself, especially during the rebellion, . . . a curse to the country" because it was impossible to "control and supervise the natives." BBNA (G33-1879), p. 188.

68. BBNA (G13-1880), p. 180.

69. BBNA (G8-1883), p. 63.

70. Charles van Onselen and Ian Phimister, "The Political Economy of Tribal Animosity: A Case Study of the 1929 Bulawayo Location 'Faction Fight,'" *Journal of Southern African Studies* 6 (October 1979): 1–43.

71. Ibid., pp. 10–11.

72. A. Epstein, *Politics in an Urban African Community* (Manchester: University of Manchester, 1958); For a more recent analysis regarding ethnicity, see William Beinart and Colin Bundy, eds., *Hidden Struggles in Rural South Africa* (Berkeley and Los Angeles: University of California Press), 1987, Chap. 3.

73. "The Faction Fights," *EPH*, 1 October, 1881.

74. E. J. Inggs, "Mfengu Beach Labor and Port Elizabeth Harbor Development, 1835–1879," *Contree* 21 (1987): 5.

75. Ibid.

76. Ibid., p. 12.

77. A. J. Christopher, "Race and Residence in Colonial Port Elizabeth," *South African Geographical Society* 69 (1987): 10.

78. Inggs, "Mfengu Beach Labor," p. 11.

79. Alan Mabin, "The Making of Colonial Capitalism: Intensification and Expansion in the Economic Geography of the Cape Colony, South Africa, 1854–1899" (Ph.D. diss., Simon Fraser University, 1984), 190. Mabin has discussed the period 1881–1886 as one of an economic downturn; "Editorial" *EPH*, 18 October 1881, for evidence of "faction fights" elsewhere.

80. "Magistrate's Court," *EPH*, 18 October 1881.

81. "Editorial," *EPH*, 11 October 1881.

82. For comments by the Xhosa man see "The Late Fight at Location," *EPH*, 14 October 1881; For the Zulu's charges see, "The Riot at the Location," *EPH*, 4 October 1881.

83. "An Encounter Between the Natives," *EPH*, 4 October 1881; "The Late Fight at the Location," *EPH*, 14 October 1881.

84. "The Late Fight at the Location," *EPH*, 14 October 1881; Often the Superintendents of Native Locations abused their positions and were corrupt. For example, see Noreen Kagan, "African Settlements in the Johannesburg area, 1903–23" (master's thesis, University of the Witwatersrand, Johannesburg, 1978).

85. "Town Council," *EPH*, 14 October 1881.

86. Ibid.

87. Vivian Bickford-Smith, *Ethnic Pride and Racial Prejudice in Victorian Cape Town: Group identity and social practice, 1875–1902* (Cambridge: Cambridge University Press, 1995), notes that by 1875 in Cape Town the way that whites categorized the "races" illustrated their knowledge of "scientific" ideas emanating from Britain, p. 67.

88. Racial science, also called pseudo-scientific racism—more precisely, a system of theories, assumptions, and methods erroneously regarded as scientific—has been applied to many of the nineteenth century studies, since the findings were often unwarranted and tainted by racism and prejudice. However, racial science has had a profound influence on the present-day disciplines of anthropology, psychology, and genetics. Moreover, in the nineteenth and early twentieth centuries, these studies were part of mainstream scientific investigation. The author believes that an understanding of past and present racism can be increased by utilizing the information to analyze how it affected the ideology and actions of people during particular historical period, rather than dismissing it as pseudo-scientific. This explanation owes some credit to Saul Dubow, *Scientific*

Racism in Modern South Africa (Cambridge: Cambridge University Press, 1995); and Dona Richards, "The Ideology of European Dominance," *Western Journal of Black Studies* 3 (1979):244; Frederickson, *White Supremacy: A Comparative Study of American and South African History* (New York: Oxford University Press, 1981); Also see Clifton Crais, *White Supremacy and Black Resistance in Pre-Industrial South Africa: The Making of the Colonial Order in the Eastern Cape, 1770–1865* (Cambridge: Cambridge University Press, 1992), on the "Other" and also racial science, pp. 127–129.

89. John Cell, *The Highest State of White Supremacy: The Origins of Segregation in South Africa and the American South* (Cambridge: Cambridge University Press, 1982), p. 1.

90. Ibid., p. 3.

91. George Frederickson, *The Arrogance of Race: Historical Perspectives on Slavery, Racism, and Social Inequality* (Middletown, Connecticut: Wesleyan University Press, 1988), p. 189.

92. Toni Morrison, "Unspeakable Things Unspoken: The Afro-American Presence in American Literature," *Michigan Quarterly Review* (Winter, 1989): 18.

93. Winthrop Jordan, *White Over Black, American Attitudes Toward the Negro, 1550–1812* (Baltimore: Penguin Books Inc., 1968), pp. 33–35, 7–8.

94. Richards, "Ideology of European Dominance," p. 244.

95. Nancy Stephan, *The Idea of Race in Science* (Ithaca: Cornell University Press, 1991), p. 6.

96. Ibid., pp. 8–9.

97. Jordan, *White Over Black* (a term used in general for apes but especially orangutans), actually the chimpanzee, was native to those parts of western Africa where the early slave trade was heavily concentrated), p. 29.

98. Jordan, *White Over Black*, p. 29; Stephan, *Idea of Race in Science*, on printing press p. 7.

99. Stephan, *Idea of Race in Science*, p. 8

100. Ibid.

101. Greta Jones, *Social Darwinism and English Thought: The Interaction between Biological and Social Theory* (New Jersey: Humanities Press, 1980), p. 147 and for a general discussion of Social Darwinism see the preface and Chap. 1.

102. Stephan, *Idea of Race in Science*, p. 5.

103. Ibid., p. 9.

104. Dubow, *Scientific Racism in Modern South Africa*, p. 9.

105. Michael Banton, *The Idea of Race* (London: Tavistock Publications Ltd., 1977), p. 52.

106. Curtin, *Image of Africa*, pp. 373–378; Dubow, *Scientific Racism in Modern South Africa*, p. 27.

107. "Town Council," *EPH*, 14 October 1881.

108. "Letter to Editor," *EPH*, 14 October 1881.

109. "Town Council," *EPH*, 11 November 1881.

110. G. S. Jones, *Outcast London* (Oxford: Clarendon Press, 1971); Nicholas Bullock and James Read, *The Movement for Housing in Germany and France, 1840–1914* (New York: Cambridge University Press, 1985); Also see Stanley D. Chapman,

ed., *The History of Working Class Housing* (Newton Abbot: David and Charles, 1971).

111. Philip Curtin, *Image of Africa* (Madison: University of Wisconsin Press, 1964); Stephan, *Idea of Race in Science*, pp. 7–8; Banton, *Idea of Race*, indicates that "It is . . . unwise to study the idea of race in isolation from two other ideas that were likewise reborn in the early years of the nineteenth century. The modern ideas of race, of class, and of nation. . . ." p. 3.

112. "Letter to Editor," *EPH*, 13 January 1882.

113. The idea and practice of deference is closely connected to the disease of honor, respect, and degradation in slave societies. See Orlando Patterson, *Slavery and Social Death: A Comparative Study* (Cambridge: Harvard University Press, 1982), Chap. 3.

114. "Town Council," *EPH*, 11 November 1881.

115. Saul Dubow, "Race Civilization and Culture: The Elaboration of Segregationist Discourse in the Inter-War Years," in Marks and Trapido, *The Politics of Race, Class and Nationalism in Twentieth Century South Africa* (London and New York: Longman 1987), pp. 71–94 esp., p. 76; Cell, *The Highest Stage of White Supremacy*; on English attitudes toward Africans, see Douglas A. Lorimer, *Color, Class and the Victorians: English attitudes to the Negro in the mid-nineteenth century* (Bristol: Leicester University Press, 1978).

116. "Editorial," *EPH*, 11 October, 1881.

117. 1883 Select Committee Report, Appendix F.

118. "Town Council," *EPH*, 15 January 1884.

119. Turrell, "Kimberley: Labor and Compounds, 1871–1888," in Marks and Rathbone, *Industrialization and Social Change*, pp. 1–44; also Alan Mabin, "Labor, Capital, Class Struggles and the Origins of Residential Segregation in Kimberley, 1880–1920," *Journal of Historical Geography* 12 (1986): 4–26.

120. BBNA (G8–1883), p. 69.

121. Ibid., pp. 61–63.

122. 1883 Select Committee Report; Mayor's testimony, 18–19, 44 and Mr. Holland, p. 16.

123. Ibid., p. 22.

124. For the effects of the 1903 legislation see Joyce F. Kirk, "A 'Native' Free State at Korsten: Challenge to Segregation in Port Elizabeth, South Africa, 1901–1905," *Journal of Southern African Studies* 17 (June 1991): 309–336; and for background to 1923 Native Urban Areas Act, see Davenport, "African Townsmen?," pp. 95–109; and Paul B. Rich, "Ministering to the White Man's Needs: The Development of Urban Segregation in South Africa, 1913–1923," *African Studies* 37 (1978): 177–91.

125. "Town Council," *EPH*, 18 September 1882.

126. "Town Council," *EPH*, 25 November 1881.

127. "Letter to Editor," *EPH*, 9 February 1883.

128. Andre Odendaal, "African Political Mobilization in the Eastern Cape, 1880–1910" (Ph.D. diss, University of Cambridge, 1983), 62.

129. Andre Odendaal, *Black Protest Politics in South Africa to 1912* (New Jersey: Barnes and Noble, 1984), p. 9.

130. 1883 Select Committee Report, Appendix F.

131. BBNA (A8–1883) Report of Civil Commissioner, Alfred Wylde for the Division of Port Elizabeth in 1882, p. 62; Also see BBNA (1882) for Native Affairs report dated July 12, 1881 by W. B. Chalmers, Civil Commissioner at King William's Town in the eastern Cape where he also uses the phrase "scale of civilization" in a discussion on the disaffection of the African population toward the British government because of a poor and inconsiderate "native" policy, p. 129.

132. Curtin, *Image of Africa,* vol. 2, pp. 373–377; Lorimer, *Color, Class and the Victorians,* p. 147.

133. 1883 Select Committee Report, 28–29; "The Location Bill," *EPH,* 5 September 1883.

134. 1883 Select Committee Report, 13.

135. Transvaal Publishing Company, *Men of the Times* (Cape Town and London: Eyre and Spottiswoode, 1906).

136. 1883 Select Committee Report, 26.

137. Christopher, "Race and Residence," p. 10; For information on the number of families that moved to Reservoir Location, see, "Town Council," *EPH,* 1 September 1891.

3

Negotiating Segregation, Political Representation, and African Rights to Land

Introduction

Because the location is a place for natives, unpleasant things were said about it. Why is the location never right? The natives have no voice at all in any matter whatever concerning them, and are therefore treated like children. What is wanted . . . is a man or men who will represent the location in the Town Council, and these men to be natives, so that whenever a question or difficulty arises, re: the location, these men . . . will be able to offer a remedy, since they will be in a position to know the requirements of the natives better than any member of Council. Most of the houses in the location are in a most dilapidated state which is most ignominious to a civilized community. . . . the natives are handicapped, and are not given a chance to improve themselves . . . One has only to look at the location regulations and judge for himself.[1]

So wrote Theo A. Don in 1891 in a letter to the *Eastern Province Herald,* a daily newspaper in Port Elizabeth. Significantly, Don's complaints reflect the anger and frustration felt by many Africans who aspired to middle class status but whose efforts were thwarted as the liberal alliance failed to fulfill their expectations of integration into colonial society. A member of the emerging black middle class, Don typified a growing number of Africans who found that colonial government legislation based on race prevented upward mobility for the Christian and mission educated blacks who had equipped themselves to compete equally with whites in colonial society.

In fact, Don's complaints speak directly to two of the major ideological components of liberalism, "progress" and "improvement."[2] Unfortunately, in the face of racist ideas, such suppositions were rapidly declining during the late nineteenth century. Thus, the popular assumption about the inevitability of man reaching a "civilized" or Western status because of "the civilizing influence of Christianity" (regardless of race and class) was in the process of changing to an assumption that emphasized cultural differences that prevented movement along the evolutionary chain of being in Social Darwinist terminology. As we have seen racial scientists such as Herbert Spencer discussed the relationship of races on the evolutionary scale and the failure of the lower species to reach the heights of the Western Europeans. Consequently, by the end of the nineteenth century, white popular opinion held that Africans would remain children and that blacks needed whites to guide and to control their lives.[3]

References to Africans as children, the lazy Africans, the "uncivilized" and so on were threaded throughout the debates and the justifications for legislation that discriminated against Africans by race. As the number of conquered Africans under colonial jurisdiction increased, so, too, did the doubts about the "inevitability of human progress" and, further, whether Africans belonged on the human scale. This ideology of the white man's burden, i.e., to civilize the lower order of humanity who were "nonwhites" and inferior, fit well with the military subjection. Thus, conquering the African independent territories in South Africa between 1887 and 1899 was of crucial importance to the colonial government's efforts to establish administrative control to facilitate the "expansion of capitalist relations."[4]

Don's complaints also reflect his grasp of the relationship of political representation, interest groups, political power, and race. In fact, Don called for the election of a black town councillor, who, he felt, would better represent the "voice," the specific interests of a black constituency who resented being treated like children rather than being treated as adults. Don's use of the word "children," in his letter, the very word that evoked a popular image of Africans as perpetual dependents and whites as perpetual rulers, in short, domination, illustrates his understanding of these popular notions influenced by racial science that more and more relegated Africans to a subordinate and child-like status. Don's conclusions illustrate that not only did many Africans reject the usual paternalism or social class subordination between blacks and whites, but it also suggests that racial dogma and practices had affected the growth of African political and racial consciousness.[5] Both group insecurity and group pride among the Western-educated and Christian Africans was giving rising to a sense of nationality, that cut across ethnic and class lines.

It is clear that Don, like other Africans, recognized this change in the ideology of certain whites that had been the "friends of the natives," from paternalistic benevolence to white racial domination. A credo of racial segregation for the benefit of the uncivilized was gaining ground among the white colonists. This is demonstrated in words from his letter, which was quoted earlier in this chapter, that "because the *location* is a place for *natives, unpleasant* things were said about it."[6] During this period, many of these unpleasant things voiced about Africans were based on the metaphors of health, disease, sanitation and the body, as well as effected by the popular images and ideas that many whites held about Africans. At the root of these ideas were beliefs about the superiority of European culture, skin color, and civilized behavior and the inferiority of African culture, skin color and uncivilized behavior according to the white viewpoint. As we shall see, the terminology that Port Elizabeth officials used to justify segregating Africans held negative assumptions that were influenced by such racial and cultural beliefs.

Nevertheless, since no black councillors were ever elected, Don's complaints obviously went unheeded. Still, his criticism indicates that Africans were deeply dissatisfied with the colonial administration as their consciousness about class, race and politics increased. They expressed this dissatisfaction and growth of consciousness through petitions, protest meetings, parliamentary voting, and the formation of organizations. This new consciousness was readily apparent when Africans and the local and central government went head to head over legislation to limit African access to the franchise, to land and to property rights in the urban area.

Most studies have emphasized the importance of government legislation between 1884 and 1898 to limit African rights to the franchise, and to land and property ownership in the countryside. Yet less attention has been paid to the impact of these laws upon Africans who lived in urban areas. Nonetheless, it is clear from the protest against the passage and implementation of these racially discriminatory laws by Africans living in towns like Port Elizabeth in the last quarter of the nineteenth century that the struggle had moved to the urban areas. Thus the twentieth century struggle over land, housing and segregation that was to grip the urban areas nationwide was already being played out.

Throughout the eastern Cape, Africans showed a remarkable degree of political consciousness in contesting the racial legislation.[7] Several pieces of legislation were passed to ensure white control and white supremacy including the 1887 franchise law and the 1894 Glen Grey Act.[8] Africans in Port Elizabeth along with other Africans and some white liberals actively protested this legislation, clearly recognizing that restrictions on the franchise and on black land rights in the countryside were a precursor to limitations on their rights to land in the towns.[9] It is noteworthy that Britain granted responsible government to the Cape colonists in 1872, making it easier for them to pass discriminatory legislation that would facilitate home rule, or settler colonial interests (also called sub-imperialism) rather than British imperialism. Yet each piece of legislation the Africans contested afforded direct experience in utilizing Western political techniques to further their own interests.

It is not surprising that, concomitant with the passage of the Glen Grey Act in 1894 which aimed to curtail African land ownership in the countryside and thereby to promote black labor, the local government in Port Elizabeth, as in other eastern Cape towns, moved to pass municipal acts to segregate Africans and bring the emerging working class under control. By skillfully linking African land and political rights, government legislation aimed to impose rural and urban residential segregation, to limit black land rights and, in general, to restrict and contain Africans whether in the countryside or in the town.

Although the Glen Grey Bill of 1894 (Glen Grey was a rural district in the eastern Cape), and the Port Elizabeth Municipal Act of 1897 were to be applied locally, they were intended to have a wider colonial effect, since they could be proclaimed in other areas. Moreover, the parallels between the two acts are striking. For example, both sought to create local political rights in the form of Native Councils in Glen Grey district and Advisory Boards at Port Elizabeth. The Glen Grey Bill and African protest against the passage of the Act and subsequently the inability of the government to enforce especially the labor aspect have been analyzed elsewhere.[10] The following section examines the attempt of Africans to retain land rights in Port Elizabeth as the Town Council sought to negotiate a new agreement with the African landholders and to remove Strangers' location. Moreover, the discussion provides a background to the passage of the Port Elizabeth Muncipal Act of 1897 another piece of legislation aimed at formally segregating Africans in housing settlements.

Land, Labor, and Segregation

As we look specifically at the 1890s and the continuing struggle over land and housing in Port Elizabeth, the conflict between the Town Council and the African property holders was ostensibly over the choice of an appropriate site to which to remove Africans living at Strangers'. But both the African population and the Town Council realized that larger issues were at stake: class, race, and the "place" Africans would occupy in colonial society. Thus, political power and representation as well as economic rights, including the right to land and property, were the subject of debate.

Underlying this debate was a change in the liberal alliance as the ideology of segregation and white supremacy gained influence. At the local level, in the towns such as Port Elizabeth, Africans expressed discontent at the municipal administration that failed to provide them with proper sanitation, land rights, and security of tenure and opportunities for up-

transport riding also ceased with the completion of the rail link from Cape Town to the goldfields in 1892. Transport riders delivered produce to the towns for shipment and also traversed the roads from Port Elizabeth to the Kimberley goldfields.

Living conditions for Africans remained deplorable. In fact, as congestion increased, the conditions deteriorated. One reason was that the Superintendent of Locations tried to facilitate separation of the "races" by directing Africans to municipal housing that was already overcrowded. Another was that Africans sought accommodation with friends and relatives in the already overpopulated areas.

The African population increased at each of the municipal and the private locations. By 1894, approximate figures indicate that the population at Strangers' stood at 1,000, Cooper's Kloof at 700, and Reservoir at 1,300. Reservoir, the new municipal location that the Council had planned would house the Africans residing at Strangers', was filled instead with new arrivals.[14] Thus, rather than alleviating the housing problem, Reservoir simply added to the dilemma since its population would also have to be relocated if the black work force was to be segregated. (See Map 1.2, #4 for view of Reservoir.)

The population at Reservoir included a mixture of educated and uneducated; petty bourgeoisie, and working class; and Africans, Coloreds, and Chinese. Also, a roadway divided the settlement into two sections,[15] and a definite correlation existed between the type of housing in each section and the degree of acceptance of European customs. On the left were corrugated iron houses, probably of a square shape, most often occupied by the "school" or western educated Africans who were more often amenable to European customs. To the right were the traditional round houses occupied by the "red" (so-called because they smeared red clay on their bodies which was an African custom frowned on by westerners) who preferred African customs.

Yet this division between the "school" and "red" Africans was not so marked that all of the European or African customs were rejected. For example, even among those living in the traditional round houses, there was evidence that Western materials were selectively utilized, since pieces of tin or sacking were used to repair their homes. Similarly, some mission-educated Africans preferred round houses because they were not only more secure and comfortable than sheet-iron houses, they were more efficient at keeping out the rain.

Since some middle class Africans lived in one-room houses in a section set slightly apart from Reservoir, a further spatial separation existed. This correlated with their perceived and actual higher status as a result of education, occupation, wages, and viewpoint on life. In contrast to the residents at Strangers', most Reservoir residents had no right to freehold title. In future years, this fact would become a source of contention between the Reservoir residents and the Town Council.

Aside from the three municipal locations, Africans lived in private locations as well as in rented rooms and in tenements located inside and outside the municipal boundaries. Land proprietors included both men and women and represented a diversity of backgrounds among the whites, Africans and Asians, including ministers, headmasters, and town councillors. The housing was often overcrowded and unsanitary, and was constructed of all kinds of material including sacking, flotsam, tin and iron.

The Gubbs' Syndicate

In 1894, Gubbs' was the largest and most populous private location that lay within the municipal boundaries, with a population totalling about 2,300.[16] According to an official government report, the majority of the African residents were designated as belonging to the "red" category. The increase in this category reflects the economic changes in the countryside, as more blacks lost land and were forced to work either temporarily or permanently for the whites in both rural areas on the farms and in the urban areas. Furthermore, the effects of a drought and the rinderpest epidemic were also being felt in the rural areas. The new arrivals migrated to Gubbs' and settled down with other longer-term African residents who had moved there in the 1860s as Strangers' filled up.

The Town Council and the syndicate that owned Gubbs', had an ongoing battle over the closure of the settlement. On one hand, the Council claimed that Gubbs' was unsanitary, and that it blocked expansion of the town. Gubbs', much like Strangers' was initially on the outskirts of town. Now situated as it was (see Map 1.2), the settlement prevented expansion of the town in the southwesterly direction, and the nearest white occupied housing was about one-half mile from Gubbs'. In fact, the Mayor of Port Elizabeth, Mr. Brooks complained that because of the unsanitary Africans, white residents refused to buy land anywhere close to the area.

On the other hand, the syndicate, consisting of three businessmen, that owned Gubbs' denied that the settlement blocked expansion of the town. Nevertheless, they offered to close the location if the Council would compensate them for the loss of rent. The rent averaged £350, and the revenue from their location shop brought in £250–300 per year, for a total of £650 annually. Since the syndicate had paid £850 for the Gubbs' property in 1889, and since they were averaging £650 per year, their profit was substantial. The syndicate received additional profits of £300 for grazing rights and the operation of a slaughterhouse.[17] Of course, the syndicate felt justified in requesting £8,000 compensation.[18] Still, it is significant that the syndicate was only offering to sell that section of the land on which Gubbs' location was situated while retaining ownership of the rest.

Although willing to compensate the Africans for their houses, the outraged councillors adamantly refused to pay the syndicate to close the location. In fact, the officials argued that since the syndicate paid a low price for the Gubbs' property and was now making a sizable profit, they needed no further compensation. Not surprisingly, this was hardly an argument that provoked sympathy from the Gubbs' syndicate. Expressing the opinion shared by many councillors in 1894, the Mayor of Port Elizabeth, said that once the syndicate closed the location, the value of the land would rise enormously, and it could be sold for £20,000, a windfall profit. Since this was the case, he questioned why the Council should be forced to pay the syndicate to close a private housing location that was not benefiting the Municipality.[19] But this was not strictly true. In fact, since Gubbs' took the pressure off the government to provide needed housing for the growing black working class, it indirectly benefitted the Municipality by aiding in the sustenance of the labor force.

Also, the Council wanted to remove Gubbs' because no lawful mechanisms existed to control the residents. In fact, precisely because Gubbs' was a private location and the municipal regulations did not apply, many Africans preferred to live there, since they could engage in recreational activities such as gambling and fighting with knobkerries, as well as brewing beer and drinking, without penalties. In contrast, these activities were deemed unlawful at Strangers' and in the other municipal locations. For the most part, however, such laws were unenforceable.[20]

Yet another reason the Council wanted to close Gubbs' was related to taxing the private locations. In 1893, the syndicate paid municipal rates of 29 pounds on the Gubbs' property.[21] Doubtless the Council was frustrated at not being able to implement the recommendation of the Municipal Health Committee that each hut on this location [Gubbs'] come under the ordinary assessment, be registered in the name of the owner, and be submitted to taxation as other dwellings were in this Municipality between the owner and the Council.[22]

The required tax would have been at least 10/- per structure for each occupant, considerably raising the town's revenue. But no legal means existed to compel Gubbs' to pay increased taxes. Therefore, a private agreement between the Town Council and the syndicate was necessary, and under the circumstances this was unlikely.

Although the Council criticized living conditions at the private locations and even passed legislation to establish segregated areas for Africans as it had done in 1883, it was unwilling to take the responsibility of providing a sanitary environment that included paying the high costs of properly housing the black workers. Thus, nothing had been done to remove—to another site—the Africans living at Strangers' and Cooper's Kloof municipal locations. Rather, the Council tried to enforce municipal location regulations that prohibited new construction or improvements on dwellings. These regulations aimed to reduce the compensation that the Council would have to pay to the Africans whenever they moved from Strangers' to a different location. But the regulations also meant that the housing was deteriorating and becoming more and more dilapidated. Not surprisingly, by the 1890s, African complaints about the poor conditions of the municipal locations were rampant. Indeed, on several occasions, the Africans initiated discussion on ways to address the sanitation problems in the black settlements and especially those Africans affected made deliberate efforts to put pressure on the local government to provide proper housing and sanitation services.

African Complaints and Municipal Administration

As we have seen prior to the 1890s, members of the aspirant black middle class in Port Elizabeth had already established political, educational, cultural, and religious associations. Many of the same people, or men of similar mind, that had formed these organizations put this knowledge to use in their attempts to pressure the local government to provide needed housing and services and to remove obstacles to upward mobility. For instance, in 1890, African leaders requested that a locations committee be formed to advise the Council.[23] Although the relationship of this committee to the local *Iliso Lomzi* or vigilance association headed by Reverend Benjamin S. Dlepu is unclear, it is likely that Dlepu belonged to both groups, since organizational membership and leadership often overlapped.

It will be recalled that a Native Improvement Association, headed by Isaac Wauchope, was operating in 1882 at Strangers'. Wauchope left Port Elizabeth to attend Lovedale Seminary and was ordained and appointed minister at Fort Beaufort in the 1890s. Following Wauchope's departure, Dlepu became one of the most prominent leaders of the educated elite and aspirant black middle class. African membership overlapped in the local vigilance association, sports clubs, debating teams, and music societies. For example, in 1886, Ross, Rwexu, Wauchope and Foley were members of the Port Elizabeth Debating Society.[24]

Dlepu, minister at the Wesleyan Methodist Church, was one of the most prominent African ministers who provided leadership to the "school" community.[25] Moreover, his rise in status was typical of many educated Africans. In 1858, at age twelve, Dlepu attended Healdtown Institute. Then, after qualifying as a teacher, Dlepu taught at Kingwilliamstown. Later he studied to be a minister; and by 1880, he was ordained by the Wesleyans.

Men such as Dlepu acted as liaisons between the municipal authorities and the African population. Since their religious training and activity in the ministry, not the least of which were verbal and written skills, equipped them for responsible positions of leadership and authority, it is not surprising that they were selected to be spokesmen for their race. Also, higher education for Africans was limited to those in teaching and theological fields. Therefore, those who completed this training enhanced their opportunities for increased salaries and status. Among the ministers at Port Elizabeth were Reverends J. W. Gawler, Anglican Church; W. P. Momoti, St. Paul's; and Gavan Kakaza and William Bottoman, both Wesleyan Methodist Church. All were active in the various African organizations and acted as spokesmen in particular for western educated Africans.

Not only did the ministers serve their congregations, organize political meetings, present resolutions to the local and central government officials, and testify before government select committees, they also generally advocated fair and just treatment for Africans. Moreover, many of the ministers criticized racial practices that deprived them of the opportunities that they had been led to believe would be open to them once they completed their studies. Also, they questioned white denigration of African culture and the notion of the inherent inferiority of blacks to whites. For example, during his ordination trial in 1884, Gavan Kakaza criticized certain religious practices such as preaching that African customs in general were uncivilized and should be discarded. Thus, after being received into the fold, he cautioned in a paper published in 1885 in *Imvo* against "throwing away as useless every custom that obtained among our forefathers and of adopting every European custom as being right simply because it is European in its origin."[26] Aside from the leadership provided by the ministers, other prominent Christian African leaders in Port Elizabeth were Frank Makwena, store proprietor, realtor, and carpenter; George Ross, store proprietor; Theo A. Don (whose remarks opened this chapter) clerk; Moses Foley, general dealer; and Elijah Mdolomba, teacher.

Most of these Christian leaders refused to reject all aspects of their African culture outright as some of the white missionaries advised them to do rather choosing to retain some of them such as the public meeting, *intlanganiso* in the Xhosa language, where open discussion and counsel on grievances continued until consensus was reached.[27] The *imiti* was a notable practice taking root that formed the basis for a democratic and popular political culture in the urban areas. During these meetings, spokesmen were elected to serve on committees or in deputations to present grievances or resolutions. Still, the chosen leaders could not simply make final decisions arbitrarily without consulting the people. In fact, to be viewed as legitimate, the leaders had to maintain frequent communication and consultation with their constituents. So grievances were discussed at public meetings, and resolutions were formulated to be presented by their spokesmen to the government. Moreover, the fact that the public meetings were often held in church buildings underscores the influence and the blending of western and African cultural practices.

Not surprisingly the major grievances voiced at the public meetings focused on the burning issues of land and security of tenure. During a political meeting in 1893 at the Wesleyan church, the liberal candidate, and the Minister of the Legislative Assembly, Mr. Jones faced an overflowing crowd of Africans. Members of the crowd including Peter Rwexu and George Ross asked Jones questions about the government's intention to issue land titles to Africans living in the towns and also complained about the local government policies that did not allow black men to claim the house in a government location as his property. In other words, Africans were not allowed to own houses in the government locations even though they had paid to build them. Many of these educated Africans voiced a wider concern that recognized the needs of the growing number of Africans entering the emerging black working class. For instance, Revd. Gawler wanted to know what Jones thought "natives should do to get better wages" since in some places they received less than 9d a day. And, Gawler continued, "The wages in the country districts were not sufficient to support a man and his family." These concerns indicate that, despite their changing class position in the colonial economy, western educated African leaders tried to represent the interests of all classes and were well aware of the possible repercussions of racially discriminatory legislation in both the countryside and the urban areas.

This is not surprising since many Africans qualified to vote because of their occupations, which included laborers, messengers, interpreters, teachers, gardeners, drivers, and clerks who were themselves wage earners and not permanently fixed in one economic class. Following the 1893 political meeting, controversy erupted between the Council and the Africans with regard to George Ross' allegation that although the town council was always grumbling about the locations being dirty, "the houses owned by the Council were the dirtiest of all."[28]

Ross' remarks caused an uproar at the Council meeting a few days later. For instance, the Superintendent of Locations, who was suppose to supervise the municipal settlements, emphatically denied that the approximately 60 houses owned by the Council at Strangers' location were the dirtiest. He insisted that "the Municipal houses as a whole were as clean and orderly as the others."[29]

Since, the municipal houses were in no better condition than the rest of the dwellings, the foregoing remark was not much of a compliment. In fact, orders had been issued for some of the Council owned houses to be pulled down. But when the residents insisted that they had nowhere else to go and would have to sleep outside, the Superintendent allowed them to stay. Upon hearing this, Mr. Wills, a town councillor, said unsympathetically, "I don't believe one of them. Let them get proper houses." Yet other councillors supported the Superintendent's decision not to evict the residents, stating that they feared an outcry and in any case it would be reprehensible. Mr. Wills, undeterred, remarked, "According to Mr. Brister, it was a pity that the ["native"] people should be turned out of their houses." And he asked, "How many white people were turned out and not one word about it?" It was all bosh, talking that way (laughter)." Councillor Wills seemed to be saying that if poor whites could be turned out, then why not blacks? Mr. McIlwraith replied that "the Town Council doesn't turn white people out."[30]

The foregoing discussion reveals the disagreements among the councillors with regard to the treatment of Africans living in dilapidated housing. Whether the councillors were feigning concern about the "natives" being put out on the street or not, their reactions point out their sensitivity to criticism from black men like Ross, who tried to force the white officials to be accountable to the needs of the African population. Furthermore, the councillors' reactions speak to a twentieth-century problem that was already becoming noticeable by the end of the nineteenth century in the towns: the problem of the "poor whites." In fact, only the year before, a conference focused on the predicament of the poor whites had been held in Cape Town, and solutions were sought to alleviate their plight. Conference delegates included members of the press, ministers, parliamentary and government representatives and the Superintendent General of Education. One speaker said, "We required a number of cheap Lovedales for whites only." The delegates agreed to form a permanent committee to seek solutions so that "the government, the church, the private citizen—one and all—should make a joint effort to raise our people, so that the European can be worthy of that leading position in South Africa which it has pleased providence to entrust to it."[31]

Another element entering the debate can be gleamed from councillor McIlwraith's comments. This was the practice of blaming the poor "natives" for their economic predicament and labelling them vagrants while being sympathetic to the poor whites and labelling them the "deserving poor."[32] That is, poor whites and poor blacks occupied the same class position and theoretically should have been treated the same. In reality, however, officials were beginning to speak about treating the poor whites differently and according them privileges, such as not being turned out of their houses because of their race.

Indeed, African leaders complained repeatedly against the Council's administration, especially its arbitrary enforcement of a municipal regulation that increased the unsanitary conditions since it disallowed improvements or repairs at the locations. In fact, a double standard existed whereby outside the locations, the mostly white property owners could make improvements, but when it came to the locations where mostly Africans lived, restrictions were imposed. The Council, fearful of having to pay higher compensation when Africans were removed, had implemented the regulation which had been in affect for several years. This regulation only added to the deterioration of the location housing. However, because the regulation was difficult to enforce, many Africans ignored the ban on improvements and repairs although they could be prosecuted.[33]

Also Africans continually requested water closets (toilets), water pipes, drainage at the thoroughfares, and yard space as well as permission to build, repair, and open shops.[34] Ironically Africans could be arrested for making repairs, renovations or opening shops without the permission of the urban officials. For the most part the Council refused the majority of requests for repairs or renovations. [35]

Such complaints put pressure on the Council, which at times responded to public criticism of its weak enforcement of sanitation regulations by requesting that the inspector step up enforcement. The procedure followed to enforce compliance required an inspection. The inspection included monitoring the number occupying the property, the construction of the housing, and the sanitation. If noncompliance was found, a notice was served, followed by a summons, and, finally, a court proceeding. Nevertheless, the response was limited since, apparently, the municipal regulations did not restrict the number of occupants, a major cause of the overcrowding.[36]

More often than not, however, racial and class discrimination influenced the justice procedure, and prosecutions were handled in a biased manner. As a result, the authorities prosecuted the poor landlords (usually Indians and, in a few cases, Africans) rather than the wealthy ones. Among the well-off landlords were several of the town councillors, including one Mr. McWilliams, an attorney, who often defended those accused of operating unsanitary and overcrowded premises.

Since so many of the Councillors derived an income from rental property, it was not in their self-interest to enforce municipal regulations by prosecuting each other. Not only would they lose money, but they would also open themselves to vindictive treatment from fellow councillors and the ratepayers. For example, when councillor McWilliams was accused during a council meeting of renting out an unsanitary tenement to Indians, he maintained that "the place was clean and healthy, there had been no sickness there and gentlemen who were talking about it have worse at their own doors."[37] Moreover, the sanitation regulations were vague and required that the occupant, rather than the owner, must keep the premises clean. Consequently, instead of the owner of the property being prosecuted, the renter was charged. In general, however, these cases were dismissed. Exact figures on rental income are unavailable, but it must have been a lucrative and stable income since so many businessmen were involved.

The government's failure to prosecute wealthy landlords exacerbated the problem of slums and did nothing toward improving living conditions for the residents. And basically, there was simply not enough housing for the growing population. If the sanitary regulations had been enforced and if all of the buildings that were "unfit for habitation" were destroyed, housing conditions would have become worse since more people would have simply crowded together. As usual, inadequate financing, poor budgeting, and the refusal to prosecute landlords restricted the Town Council's ability to provide adequate housing.

At the same time that Africans criticized the Council, they tried to clean up their own living areas. Unfortunately, they were often undermined. So even though Africans paid taxes for rubbish removal, only sporadic pick-ups were made. Residents at Strangers' location tried to assist with refuse removal by collecting the rubbish and placing it at a central collection spot. But because the rubbish boxes had no lids, these efforts were viewed as a hindrance, and the Council's Health Committee complained about the unsanitary "natives." In fact, one Councillor complained that the rubbish in the lidless boxes simply blew all over, spreading dirt and disease.[38] Even when the rubbish was piled in dumps, removal was so sporadic that it served little purpose.

Housing and sanitation conditions were worsened by the general practice among whites of using sections of the African settlements as dumping grounds. It is clear that much of the town rubbish was transported to the property on which Gubbs' location was situated and then dumped. So rather than any rubbish from Gubbs' being transported from the location, "It [Gubbs] was being used as a general dumping ground."[39]

The Council's restrictions on building also affected the business opportunities of those who aspired to be part of the black middle class. That is, such restrictions limited their upward mobility and opportunities to increase their capital. Although many African men and women went to the expense of hiring an attorney to apply to the Council for a building license, they were routinely refused permission to build.[40] Also, many Africans believed that the Council did not have the legal authority to restrict building construction. Their belief was reinforced when a few years later a parliamentary select committee was appointed in 1896 to review a municipal bill. The select committee ruled that indeed these Council restrictions were illegal.

Struggle Over the Location Site

In 1894, these were the circumstances when the African leaders and the municipal officials began to negotiate over the removal and resettlement of the Stranger's location residents to a new site. Both the African leaders and the municipal officials were willing to regulate land and occupation, but how to go about it and in whose interest were the primary questions. Johnston's comments about the twentieth century disadvantaged in capitalist societies who struggle against distancing processes that impose residential segregation fit the predicament of the African leaders in Port Elizabeth. Johnston states that they [the disadvantaged] wanted to improve their relative status within the system, "and to prevent the manipulation of space by the affluent whites, and to equalize inter-group life experiences and opportunities by creating a new spatial morphology. . . . Their conflict is over how the city is constructed and reconstructed as a spatial organism; it was a political conflict."[41]

Clearly, many of the aspirant African middle class desired land and property rights. Also, they wanted to be located at a permanent site and to exercise a role in local government administration, including through an elected advisory board. The attitude of Africans toward residential segregation was in contrast to the 1883 opinion of the black petitioners opposing the Native Strangers' Location Bill. It will be recalled that they wanted to remain in close proximity to Europeans for the "civilizing" affect. Still, many Africans seemed to be far less concerned with separation from whites if they could maintain or gain particular privileges such as land, property, political, and entrepreneurial rights in their own settlements. For instance, six years before, the Strangers' location residents had already indicated they would move but only to the Reservoir site.[42]

As we have seen, the racial discrimination increasingly encountered by "school" Africans had influenced them to form their own political, religious, social, and economic organizations. Furthermore, black unity across ethnic and religious lines was becoming a popular call to combat legislation according to class. The class consciousness of the leadership was honed by pass struggles with the local and central government. Consequently, it is likely that disgust with the municipal policy of neglect influenced the propensity of Africans to move to another settlement even if it was segregated.

In contrast, the Council wanted to remove the Africans from the valuable land on which the locations were situated and to avoid paying large sums in compensation as well as prevent increased numbers of Africans from becoming landowners. Clearly, the Council preferred to have the black work force settle in a permanent location, yet somehow found it difficult to supply a suitable site and proper housing. In the fast-growing urban areas, a related problem was how to structure the housing of the urban population without completely alienating the African workers who preferred being in walking distance to work.

Furthermore, consideration had to be given to the preferences of the white ratepayers who disliked living in close proximity to Africans for reasons of racial and cultural biases, as well as the fear that their moral, health and property values would decline. Moreover, some white employers of black laborers feared that a move to a site further away from town might drive away the workers. Of particular importance were the "civilized" Africans who provided the largest section of the permanent workforce and who sought to hold the whites accountable for equal treatment according to British liberal principles. It was also this group that would be most likely to protest the local government's plan. Clearly both the African leaders and white officials had their own agenda, and both approached the negotiations in a cautious, but determined, manner. By this time, the conflict was no longer over whether or not Africans would be segregated. Rather, the issue was the terms of that segregation, and especially which and how many Africans would be counted among a black land-owning class in the towns.

It was for this reason that in 1894, eleven years after the passage of the Native Strangers' Location Act, the Port Elizabeth Town Council unveiled a plan for the removal of Strangers' location. Black and white clergyman, councillors and "native" delegates all attended the conference to discuss the location plan. Another reason for the removal plan was the wider colonial political and economic structural changes that seemed to indicate that the African population in towns would continue to rise.

As we have seen the African population had increased by nine thousand, probably even higher since black migrants enroute to other territories continually passed through Port Elizabeth and doubtless some settled there. Transformations in the South African economy influenced by the mineral discoveries, harbor and railway construction and the suppression of independent African polities, drove more Africans into the colony to work and undermined their bargaining position. Prior to the 1890s, as Switzer relates "Many Ciskei Africans chose not to work for low wages, demanding 36 shillings a month and food that had been paid on public works projects in the 1850s." This choice became almost non-existent for many African men and in most cases, the wages for unskilled workers dropped, and employers sought to gain more control over their employees. However, "Cape Africans working in the port cities and on the railways still received relatively higher wages than African labor on white farms or on the diamond and gold mines during the 1880s, but these preferred sectors of employment were much less competitive in the 1890s."[43] The newly arrived migrant workers during the 1880s to the early 1890s to Port Elizabeth were primarily Xhosa men, largely unskilled, likely to reside at Gubbs' location, save their wages and return home to farm and raise stock. In other words, they were unlikely to be western educated Christians aspiring to permanent residence and land ownership. It is within this context that we must examine the removal plan.

Although prior to this time the Council had discussed the removal of the location, two obstacles prevented serious consideration. These were (1) the inability of the Council and the Africans affected by the 1883 Native Strangers' Location Act to agree on a suitable site for a new location, and (2) inadequate funds for compensation to Africans for their houses and to ministers for the church and school buildings serving the black population. The foregoing were requirements of the 1883 Act.

The first obstacle for the Council was partially resolved when the colonial government allocated a substantial piece of land to the Municipality to be used as an African settlement. This decision was made in line with increasing local government endeavors backed by the Cape colonial government to remove the Africans from the towns and impose residential segregation. Such segregation had been accomplished in two other eastern Cape towns, East London and Kingwilliamstown. And when the Council decided to use municipal funds to compensate Africans and their churches and schools, the second obstacle was removed. Consequently, the way seemed open for the removal of the Africans living at Strangers' and Cooper's Kloof as well as Gubbs' private location to a segregated settlement.

At the meeting Mayor John McIlwraith explained the various conditions whereby Africans at the three municipal locations occupied land.[44] At both Cooper's Kloof and Reservoir, the residents, with a few exceptions, could be expelled at any time since they had no right to land titles. Under Act 17 of 1883, however, the residents at the Strangers' location could be moved only after being given ninety days' notice, compensation, a new site, and land ownership titles. Therefore, unless a contrary agreement was reached, the removal and compensation payments would only affect Africans living at Strangers'.

To solve the problem of a location site, the mayor proposed two options. The first was to remove all of the "natives" living in the municipal locations to a site at the North end of the town near the beach. All Africans from the three municipal locations would be required to move there, and about £20,000 pounds in compensation would have to be paid. This option would require a Parliamentary Act to annul the 1883 legislation, which sanctioned removing Strangers' location residents only to the Reservoir site and no other. The second option was to move Africans to the Reservoir location. The cost of this move was about £4,000 pounds. Here the Council would erect dwellings and rent them out to tenants. Since this move would fulfill the original 1883 Act, there would be no need for a Parliamentary Act.

Despite the considerably lower cost of the latter option, the Council and white townspeople generally preferred the North End site primarily because it was further from the town. Such a move would place the African population out of sight and perhaps, for a time, out of mind. Also, because the site was a good distance from the town, the land value was much less compared with that of the three municipal locations that were on prime real estate. In addition, the land would accommodate all of the Africans residing in the municipal locations, not just the Strangers' residents. Moreover, the mayor promised an incentive of liberal compensation and perpetual site titles to all Africans who moved there. Thus, the "native" problem could be solved for several years.

Because many of the Reservoir residents had settled there after the 1883 legislation rather than before, they were not legally entitled to freehold land. Therefore, this site was problematic, and other arrangements would have to be worked out if residents refused to move from Reservoir to the North End site. In addition, if the Africans at Strangers' and Cooper's Kloof chose Reservoir, the current residents might have to be removed to prevent overcrowding. Finally, Reservoir was still too close to town, which meant that the Africans would probably have to be moved again—another costly procedure. To deter Africans from choosing Reservoir, the mayor emphasized that if they moved there, the Council would refuse them land titles. In his proposal, the mayor stated that he knew that the North End site would "in all probability be opposed by large and influential sections of our native community, through memorial and other means, which would involve the Council in a large initial expenditure."[45]

The mayor was right! Immediately after he explained the proposition, controversy erupted. While white support for the North End site was almost unanimous so, too, was African opposition. On general principle, the Africans objected because, even before the meeting, the Council, had already narrowed the possibilities down to two sites without consulting the black population involved. In essence, the Mayor had already chosen for them. But perhaps more importantly, Africans living at Strangers' location preferred the Reservoir site and having already made up their minds, despite the Mayor's threat to refuse them titles, they arrived at the meeting ready to voice their opposition in no uncertain terms.

Many Africans were well aware of Mayor McIlwraith's proposition, since it had previously been discussed at a March Council meeting and the proceedings were printed in the local newspaper. Consequently, Africans held a large meeting in April, during which about 400 male adults agreed upon a resolution. So by May, they were prepared to answer the Mayor's proposal. Mr. Ross read the resolution in which Africans agreed to move to the Reservoir site as long as the terms of the 1883 agreement were enforced, namely, "that compensation be given to the present siteholders and titles to the sites in the said location."[46]

Several other Africans expressed concern about the proposed North End site.[47] For instance, Revd. P. Momoti said "Africans did not maintain their health near the sea so perhaps a new site could be proposed." Mr. Mdolomba declared forcefully that "he for one would not live there." Revd. J. Pritchard, the well respected white minister at the Edward's Memorial Congregational Church (the largest serving Africans), said "With regard to the sea, they found that native people living close upon the sea were unhealthy, and a great many of them suffered from consumption."

The Council ignored most of the opinions of the Africans as well as the resolution. Moreover, the Council responded by trying to prove to Africans that the site was healthy. To this end, a health commission was formed consisting of four doctors and Council members to report on the medical safety of the proposed North End site. Although the doctors could not reach a unanimous conclusion, three did approve the site. Drs. P. O. Considine, Walter T. Harris and John George Uppleby,—all longtime residents of Port Elizabeth—agreed that Africans were susceptible to pulmonary disease because they wore insufficient clothing and "the sea air contains a large amount of moisture and not because of any special locality in or near the town."[48]

The three doctors concluded that the soil at the new site would allow for proper drainage, and that since the wind blew in a southwesterly direction, windblown debris would present no danger to the town. Still, Dr. J. Alexander Bruce, a recent arrival to town, and apparently not yet cognizant of his role as a government official, recommended against the site. In fact, he insisted that the southeast winds would hit the proposed site full force and that the sand, when wet, would turn into a swamp. Bruce said that these conditions were conducive to bronchitis and pulmonary complaints.[49] In effect, his report supported the fears of the Africans about the unhealthiness of the site.

At another meeting, the African audience exhibited unanimity against moving to the North End site. This occurred when Mr. Williams, a town councillor, held a meeting at Reservoir with about 150 African location residents in order to learn their opinions. Their sentiments were more than likely shared by others. Once again Theo Don, whose forceful statements opened this chapter, spoke in earnest declaring, "You may build high walls to prevent both south-eastern and land winds; we won't go to the water, we won't go to the sand, we won't go to the bush to kill snakes for you."[50]

When Councillor Williams went to the Reservoir location, an African delegation that had visited the site at North Beach had already reported to the residents. Also, the Africans knew the conditions of and the resolutions against the proposed site taken at the meeting two weeks before. Apparently Williams was attempting to find out if all the Africans were in agreement. In addition, Williams was probably trying to sweeten the pot, and also perhaps hoped to create dissension among the Africans, for he explained that all those who moved to the site at North Beach "within twelve months would be granted extra favors, and so on."

It was then decided that a vote should be taken. An African man said, "All those who are in favor of the North End site should stand on one side, and all those who are in favor for the Reservoir should sit down."[51] Not one [man] moved, strongly signifying unanimous support for the resolutions and against North End and Councillor Williams and his attempt to create disunity. The meeting ended on this note.

Africans continued to voice numerous objections to the North End site. At a public meeting of Africans on September 16, 1895, at the Wesleyan Church, the major objections to the site were succinctly expressed in several resolutions.[52] The reoccurring theme in the resolutions was that the increased distance from town would cause numerous problems. First, Africans resolved that the proposed site was too far from town. Africans might be late to work and this could create problems between the master and servant. Also the distance was so far that young women would have to leave work early so as not to be out pass 7:30 p.m. since they would have to return home alone. Because the site was in an unsavory area, the women were at higher risk from "rascals which would result in a great amount of immorality."

The fears of the Africans were not unfounded nor unusual. Deborah Gaitskell wrote about the concerns of African parents with regard to their daughters and the immoral urban environment. Indeed, many Africans living with their families in town feared that the urban area would corrupt not only their daughters, but also their sons.[53] These anxieties were heightened because the proposed site was adjacent to streets such as Alice and Evatt (near North End) where bars, prostitution and crime was prolific. So much so that even the police were afraid to patrol the area.[54] (See Map 1.2.)

The next resolution was concerned with wages and transportation. The Africans pointed out that "the present wages to natives could not warrant the expense of trams, etc." Since this raised the question of the rate of wages paid by the white employers, it was extremely volatile. Moreover, as a result of being forced to move, it was possible that Africans might demand higher wages to pay the added travel expenses. Also, the workers could even refuse to go to work at all. From the previous chapters we are aware that black laborers were willing to strike, especially dockworkers, and that the town was almost totally dependent on the black workers. The threat of higher wages or a strike could lead employers to side with the Africans against the council in order to prevent the move. Certainly the council did not want to even hint that the white townspeople should have to pay higher wages and a strike was unthinkable. Complaints by whites about money wasted by the local government were legend. If the proposed removal of Africans led to a demand for higher wages, the town councillors would be blamed. In any case, the municipality was one of the largest employers in the town so they most likely would have to pay increased wages as well.

The final resolution brought vehement objections to the North End site because it was so near the beach. Again, they reiterated concerns about their health and its decline if they virtually lived in the sea and had to build their houses on sand.

In any case, African opposition to the Port Elizabeth Council's plan to remove blacks to the unpopular site was so successful that one observer commented that "the Africans seem to have them [the municipality] over a barrel."[55] African resolve stemmed from a realization that the government initiatives to impose restrictions by race were attempts to create a "native" policy to ensure white supremacy and black subordination.

While Africans agitated against the North End site, a group of whites from Ward 7, situated close to the Reservoir site, sent a resolution to the Council to protest against Africans being moved from Strangers' to Reservoir. The whites complained that the area would simply be inundated with more "natives."[56] In fact, they resolved that the move would endanger the health of those whites living at North End on the hill section and that it would cause depreciation of property. Finally, the whites stated that relocation would not settle the location question permanently even though heavy expenditures were required.

By November 1894, African opposition had forced most councillors to agree that it would be impossible to compel the Africans to move to the North End site. In the end, the Council resolved to purchase land near the Reservoir site and induce Strangers' residents to move there.

For the next two years, the debate continued.[57] Finally, in 1896, the Council and the Africans at Strangers' location reached a *tentative* agreement on a site. Included were clauses dealing with an advisory board, compensation, transportation and individual land rights. The following resolutions were considered for adoption.

The 1896 Resolutions

1. That the land at the N.E. side of the racecourse be occupied as the site for the new Location, and be surveyed into plots.
2. That the siteholders in the present Strangers' Location have the plots 40' by 60' first, with individual title (vide Bill) subject to a quitrent of twenty shillings (20/-) per annum, per plot, and that the person holding the ground under this Clause shall have no power of alienation without the consent of the Port Elizabeth Municipality in writing obtained, except to their heirs or legal successors.
3. That suitable sites be given to the three existing churches, Edward's Memorial, Wesleyan and Church of England, for their parsonages, church and school buildings.
4. That the water be laid on at once.
5. That compensation be mutually agreed upon by siteholders and Councillors for their present buildings, and that after such a settlement they be allowed to remain in the houses a reasonable time until their new places are ready for occupation.
6. That the churches, parsonages, and schools be completed before the final removal of the people, so as not to cause cessation in the work of such institutions.
7. That the Town Council put itself into communication at once with the trustees of the existing churches regarding the compensation for the property, so that the work of building the places be proceeded with on the completion of the plan.
8. That the Council use their influence to obtain an assurance that the tram will run to the racecourse, and that it will convey Native passengers at a reduced charge.
9. That sites be allotted to all Native applicants (40' X 40'), at present residing in Port Elizabeth outside the Locations.
10. That the Council sanction the establishment of a Board of seven Native residents to assist, subject to the Town Council's approval, in keeping order in the Location.
11. That these proposals, if agreed upon by the Council, be sent to the Reverends J. Pritchard, C. M. Parnell and Gavan Kakaza, together with the resolution of the Council to lay before the people.
12. That the Council request these gentlemen to have a meeting of the siteholders of Cooper's Kloof, with a view of getting them to move into the same site, and on the same terms, as stipulated in Clause 2.
13. That the siteholders holding two or more sites in [Strangers'] Russell Road Location, receive title to two plots in the new location, on the terms specified by Clause 2.

14. That subsequently the Reverend gentlemen intimate to the Council by a resolution of the Natives interested, their approval of the site suggested and willingness to comply with these proposals.

The site proposed was at the Northeast side of the racecourse adjacent to the Reservoir location. Africans living at Strangers' would receive compensation and a 40-foot-by–60 plot at the new site subject to a rent of twenty shillings per annum. Also, they would be able to remain in their homes until the buildings were completed and water was installed. In addition, the churches and schools would also receive compensation and plots at the new site. Any African living outside the locations could apply for a site but was not compelled to do so. Furthermore, if they approved, siteholders at Cooper's Kloof would be included in the agreement and receive land rights. The Council was to "use their influence" to arrange tram service to the RaceCourse site at a reduced rate. Moreover, a Native Advisory Board consisting of seven members would assist to "keep order" in the new location. The resolutions were to be sent to the ministers of the native churches and decided on at a public meeting.

Overall, Africans were enthusiastic about these resolutions, which were presented at public meetings held at the Town Hall. Still, the Africans had one objection. They wanted the right to sell or transfer their new land only to other blacks. Apparently they had learned from experience how easy it was to lose their land to whites, through legal and illegal means. In this case, they hoped to use the white man's law to protect their interests. Thus, the Town Council agreed to a change in the land transfer clause.

Significantly, the Port Elizabeth Town Council was applauded for taking the lead in addressing the problem of native locations in urban areas by proposing to survey lots and give land titles to Africans. In the *Imvo,* Jabavu duplicated the entire agreement—heralding it as the proper solution to "improve the natives."[58] He recommended that other town councils follow suit and further remarked on the unusual policy proposed by the Council of "laying water to the people and to provide them within certain limits with some sort of self-government."[59]

The latter was a reference to the proposed native advisory board. It is noteworthy that the advisory board was meant to meet the demands of progressive Africans for more say in local government. This was in contrast to Glen Grey, which aimed with the Council system to "substitute an advisory role in local government for participation in the colonial political process."[60] Jabavu enthusiastically concluded that "A scheme has . . . been propounded of giving individual tenure to our people, thus enabling those able to do so to improve their dwellings without fearing the

Sword of Damocles of removal at the sweet will of an ignorant, prejudiced Council."[61]

The Port Elizabeth Municipal Act

A year later, Jabavu was considerably less jubilant and, in fact, strongly criticized the Port Elizabeth Council. The change in opinion was influenced by the municipal bill that the Council submitted to the Cape parliament in 1897. If passed, the Bill would annul the 1883 Act, neutralize the 1896 agreement and authorize the Council to remove the Africans and the municipal locations.

In effect, the Bill proposed a complete overhaul of municipal laws that would considerably increase the Council's powers, especially in relationship to native locations. Under the Act, the Council would hold complete jurisdiction over any new location and could also remove it as long as the residents, even Africans with land rights, were allotted living space elsewhere. The law would allow for Strangers' to be closed down and, for that matter, any other government-administered location within the municipal boundaries. Also, regulations could be framed to control these locations situated on both municipal land and also on privately owned land. Nowhere in the proposed bill was there a clause protecting rights to land titles, compensation, or security of tenure for Africans. This is why Jabavu wrote so scathingly about the Port Elizabeth council less than a year after praising it highly, concluding that the "continued tenure of the Natives should not depend on the whims and fancies of the council."[62]

Given these circumstances, it is puzzling that the town council made the agreement in July 1896. Could it be that the councillors, the townfathers, knew that the municipal act would annul the agreement and had already decided to pursue new legislation that would allow the Council to remove the African locations without fulfilling the contract with the disagreeable residents? There is no specific evidence on this point. However, circumstantial evidence seems to support the supposition that the municipal bill was the Council's ace in the hole. For example, in 1896, the land agreement was made, and in May 1897, the municipal bill was sent to Parliament. Since it usually takes several months for legislation to be composed, analyzed, and revised, it seems likely that the council already knew in 1896, that they would be sending the municipal bill to parliament, and that once it became a law, previous accords with the black population in regard to the location removal could be annulled. Moreover, even if the agreement stood, the new law would allow for future removals. This is not to say that the only reason for the 1896 promise was because the council knew it could renege. Rather, the council played its hand much like a gambler that has an ace in the hole, savoring it, until it was needed to assure winning.

Still, the language of Mr. Holland, a town councillor, in testimony before the select committee implied that the Council intended to fulfill the 1896 agreement. Holland testified that "the natives will receive permanent title, under a quitrent of 4 pounds per year at the new site, and compensation for their houses." He continued that they wanted to remove the natives to "one great location under perfect supervision, so that the locations will no longer be a nuisance and a danger to the white population of the town."[63] Similarly, the Mayor maintained that the Council's intention was to honor the agreement to supply land, titles, and compensation. Yet despite the espoused good intentions, the law would not compel the Council to uphold the agreement.

For many of the African residents who had agreed to move to the Racecourse location, the proposed bill could destroy all that they had negotiated for with the Council over a two year period, especially the land rights, the security of tenure, and the local representation. Whereas before it may have seemed that the Africans had the Council over a barrel, now the barrel had been turned and the prospective black landholders were on the bottom.

So at the request of Reverend Pritchard of the Edward's Memorial Church, Mr. Jones, the Member of the Legislative Assembly (MLA), spoke against the Bill when it came to the Cape Parliament. He pointed out that, if passed, the Act would empower the Municipality to remove the locations without offering compensation or giving titles. Jones further explained that some Africans at Reservoir and those who had agreed to move to the Racecourse location wanted to be excluded from the Act to ensure that they would not be deprived of their land titles. Moreover, he requested that the Committee "provide in the Bill that these people shall not be removed within a limited time, and that when they are removed" their land rights are safeguarded.

It was no small matter for Jones to take this position. In fact, since the liberal tradition was on the decline, it was possible that he was committing political suicide since he was going against the Council on behalf of the Africans. However, Jones had long been allied with the African voters and retained his seat with their support. On this occasion, the town councillors heartily criticized him for "opposing the Municipality in regard to this matter of the natives," and they threatened to formally censor him. And Mr. Gumpert forebodingly added, "They should remember this for the next election."[64] It is worth noting that these were not empty threats since Jones was ousted from office in 1898, and during the election campaign, his opponents often cited his record in defending the natives.[65] It is significant that although no Africans testified before the select committee, Frank Makwena was in Cape Town lobbying against the Bill and he telegraphed back that the Mayor was telling lies about the location shop. He also promised to call a meeting upon his return to give the details although the sources remain silent on this issue.[66]

If the bill passed, the municipality would be able to regulate private locations. Thus, the Gubbs' syndicate was also opposed to the Bill because it feared the Council would close the location without paying compensation. Moreover, Albert Walsh, a syndicate member, argued that if Gubbs' were closed, the "natives" would go to the municipal locations and the syndicate's earnings would go into the pockets of the Council.[67]

The Council was anxious to gain control over the private locations and, in particular, Gubbs'. If passed, the legislation would allow the Council to regulate sanitation, the sale of "kafir" beer and the right of police entry. The floating population, especially the criminal element, could be endorsed out of the town and a more productive workforce encouraged. Also, the Municipality intended to survey the public land it owned adjacent to Gubbs' and to put it up for sale or lease.

In this regard, Councillor Holland maintained that the property at the private location (Gubbs') is no value to white people while the location is there. Indeed, the Council envisioned a prosperous growth area once the Gubbs' location was removed where the "landed property owners," many of them town councillors would profit from an investment in and development of the property adjacent to Gubbs'. This land was already considered some of the most valuable in Port Elizabeth, and it could be "cut up into building lots and people would build there."[68] In the last several years there had been phenomenal building construction in the direction of this settlement; and it had ceased only because the whites believed that a distance of one and one-half miles was too close to the African population. Moreover, the probability of an extension of the electric tram would be a further inducement for building up the area. For all of these reasons, the councillors thought it perfectly legitimate to close Gubbs' and remove the native residents to one settlement so whites could use the land and the revenue could enlarge the town coffers.

As had been done in other places, the Council used the metaphor of public health, sanitation, and disease to argue for the bill, charging that both municipal and private locations were a danger to the well-being of the town. At this time, typhoid (also called enteric fever) was prevalent. During an outbreak in 1896, municipal officials pointed the finger at Gubbs' and commissioned an investigation into the causes of typhoid. The timing of the study coincided with the Council's decision to submit the municipal Bill to the Cape Parliament. Although the Municipality expected the findings to strengthen its case for the removal of the locations, the findings did not substantiate their claims.

Dr. George Turner, the Medical Officer of Health (MOH) for the Colony, conducted the investigation. His study covered the four-month period from September 1896 to January 1897.[69] Within that time, 236 people out of a total population of 28,451, had contracted the disease. Of this number, 60 died, 26 whites and 34 Colored (including Africans). After a thorough study, Turner concluded that the locations were not the cause of typhoid. Rather, the inadequate drainage and sewage system seemed to be the culprit. In fact, typhoid is an acute, infectious disease acquired by ingesting food or water contaminated by excreta; it is characterized by fever or an intestinal disorder (formerly considered a form of typhus).

It should be pointed out that the insufficient water supply and lack of a proper drainage system was a real problem for the whole town. The fluctuation of the water level, whether above or below normal, was of major concern and a topic frequently reported in the local newspaper. Because the whole town's supply came from one source, Van Staaden's Reservoir, the water level was extremely important. Van Staaden's was located several miles from the town, and many of the Council's discussions were related to how to generate another water supply. Also, plans to build a dam and proper drainage system for the town had been drafted, but they were never executed because the funds had to come from the ratepayers or a government loan. The ratepayers did not want to pay, and the municipality was unwilling to secure a loan because it was already in debt to the central government for a water-filtering system installed a few years earlier.

Added to the poor water supply and inadequate drainage was the unclean water from the Baakens River, the same river where the dust had settled, blown and mixed with excreta that came from almost every direction. This was also the same river where hawkers (street sellers) washed their milk bottles and refilled them with milk, which were then sold to whites. The poor sewage and toilet facilities, some situated close to the food preparation area, existing throughout the town assisted the spread of the disease.

To say the least, Dr. Turner's conclusions were, as one councillor noted, "disappointing" especially since a medical study carried out a year earlier claimed that unsanitary Africans were the cause of the typhoid disease.[70] In that study, two Port Elizabeth medical men, Dr. Harris and Dr. Ensor, concluded in September-October 1895 that the municipal locations and Gubbs' were causing the spread of typhoid as the wind blew "sundried fecal matter . . . over the town."[71] In fact, Ensor recommended removing all of the locations. But Ensor, like other medical men before him—may have had political reasons for supporting the removal of the locations. For example, at the Kimberley diamond mines in 1884, the diamond mineowners in collusion with medical doctors suppressed the news of smallpox saying it was some other disease that was not smallpox and not contagious for fear that the workers would leave and prices of fuel and provisions would rise.[72]

The town councillors and other influential whites held different opinions about who or what was to blame for the disease. Some found it convenient to blame the blacks for the disease even though they recognized that other factors were influential. For example, one councillor blamed the typhoid cases in his family on "the position of the locations above the town" and "the filthy habits of the natives. . . ."[73] And although all of the townspeople used the bucket system, another councillor thought that the wooden buckets used to collect night soil might be connected with the prevalence of typhoid. On the other hand, the mayor pointed out, "Typhoid is prevalent in some of the best neighborhoods, not in the dirty localities." Moreover, the editor of the *Eastern Province Herald* blamed the prevalence of typhoid on the poor drainage system and the composition of the Council. He argued that the town councillors were at fault because they were apathetic and "utterly unable even to touch the fringe of the question." And, he charged that they ignored the sanitary question because "they were too busy bickering among themselves about nothing to address this dangerous question of sanitation and removal."[74] These diverse opinions give an indication of the controversy and lack of consensus among whites surrounding the question of sanitation, Africans, and where they should live.

As mentioned, Dr. Turner did not find that the African settlements were the source of typhoid. Nonetheless, he deferred to the recommendation of Dr. A. J. Gregory, the Assistant Medical Officer of Health (MOH) for the Colony. In October 1896, Gregory and Dr. Uppleby, the MOH for Port Elizabeth carried out an extensive inspection of the three municipal locations and Gubbs'. Gregory also concluded that even though the African locations were "untidy, dirty, and unsanitary . . ." they were not the cause of typhoid fever. Yet, he recommended that the Council abolish "the present scattered and ill-planned locations for one large, properly laid-out Location, upon a new and suitable site. . . ."[75] Also, in a November 1896 report on typhoid, Uppleby stated that Gubbs' location should be closed and the natives moved.[76]

But by the next month, Dr. Uppleby was hardly in a position to point any fingers, since the nine cases of typhoid he diagnosed at one particular site were not contracted at the African locations; rather, all of them were at his home. Five of those contracting the disease were Uppleby's relatives, and four others were friends who had attended a birthday party for his daughter.

In response to "unkind remarks," Dr. Uppleby felt compelled to explain in his December report how the typhoid was contracted. He stated that the five cases contracted at his house resulted from the people drinking unboiled milk and concluded that there was no connection between these five cases and the four who later contracted the disease. Rather, Uppleby concluded that this was a COINCIDENCE.[77]

It is unlikely that many Africans accepted Dr. Uppleby's explanation. And since Uppleby's report appeared in the local newspaper, we can be sure that some Africans knew about the typhoid cases. They probably also concluded that, under the circumstances, Uppleby could hardly point a finger. To the contrary the doctor's case supported what many Africans had been saying all along: Typhoid affected all sections of the town, not just the locations.

Prior to the outbreak at Uppleby's, and doubtless in response to the comments made by whites at the Town Council meeting, an African correspondent had challenged the doctors' conclusions and negative imputations in general that pointed to the locations as the cause of typhoid. First, the correspondent maintained that typhoid "breaks out in the most aristocratic portions of the town, Bird and Clyde streets, and Western road." Moreover, he said, "These portions of the town can in no way be affected by prevailing winds from locations."[78]

Also, Africans questioned the conclusion of whites that native locations in close proximity to the town were objectionable. It this were so, one African said, then why not "improve these objectionable locations" with the balance left over after expenditures on Strangers', Cooper's Kloof, and Reservoir. He based his remarks on the Superintendent of Locations revenue report that posted an income of £1,272 13s 6d, and expenditures of £590 11s for the municipal settlements, an obvious income credit. Further, this commentator objected to the racial generalities that European observers often made about the locations and "natives." For instance, he declared that if the locations were objectionable because of the low class of natives that live at these locations, "Then we say there are low Europeans who would not hold a candle to the Native." In conclusion he said, "What we want is justice, and nothing but justice and fair play to natives."[79]

The foregoing broached two issues that Africans would continually raise: (1) how the government justified using location revenue not for the African locations but for the white areas, and (2) challenges to the racist dogma that whites were superior to blacks because of skin pigment when there were obvious class differences. Further, the previous commentator spoke to the quandary of the colonial and later the Union government, which was how to pay for segregation and how to justify segregation.

Despite the opposition, it is not surprising that the Port Elizabeth Municipal Bill was passed in June 1897. In the end, the failure of the medical doctors to agree was less important than the government's overall policy initiative to bring Africans under control through imposing residential segregation. Furthermore, members of the Select Committee were themselves government officials who sympathized with the Council's quandary in solving the native location problem.

The Select Committee ignored Mr. Jones' plea and instead empowered the Municipality to "establish locations of natives on any part of the municipal lands, and to remove the same . . . ." No mention was made about retaining land titles if the Africans were moved. Rather, it was plainly stated that if the Municipality removed any native location, the Council "shall thenceforth hold the said piece of land free and unencumbered, and may sell and alienate the same."[80] In essence, the Council could close and regulate both municipal and private locations, remove the residents and use the valuable land as they pleased.

Conclusion

Despite the passage of the Act, no locations were closed or removed. Africans did not move to the Racecourse site for several reasons. On the one hand, they refused to move from Strangers' location until water was laid on at the new location.[81] But the Council had made few real plans to accommodate Africans and their failure to provide water underscores this lack of planning. None of the locations had a drainage system. As for water, since there were only a few water taps at Strangers', Africans from all of the other locations, both municipal and private, congregated there to collect water. In many cases, they had to cart the water for long distances. Moreover the councillors lethargy illustrates that their interest lay in moving Africans off the valuable land and to use it for other purposes rather than drawing up plans for constructing proper houses, allocating water, or providing sanitation facilities.[82]

On the other hand, not until 1899 did the Town Council begin offering compensation and arranging for Africans to select lots.[83] Apparently, the will to implement the law was lacking, and the Council's strength was sapped by the process of getting it passed. Furthermore, the compensation money was to be paid from the sale of the Strangers' location land, so arrangements had to be made. But the situation languished as life proceeded with everyday encounters between the Superintendent of Locations and beer brewers; as Africans constructed buildings and opened shops without permission, the Council continued to be lax in enforcing sanitation regulations, and nothing was done about the move.

As for Gubbs', its population kept growing, and a brief debate about paying the syndicate to close the location ensued, but white criticisms forced the Council to table the idea. But perhaps the most immediate reason for the status quo was the South African War that broke out in

1899–1902. As a result, the military authorities took possession of a portion of the Racecourse site thus preventing the removal of Africans.

So the segregation envisioned by the local government officials did not materialize, and neither did formal limitations on the use of space. Moreover, the possibility of property and land ownership, and local political representation for Africans was placed on hold. Still, the creation of formal residential segregation was moving into a different stage. Also moving into a different stage was African initiative to take a part in broader-based economic ventures as a means to upward mobility and independence. In fact, several members of the aspirant black middle class formed an economic cooperative with a pan-African base. The following chapter examines this project.

Notes

1. "Town Council," *EPH*, 9 June 1891.

2. D. M. Schreuder, "The Cultural Factor in Victorian Imperialism," *Journal of Imperial and Commonwealth History* 4 (1976):283–317; Dona Richards, "The Ideology of European Dominance," *Western Journal of Black Studies* 3 (1979): 244–251; Brian Willan, "An African in Kimberley: Sol T. Plaatje, 1894–1898," p. 234, in Shula Marks and R. Rathbone, eds., *Industrialization and Social Change in South Africa* (New York: Longman, 1983), for a discussion on the elements of the ideological milieu of the African petty bourgeoisie in Kimberley.

3. Greta Jones, *Social Darwinism and English Thought* (New Jersey: Humanities Press, 1980), p. 147; Richards, "The Ideology of European Dominance," states that the European idea of Africans or other non-European cultures as children was not a new one. However, the evolutionary interpretation by the mid-nineteenth century was new.

4. Marks and Rathbone, eds., *Industrialization and Social Change*, p. 12.

5. Don's opinion was contrary to the opinion of some of the other African leaders. For example, in 1898, J. T. Jabavu cautioned against electing Africans since they were not savvy enough to hold office. His conclusion was embedded in the paternalistic relationship between white and black liberals; See R. Hunt-Davis, Jr., "School vs. Blanket and Settler: Elijah Makiwane and the Leadership of the Cape School Community," *African Affairs* 78 (1979): 12–31.

6. "Town Council," *EPH*, 9 June 1891.

7. Stanley Trapido, "African Divisional Politics in the Cape Colony, 1884–1910," *Journal of African History* 9 (1968): 79–98; Andre Odendaal, *Black Protest Politics in South Africa to 1912* (New Jersey: Barnes and Noble, 1984).

8. *Statues of the Cape of Good Hope*, Act No. 25 of 1894, to Provide for the Disposal of Lands and for the Administration of Local Affairs with the District of Glen Grey and other Proclaimed Districts.

9. "Native Opinion," *Imvo*, 20 July 1887; "The Registration Act-Public Meeting of Natives," EPH, 23 September 1887. On the same date Africans at King-

williamstown held a meeting of the Native Vigilance Association, and resolved to adopt the resolutions voiced at Port Elizabeth. The Native Electoral Association, formed in 1883, probably consisted of the Vigilance Associations in the Eastern Cape and functioned as a pressure group. James Rose-Innes said that the Association declared in his favor for his first campaign in 1884, in B. A. Tindall, *James Rose-Innes, Autobiography* (New York: Oxford University Press, 1949), 52; According to Jabavu, there were over 100 members in August 1885, see "Editorial," *Imvo*, 5 August, 1885.

10. For example, Theo Don wrote two letters to the editor of the *EPH*, "A Native on The Glen Grey Bill," 3 September, 1894, and "The Glen Grey Bill," *EPH* 7 September 1894; For other Port Elizabeth African reaction see "Meeting with Jones," *Imvo*, 24 October 1894. At this meeting to protest against the passage of the Glen Grey Act held in Port Elizabeth, Charles T. Jones, the M.L.A. for Port Elizabeth, and usually a staunch opponent of "class" legislation declared that the Queen was not disposed to use the veto. Jones, a merchant, had been widely supported by the African voters since 1884. His position was representative of the staunch liberals also called the "friends of the natives."; John X. Merriman, James Rose-Innes and J. W. Sauer, all "friends of the natives" voted against the bill on the third reading. See Richard Parry, "In a Sense Citizens, But Not Altogether Citizens: Rhodes, Race and the Ideology of Segregation at the Cape in the Late Nineteenth Century," *Canadian Journal of African Studies* 17 (1983): 385–386; Les Switzer, *Power and Resistance in An African Society: The Ciskei Xhosa and the Making of South Africa* (Madison: University of Wisconsin Press, 1993), p. 102; Trapido "African Divisional Politics," pp. 79–98.

11. Alan Mabin, "The Rise and Decline of Port Elizabeth, 1850–1900," *International Journal of African Historical Studies* 19 (1986): 295.

12. Ibid.

13. Colin Bundy, *The Rise and Fall of the South African Peasantry* (Berkeley: University of California Press, 1979), esp. Chap. 3 for explanation of the opportunities for the African peasantry, the growth of social stratification and factors leading to proletarianization between 1870–1890 in the Cape, pp. 65–108. Then in 1896–97, the rinderpest (cattle disease) struck reaching epidemic proportions. It left thousands of cattle dead and many Africans anxious to replenish their stock and thus willing to enter wage labor in the towns.

14. "Town Council," *EPH*, 1 September 1891; Christopher, "Race and Residence," gives a different estimate; under the 1883 agreement, only about twenty families moved from Strangers' to Reservoir; Approximate figures for the municipal locations are from "The Location Question," *EPH*, 7 November 1894.

15. "The Locations—at the Reservoir Location," *EPH*, 16 October 1895.

16. These figures calculated from approximately 3,000 persons in 1897, compared to 1,800 persons in 1884, See Cape of Good Hope, Report of the Select Committee Report on the Native Reserve Locations Bill, A22-1902 (hereafter 1902 Select Committee Bill Report).

17. Cape of Good Hope, Report of the Select Committee on the Port Elizabeth Municipal Act Amendment Bill (Cape Town: Cape Times Printing Works), A9-1897 (hereafter 1897 Port Elizabeth Municipal Act), p. 27.

18. This was because land speculation was rampant, and once it was known that the municipality was an interested purchaser, the individual owner or syndicate often raised the price considerably. For an example, see "Town Council," *EPH*, 3 November 1898. The municipality wanted Corcoran's private location closed. Thus, Corcoran offered to sell the property to the Council for £10 per hut, the equivalent, he maintained, of the taxes he paid on them. The Council refused to pay what they considered to be an exorbitant price, so Corcoran's stayed; Also on the Johannesburg Municipal Council and property owners, see Noreen Kagen, "African Settlements in the Johannesburg Area, 1903–1923" (master's thesis, University of the Witwatersrand, 1978), p. 73.

19. "Town Council," *EPH*, 21 August 1891.

20. For example, at Strangers' location on a Saturday night, Africans fought with knobkerries from 11:30 p.m. to 3:30 a.m. until they were dispersed. "Town Council," *EPH*, 27 April 1896.

21. 1897 Select Committee Report, p. 34.

22. "Town Council," *EPH*, 1 December 1894.

23. Editorial, *Imvo*, 19 June 1890, and "Port Elizabeth Leads," 3 July 1890.

24. Revd. Dlepu was ordained in 1881. See T. D. Mweli Skota, *The African Yearly Register: Being an Illustrated Biographical Dictionary (Who's Who) of Black Folks in Africa* (Johannesburg: R. L. Eddon and Co., Ltd., 1933), p. 146; "E Bhayi," *Imvo*, 4 November 1891; For opera company and debating society, see "*Imvo e Bhayi*," *Imvo*, 4 August 1886 cited in Odendaal, "African Political Mobilization," pp. 292–293.

25. School people is defined here as *abantu basesikolweni* "those who entered the cash economy, possessed some formal education, were Christians, or had otherwise assimilated prominent aspects of European culture," following Hunt-Davis, "School vs. Blanket and Settler," p. 12.

26. George Wallace Mills, "The Role of African Clergy in the Reorientation of Xhosa Society to the Plural Society in the Cape Colony, 1850–1915" (Ph.D. diss., University of California, Los Angeles 1975), pp. 55–56. Mills relates that Isaac Wauchope also launched a defensive counterattack against the "unrelenting denigration and disparagement of traditional culture and customs," p. 58.

27. These public meetings were grounded in the Nguni political counsel system, which allowed for the Chief to be assisted or advised by a small group of councillors, then a governing body or a larger council of hereditary headmen, then if necessary a general assembly of initiated men considered the matter where freedom of speech was allowed. Among the Xhosa the public meeting was more likely called in matters of war and first fruit ceremonies. The Basotho called a full assembly meeting (*pitso*) when the occasion demanded, pp. 181–184. I. Schapera, ed., *The Bantu-Speaking Tribes of South Africa.*

28. "The Political Campaign," *EPH*, 1 November 1893, this note is for quotes in this paragraph and the previous paragraph on the political meeting between Jones and the Africans.

29. "Town Council," *EPH*, 10 November 1893. Some of the Council houses were bought from the Africans when they moved in 1884 from Strangers' location to Reservoir location. Also, about twenty had been built as model dwellings.

30. Ibid.

31. "White Barbarians," *EPH*, 21 December 1892. Also see 28 December 1892; 2, 16 January 1893, and 10 December 1894.

32. Vivian Bickford-Smith, "Dangerous Cape Town: Middle Class Attitudes to Poverty in Cape Town in the late Nineteenth Century," *Studies in the History of Cape Town* 4 (1981): 47.

33. "The Locations—Our Special Commissioner at Work," *EPH*, 30 September 1895.

34. On one occasion, Revd. John Pritchard, the white minister at the largest church for Africans in Port Elizabeth, Edward's Memorial, Congregationalist Church, complained about the rain accumulating in the thoroughfares near Strangers' location. He suggested that a drainage ditch be installed, since after each heavy rainfall the location flooded. But, the Board of Works summarily recommended against the work being done, doubtless deterred by the projected cost of £100, "Town Council," *EPH*, 21 August 1891; The Christian Africans also requested that the Council support parliamentary legislation for the suppression of making, selling, and drinking of "Kafir" beer and other intoxicating liquors, "Town Council," *EPH*, 30 June 1893; Africans also requested that water-pipes be brought closer, "Town Council," *EPH*, 2 September 1894.

35. Still, on one occasion the Council agreed to the demands. This was the case of the water closets. The problem arose when the municipality failed to provide public water closets, and many Africans were arrested for "committing a nuisance." So the Africans sent a deputation to the Council to complain about these arrests. Upon the request of the Africans, the Council agreed to provide water closets. But since they were "erected in the open air," some of them close to the street, there was no privacy. Thus, most Africans refused to use them. For request see "Town Council," *EPH*, 9 December 1892; "The Location," George A. Ross to editor, *EPH*, 13 November 1893.

36. "Our Notebook," *EPH*, 19 June 1893.

37. "Town Council," *EPH*, 10 August 1894, for example, an Indian who owned property on South Union Street, the same street where Councillor McWilliams owned property, was prosecuted for running an overcrowded tenement. In contrast, when the sanitary inspector reported to the town council that the building owned by McWilliams was also in a dilapidated condition, there was no prosecution; see "Magistrate's Court," *EPH*, 29 August 1894. Also, African and white missionary landlords were cited for unsanitary conditions; for instance, in November 1895, Frank Makwena, Reverend Stephen Gous, and the mission buildings were served with notices to clean up their premises, "Town Council," *EPH*, 8 November 1895.

38. "The Locations—Our Special Commissioner at Work," *EPH*, 20 September 1895.

39. Ibid.

40. Whiley Pikoli received permission to build a house at Reservoir location only after applying twice through an attorney, "Town Council," *EPH*, 1 March 1895; 24 May 1895; Africans were also prosecuted for building without permission, or threatening the officials, see "Magistrate's Court," *EPH*, 30 August 1895; 20 January 1896, "Town Council," *EPH*, 29 May 1896.

41. R. J. Johnston, *Residential Segregation, the State and Constitutional Conflict in American Urban Areas* (New York: Academic Press, 1984), pp. 16–17.

42. In January 1894, some Africans from Reservoir location petitioned the Council for title to their sites. Apparently they had moved there from Strangers' location as part of the 1883 agreement. See Reservoir petition in CAD, 3/PEZ 6/1/1/1/209, 2 January 1894; "Town Council," *EPH*, 7 November 1894.

43. Switzer, *Power and Resistance in an African Society*, p. 108.

44. "Town Council," *EPH*, 11 May 1894; CAD 3/PEZ 1/2/1/6, Committee Minutes August 1893 to May 1896.

45. "Town Council," *EPH*, 16 March 1894.

46. Ibid.

47. The following quotes in this paragraph are all from "Town Council," *EPH*, 11 May 1894.

48. "Town Council," *EPH*, 31 August 1894.

49. Ibid.

50. "Letter to Editor," *EPH*, 26 September 1894.

51. Ibid.

52. The following resolutions were taken at the meeting, "Town Council," EPH, 19 September 1894; Council's reaction, see "Town Council," *EPH*, 27 September 1894.

53. Deborah Gaitskell, "Wailing for Purity: Prayer Union, African Mothers and Adolescent Daughters, 1912–1940," in Marks and Rathbone, *Industrialization and Social Change*, pp. 338–357; Van der Horst, *Native Labor*, p. 89.

54. "Town Council," *EPH*, 11 May 1894. According to J. Redgrave, *Port Elizabeth in Bygone Days* (Wynberg, Cape Town: Rustica Press, Ltd., 1947), the North End area especially Evatt and Alice streets, were two of the oldest established streets located alongside the railroad. From the "early days they were lined with low disreputable houses chiefly inhabited by the lower class of Irish and Malays," and the "quarter" became known as "Little Irish Town" because of its "bad reputation and gay, fast, and furious life." p. 135.

55. "Editorial," *Imvo*, 9 July 1896.

56. "Town Council," *EPH*, 7,9 November 1894 and 27 September 1895.

57. Another site chosen by the Council was rejected. This time, African representatives were selected to tour the site. Among them was Ross, and Revd. W. Momoti. When Ross and Momoti reported back to the location residents they vehemently objected and proceeded to pass more resolutions against moving to the site. See, "Town Council," *EPH*, 27 September 1895.

58. "The Location Question-The Problem Solved at the Bay," *Imvo*, 9 July 1896.

59. "Town Location Question," *EPH*, 23 July 1896.

60. Parry, "In a Sense, Citizen," p. 386.

61. "Model Locations," *Imvo*, 6 August 1896.

62. "Mr. Jones, M.L.A. and the Natives," *Imvo*, 26 June 1897; The Act would give the towns the same powers to remove locations as possessed by farmers under the private locations Act, Port Elizabeth Municipal Bill Select Committee Report, A9-1897, p. 14.

63. 1897 Select Committee Report, p. 15.

64. For Jones' testimony, see 1897 Select Committee Report, p. 63, and for town councillors comments, see "Town Council," *EPH*, 21 May 1897.

65. For example, see "Electoral Division or Blackocracy," *EPH*, 12 April 1898 and "The Port Elizabeth Poll," *EPH*, 19 August 1898.

66. "Town Council," *EPH*, 17 May 1897;

67. 1897 Select Committee Report, p. 19.

68. 1897 Select Committee Report, Holland, pp. 16,40; Wynne, pp. 42,48.

69. Cape of Good Hope, Reports on the Public Health for the Year 1896, including reports of District Surgeons, Local Authorities and Medical Inspectors (Cape Town: W. A. Richards and Sons, Government Printers, 1897), G5-1897, especially Annexure I–XII.

70. So said Councillor Fettes, see "Town Council," *EPH*, 18 September 1896.

71. "Dr. Ensor's Report," *EPH*, 16 October 1895; In a nutshell, Ensor touched on several issues that influenced the removal and housing of the working class in the nineteenth and twentieth centuries, issues that had plagued London as well as other cities in Europe, America, Africa, and Asia. These included, "a rapid growth population to a supreme shortage of housing and severe overcrowding" and "the continual dislocation caused by street, commercial and railroad building." See A. S. Wohl, "The Housing of the Working Classes in London, 1815–1914," in *The History of Working Class Housing* edited by Stanley D. Chapman (Newton Abbot: David and Charles, 1971), pp. 13–54, for similar blame and treatment directed by the officials toward the white working class tenants. It was always the poor who were dislocated into yet another area that would more often than not again be claimed by the authorities. p. 16.

72. Rob Turrell, "Kimberley: Labor and Compounds," in *Industrialization and Social Change*, p. 60.

73. "Town Council," *EPH*, 9 November 1891.

74. "Port Elizabeth Drainage," *EPH*, 11, 15, 18 January 1897; "Editorial," *EPH*, 16 October 1895.

75. Report on the Public Health, G5-1897, Annexure VI, Report on Typhoid.

76. "Town Council," *EPH*, 10 November 1896.

77. "Town Council," *EPH*, 25 December 1896; Dr. Turner, MOH for the Colony, stated that the food eaten at Dr. Uppleby's home was contaminated as a result of being kept in a room where there was a drain to take water to the sewer and the airborne germs infected the food. See Appendix 5, G5-'97

78. "Location Question, Native Point of View," *EPH*, 19 September 1894, the last statement was a reference to Dr. Ensor's conclusions.

79. "Location Question, Native Point of View," *EPH*, 19 September 1894.

80. Cape of Good Hope Laws, Act to repeal Port Elizabeth Municipal Act, p. 3835. The Act amended the municipal constitution thereby revoking the previous municipal acts of 1868, 1873, 1877, 1883, 1883, 1886 and 1890.

81. "Town Council," *EPH*, 1 December 1898; Also see "Town Council," *EPH*, 21 September 1891 for information on water supply and Council's financial problems.

82. Jabavu commented in 1896 that he thought it a mistake that no plan was included for the type of housing to be constructed at the new location. He recommended a three-room cottage as an ideal model building.

83. CAD, 3PEZ 6/1/1/1/209, See List of Siteholders at the Race Course location proposed by Mr. Newcombe in July 1900, Strangers' and Cooper's Kloof, 3 March 1901; Town Clerk records; and Meetings of Location Committee and natives re: the valuation of their huts, April 1899.

4

African Americans, Black South Africans, and the Economics of Pan-Africanism

Introduction

In the early 1890s a small nucleus of African Americans and Africans living in Port Elizabeth established a multiregional economic (union or co-operative) *manyano* called the African and American Working Men's Union (AAWMU). The name reflected the Union's transAtlantic, pan-Africanist orientation as well as the working class background of the men and women to whom the organizers attempted to sell shares. The Union purchased land, on which a trading store was constructed in 1893; the store remained solvent at least until 1908, and property was listed in the Union's name as late as 1930.

The Union's goals were to provide management training to facilitate the establishment of black-owned businesses throughout the region, create jobs for men and women, and promote black unity and racial uplift.[1] Another goal was to build a strong economic base in the hope that this would counteract not only the economic discrimination but also the social ostracism, such as indignities, insults, and injustice to which Blacks were increasingly subjected in the 1880s.

These physical and socio-psychological attacks on the body and the spirit of Africans were manifestations of an ideology among whites that aimed to generally humiliate Africans in South Africa in order to emphasize white superiority and domination vis-à-vis black inferiority and subordination. For example, Africans routinely faced mistreatment when travelling on the railway trains; the white station attendants were rude when issuing and collecting tickets and sometimes verbally and physically abused black passengers, by pushing and shoving them. Also Africans were forced to step off sidewalks when approaching whites in deference to their supposedly "civilized" and superior status. The deferent behavior that whites demanded from blacks was an example of the power relations associated with inequality of power and domination emerging in the colonial context. Orlando Patterson has discussed three facets of power relations and domination including the first which is social and involves the use or threat of violence in the control of one person by another. The second is the psychological facet of influence, the capacity to persuade another person to change the way he perceives his interests and his circumstances.[2] In both examples we can discern the changing relations of power and domination, that is, the violence and intimidation of the whites and how their actions in the first instance might lead Africans to follow discriminatory actions in the interest of protecting themselves from the physical and verbal abuse of the white colonists.

The members of the AAWMU hoped that by establishing themselves economically they would be able to improve not only their socio-economic position in the colonial society but also show the whites that African men and women deserved respect, equal treatment, and equal opportunities. The American Negroes (this term was used until the 1960s in regard to African Americans), having experienced similar treatment from whites in America, shared these views.

In the United States free Negroes facing increased racial segregation in the late eighteenth century began to create separate and independent socio-economic and political institutions including benefit societies, churches and schools. Similarly, in South Africa by the 1870s, Africans began forming their own social, educational, and political organizations to represent their interests. As we have seen these included the first political association the *Imbumba Yama Nyama*, established in Port Elizabeth in 1882 that attracted members from different ethnic, religious and class backgrounds.

The AAWMU founders also espoused political objectives. They aimed to use their economic base to gain political power at least at the local level. There was talk of a black town, a black mayor, and black councillors. In America, too, after the Civil War and reconstruction, racial hostility and discrimination influenced blacks to establish all-black towns such as Mound Bayou, in Mississippi.[3] Their shared concern about political methods to resist discrimination was not surprising, given that racial injustice at the hands of whites was experienced by both Africans and those of African descent living in South Africa, although sometimes the level of discrimination could be affected by such factors as the darker or lighter hue of the skin, one's educational background, the clothes one wore, one's gender, and whether or not one could understand or speak English or Dutch. Without a doubt, Africans and Negroes resented the superiority complex of the white colonists, which increasingly drew color distinctions.

Yet resentment by this aspirant black middle class about racial discrimination did not result in them turning away from white society or in anti-white racist sentiment. Instead, blacks showed an increased inclination to participate in the white-controlled, colonial capitalist economy. This may seem a contradiction, but in fact both the Africans and African Americans had been educated to believe that the "civilized" were entitled to compete equally, both politically and economically, and to co-exist socially, regardless of race. However, many blacks seemed willing to compromise on social equality, at least temporarily, thus sharing that aspect of the Booker T. Washington philosophy, "separate as the fingers in social matters but as close as one hand in economic concerns." But as liberalism declined at the Cape, undermining the white and black liberal alliance, and it became clear that the Western and Christian teachings were tarnished by the concrete practices of racial discrimination, the Western-educated blacks began to look for new allies to pursue their aspirations within the "race."

In more lyrical terms, these black men and women were experiencing what Richard Wright called in the 20th century, "double vision." Although Wright was speaking of how the color line on one hand and the intellectual Western education on the other divided Africans from both Western society and from African society [forcing them to live in two worlds] the words apply here.

> speaking as a western man of color. . . . My position is a split one. I'm black. I'm a man of the west . . . I see and understand the West . . . but I also see and understand the anti-Western point of view. How is this possible? This double-vision of mine stems from my being a product of Western civilization and from my racial identity which is organically born of my being a product of that civilization. Being a Negro [or African] living in a White Christian society, I've never been allowed to blend in a natural and healthy manner with the culture and civilization of the West. This contradiction of being both Western and a man of color creates a distance . . . between me and my environment. I'm self-conscious, I admit it. Yet I feel no need to apologize for it. Hence, though Western, I'm inevitably critical of the West. My attitude of criticism and detachment is born of my position. Me and my environment are one, but that oneness has in it, at its very heart, a schism.[4]

This "double vision" forced them to view life both as people discriminated against because of their skin color and as people educated to aspire to inclusion in the broader white-dominated and-controlled society. They lived in two worlds, and in the Western world, a double standard based on race operated to prevent blacks participating fully. Thus, the badge of color worn by the blacks allowed only for a partial blending into the white society, since many whites had determined that a dark-skinned color was the outward sign of inferiority. Racial discrimination against blacks also promoted criticism, protest, and bitterness and eventually the formation of separate organizations such as the AAWMU. This was contradictory behavior, forming separate organizations, to facilitate assimilation into white colonial society.

The AAWMU is significant because it is the first and earliest evidence of the formation of a pan-Africanist economic alliance between African Americans living permanently in South Africa and black South Africans. By pan-Africanism I mean the awareness of Africans living in Africa and people of African descent wherever they are living, that based on their common oppression because of western European slavery, colonialism, and imperialism, they share experiences and struggles and should combine whenever possible to work to prevent further exploitation and to build unity and organizations to enhance the position of the peoples of Africa and those of African descent.[5] As Michael West points out, pan-Africanism was judged too hastily by those claiming that it was irrational in its approach to economic concerns.[6] He continues that numerous attempts were made in the nineteenth century to promote economic pan-Africanism but with little success. The formation of the AAWMU was yet another economic venture, and it was relatively successful for its time.

The religious, educational, and cultural pan-Africanist connections between Africans and African Americans in South Africa are relatively well known after the mid-1890s.[7] Much of the scholarship on them focuses specifically on religious organizations, especially the Ethiopian, which is the name often used in discussing the African independent church movement; or educational issues, such as the attendance of Africans at black American colleges in the United States; or cultural connections, such as the McAdoo Singers). The AAWMU adds economic avenues of co-operation between African Americans and Africans in South Africa to this list.

The African Americans and the Africans who established the Union were Christians who shared certain beliefs, expectations, and aspirations based on Christian principles and teachings. Their establishment of the Union shows once again how the Christian teachings and western influences could be turned against their white proponents and used to challenge racial discrimination and white supremacy. These activities challenge the idea that black liberals were willing to wait patiently until they were deemed "civilized" and "advanced" enough by the whites to be accepted into the white colonial society. It also shows that during this period, Christian and western-educated Africans developed economic organizations and alliances independent of white liberals as support for the Cape liberal tradition declined.

The formation of the AAWMU also informs us about the class position of the African leadership in Port Elizabeth. The Unions' African leaders were members of the emergent black middle class. All of them had rights to land and property in the town as a result of the 1883 Native Strangers' Location Act.[8] More about the ideology of this group can be learned by analyzing the background that led to the formation of the AAWMU. Moreover, the establishment of the Union adds to the body of knowledge about the economic strategies Africans were using to challenge the ideology and intensifying practices of racial discrimination and segregation in South Africa. Finally, it provides information about local and regional efforts by Africans to promote black unity and cross-ethnic and cross-class alliances to gain economic autonomy.

The union was formed during the transition years when South Africa was moving from commercial to industrial capitalism. Especially after the mineral discoveries, the colonial governments attempted to structure the subordination of Africans and promote the growth of an African working class while simultaneously limiting the growth of a black middle class. The Cape colonial government passed racially discriminatory laws to segregate Africans residentially, eliminate black rights to the franchise, prevent land and home ownership in the town and countryside, and limit economic opportunities.[9]

The formation of the AAWMU challenged these government initiatives. The attempt of the aspirant African middle class to ally on the one hand with the "Negro" Americans living in Port Elizabeth and on the other with the emergent African working class underscores the racial and defensive forces bringing together these groups despite their class and ideological differences. The Union was viewed as an economic vehicle to unite Africans so that they could gain political power, and also enhance their social position, thus it exhibited a nationalist component that could become one of the building blocks for twentieth century African nationalism.

Background to the Formation of the AAWMU

Until the 1890s, Port Elizabeth remained the second largest city in the British Cape colony. In the 1880s, an increasing number of workseekers, primarily of Xhosa extraction but also Sotho and Zulu, began entering the city to work or passing through it enroute to the diamond and gold mines. In 1891, the total population was 23,266, including about 13,538 Europeans and 5,000 Africans; although the Mfengu Africans had began to settle there in the 1840s, the majority by the 1890s were Xhosa.[10]

One of the largest mission-educated African populations continued to live and work in the town permanently rather than as temporary migrant workers. Many were second-and-third generation urban dwellers, having been born and raised in the town. They lived in family settings, and by the 1890s, members of this class numbered about 1800.

It will be recalled that by the 1870s, this group was developing political and social consciousness as many became involved in church activities, sports clubs, temperance lodges, and benefit societies. They also sponsored concerts, debates and tea meetings. They were concerned as well with Africans receiving fair wages, the poor and segregated living conditions, working conditions, and the abuse of Africans political, economic, and civil rights. The African leaders also expressed concern about the safety of young African men and women, and immoral behavior in the towns.[11]

The basis for the liberal alliance continued to erode as independent black polities around the Colony were conquered and the number of Africans under colonial jurisdiction increased. A new policy was needed that increased labor, encouraged Africans to work for wages, and subordinated them to whites. Thus, there were government initiatives for segregation and a rise in racial discrimination in the social, economic, and political arenas. The aspirant black middle class was caught in the middle of this change as their privileges were eroded and doors were closed. White supremacy and domination had no room for an emergent black middle class that, among other things, would compete with whites for land and capitalist enterprises. The liberal alliance, weakened as it was, seemed to offer fewer avenues for fulfillment. The promise of equal opportunity, if Africans became "civilized," which included becoming Christian and educated by Western standards, were transitory. Instead, racial discrimination, prejudice, and inequality were increasing.

African Businesses and Black Consciousness

A major aspiration of many in the emergent black middle class throughout South Africa was to own land and businesses. However, the bulk of the land, property, and industrial and commercial businesses in Port Elizabeth were controlled by whites, thus hampering commercial activity for Africans. Business interests and the municipal councillors allied to reduce competition from Africans. Outside the African municipal locations, a few Africans occupied or owned property where they, in turn, rented rooms or supplied room and board. For example, Frank Makwena acted as a real estate broker for a woman whose property in 1895 was cited for dilapidation.[12] They had gained this foothold in the commercial economy in spite of periodic municipal government attempts to impose formal residential segregation. Not surprisingly, it was difficult to rent or buy land particularly because land values were rising and most whites did not want Africans living near them for fear of disease, let alone operating business establishments.[13]

Local government also tried to restrict competition from the growing Indian population whose numbers by 1891, though not conclusively known, were perhaps 500. But since the government proposed the establishment of Indian bazaars in 1895, the population and number of successful traders must have been growing. Indian traders were primarily situated away from the main business district because of racial discrimination and high property prices.[14] They were also denied permission to trade in the African locations. Yet, informal street trading or hawking was controlled primarily by the Indian traders, although a few African men and women also engaged in this form of trade.[15]

It is noteworthy that the town officials did not allow the Africans to attend town market thus denying them the opportunity to compete with the European and Indian traders. The town councillors wanted to extend this restrictive policy to all Indians. Expressing the general opinion of the all white Council, about market operations, Mr. Gates complained of the way in which the Indians crowded at the front. This resulted in the Indians getting all the good stalls and the Europeans being forced to the back. He thought they [the Indians] should be made to take a back seat and make room for the Europeans. Then, a Mr. Winters suggested that no Indians except buyers be allowed in the market. Not surprisingly, both Gates and Winters were supported by the other town councillors. It is worth noting that Gates and Winters were complaining about the initiative of the Indian traders, a positive attribute that normally draws praise.[16]

In contrast to the opportunities offered to white businesses, African businesses were restricted mostly to the municipal housing settlements, but even there the Port Elizabeth Town Council tried to impose limitations. In Port Elizabeth itself, the Council attempted to prevent Africans owning land and pursuing economic ventures even in proscribed areas. For example, it imposed a restrictive policy on building construction at the African locations. The municipal scheme of limiting construction unless there was governmental approval was instituted when attempts were being made to remove Strangers' location in 1883.[17] From the Council's viewpoint, which assumed that the location would be removed at some future date, continued improvements would require that the government would have to pay more compensation to the residents displaced. Therefore, the decision was made to limit any new construction by refusing to issue building licenses.

The foregoing practice left the location residents in a difficult position, never knowing when they would have to abandon their homes and move. Many Africans criticized the Council's arbitrary building policy, pointing out that it was an obstacle to self-improvement and also that it contributed to the dilapidated appearance of the municipal locations as well as to overcrowding. The Council's building restrictions were an impediment to free enterprise for would-be black capitalists. It prevented their erecting structures or small business enterprises, limited their upward mobility, and stunted their opportunities to increase their capital. Moreover, the Council's approval of applications was influenced by recommendations of their Location Committee (made up of Council members), which in 1893 agreed that construction would be allowed so long as a written guarantee was submitted that the Council would not have to pay compensation.[18]

Yet at times, the decision seemed to be strictly arbitrary, depending on whether or not the applicant was in the good graces of Council members. Consequently, obtaining a building license was extremely difficult. For example, in March 1895, when Whiley Pikoli wanted to build a house at Reservoir, he went to the expense of hiring an attorney to send a letter of application to the Council.[19] Still, the Council refused. When Pikoli's application was resubmitted in May, it succeeded with the support of the Location Committee.[20] Nevertheless, such success was unique.

In contrast, there were many less fortunate cases, like that of James Magenta who in 1895, was refused permission to erect a building on his site. Apparently some altercation had occurred between Magenta and the location officials, and his building materials were carted away. Magenta hired solicitors to represent his case to the Council. The Council recommended that his building supplies be returned but that he be refused permission to erect the structure. Also, they warned that "should he insist on doing so, he is to be informed that next year no site certificate will be issued to him and he will be expelled from the location."[21]

Magenta must have lived at Reservoir or Cooper's Kloof, where tenure was less secure, as opposed to Stranger's location, where several hundred residents had land rights and thus could not be evicted. The government's threat to expel Magenta from his residence shows it had some degree of control over Africans dependent upon governmental housing, a predicament that would plague Africans in the twentieth century.[22]

Despite government restrictions, some Africans were able to open businesses. Therefore, by 1891, the Africans in Port Elizabeth held "seven black-owned shops" and a butcher's business.[23] These had been established with some difficulty because, as Mr. S. Khata emphasized at an AAWMU meeting, at first the men who established shops were victims of mockery, "even birds laughed at them," but by 1891 they were well-established and even enjoyed a little bit of respect.[24] Exactly who mocked the African business owners is unclear, but since the local whites did not relish competition from black entrepreneurs, it was no small accomplishment for blacks to establish these businesses.

A case of one African named John Perry indicates what aspirant African businessmen faced and the way in which they were at the mercy of the white officials who mocked them.[25] Perry had constructed a residential building at the North End of town that had been found unfit for human habitation by the municipal sanitary inspector. Cited to appear before the Council, Perry submitted a written statement arguing that the tenants were quite satisfied even though the building was incomplete. Perry was given two months to repair it to the Superintendent's satisfaction. During the discussion of the case, some of the councillors made fun of Perry's building and the length of time it took to construct. For example, councillor, G. Brown said that the structure was erected all backward because first the roof was put up on studs, then the foundation, and then the walls. (Laughter). For Perry this probably made sense, because it could be occupied when a roof was up and also the building materials could be protected from the natural elements.

Moreover, Perry began constructing the building in 1880. The inordinate length of time, it took to erect it, from 1880–1896, indicates that Perry probably faced similar difficulties competing with white businesses as did black businessmen in America including, "1) . . . procuring capital and credit, 2) inadequate training, 3) poor and restricted geographical locations."[26] These problems meant that Perry could not compete with white businessmen in the same field as to price and services. But Perry had few defenders since he was not part of the inner circle of businessmen that could enforce the laws arbitrarily. Although Councillor Griffin, his one defender noted, "the Council always picked out the weakest men. There were councillors who had premises equally as bad as Perry's." With this comment, there were shouts of "Names! Names!" but none were given.[27]

In any case, Africans continued to build, even without government permission. Thus, Africans at both Strangers' and Reservoir Locations went ahead and erected buildings for businesses such as butcher's and general dealer's shops in defiance of the regulations. For example, in 1893, John Zwaartboi, a houseowner in Strangers' location added a room constructed of wood-and-iron slabs and asked for the Council's permission after the work was completed.[28] Similarly in 1891, John Kama put up a butcher's shop at Strangers' location without a license.[29] A few years later, Mani Mlandu opened a general dealer's shop at Reservoir.[30] When the councillors were told, they ordered the superintendent of the municipal locations, Mr. Newcombe, to close the shops. But he was not always able to enforce the regulations because of inadequate and unreliable police help and resistance from the occupants. In fact, Newcombe often complained that Africans continued to erect buildings even after he advised against it.[31]

While some Africans challenged the regulations by constructing buildings, many others questioned the Council's authority to impose such seemingly arbitrary restrictions. Indeed, there was some legal basis for the doubt they raised. Although space does not allow me to pursue the details of the municipal councils' legal authority in the 1890s, it is noteworthy that the Cape central government in 1896 claimed that the Port Elizabeth municipality never had the legal power to restrict building construction in the locations. Obviously white economic jealousies lay behind this stretching of official authority. Also, and even more revealing regarding the Council's economic motives for their restrictions on African businesses, was the fact that the Council itself owned a general store at the Reservoir location and was trying to maintain a monopoly.[32]

The store was leased to Frank Makwena, a BaSotho, trained at Lovedale as a carpenter. Like so many other young western-educated Africans, Makwena found problems practicing the skills he had learned because of racial discrimination, which limited white clientele and the lack of demand among his own people. So he took a job in a store. In November 1893, Makwena leased the general store at Reservoir from the Council.[33] Since Makwena requested in May 1895 that the Council keep its bargain by closing several stores at Reservoir that were competing for business, it seems that he must have been promised a monopoly.[34] Although the councillors denied his implied allegation, they ordered the businesses closed because the proprietors had not been issued proper building licenses.[35] But evidence from none other than the Town Council's own attorney came to light pointing out the intention to grant a monopoly to whomever rented their general dealer's store. The attorney explained that, "the Town Council granted the lease of the ground upon which the shop stands to a person who was to retail goods at certain prices, granting this person sole right, and if other persons could open shops, the Town Council would in terms of their own agreement lay themselves open to an action for damages."[36] To fulfill this promise [to the lessee], they tried to prevent African competition by restricting building. But the monopoly brought complaints from African residents who said the Council's policy put them at the mercy of the one shop keeper.[37]

These complaints probably emanated from members of the aspirant black middle class who were themselves attempting to open small businesses as well as African consumers in general trying to save money by selective buying, especially of essential goods. Also, it is likely that Africans would support maintaining some control over institutions in their immediate environment.

Undoubtedly, the Council's promised monopoly was at the expense of the location residents. They wanted to control the number of African businesses competing with not only the Council's leased location shop

politics had been a disaster for blacks in the United States South and what a blessing it was that they were no longer involved."[56]

Prior to the direct cultural and religious contact, however, John T. Jabavu, the premiere South African leader in the nineteenth century, and editor of the African newspaper *Imvo*, encouraged the influence of American "Negroes." For example, he urged his readers in 1889 to "study the socioeconomic conditions of American blacks in order to appreciate the importance of acquiring an education and with it the ability to buy property."[57]

It is noteworthy that the self-help ideals voiced by AAWMU's leaders were the product of a variety of internal and external influences. Among the external influences was Booker T. Washington, the prominent African American leader known for his self-help ideology, who was an inspiration to many. Interestingly, both white and black claimed Booker T. Washington as an inspiration. Many South African whites interpreted Washington's message as supporting white supremacy because he cautioned against involvement in politics and supported a "slow" move toward civil rights. Africans, on the other hand, were inspired to economic upliftment but largely rejected the idea of withdrawing from politics.[58]

Internally the inspiration to develop self-help strategies flowed from the English and German missionaries in the Eastern Cape, and the mission society also fostered organized trade. In particular, the stores established first on mission stations and later in the urban locations provided an example of the benefits to be derived from economic co-operation. And some Africans quickly responded to consumers' needs by opening shops at the mission stations.[59]

On the contrary, Bundy claims that around 1835 at the Cape, some missionaries envisioned African converts as landowners, producers, workers, and consumers, but for the most part these perceptions did not include the African as self-employed.[60] This may have been true in the Cape in 1835, but in Natal the Africans developed farm co-operatives as early as the 1860s.[61] By the 1880s the missionary and white liberal emphasis shifted pushing Africans out to wage labor.

Doubtless the formation of the AAWMU was also influenced by indigenous ideas about communalism, co-operation, and mutual responsibility among the Nguni-speaking people, including the Xhosa, Zulu and Mpondo. For example, communal work parties in which members of the community co-operated in agricultural or building activities such as clearing the land and were offered in return food and beer, were widespread.[62] The principal of co-operative work, which is rewarded immediately with beer and which also includes the societal sanction of reciprocity, was present prior to the arrival of the Europeans.[63]

The formation of the AAWMU by members of the aspirant black middle class reflected an ideological shift away from dependence on liberal whites and a move toward pan-Africanism and nationalism. The four men founding the AAWMU, two African and two African Americans, had several common elements contributing to their shared ideology. First was Christian religion and Western education. The English language facilitated communication and the idea of Christian spiritual brotherhood. Second was class position, as all were part of the emergent middle class. Third was color and race solidarity. Fourth was racial discrimination perpetuated by the whites, and fifth was the belief in cultural and economic pan-Africanism and political rights.

The similar ideology shared by these Christian blacks was based on the realization that the promise of Christian brotherhood was thwarted by racial discrimination and segregation, white domination and oppression, Jim Crow laws in the United States South, and de facto segregation in the North. In the South African colonies, there was also the rise of the ideology of segregation and racially discriminatory practices.

A shared experience of black South Africans and African Americans was their exposure to racial discrimination on the public transportation system. This occurred on the railway system in particular because of the possibility of body closeness and eye contact, that is, as the proximity of black to white increases, the tolerance level of whites decreases, resulting in unparalled hostility by whites.

This hostility was acted out by whites in physical attacks against blacks in order to emphasize their power and control or lack of it, and also to degrade and humiliate the victims. Apparently the whites feared, among other things, that blacks would pollute the railway cars.[64] Also, some of the white railway officials seemed to think that blacks ought not to use the same transport system. Moreover, if some blacks did not understand the workings of the system, such as the correct fares to a specific point, the use of tickets, and the seating arrangements, the officials sometimes accused them of being too dumb to understand or of trying to cheat on fares. Some of these officials took it upon themselves to teach black passengers through physical abuse.

Not surprisingly, Blacks resented this racial discrimination and segregation as a "humiliating disgrace."[65] A good example of a case of railway discrimination occurred in 1885 at Port Elizabeth. It involved a young black man enroute from Port Elizabeth to Grahamstown who was assaulted by a white railway attendant, arrested, and released the next morning without charge. This incident of racial discrimination might have gone unnoticed if not for the fact that the young black man was the brother of Isaac Wauchope, the court reporter for the municipal court at Port Elizabeth, chairman of the Native Improvement Association, and a leading member of the emerging black middle class.

Briefly, the incident unfolded as follows.[66] Peter Wauchope left Port Elizabeth by the Thursday night train arriving in Grahamstown on Friday morning. Apparently when handing his ticket to the ticket guard, Peter dropped a coin. When he bent down to pick it up, a shunter (the attendant who switches the cars from one track to another) "came up and, without asking for an explanation, began to kick and strike at Peter . . . and even followed him into the carriage. Shunter Ellenton then locked the carriage door, saying, 'I am not done with you yet, my man.'" When the train reached the end of the line, Wauchope was marched off to jail. Ironically, Ellenton harassed and assaulted Wauchope but Wauchope, not Ellenton, was arrested for being the object of assault. The next morning Wauchope was taken before the Grahamstown Magistrate and released without charge.

Issac Wauchope immediately went to his brother's defense and filed a complaint at Port Elizabeth with the Railway Department against shunter Ellenton. After investigating the case, Inspector Brown of the Port Elizabeth Railway Department sent a letter to Wauchope, informing him that he "regretted the occurrence and . . . the attendant had been dismissed for his rude behavior." Wauchope responded with a letter to Brown in which he praised the Railway Department and Brown for "carrying out the strictest justice in order to secure the protection of the public without distinction of color." Wauchope pointed out that:

> My brother's case is but one of many in which the native traveller is taken advantage of by some of the so-called railway officials, and the only reason I can assign for the fewness of complaints is, not that their complaints would not be attended to if lodged with the proper authorities, but because they think that the bullying and knocking about which they receive are part of the duty of the officials, and that therefore it would be futile to complain against a man who simply performs his duty. I am perfectly aware of the annoyance given to the Railway officials by Native passengers who are, in most cases ignorant of the rule of the Railway department; but there is ample provision in the railway law for the protection of those whose duty it is to protect life and property so that Mr. Ellenton had no need to commit an assault. . . . You have cleared the Railway Department of a very serious charge, namely, of only protecting those of the public who have a white skin, and leaving the many of color out in the cold.

It is obvious that Wauchope absolved the railway department, based on the successful resolution of this one incident of racism. Similarly, it is also clear that white railway attendants almost routinely harassed and assaulted Africans. The response of Wauchope is representative of members of the petty bourgeoisie who found it expedient to use non-offensive or accommodating language in the hope that British justice as promised and practiced toward white citizens would be color-blind when it came to the "civilized" Africans. Thus, when such incidents occurred that tested the system of justice and pitted views on race and class against one another, a favorable resolution was often seen as a moral victory.[67] Similarly, in a broader sense, the alliance between white liberals and Western-educated Africans was tested by such incidents, since belief in the British system of justice was based on the teachings of the whites. And if these beliefs about justice were found wanting, it is likely that the rest of the Christian and moral teachings would be questioned.

It is noteworthy that in defending his brother, Wauchope downgrades the ordinary so-called "uncivilized" African when he says they do not complain because perhaps they think that the bullying and knocking about are part of the duty of the officials. This statement is clearly not to be taken seriously, since it is ludicrous to think that anyone would accept that attacking them was the job of an official unless they believed that they were inferior and therefore deserved such treatment.

Rather, the statement is meant to imply that the ignorant "natives" would not know the difference between just and unjust treatment. In saying this, Wauchope is building a bridge between him and the white official who are both "civilized" to the exclusion of the "uncivilized." And herein lies one of the problems between the emerging black middle class and the ordinary Africans: the class divide influenced by Western education and religious beliefs and inculcated by the converted African or the *kholwa* skewed their views of Africans, who preferred to continue their own customs and not to accept Western values or missionary education.

African Americans also faced similar racial discrimination from railway officials. This was especially true for blacks who were of darker skin color since the act of discrimination was committed before the whites knew if they were insulting local blacks or international blacks from such places as The United States or the Caribbean.

This was a matter of importance, since on one occasion, "On January 15 [1893] a black man named John Ross, who worked as a laborer in the construction of the Delagoa Bay railway, was verbally abused by a white employee and when he ventured to answer back, he was tied up and given fifteen lashes for being 'impudent'."[68] It seems that the sentence was executed without a trial which apparently was the usual treatment meted out to Africans. Ross, it turns out, was a black American, and he subsequently issued a claim for ten thousand dollars $10,000 for damages against the South African Republic, backed by the U.S. Department of State. The case was settled. Thereafter black Americans, Keto declares, were given an "honorary white" status in the Transvaal which he implies meant that they were no longer molested. After the South African War ended in 1902, a new policy of requiring identification emerged. He continues that Bishop Turner reported in June 1, 1898, that black Americans could also ride where they chose on the public railway trains and stay in any hotels, while native Africans were forced to ride in third class cars and refused hotel rooms.[69]

Turner's experience was clearly influenced by the Ross case and perhaps even by his own ministerial position. Richard H. Collins, a black American singer and member of the McAdoo Troupe, had a less pleasant experience in March 1898 in Durban, Natal. He was confronted by a white trooper at the railway platform bar who questioned his right to be there because he was confused as to Collins' nationality. The trooper had already encountered several colonial "dressed natives" (This is the term whites used for Africans who generally wore Western clothes and observed western customs) who produced badges of exemption and asked for a drink. But Collins refused to co-operate, saying he was an American citizen and had every right to be in the bar and to drink as much as he liked. The trooper tried to arrest Collins. A scuffle ensued, and with help from the railway clerk, Collins was arrested; he was later released on five pounds bail. Through the intervention of the American consul in Durban, the court proceedings set for the next morning were suspended.[70]

It is worth noting that J. T. Jabavu, editor of *Imvo,* in musings about his railway trip from Kingswilliamtown in the eastern Cape to Natal in 1891, indicated that the white passengers avoided him like the plague so he had a whole compartment to himself with plenty of elbow room.[71] Thus, restrictions were less rigid. By 1898, there were reports of assaults by railway officials. For example, P. Xiniwe was "run in" and held for three hours apparently for being on the platform to see a friend off. The implication from the newspaper report is that the official and Xiniwe had words because Xiniwe acted "impudent."[72] Ironically, these were the same words used about Ross, the black American in the 1893 incident.

Thus, blatant harassment continued, in particular of welldressed and western educated Africans. These types of experiences help to explain the empathy drawing blacks toward each other and influencing them to establish organizations such as the AAWMU. Included among the founding members of the AAWMU were two wellknown local African spokesmen in Port Elizabeth, George A. Ross, trustee, and Moses Foley, secretary. Ross was a small businessman, and Foley was a store clerk. Ozias Henderson, an African American was the Treasurer, while Henry Phipps, described as an African American and also as a West Indian, was the manager. Before settling in Port Elizabeth, both Henderson and Phipps had been boatmen or sailors, with the latter having lived there for over four years.[73] J. T. Jabavu was at this meeting and supported the Union.

The philosophy associated with the formation of the co-operative is il-lustrated by Foley, one of the leading spokesmen. The goals of the co-op-erative were not only commercial success but also to "uplift" economic activity through self-help by teaching management training; by hiring African women who otherwise "toiled in the kitchens of the white women"; and by uniting the black community.[74] Many of the same "up-lift" sentiments had been voiced when the *Imbumba Yama Nyama,* the first political association, was founded and its leaders such as Reverend B. Dlepu also supported the AAWMU.

August Meier notes that similar self-help ideals became more popular among American "Negroes" in the decade before the Civil War and again in the years following Reconstruction. He states that:

> the years following Reconstruction were characterized by an increasing em-phasis on economic activity as a factor in solving the race problem. This view was usually part of a larger complex of ideas that included racial sol-idarity and self-help. It was based upon the assumption that by the acqui-sition of wealth and morality—attained largely by their own efforts—Ne-groes would gain the respect of white men and thus be accorded their rights as citizens.[75]

This ideological outlook was prevalent as well among the Christian Africans in South Africa in the 1870s as they formed political and social self-help organizations. Meier continues, "At times the emphasis on race pride and solidarity approached a kind of nationalism."[76] Some Negro leaders supported separate institutions, although this idea was usually regarded as being a tactic in the struggle for ultimate citizenship rights . . . at least temporarily until real equality and integration could be achieved.[77] Supporting this view was Phipps, the African American speaking at a commemoration day ceremony for the AAWMU store opening; he "stressed the fact that Americans were always prepared to help Africans. But . . . racial integration was the only solution to South African problems."[78] In a corresponding statement, Francis L. Cardozo, an African American leader: "advocated separate schools and churches only as a means to an end . . . until Negroes could enter white institu-tions on terms of complete equality, he thought it preferable to maintain segregated institutions. . . . Though Negroes were willing to accept seg-regation as long as they were accorded some status and control over their affairs. . . ."[79]

Significantly, an American Negro who attended a political meeting in Port Elizabeth in 1898, for the re-election of the member of the Legisla-tive Assembly, expressed views similar to those of Cardoza. It seems likely that the Negro described was Ozias Henderson, discussed earlier, a founding member of the AAWMU. He and his wife, Eliza, were still residing in Port Elizabeth in 1898. Henderson opened the Resolute Boarding House in September 1896, for black travellers "who would like to find a home away from home to relax."[80] It seems tenable that some of the eight black Americans living at the Reservoir location in 1904 may have at some point stayed at his hotel.[81] In any case, at the meeting, "the Negro" stated that "in America they did not hug the white race and though he agreed in this country a line should be drawn between the white and colored children, the latter should be given a chance to excel."[82]

On another note, the African leaders in Port Elizabeth held a high opinion of American Negroes and sympathized with their previous enslavement in America. According to P. Rwexu, an AAWMU member and leader in Port Elizabeth, "Africans and Americans . . . are blood relatives, because Americans are also Xhosas who were snatched from Africa and enslaved in America."[83] In the same vein, George Ross raised the rallying cry of pan-Africanism when he stressed that "Africa was for Africans, not Europeans."[84]

The phrase "Africa for the Africans" had already been used in the 1860s and 1870s by two well-known American Negro emigrationists of the period, Martin Delaney and Bishop Henry Turner, mentioned earlier. In fact, Turner was elected vice-president of the American Colonization Society in 1874. In the twentieth century, the phrase and nationalist sentiments were revitalized by the Marcus Garvey movement in the United States and in South Africa.[85]

Moreover, Mr. Hendry, one of the African Americans involved, expressed mutual pan-Africanist sentiments when he declared as follows: "they both had the same people, [and] were the last [chosen] of the races. In history there was no queen like the one from Sheba. She had been African. They should climb the ladder of advancement together and, when they reached the top, spit on the whites."[86] These were radical words and strongly illustrate the movement towards pan-cultural nationalism.

Clearly the co-operative was viewed not only as an economic development venture but also as a nation-building strategy that would liberate Africans from economic dependence on whites. The leaders called for Africans to join, whether literate, non-literate, rich or poor, and to help develop the "nation."[87] Africans were anxious to control their own businesses, not only for the capital to be made but also, according to an AAWMU trustee, to "get out of slavery . . . [so that] the money that black people work for must go back to their black people. We want to establish businesses which will be controlled by black people."[88] Talk of reinvestment in the "nation" is a familiar refrain in economic co-operatives such as the AAWMU that combined African nationalism and economic pan-Africanism.[89]

At one meeting to explain the Union's mission, Ross emphasized that Blacks had a little bit of respect because of their businesses. Nonetheless, he said that the businesses were not on such firm ground that they could survive without black support, and such support would enrich the black race and restore its dignity. He ended with an analogy "that even in the Xhosa tradition, a pauper and coward are unrespectable."[90]

Similarly, Moses Foley, insisted that Africans could also be about "training one another in business management." He said that several businesses failed, not because of the proprietors lack of education but because they had limited knowledge about management. Foley continued that a formal Western education did not guarantee success in business. Rather, he gave an example of an uneducated African man who was more successful than the Western-educated because he knew how to use his brains and had a nose for business."[91]

Furthermore, Rwexu complained about Africans being called not by their given names but rather "John, Jack or Jim . . . even small white boys can be heard to call an elderly black man "boy." In America, African Americans too were exposed to a generalized humiliation to promote white supremacy, which included calling them "boy" and "girl" despite their ages and never addressing them by their given names nor as Mrs. or Mr., both during the period of slavery and after.[92] Rwexu continued, that: "Even after working for thirty years in a warehouse, a black person will be the one whose job it is to close shutters whilst there is white trash and small white boys who just came on recently and know absolutely nothing about the job. To the men who initiated this idea [of the trade union], the lingering question was "How long is this state of affairs going to remain so?"[93]

Therefore, the Union was established to address the problems of lack of occupations, discriminatory hiring practices, and inadequate social, economic, and political power. The directors hoped that the union would lead to a degree of political independence. In the words of George Ross of Port Elizabeth, "I'm not ashamed to say in no time [that] this Union will hear people saying—there is a black town, with a black mayor and black councillors."[94] Clearly, Ross envisioned the possibility for a political power base if the economic arm of the Union was successful. Also, he was probably thinking about such areas as Queenstown, where Africans had formed a Village Management Board which allowed for some independence in local matters.

Already in June 1891, an African named Theo Don had criticized the Port Elizabeth Town Council and called for native councillors to represent the interests of Africans because "these men . . . will be able to offer a remedy, since they will be in a position to know the requirements of the natives better than any [European] members of Council."[95] Although many of the African voters vehemently exercised their voting privileges in parliamentary elections by organizing and attending pre-election meetings to hear the platform of the white candidates and also to discuss their voting strategy and preferences, none had called for an African to sit on the local Council.[96] However, requests had been made by African leaders for the Council to recognize a Native Vigilance Committee appointed by Africans as the official representative of Africans in Port Elizabeth. Only the year before, in June 1890, the Municipality had agreed.[97] Don's complaint indicates that an African advisory committee was not enough. Thus, the idea of political representation was not novel, but the formation of the union as a vehicle to facilitate political power was new. The appeal to the audience at one of the meetings to support black people instead of "sending insurance money overseas and to Cape Town [and] trusting whites whom they don't even know" summed up these sentiments.[98]

The Union's Shop

Rwexu, who later became a Union trustee, and others hoped that Union shops would be established in many areas outside Port Elizabeth. Five thousand shares were advertised at one pound each, and meetings were held throughout the region to recruit shareholders. Ministers, businessmen, and ordinary people attended the meetings at Uitenhage, Grahamstown, Kimberley, Aliwal North, and Kingwilliamstown. Shareholders joined at most of these places as well as at Bechaunaland, Herschel, Cradock, East London, Middledrift, Peddie, Cala, Butterworth, Lesseyton, and Queenstown.[99] The Union secured the services of solicitors Innes and Elliot, and the funds were deposited at Standard Bank.

Meanwhile, by 1893, about 2,500 shares were still to be sold because "there had been disagreements on what they had set as requirements."[100] Nonetheless, enough of the 500 shares marketed had been bought to finance the opening of the first store at Port Elizabeth. The shop was built entirely by Africans on a site owned by the union. The difficulties the Union encountered in securing the store site illustrate the discrimination faced by the co-operative and African entrepreneurs in general in the Cape at that time. In one instance, for over a period of a month, they continually visited Oddfellow's Hall, a prospective site at Russell Road, hoping to rent it. Apparently the site owners thought that the Africans wanted to open a coffee shop, but "when the English people realized later what it was for, they were shocked to death and refused flatly. Even today, that house stands empty; they don't want to give it to black people."[101] The same thing happened when Africans tried to rent a house at

Russell Road site. One member of the co-operative commented, "I mean the English have made a solid blockade."[102] After unfruitful attempts to rent a building from white owners, the AAWMU officials purchased a sports field on which to erect the store.

When the Union opened the store, it was able to fulfill its goal to create jobs for the "nation," since its entire staff was African. The shop's stocks were purchased from overseas. These included clothes and equipment ordered by sports clubs and church ministers. Among those ordering supplies were Messrs. Dlepu, Masiza, and Kakaza, all of them Methodist ministers in Port Elizabeth. Also the Union bought and sold—presumably from African farmers—hides, wool, and food.[103]

From a financial standpoint, the Union was a moderate success. In fact, the half-yearly reports in 1893 and 1894 "showed an increase in the after expenses balance, which stood at £630 in December, 1894."[104] In 1908, the Union was still holding shareholders meetings, but details about its operations are unavailable. Also as late as 1930, property was listed in its name at Korsten, a freehold property black township in Port Elizabeth. Apparently the AAWMU opened no other stores.

Yet in January 1900, the Union must have been relatively prosperous, since it was still functioning and even able to assist in altruistic endeavors. Thus, when a call went out for assistance to war refugees during the South African War, between 1899 and 1902, the women of six branches of the African Women's church union worked hard to gather donations of food and clothing. And it was Mr. Foley, trustee of the AAWMU, who "devoted himself to the cause taking from his shop a huge amount of stock."[105]

Tensions

It appears from the available data that a disagreement between one of the AAWMU African American co-founders and the African leadership apparently, about membership and share requirements, led to a rift. Ozias Henderson, named as treasurer in the original advertisement announcing the formation of the Union, withdrew, and the position was taken over by P. Rwexu.[106] Apparently the officers' positions were only temporary until shares were sold and elections for permanent officers were held among the shareholders. Yet after Henderson withdrew, H. Phipps, the other African American named as the original manager, continued in that position at least until April 1892. By September of that year, all of the trustees and directors were Africans.

Perhaps another reason for Henderson's withdrawal was a preference by the African shareholders for the Union trustees to be people whom they recognized and trusted and who also had business experience. Understandably some were fearful of losing their investment and wanted to make sure that the trustees had business experience and that there was proper insurance to cover any losses. Once the prospective investors were assured that the Union's funds were properly insured and deposited in a bank, this worry was allayed. In any case, at one meeting the audience was informed that whomever was elected to the trustee positions would be people they would be able to trust.

The impression one gets from reading the reports of the AAWMU meetings is that the Africans knew Foley and Ross and also that they had business experience, while Henderson and Phipps were unknown and did not.[107] Consequently some Africans may have doubted the ability of the "Negro" ex-sailors to operate a business concern. Thus, at one meeting, a Mr. Mantsayi inquired about what type of work Mr. Phipps did, and when Ross answered that Phipps was a sailor, there was laughter from the audience of African men. However, the ex-sailors may have had funds to invest, which could have compensated for their lack of business experience. In a recent discussion on black seamen, Cobley notes that perhaps half the sailors in the United States merchant fleet were black and that their monthly wages in the 1880s averaged from £2,15 shillings to £3. He concludes that a sizeable amount could be saved from these wages and also from profit-sharing if the seaman worked on small ships. Thus by the time a sailor's seafaring days were over, he could have capital that he could invest ashore. Moreover, it was the black seamen who were more likely to be politically conscious, because the racial discrimination they faced on and off ship promoted a closely knit fraternity.[108]

Furthermore, lack of finances probably played a role in the withdrawal of the Americans. Ross and Foley were selected to travel to surrounding regions to recruit shareholders, which was a relatively expensive project. To send all of the officials would have been too costly. Also, the language might have been an important factor, since at the recruiting meetings amaXhosa was most often spoken.

It is noteworthy that the rift was not so wide as to cause a permanent split between the African Americans and the Africans. Several African Americans were at the store opening in March 1893. Only Ozias Henderson did not attend.[109]

Another criticism of the AAWMU was not so easily put to rest. This complaint came from Frank Makwena, one of the AAWMU shareholders who was highly disparaging of the officials' decision to hire George Ross full time, which had led Ross to resign from his clerk's position "even before the business started."[110] It seems that Makwena felt this move was premature until the store was opened and profits accumulated. Makwena was not alone in doubting that the AAWMU would be fiscally sound. There was support for Makwena's position and for further charges that two AAWMU trustees, Moses Foley and Nisini Mbambani, not only had poor morals but were also untrustworthy. This criticism led to sharp rebuttals from Foley and Mbambani, who demanded that proof be offered to substantiate the accusation or an apology.[111]

The foregoing illustrates that it took a while for Africans to have confidence in the venture. Nonetheless, as we have seen, support emanated from several regions. Yet the conflict between Makwena and the AAWMU led to a split and the establishment in 1896 of the Basotho Pioneer Trading Company, suggesting an ethnic split between the majority of the AAWMU, who were Xhosa speakers, and the Sotho.[112] As mentioned earlier, Makwena was Sotho speaking. He was declared the general secretary and the senior treasurer of the Sotho union. Nonetheless, the leaders stressed that the Union was open to all blacks, not just speakers of seSotho.

However, before concluding that the split was primarily ethnically based, it is worth recalling that Makwena had leased the Port Elizabeth Council's general store in 1893, and this competing business interest may have been related to his dissatisfaction with the AAWMU. In 1892, Makwena was a disgruntled AAWMU shareholder; a year later he was renting the Council store at Reservoir location. Then, in the latter part of 1896, he, along with several others, started the Basotho Union. This was the same year that the Council's store monopoly was declared illegal by the Cape government's parliamentary Select Committee appointed by the Cape government to review the Port Elizabeth Municipal Bill. Thus, it may be that Makwena, an ambitious businessman, was acting less for ethnic reasons than to boost his personal career and fortunes.

Another offshoot of the AAWMU was the African Trading Association, established in Kingwilliamstown by Paul Xiniwe. Xiniwe was a relatively wealthy African businessmen who originally had worked in Port Elizabeth until around 1888. He then moved to Kingwilliamstown and established several stores and eventually a double-storied "temperance" hotel in 1894. The African Trading Association's aims were to purchase land and establish businesses.[113] Similar to Makwena, one of the influences on Xiniwe's decision was personal ambition. But the support from other Africans also indicates that these men were fulfilling a need among the aspirant African middle class. Support for this trading association was cross-regional and included two of the leading African ministers and leaders in Port Elizabeth, B. Dlepu, also a supporter of the AAWMU, and W. Bottoman.[114]

Inspired by the AAWMU, Africans as far away as Natal also considered opening a working men's union. Natal's local African newspaper welcomed the possibility because "so far [the] Indians have enjoyed all the Africans' money" and "also the young men will have the opportunity for work, if this succeeds."[115]

Conclusion

Although the AAWMU union was unable to accomplish its many lofty goals, its formation was a landmark for this period and its success in Port Elizabeth was significant. In particular, several important features of the union are noteworthy. First, political consciousness that transcended ethnic and class background as well as nationalist tendencies, was evident in the operation and philosophy of the leadership. The mixture of pan-Africanism, African nationalism, and commercial capitalism, combined with the notion of incorporation into the wider economy, was a driving force for the establishment of the AAWMU. A parallel is found among African Americans who also demonstrated their belief that success in capitalist ventures was one avenue through which to uplift the "race."

The initial participation of the African Americans illustrates the early influence of pan-Africanism and similarities in African and African American political thought. Also illustrated is the willingness of the emerging black middle class to seek alliances outside of white liberal circles and a belief in their own initiative and independence. Their recognition of the linkage between economic independence and political rights and power would be a reoccurring theme voiced by the African leadership in the twentieth century.

Notes

1. These exact same sentiments were expressed at the Colored National Labor Convention organized by a ship-caulker, Isaac Myers, and held in Washington, D.C., in December 1869, see August Meier, *Negro Thought in America* (Ann Arbor: University of Michigan Press, 1966), p. 9.

2. The third is the cultural facet of authority, "the means of transforming force into right, and obedience into duty which . . . the powerful find necessary to ensure them continual mastership." p. 2, Patterson, *Slavery and Social Death*.

3. August Meier, "Booker T. Washington and the Town of Mound Bayou," eds., August Meier and Elliott Rudwick, *Along the Color Line: Explorations in the Black Experience* (Urbana: University of Illinois Press, 1976) pp. 217–223.

4. Colin Legum, *Pan-Africanism: A short political guide* (Westport, Connecticut: Greenwood Press, 1962), p. 99.

5. Many authors have attempted to define pan-Africanism. My definition is formulated from reading Ronald W. Walters, *Pan Africanism in the African Diaspora: An Analysis of Modern Afrocentric Political Movements* (Detroit: Wayne State University Press, 1993), see his Intro.; Legum, *Pan-Africanism*, p. 14; Esedebe, *Pan-Africanism: The Idea and Movement, 1776–1963* (Washington: Howard University Press, 1982), p. 3.

6. Michael O. West, "Pan-Africanism, Capitalism and Racial Uplift: The Rhetoric of African Business Formation in Colonial Zimbabwe," *African Affairs* 92

(April 1993): 263–283; Also of interest in this respect is the research of Keletso E. Atkins, *Questionable Haven: South Africa as an Immigration Site for Freed Slaves and their Descendants from North America,* book manuscript in progress.

7. See for example, Peter Walshe, *The Rise of African Nationalism in South Africa* (Berkeley and Los Angeles: University of California Press, 1971), Chap. 1.; J. M. Chirenje, *Ethiopianism and Afro-Americans in Southern Africa, 1883–1916* (Baton Rouge and London: Louisiana State University Press, 1987); Clements Keto, "Black Americans and South Africa 1890–1910," *Current Bibliography on African Affairs* 5 (July 1972): 382–406; Richard Ralston, "Africa, Africans, and Afro-Americans: Cultural and Political Interchange," *African Directions* (Spring, 1978): 48–58; R. Hunt Davis, Jr. "The Black American Education Component in African Responses to Colonialism in South Africa: 1890–1914," *Journal of Southern African Affairs,* 3 (January, 1978): 65–83; Veit Erlmann, "A Feeling of Prejudice, Orpheus M. McAdoo and the Virginia Jubilee Singers in South Africa, 1890–1898," *Journal of Southern African Studies,* 14 (April 1988): 331–349; David Coplan, *In Township Tonight* (New York: Longman, 1985); Andre Odendaal first discussed the AAWMU in his dissertation, "African Political Mobilization in the Eastern Cape, 1880–1910" (Ph.D. diss. University of Cambridge, 1983).

8. Joyce F. Kirk, "Race, Class, Liberalism, and Segregation: The 1883 Native Strangers' Location Bill in Port Elizabeth, South Africa," *International Journal of African Historical Studies,* 24 (1991): 293–321.

9. Included in this legislation were the franchise changes in 1887 and 1892 aimed at restricting African voters; the Glen Grey Act limiting land ownership and proscribing labor, and the 1883 Native Strangers' Location Act in which the Port Elizabeth Town Council attempted to remove Africans from the town center to a circumscribed area.

10. According to the census, there were 3,455 "Kafirs" (Africans); included in this African group were 2,359 Xhosa, 1,399 male and 960 female and also Thembu, Tswana, Zulu and Sotho. The officials counted the Mfengu (Fingo) separately and they numbered 990, 616 male and 374 female. Cape of Good Hope, Results of a Census of the Colony (G6-1892, hereafter 1892 Census.)

11. Andre Odendaal, *Black Protest Politics in South Africa to 1912* (New Jersey: Barnes and Noble, 1984), p. 9.

12. "Town Council," *EPH,* 8 November 1895. This information is primarily from Magistrate court cases brought against landlords, including Africans, for dilapidated dwellings in the *EPH,* especially in 1894 and 1895. For example, see "Magistrate's Court," 10 August 1894.

13. Maynard Swanson, "The Sanitation Syndrome: Bubonic Plague and Urban Native Policy in the Cape Colony, 1900–1909," *Journal of African History* 18 (1977): 387–410.

14. They were included in the 1891 census among the 5,273 "mixed and others." By 1904, the Chinese and Indian population was 779, and by 1910, 112 of the 166 grocers in Port Elizabeth were Asian, as were 23 of the 54 butchers. A. J. Christopher, "Race and Residence in Colonial Port Elizabeth," *South African Geographical Journal* 69 (1987): 8.

15. The Port Elizabeth Town Council was considering requiring vegetable hawkers, many of them Indian, to carry badges in 1893. "Town Council," *EPH*, 20 January and 3 February 1893. The business of "hawking" was an enterprise that was much criticized by the whites. Numerous reports indicate that by the 1900s, white criticism and resentment was at its height against blacks and Indian hawkers; Ruth Tomaselli, "Indian Flower Sellers of Johannesburg: A History of People on the Street," Belinda Bozzoli, compiler, *Town and Countryside in the Transvaal (Johannesburg: Ravan Press, 1983)*, pp. 215–239.

16. "Town Council," *EPH*, 15 May 1896.

17. Cape of Good Hope, Report of the Select Committee on the Port Elizabeth Native Strangers' Location Bill, A10-1883.

18. CAD, 3/PEZ 1/2/1/5, Location Committee Minutes, April 20, 1893.

19. "Town Council," *EPH*, 1 March 1895.

20. Cape Archives Depot (CAD), 3/PEZ 1/2/1/6, Location Committee Minutes, 21 May 1895 and "Town Council," *EPH*, 24 May 1895. Less successful were a Mr. Masiz, denied permission to construct a bakehouse in 1895, and a woman named Nonati who was refused permission to add a kitchen in 1896.

21. "Magistrate's Court," *EPH*, 30 August 1895.

22. J. Rex, "The Compound, Reserve and Urban Location-essential institutions of Southern African Labor Exploitation," *South African Labor Bulletin* 1 (1974): 4–17.

23. "Umanyano Lwabasebenzi," *Imvo*, 5 November 1891. Translated by M. Ntwasa.

24. Ibid.

25. Information in the next paragraph is from "Town Council," *EPH*, 3 July 1896.

26. St. Clair Drake and Horace R. Cayton, *Black Metropolis: A study of Negro life in a Northern City* (New York: Harcourt, Brace and World, Inc., 1962), p. 437.

27. "Town Council," *EPH*, July 1896.

28. CAD, 3/PEZ, 1/2/1/5, Location Committee Meeting, 20 April 1893.

29. "Town Council," *EPH*, 6 November 1891.

30. "Town Council," *EPH*, 30 June 1893.

31. "Town Council," *EPH*, 2 February 1894. In fact, the Superintendent of Native Locations reports indicate that Africans continuously defied the regulations. See "Town Council," 30 October 1890, 6 November 1891 and 30 June 1893, 10 August 1894.

32. Cape of Good Hope, Report of the Select Committee on the Port Elizabeth Municipal Act (A9-1897) p. 6. (hereafter 1897 Select Committee Report)

33. "Town Council," *EPH*, 24 May 1895.

34. "Town Council," *EPH*, 29 May 1895.

35. "Town Council," *EPH*, 24 May 1895.

36. 1897 Select Committee Report, p. 68.

37. Ibid.

38. To be eligible, one had to be a male, twenty-one years old, earning £50.00 per annum (or £25 with free room and board), or occupying any property worth £25.00. In an attempt to disfranchise African voters, the qualifications were

changed in 1892 to £75.00 property ownership or earning £50.00 per annum and able to fill out an application form in English or Dutch.

39. Swanson, "The Asiatic Menace: Creating Segregation in Durban, 1870–1900," *International Journal of African Historical Studies* 16 (1983): 405.

40. Isaac Wauchope was a shareholder and had lived in Port Elizabeth several years and was a major leader there until he left around 1888 to return to Lovedale Seminary to complete a degree. Afterwards he worked in Fort Beaufort as a minister. It is noteworthy that by the 1870s Africans had already begun self-help, and educational organizations. Foley, Makwena, Ross, Dlepu, and Rwexu will be discussed in the body of the paper.

41. Iain Edwards and Tim Nuttall, "Seizing the Moment: The January 1949 riots, proletarian populism and the structures of African urban life in Durban during the late 1940s," University of the Witwatersrand, History Workshop, "Structure and Experience in the Making of Apartheid," 1–10 February 1990. They discuss the co-operative movement in Natal and argue that a potentially militant organization and ideological thrust was on the rise. p. 12.

42. It is interesting that the phrase "Africa for the Africans" is associated in general with pan-African movements. Shepperson concludes that the phrase emanates from the 19th century, perhaps Martin R. Delaney or even before that to the Sierra Leone settlement, in West Africa, established by the British for Africans who had been enslaved but were rescued or "re-captured" by a British patrol set up to enforce the 1808 abolishment of the trans-Atlantic slave trade by Britain and the United States. These African recaptives were freed and resettled at Sierra Leone. The phrase "Africa for the Africans" is also closely associated with the Back to Africa forces, whether organizational or individual, such as the American Colonization Society, Peter Walshe, "Pan-Africanism: Some historical notes," 23 *Phylon* (1962): 350; See Chap. 1 of Walters, *Pan Africanism in the African Diaspora.*

43. Coplan, *In Township Tonight*, notes that black Americans were at the goldfields in the nineteenth century, p. 13; Alan Cobley, "Far From Home: The Origins and Significance of the Afro-Caribbean Community in South Africa to 1930," *Journal of Southern African Studies* 18 (June 1992): 353; According to Tony Martin, *The Pan-African Connection: From Slavery to Garvey and Beyond* (Dover, Massachusetts: The Majority Press, 1983), pp. 141–42, Alexander's wife was the product of a Cuban father and Javanese mother. In the 1920s, their son, David William Alexander, was a minister and supporter of the Universal Negro Improvement Association (UNIA); Alexander later became Archbishop of the African Orthodox Church, see Richard Newman, "Archbishop Daniel William Alexander and the African Orthodox Church," *International Journal of African Historical Studies* 16 (1983): 615–630.

44. Harry Dean, *The Pedro Gorino: The Adventures of a Negro Sea Captain in Africa and on the Seven Seas in his Attempt to found an Ethiopian Empire* (New York: Houghton and Mifflin, 1929).

45. Erlmann, "A Feeling of Prejudice," p. 343; Chirenje, *Ethiopianism and Afro-Americans*," states that the troupe arrived in South Africa in May 1890, p. 35.

46. "Isikumbuzo Somanyano," *Imvo*, 29 March 1893, translated by T. Mda and C. B. Bosiki. At the opening of the co-operative store Mr. Rwexu stated that it was noteworthy that the first African Choir or South African Choir was started in Port Elizabeth.

47. "The Jubilee Singers," *Imvo*, 21 August 1890, translated by P. Huna.

48. Ibid.

49. "*Leselinyana*," 15 January, 1891, cited in V. Erlmann, "A Feeling of Prejudice," p. 345.

50. Ibid.

51. Erlmann, "A Feeling of Prejudice," p. 344.

52. "Education Through Books," *Imvo*, 29 August 1889.

53. Chirenje, *Ethiopianism and Afro-Americans*, p. 4.

54. Chirenje, *Ethiopianism and Afro-Americans*, p. 52; For information on black South Africans attending black American schools see Walter L. Williams, *Black Americans and the Evangelization of Africa, 1877–1900* (Madison: University of Wisconsin Press, 1982), esp. Chap. 8 and Appendix G.

55. Chirenje, *Ethiopianism and Afro-Americans*, pp. 52, 59–69 for Turner. For evidence of earlier secessions from white congregations in South Africa see, Chris Saunders, "Tile and the Thembu Church," *Journal of African History* 11 (1970): 553–570; Nehemiah Tile seceded from the Wesleyan Methodists in 1883, both a political and religious act. Tile was advisor to the Thembu paramount chief, and this involvement was unacceptable to the Wesleyan church ministers and the colonial administration, see Sylvia Jacobs, *Black Americans and the Missionaries in Africa* (New York and Westport, Connecticut: Greenwood Press, 1982), p. 178.

56. *Imvo*, 30 December 1886; The author of *The History of the Negro Race in America from 1619–1880* (New York: G. P. Putnam's Sons, 1882), was George Washington Williams.

57. "Editorial," *Imvo*, 14 October, 1890.

58. This is hardly surprising, since Washington was so influenced at Hampton Institute by Professor Armstrong, a Scotsman raised on the self-help ideals of the Scottish church. "People's Advocate," 30 August 1879 and 29 September 1883, cited in Meier, *Negro Thought in America*, p. 100; Also see pp. 100–118 on Washington's philosophy. For white American opinion of Washington's message, see Louis R. Harlan, *Booker T. Washington: The Making of a Black Leader, 1856–1901* (New York: Oxford University Press, 1972), pp. 222–224; For white South African opinion see correspondence in Phyllis Lewsen, ed., *Selections from the Correspondence of John X. Merriman*, vol. 3, 1899–1905 (Cape Town: Van Riebeeck Society, 1966), p. 359 indicating that John X Merriman, a Cape liberal and political leader, greatly admired Washington; Later in the early twentieth century, John Dube— sometimes referred to as the Booker T. Washington of South Africa, established Ohlange in Natal in 1901, based on the Tuskegee model. See R. Hunt Davis, Jr., "John L. Dube: A South African Exponent of Booker T. Washington," *Journal of African Studies* 2 (1975–1976): 497–529.

59. In 1850, Reverend T. Helm a missionary at Zuurbrak expressed pride because African men were opening stores; see Joseph John Freeman, *A Tour in South Africa* (London, 1851), cited in Stanley Trapido, "Friends of the Natives: Mer-

chants, Peasants, and The Political and Ideological Structure of Liberalism in the Cape, 1854–1910," *Economy and Society in Pre-Industrial South Africa*, eds. Shula Marks and Anthony Atmore (London: Longman, 1980), p. 250.

60. Colin Bundy, *The Rise and Fall of the South African Peasantry* (Berkeley: University of California Press, 1979), p. 40; Norman Etherington, "Mission Station Melting Pots as a Factor in the Rise of South African Black Nationalism," *International Journal of African Historical Studies* 9 (1976): 601–602.

61. Etherington, "Mission station melting pot," pp. 601–602.

62. Brian M. Du Toit, "Co-operative Institutions and Culture Change in South Africa," *Journal of Asian and African Studies* 4 (October 1969): 278.

63. I. Schapera, "The Old Bantu Culture," *Western Civilization and the Natives of South Africa: Studies in Culture Contact*, edited by I. Schapera (London: Routledge and Kegan Paul, Ltd., 1967), pp. 3–36.

64. G. H. Pirie, "Racial Segregation on Johannesburg trams: Procedures and Protest, 1904–1927," *African Studies* 48 (1989): 37.

65. August Meier and Elliott Rudwick, "The Boycott Movement against Jim Crow Streetcars in the South, 1900–1906," Meier and Rudwick, *Along the Color Line*, p. 270.

66. The following description, unless otherwise noted, is from "Railway Incident," *Imvo*, April 1885.

67. Neville Hogan makes this point in discussing the ambiguity of the liberal alliance and Africans in "The posthumous vindication of Zachariah Gqishela: Reflections on the politics of dependence at the Cape in the nineteenth century," in Marks and Rathbone, *Economy and Society*, pp. 275–292.

68. Keto, "Black Americans and South Africa," p. 387.

69. Ibid., p. 388.

70. Erlmann, "A Feeling of Prejudice," p. 331.

71. "Stray Notes of a Natal Trip," *Imvo*, 21 May 1891.

72. "East London Negrophobia," *Imvo*, 28 February 1894.

73. "Qonce (KWT) and the Port Elizabeth Union," *Imvo*, 10 March 1892; Esedebe, *Pan-Africanism*, pp. 48–49 indicates that the name Phipps may be of Trinidadian origin. For example, an R. E. Phipps, a Trinidadian barrister is listed as the secretary for the West Indies, the Pan-African Conference Committee established around 1900 to organize the second pan-African congregation in London, England. F. J. Peregrino, was the secretary for South Africa, but he apparently did not attend the conference. However, H. Sylvester Williams was there; he later migrated to Cape Town, South Africa, as did Peregrino.

74. "Umanyano Lwabasebenzi," *Imvo*, 5 November 1891, translated by M. Ntwasa.

75. Meier, *Negro Thought in America*, p. 42.

76. Ibid., p. 53.

77. Ibid., p. 48.

78. "Umanyano Lwabasebenzi," *Imvo*, 5 November 1891, translated by M. Ntwasa. The commemoration ceremony originated with African women who planned to make it an annual event to celebrate the union being established. The celebration included dinner, speeches from the men, both African and African

American songs, and profuse thanks to the female organizers, "Isikumbuzo Somanyano," *Imvo,* 29 March 1893.

79. Meier, *Negro Thought in America,* p. 50.

80. "Ikaya Laba Hambi," *Imvo,* 10 September 1896, situated at Russell Road near Strangers' location. Translated by T. Mda.

81. CAD, NA598 B1525, J. A. Verschuur, ARM New Brighton to RM, NB, 17 November 1905, Attached list of occupants at Reservoir Location in May 1904. Eight black Americans rented housing including 2 adult males, three adult females and 2 female children in one dwelling while another adult male live with several other people.

82. "Mr. Jones at South End," *EPH,* 26 July 1898.

83. "Umanyano Lwabasebenzi," *Imvo,* 5 November 1891, translated by M. Ntwasa.

84. "Isikumbuzo Somanyano," *Imvo,* 29 March 1893, translated by T. Mda and C. B. Bosiki.

85. For Garvey movement, see Robert Hill and G. Pirio, "Africa for the Africans: The Garvey movement in South Africa, 1920–40," in *The Politics of Race, Class and Nationalism in Twentieth Century South Africa,* eds., Shula Marks and Stanley Trapido (New York: London, 1987), pp. 209–253; Esedebe, *Pan-Africanism,* pp. 25–41 on Blyden. Delaney favored emigration to Nigeria while Blyden favored Central America; see Meier and Rudwick, *Along the Color Line,* p. 196.

86. "Isikumbuzo Somanyano," *Imvo,* 29 March 1893.

87. "Abathunya babarwebi e Kimberley," *Imvo,* 25 February 1892, translated by C. B. Bosiki; "Umanyano Lwabasebenzi," *Imvo,* 5 November 1891, translated by M. Ntwasa.

88. "Umanyano Lwabasebenzi," *Imvo,* 5 November 1891, translated by M. Ntwasa.

89. West, "Pan-Africanism, Capitalism and Racial Uplift,"; Hill, "Africa for the Africans," Edwards and Nuttall, "Seizing the Moment,"; August Meier "The Development of Negro Business and the Rise of a Negro Middle Class," in Meier, *Negro Thought in America,* pp. 139–157.

90. "Umanyano Lwabasebenzi," *Imvo,* 5 November 1891, translated by M. Ntwasa.

91. Ibid.

92. Kenneth Stampp, "The Daily Life of the Southern Slave," *Key Issues in the Afro-American Experience,* edited by N. Huggins, M. Kilson and D. Fox (New York: Harcourt Brace Jovanovich, Inc., 1971), vol. 1. p. 119.

93. "Umanyano Lwabasebenzi," *Imvo,* 5 November 1891, translated by M. Ntwasa.

94. Ibid.

95. "Letter to Editor," *EPH,* 9 June 1891.

96. For accounts of election meetings organized by Port Elizabeth Africans, see "Iliso Lomzi Ebhayi," *Imvo,* 26 February 1891 and 12 March 1891.

97. "Native Opinion," *EPH,* 19 June 1890.

98. "Umanyano Lwabasebenzi," *Imvo,* 5 November 1891, translated by M. Ntwasa.

99. See the following dates in *Imvo*, "Umanyano Lwabasebenzi," 5 November 1891, translated by M. Ntwasa; "Abathunya babarwebi EKimberley," translated by C. B. Bosiki; 25 February 1891; "Qonce and the Port Elizabeth Union," 10 March 1892, translated by T. Mda; "The African and American Working Men's Union," 21 April 1892; "I Qonce no manyano lwase Bhai," 10 February, 1892, and "I Qonce no manyano lwase Bhai," 10 March 1892.

100. Ibid.

101. "Umanyano Lwabaebenzi," *Imvo*, 5 November 1891, translated by M. Ntwasa.

102. "Indaba E Bhayi in Port Elizabeth," *Imvo*, 27 October 1892, translated by M. Ntwasa.

103. "The African and American Working Men's Union," *Imvo*, 28 May 1891, translated by T. Mda.

104. Statement of the AAWMU, quoted in R. L. Kawa letter to the editor, *Imvo*, 19 December 1894, translated by T. Mda.

105. "Port Elizabeth," *Imvo*, 15 January 1900, translated by T. Mda.

106. "Qonce and the Port Elizabeth Union," *Imvo*, 10 March 1892. For announcement of officers see"Roxisa, Roxisa," *Imvo*, 1 December 1892.

107. "Qonce and the Port Elizabeth Union," *Imvo*, 10 March 1892, translated by T. Mda.

108. Cobley, "Far From Home: The Afro-Caribbean Community," p. 352.

109. "The Worker's Union, African and American Working Men's Union," *Imvo*, 16 February 1893; for commemoration see "Isikumbuzo Somanyano," *Imvo*, 29 March 1893, translated by T. Mda and C. B. Bosiki.

110. "A Reply to Mr. Wauchope," Letter to Editor, signed by shareholder *Imvo*, 14 July 1892; translated by Z. K. Kwinana.

111. "Umanyano Lwabarhweri," Letter to Editor, from Issac Wauchope, *Imvo*, 23 June 1892; translated by M. Ntwasa, "Umanyano Lwasebhayi," Letter to Editor signed Bobelityeni (probably a pseudonym), *Imvo*, 19 May, 1892, translated by T. Mda; Makwena's letter referred to in *Imvo*, on October 27, 1892 for charges against Foley and Mbambani. For refutation see "Letter to the Editor," from M. D. Foley and N. Mbambani *Imvo*, 1 December 1892, translated by Z. K. Kwinana.

112. "Basuto Pioneer Trading Co.," *Imvo*, 30 July and 10 September 1896.

113. "Intlanganiso Ngamashishini," *Imvo*, 16 January 1896 and "Umanyano Ngamashishini," 16 April 1896; "Umanyano Ugenihlaba," *Imvo*, 28 May 1896; The *Imvo*, noted that Xiniwe purchased the building from G. B. Christian and Co., for about £2,000, 14 March 1894.

114. Ibid.

115. "Umanyano Lomsebenzi," *Imvo*, 22 August 1894.

5

Public Health, African Women, and the 1901 Black General Workers' Strike

Introduction

Between the years 1901 and 1906, African women in Port Elizabeth on at least two occasions played a pivotal role in resisting colonial government laws that were clearly racially based and aimed at undermining the rights of Africans in the urban areas. The first occasion was the 1901 three day general workers' strike. The second occasion was the attempt in 1905 to remove Africans from Korsten, an area where Africans held rights to land independent from the local and central government. In this chapter we explore the background to the role of African women in the 1901 strike and in the following the struggle against the removal from Korsten, both a response to racially discriminatory laws to impose segregation. The information in the next two chapters drawn primarily from the local newspapers during that period, written in both English and Xhosa, includes for the first time an analysis of African women and their role in the resistance to segregationist legislation.

On June 10, 1901, the majority of the Africans working in Port Elizabeth went on a three-day general strike to protest against the implementation of a proclamation ordering that no travel passes be issued to "natives" and colored persons living in town unless they had been inoculated for bubonic plague. The strike included male workers at the port, railway, military, and business stores and, significantly, female domestic workers. This was the biggest general strike by Africans before the now infamous dockworkers strike in 1918 at Cape Town led by Clements Kadalie of the Industrial and Commercial Workers' Union (ICU). The 1901 strike is the earliest information available for South Africa that shows the participation of black female workers. Moreover, these women were domestic workers who as has often been stated, are the most isolated and difficult to organize and, thus, the least likely to be involved in labor protest. While this may be true for a later period, generalizations such as these must be supported with historically specific data.

An analysis of the strike illustrates that at an early stage, Africans transcended their class and gender differences in protest against racial discrimination. Africans from both the middle class and the working class—motivated by social, economic, and political factors—formed cross-class alliances. They used their labor power to engage in popular protest in urban areas; thus we see the beginnings of racial and class consciousness among both middle and working class blacks. The strike is also concrete evidence of what could happen as segregationist legislation accelerated and the liberal alliance between blacks and whites continued to decline. Its decline and the consequent decreasing dependence by the emergent black middle class as well as the growing dissatisfaction of blacks in general with racial discrimination opened up the possibilities for a racially based alliance between members of the black middle class and the black working class.

The general strike by Africans was the culmination of a long string of complaints by both white and black interest groups at Port Elizabeth against the implementation of preventive plague measures by the Cape government. Scholars have pointed out how colonial governments have used Public Health laws to impose segregation on colonial populations in Africa and elsewhere often based on the notion that the whites must be protected from the "dirty, unhealthy nonwhites." In other words, popular ideas grounded in beliefs about racial inferiority and superiority, resulted in the whites blaming the natives for the outbreak of the disease. Thus, the description of the reaction of the colonial government to the threat of the bubonic plague in Cape Town and Port Elizabeth may have a ring of familiarity. Yet, each case has its own historical specificity and with this in mind let us now explore the events in the Cape colony.

During the years of the South African War, 1899–1902, the Cape colonial government was increasingly drawn into "native" affairs at Cape Town and Port Elizabeth as a result of the outbreak of bubonic plague. The plague broke out in 1901, first at Cape Town where the colonial government applied the Public Health Act to force Africans to move into Uitvlught, a segregated location built especially for Africans. This was indeed a significant event. The wholesale forced removal of the African population from the town settlement resulted in the first formal segregated black "township" in the Cape Town area and set the tone for the legal segregation of blacks for the next ninety years.

The different political socioeconomic conditions of the African population at Port Elizabeth precluded the immediate establishment of an African location. Instead of a black "township," the Cape government offered to help to establish a Plague Board Committee, which it would finance and administer, to oversee the operation of plague preventive efforts at Port Elizabeth.

But once established, the Plague Board's recommendations to the Port Elizabeth Town Council to enforce the Public Health Act in order to wipe out the disease, drew the opprobrium of both white and black interest groups. Consequently, the Board's efforts were effectively undermined by (1) African resistance in the form of strikes, boycotts, and migration to living spaces outside the government's jurisdiction; (2) local and central government administrative, jurisdictional, and individual rivalries; (3) local government corruption, and (4) general apathy among the whites.

The opposition tactics at Port Elizabeth against the central government's segregationist initiatives foreshadowed similar methods used by Africans in the twentieth century. Africans used rallies, boycotts, and strikes in nonviolent protest against the implementation of racially discriminatory laws at the local, regional and national level. Also, the local government failed to enforce segregationist legislation, and white apathy including among employers continued to pose obstacles to the implementation of a nationwide "native" policy of segregation and apartheid.

The Public Health Act,
Bubonic Plague, and Formal Segregation

The actions leading up to the South African war have been well documented.[1] Ostensibly the British Colonial Secretary, Alfred Milner, and President Paul Kruger of the South African Republic attempted to negotiate an agreement that would allow political inclusion of the *uitlanders* (foreigners). However, since British imperialism was the driving force, the outcome was predictable; after much negotiation, a stalemate was reached and in October 1899, the South African Republic declared war on Great Britain.

Although the actual fighting never reached Port Elizabeth, the presence of a British military unit did affect how and when residential segregation unfolded.[2] It will be recalled that the 1896 housing agreement between the Town Council and African landholders (discussed in Chapter 3) was to be implemented once water was made available for the land site set aside for the new segregated African location. However, during the war, a part of the land was used as a military camp, thus preventing the implementation of the agreement. Another factor that profoundly affected the establishment of residential segregation was the involvement of the Cape central government in the housing issue.

Housing the African population in urban areas was generally the responsibility of the local government. Even though the central government usually supported local attempts to residentially segregate Africans, for example by advising on draft municipal legislation, once Parliament passed the legislation, it was up to the local government to implement it. However, in 1901, the Cape central government was drawn almost inadvertently into the local struggle over land and housing at Cape Town and also at Port Elizabeth. That is, it was through default rather than a well-thought-out policy to establish residential segregation that the central government became entangled in local land and housing politics. This is not to say that an ideology of segregating blacks from whites was new in Cape Town. It was not. Complaints about "the unsanitary, half-civilized" Africans were voiced in 1899 by the Cape Town medical officer of health and others and along with them suggestions that Africans be confined in a location, although nothing concrete was done. But the plague threat represented an opportunity for the Cape government to take advantage of the existing racial prejudice and previous urgings in Cape Town to isolate the Africans from the rest of the population. But in attempting to separate the blacks from the whites for health reasons, the central government was drawn into providing housing and administering locations for Africans.

Near the end of January, 1901, the bubonic plague broke out in Cape Town. Its first victim was a European clerk employed at the docks where military stocks brought from India and Argentina were piled. Despite the fact that the first plague victim was European, the white colonial authorities, influenced by racial stereotypes and prejudiced beliefs that chronicled the inferiority of Africans concentrated on the potential threat they believed emanated from the "diseased Africans."[3]

Under municipal law, Cape Town had no authority to force Africans to move from their homes nor to set up a segregated location, and since Parliament was suspended during most of the South African War, new legislation could not be passed to provide for the administration of urban African locations. To circumvent this obstacle, the government used the Public Health Amendment Act of 1897, under the regulation to "check the spread of infectious disease," to establish a segregated housing site and to force Africans from Cape Town to move into it. Any blacks refusing to move there could be fined or imprisoned. Despite this threat, Africans did not voluntarily enter the quickly constructed *Uitvlugt* (later renamed *Ndabeni*) location outside of Cape Town but were forced under armed guard.[4]

In contrast to Cape Town, the attempt to force Africans at Port Elizabeth to move into a segregated settlement was far less successful. One of the most important deterrents was the conflict between the central and local government over who was to be responsible for administering and financing the efforts to eradicate the plague. To understand how this conflict developed, we must examine the sequence of events that occurred in Port Elizabeth immediately following the news that the plague had hit Cape Town.

With the outbreak of the disease at Cape Town, communication quickly commenced in February 1901 between the Colonial Secretary, Thomas Lynedoch Graham and Mayor John Chambers Kemsley of Port Elizabeth regarding the necessary plague precautions. The Municipal officials requested that the central government take complete control of the preventive measures. Second, they requested that the 1897 Health Act be promulgated as it had been at Cape Town, which would provide for setting up a segregated location for Africans. The Colonial Secretary's office of the central government refused and notified the Mayor that while the government would finance precautionary measures, it could not supply personnel to direct the campaign against the plague nor set up an African location. Instead, it was suggested that the Municipality appoint a plague committee, retain doctors and nurses, and prepare the Lazaretto (building to quarantine those with a contagious disease). The Municipal Council could do little but follow these suggestions by initiating a cleaning campaign throughout the town.[5]

The First Plague Case at Port Elizabeth

This was the state of affairs when the first plague case was found on April 16, 1901, at Gubbs' private location. Only recently Dr. Simpson, while visiting Port Elizabeth, had sharply criticized Gubbs' as wholly unsanitary and recommended that it be demolished. But, in fact, the victim, an African male, worked for the Harbor Board at the stacks on the beach; this is where he had contracted the disease and subsequently taken it to his home at Gubbs'.[6] Consequently, it was not Gubbs' but the Harbor Board that was the source of the infection, much like the dock was the source of the plague at Cape Town.

The initial response of the Municipal officials indicates their lack of preparedness, despite the cleansing campaign, as well as their unwillingness to coordinate the operations against the plague. The officials sent a telegraph to the Colonial Secretary's office requesting that it "would undertake the housing of the natives in one location, and approve the adoption of similar measures in dealing with the natives as obtains in Capetown."[7]

The Municipality was eager for the central government to take over the administration of the plague and to establish an African location. While the obvious motive was to effectively eradicate the plague, there were others. Among these was the desire to avoid the high financial costs that both efficient plague administration and the establishment of a segregated location for Africans would require. In addition, and significantly, if the central government agreed to build an African location, it would relieve the Town Council of its obligation to fulfill the 1896 housing and freehold land agreement with the approximately 300 African families concerned.

Clearly, in the minds of many whites, the outbreak of the plague provided an opportunity for settling all of their complaints against the Africans. This propensity can be discerned from the words of the Mayor, who stated at the special Town Council meeting called in response to the news of the first case of plague that "the opportunity now presented itself of placing the native question in Port Elizabeth on a proper basis. They must stop natives *travelling by tram, walking on the footpaths and living all over the town.* The present was the occasion for thoroughly dealing with the native question in all its aspects."[8]

The Mayor's statement did not specifically mention checking the spread of the bubonic plague but rather focused on Africans using public facilities such as the tram, walking on the sidewalks, and living all over the town; his response implied an intent to control the movements of Africans and to ensure white supremacy in the public/social realm. Dealing with the "native question" from the standpoint of white supremacy required demanding subordination from the subjected population in all arenas, however mundane. That is, using the public transport system and walking on the sidewalk—ordinary, everyday activities—were viewed through a racial lens and linked with choosing one's residence. Thus, the public and the private domain were linked and the right of Africans to use both was to be controlled. Moreover, merchant and commercial capitalist interests could finally obtain the highly valued land they coveted on which Strangers' and Cooper's Kloof location were situated in the center of town. Thus, previous areas of struggle such as public transport, use of the sidewalk, and residential segregation of black and white, were further strained with the threat of bubonic plague.

The Cape central government agreed almost immediately, after the first plague case was reported from Port Elizabeth, to take over the plague administration. Thus, a plague board was established to oversee the effort necessary to prevent an epidemic. However, virtually from the beginning there were strong disagreements, expressed in verbal gymnastics, acidic language, and animosity between the local government and members of the Plague Board who represented the central government. The primary reason was divided authority, which prevented the Plague Board from enforcing local sanitary regulations without the cooperation of the Town Council. Meanwhile, the Council often failed to apply the plague regulations because of vested interests.

The problem was that since the Plague Board was appointed by the Colonial Secretary's office, its authority emanated from the Cape central government rather than the Port Elizabeth local government. This meant that the plague board did not have complete authority to proceed in carrying out a cleansing program, because the local government retained control of implementing the sanitary procedures. So, unless the local and central government committees co-operated and enforced the plague regulations the campaign was unsuccessful. This divided authority led to a tug-of-war between some members of the Town Council and the Plague Board over administering and enforcing the plague regulations. At issue in particular was who would pay for specific procedures and whether or not the local officials were willing or unwilling to speedily or laconically implement Plague Board recommendations.

Plague Administration

The Plague Board was established on April 22, 1901, under the Public Health Act to advise on how to handle the plague. The nine white male Board members included the Mayor, who was appointed by the Colonial Secretary, two town councillors elected by their peers, and six other members, all nominated by the central government.[9] At the first meeting the Chairman, Mr. J. T. Wylde, the Resident Magistrate, read a letter from the Colonial Secretary's office enumerating the Board's powers. It was empowered to be the Executive Body "in all matters concerning the measures to be adopted for checking the progress of and for suppressing the disease," and it was directly responsible to the Cape central government and was instructed that "it will not interfere with the ordinary sanitary work of the town which [will] be carried on by the Council. . . ."[10] Thus, the Board was charged with making recommendations to eradicate the plague, which would then be administered by the local officials.

The Board set to work immediately establishing an operating framework.[11] Heading the list to prevent further cases of the plague was cleansing the city and relieving overcrowding. The measures necessary to clean the town required the cooperation of several separate local bodies, each with its own jurisdiction. Whereas Port Elizabeth was administered by the Town Council, nearby Walmer Township had its own Town Council, and the Harbor Board administered the docks and the Divisional Council the district.[12] Relative to local matters, the Plague Board was primarily an advisory board. Thus, it could only request co-operation and recommend procedures to these local agencies to prevent the spread of the plague, which became a key factor in the conflict that followed.

After some disagreements about how best to cleanse the city the Councillors and the Plague Board eventually, came to the view that paramount in correcting the ills of unsanitation and also in preventing the spread of the plague was the question of overcrowded dwellings. As the war brought military personnel, war refugees, and laborers the population swelled. Lack of housing, always a problem, and overcrowded unsanitary dwellings reached unparalled proportions. Housing was so scarce that dilapidated buildings that had been declared unfit for human habitation and closed by the Council were reoccupied. Two reports from the top plague officials in the Colony on overcrowding in the town give an indication of the severity of the problem. According to Dr. J. G. Blackmore, the chief Plague Medical Officer, brought in from Cape Town, Port Elizabeth was: "disgracefully overcrowded, and large numbers of buildings now used as dwelling places are absolutely unfit for human habitation, either through structural or sanitary defects . . . and if the people inhabiting them were turned out, and the overcrowding in the remaining houses were done away with . . . some thousands of people in Port Elizabeth would be rendered homeless."[13]

Blackmore listed four reasons for the unsanitary conditions: (1) overcrowding, (2) absence of proper drainage, (3) defective methods of scavenging, and (4) neglect in the past to observe building regulations. Among the ways to correct these sanitary defects, he said, was to establish a location under government supervision for the "natives" outside of the town. By doing so, maintained Blackmore, most of the overcrowding would cease and building regulations could then be enforced. Although he recommended rat destruction and human inoculation, Blackmore warned that until the "natives" were removed, the town would remain unsanitary.

Dr. Simpson, newly arrived from Cape Town submitted the second report a few days later. Simpson agreed with Dr. Blackmores' conclusions and emphasized that the way to solve the problem of overcrowding was to set up "native" locations. Simpson was referring to Africans, but he did not stop with this suggestion, concluding that a location should also be set up for Asiatics (sic). However, he emphasized that "the conditions were not the same as at Capetown . . . [and] they have not needed to evacuate premises wholesale owing to plague."[14]

Simpson's remarks regarding the number of plague cases indicates one of the reasons why the central government continued to refuse to establish an African location at Port Elizabeth. Overall the number of plague cases at Port Elizabeth had been far less than at Cape Town. Thus, up to August, 1901, when Blackmore and Simpson issued their reports, 34 plague cases, 14 fatal, had been diagnosed at Port Elizabeth in a four-month period compared to 81 cases at Cape Town in one week.[15] Yet another reason for the central government's refusal was African protest in Cape Town.[16]

The government's refusal was a complete reversal, for when the first case of plague was diagnosed at Port Elizabeth, Colonial Secretary Graham, during a visit there in April had boiterously insinuated that the central government could set up a location for Africans almost overnight just as they had at Cape Town.[17] A few months later, as African resistance heightened at Cape Town, and the astronomical financial costs to establish Uitvlught became clear (it cost the government about £100,000), the government's attitude changed. As a result, although not denying his earlier statement, the Colonial Secretary insisted that he had also pointed out to the Port Elizabeth Town Council the necessity of a Parlimentary Act to appropriate the necessary expenditures to establish an African location. Therefore, nothing could be done until Parliament passed an Act, and Parliament was not meeting during the war years.

While the debate continued between the central and local government over the establishment of an African location at Port Elizabeth, the Plague Board sought ways to reduce overcrowded and unsanitary dwellings. But opposition ensued when the Board proposed that the Council conduct midnight raids to ferret out and evict the people living in the overcrowded dwellings. The Council refused, claiming that no authority existed under the Municipal regulations for them to evict tenants unless alternative housing was provided.[18] Undoubtedly the Council realized that evictions would only compound the problem, since if no alternative housing existed, the evicted simply crowded in elsewhere. Some officials also feared that if Africans were moved out of the overcrowded dwellings, "poor whites" might take their place.[19]

As the argument heated up between the Town Council and the Plague Board, the question of whose responsibility it was to provide alternative housing became a major issue. Their responsibility, the Plague Board argued, was not to provide alternative housing but instead to prevent further plague cases by disinfecting the unsanitary premises and inoculating and removing the patients. In contrast, the Board claimed that under the municipal regulations, it was the Council's responsibility to provide alternative housing while dwellings were being disinfected and also to demolish dwellings that the Board had declared unfit for human habitation.[20]

Another factor, although often hinted at but seldom openly discussed and yet of major consequence in influencing the Council's unwillingness to demolish overcrowded dwellings, was local government corruption. It seems that the Council was trying to protect the vested interests of the Town Councillors who were slum landlords. To evict tenants and close these unsanitary dwelling would reduce their revenue. This was an important factor and one that deserves considerable attention, because it significantly undermined the efforts to eradicate the plague.

Local Government Corruption and Slum Landlords

It has been written that one man's slum is another man's castle. Yet in the period between 1880–1910, whether in South Africa, England, Germany, or the United States, the term "slum" usually denoted a crowded or densely populated area with dirty, dilapidated dwellings where the poor lived.[21] In Port Elizabeth various classes and races of people lived in slums because of poverty, racial discrimination, lack of housing, the need to be near work, and the need to save money. As of 1900, no special housing had been built for white workers, and the working class in general attempted to live near their workplace. Consequently, although informal ethnic and racial separation existed, racial segregation was not the norm and many residents lived intermixed in areas without regard for ethnic and racial differences.[22]

Methods of eliminating slum housing in Port Elizabeth almost invariably included the use of public health regulations and prosecuting slum landlords. Both these methods were tried in Port Elizabeth to aid sanitation, to relieve overcrowding, and to rid the town of the plague. But these solutions worked hand in glove and had to be enforced by the Town Council. Yet as we have seen, it was common for Town Councillors in Port Elizabeth, who were owners of considerable amounts of slum property, to use their influential position to circumvent municipal health and building regulations.[23] Although prosecutions of slum landlords did occur, the tendency was to focus on the small, defenseless landlords and to ignore the wealthier and fortified landlords on the Council. But the Plague Board brought in new players from the outside who had no vested interest in promoting circumvention of the health regulations. Thus, when the Council refused to comply when the Plague Board advised that property declared unfit for human habitation must be demolished, a major conflict resulted. Of course, other private business interests would also be less than thrilled with the enforcement of health regulations requiring them to pay to improve sanitary conditions. But ultimately the question became: Would the local government and private interests be stronger than the central government officials and their supporters whose job it was to prevent the spread of plague, which included enforcing eliminating slum housing? Or put simply, would the Town Councillors censore themselves?

Some of the affluent slum landlords often owned several properties or "private" locations (African settlements situated on privately owned land rather than government land), either individually or as part of a syndicate or organization. For example, as we have seen, a three-man syndicate owned Gubbs' location. Many "private" locations smaller than Gubbs' existed whereby an individual property owner allowed Africans to build their own dwellings and then charged them site rent. In some cases the housing was provided, and as many people as possible were crammed inside. By law these dwellings were suppose to meet safe building and health codes or be demolished or closed while being repaired. However, the Town Council often failed to enforce these regulations.

In 1901 when the Plague Board recommended enforcement of sanitary regulations, several Town Councillors were owners of slum property. For example, Councillors A. C. Reed, L. McKay, J. H. Gates, James Newton, and T. O'Brien were all connected with slum property, either as landlords or agents.[24] A. C. Reed, in particular, a Town Councillor from 1901–1903, was a thorn in the side of the Plague Board. Reed and his brothers, W. J. and G. T., owned property in several areas registered under the name of the Reed Brothers Combination. They were pursuing the family business, as their father, James Samuel Reed, who owned many slum houses, some of them used as brothels. On numerous occasions the Reeds were cited for violating Municipal Health Regulations by operating unsanitary dwellings unfit for human habitation.[25] These offenses drew fines but the buildings were seldom demolished and continued to be used.

Perhaps the most notable case involving James Samuel Reed, 80 years old at the time, was his summons in 1903, on eight counts, for violating municipal regulations by occupying condemned property and also allowing it to be used as a brothel. Only one month previous Reed had been convicted on a similar charge of renting property to be used as a brothel. The condemned properties were situated in areas of the town known for an unsavory lifestyle, including Lespade Street, Frederick Street, and Elizabeth Street (located southeast of Evatt street and Alice street on Map 1.2). Through his attorney Reed pleaded not guilty and stated that he did not know that prostitutes occupied the houses. However, one Rebecca Stein, residing at #5 Lespade Street, was registered as a prostitute and carrying on business there. When asked "to whom do you pay rent?" she replied: "To Mr. Reed, generally. . . ."[26]

Despite Reed's disclaimer, the prostitutes had apparently lived in the dwellings for several months and were charged an exploitative rent of £4 monthly, double the normal rent. It seems that Reed's agent had only notified the women to move out one month before the dilapidated property had been condemned. The case continued for four days and received considerable public attention. Eventually Reed was sentenced to pay £15 or serve two months on each of six counts. For the other two counts Reed received a reduced sentence of £1 or seven days *gaol* on each count. Ironically, the reduced sentences on the last two counts resulted when civil charges were brought against the prostitutes and they were ejected from Reed's buildings. Once the prostitutes were evicted, Reed's lawyer requested a reduced sentence on the charge of residing at condemned property since the building was no longer occupied.[27] In this case the female prostitutes were penalized by the law for earning their livelihood while the male slum landlord was rewarded with a reduced sentence for closing the condemned property.

The Reed Brothers Combination owned one property in particular that became the object of a lengthy struggle between the Town Council and the Plague Board. The case elucidates the different factors at work among the officials as they tried to protect their vested interests as well as how entrenched and deep-rooted the corruption was. This property, known as Reed's Red barracks, was apparently part of a "private" location. It was rented out to Africans and consisted of five, single-storeyed tenements located at Reed and Diesel Street.[28] On 1 September 1901, the Plague Board found four plague cases at one of the houses. The Board declared Reed's Barracks unfit for habitation and evacuated the tenants.[29] However, the Council refused for five months to declare Reed's Barracks unfit to be occupied. So not until February 1902, and after much pressure including several reports from health officials, did the Council declare Reed's Barracks unfit to be occupied.

During those five months separate reports were filed about Reed's Barracks from the two doctors attached to the Plague Board, the Secretary of the Plague Board, the Medical Officer of Health for Port Elizabeth, the Chief Sanitary Inspector, and the Town Engineer. All were unanimous on the unsanitary, dilapidated condition of Reed's Barracks and recommended that it be declared unfit by the Council and demolished. In one report Mr. S. Henry Kemp, the Sanitary Inspector, newly imported for the job from England, stated on 24 January 1902 that "The (Reed's Barracks) are in such a dirty, damp and dilapidated condition as to be incapable of being rendered fit for use as a habitation. The dampness can be traced 38 inches up the main walls in some places. The condition of the sub-soil is beyond description, and I have no hesitation in recommending the demolition of the premises."[30]

In the face of these numerous unfavorable reports the Council was compelled to condemn the property and declare it unfit. Remarkably, even then Reed and his supporters were able to stave off demolition. Reed argued that both the plague inspectors and the municipal sanitary inspector had shown partiality in condemning properties and that "he could show the brickwork was in good condition and on a very dry erf."[31] He won enough Council support so that the "Council negated the reports of the Medical Officer of Health and the Sanitary Inspector and agreed that he might repair the buildings."[32]

That same day the Sanitary Inspector resigned in protest, citing the Town Council's decision. It is worth noting that Sanitary Inspector Kemp was a recent arrival and had not developed a close-knit relationship with the other health officials nor the town councillors. In short, Kemp was not yet incorporated into the local system of politics and corruption and hence had far fewer vested interests in retaining his job.

Perhaps if the suggestion of a letter writer to the local newspaper was heeded the slum landlord problem might have been handled differently. It said "that if the plague should come to Port Elizabeth, arrangements should at once be made in the forefront of the fight against it, by dooming them [the slumlords] to dwell among their tenants."[33]

Meanwhile, the Council's position on Reed's Barracks led to a standoff between the Town Council and the Plague Board. Consequently, Reed was unable to make any repairs since the Plague Board obstinately refused to observe the Council's decision. So although Reed's Barracks remained standing, it was not reoccupied. Action was finally taken after a year and a half had elapsed as a result of pressure from the Medical Officer of Health for the Colony, Dr. Gregory. He visited Port Elizabeth at the invitation of the Plague Administration in March 1903 and strongly criticized the Council for its "neglect of duty" in failing to eliminate the plague and the unsanitary and overcrowded dwellings. Gregory specifically cited Reed's Barracks, which he said "ought to have been demolished months ago."[34]

Responding to the pressure, the Mayor appealed to the Councillors to heed the medical and sanitary officers' reports and to "act without fear, favour, and prejudice."[35] They did, by voting to demolish Reed's Barracks. Significantly, Reed resigned shortly after Dr. Gregory's visit, and the dwellings were demolished in April 1903.[36] The struggle involving the Plague Board, the Town Council, and the slum landlords was by no means over, but one of the worst offenders was momentarily quelled. The destruction of Reed's barracks did not eliminate the problem of overcrowding and unsanitary dwellings, however. Reed had been a convenient scapegoat, but he was not the only landlord who exploited the demand for cheap housing. Consequently, overcrowding would not be alleviated as long as the structural conditions producing it remained.

Africans and the Plague

At the time the plague struck Port Elizabeth in 1901, the African population was approximately 10,000, mostly Xhosa speakers while the white was 19,000 and the Colored was 13,000. Africans lived in a variety of housing settlements but primarily at Strangers', Cooper's Kloof and Gubbs'. In response to the first plague case at Gubbs' many of the preventive measures against the spread of plague targeted Africans, rather than the whole population. For example, within hours of the first case being found at Gubbs' the entire location was quarantined. Dr. Galloway, the Municipal MOH, "asked for the guard, the Council endorsed the request and the [Military] Base Commandant"[37] called out the Town Guard. Although details are scarce, it can be imagined that the Guards were stationed at strategic points to prevent Africans entering and leaving Gubbs'.

Not surprisingly, "grave complaints" greeted this official well-coordinated, swift, and panicked response. Exactly who complained is not stated in the local newspaper report, although it seems logical to surmise that many white businessmen, housewives, and merchants as well as African workers, clergy, and householders must have criticized the actions of the authorities. White employers would complain because it could potentially interfere with their workforce. As one Town Councillor responded to a suggestion that Gubbs' be closed, "the Council [should] take time and be cautious in coming to any decision. They must not bar healthy people from continuing their occupation. If they closed Gubbs', they would stop the work of the port."[38] Blacks would complain about the Town Guard being called out to guard Gubbs' because the decision was based on the "class" or racial assumption that Gubbs' was the source of the disease and furthermore that using force to contain the African population would stop its spread.

That Gubbs' was not the source of the plague was already known, since it was reported in the local newspaper that dead rats found at the Harbor Board were infected with bubonic plague almost a week prior to the first victim at Gubbs'.[39] In any case, the complaints must have indeed been grave, since the Town Guard maintained their posts for only one night.

But even though the white officals knew that Gubbs' was not the source of the plague, they responded by targeting the residents. Thus, Dr. Galloway recommended "that a hut-to-hut visitation take place and every occupant of the [Gubbs'] locations should be medically examined and as many as possible inoculated!"[40] Furthermore, to minimize the spread of the disease, he advised daily inspections for twelve days of each person at Gubbs'. It was unlikely these recommendations would be implemented, however, because of scarcity of staff to inspect the residences of over 4,000 people living at Gubbs'.

The Mayor, and he was not alone in this opinion, proposed removing the "natives," closing Gubbs', and burning it to the ground.[41] Ironically, Mr. A. C. Reed, a member of the Reed Combination, previously mentioned, concurred that "Gubbs' had always been a menace to the town and the sooner it was burnt out the better." However, cooler heads prevailed when Dr. Galloway reminded the Councillors that although Gubbs' was unsanitary "the infection was in the Harbor grounds and precautionary measures must be adopted there." Although Galloway knew that the infection did not originate at Gubbs' he still said that they must also tackle the question of so many "natives" living in the town. So, once again, the question of segregating the "natives" became an important issue.

The issue of Africans using public transport was also discussed at the meeting. The Council decided to write to the tramway company and the railway line requesting that they no longer carry "native" passengers. In addition, they would request that the Cape government establish a *separate native location* for Africans. The aforementioned recommendations and comments were made without contacting or speaking to African leaders or their representatives. Only Mr. Walsh, a member of the syndicate operating Gubbs', was approached, and he promised assistance in providing safety for the residents.

Meanwhile, the alleged plague victim was quarantined at the isolation camp along with those who had been in contact with him. Yet two days later it was unclear if the African from Gubbs' was truly plague infected. Doubts were cast on the plague diagnosis when it became known that the victim had been ill for several weeks, suffering from a disease that many other beach workers contracted.[42] Eventually a local newspaper reported that the case was verified as plague, but doubts continued. These doubts were evident in the reaction of both blacks and whites to the policy of plague inoculation.

Inoculation was among the precautions recommended by Dr. Galloway. However, the Plague Board's informational campaign to educate not only Africans but all of the townspeople about the importance of being inoculated, was mostly unsuccessful. Separate meetings were held with whites, Malays, and Africans. At the meeting between Africans and the Plague Board, held at Edwards Memorial Hall in early May, about six or seven hundred Africans attended. The Plague Board chairman tried to "impress upon the natives the paramount . . . importance of being innoculated."[43] Africans were not, in large numbers, sufficiently convinced, for hardly anyone volunteered to be inoculated.

Many people had probably heard the gossip that the first case diagnosed as plague was suspect. Another, more ominous, rumor emanating from Cape Town had it that those who submitted to inoculation were dying. Doubtless this rumor was related to the widely publicized story of the two Miss Kaysers, European nurses at *Uitvlught* Hospital in Cape Town, who, after being inoculated, died. The explanation that the vaccine was improperly sealed and therefore the contents were unsterile did not dispel this notion.[44] Furthermore, even some of the medical doctors in Port Elizabeth held doubts about the disease being plague and themselves refused to be inoculated.[45]

Much of white apathy was accountable to the medical doctors' emphasis on African inoculation rather than all racial groups. Both Dr. Simpson and Dr. Smartt, the Commissioner of Public Works for the Colony, while visiting Port Elizabeth immediately after the outbreak of plague implied that Europeans were less likely to contract the disease. For example, in April, Smartt stated that "the plague did not attack the better class of people who lived under decent conditions."[46] Also, both Drs. Smartt and Simpson emphasized that smallpox was much more dangerous and contagious than the plague, and even without inoculation, said Dr. Smartt, a plague infected person was less likely to transfer the disease if the person was already healthy. Given these types of comments from respected doctors, the apathy is not surprising. Also, the small number of cases diagnosed since the first victim in April, five in all (one doubtful), also influenced the apathy about inoculation. Thus, by June 1 only about 225 people, among them 111 Africans (including Coloreds), one Asiatic, and 113 Europeans had been inoculated and 27 of these were reinoculations.[47]

The Strike

In an attempt to force Africans to be inoculated, a new plague regulation was issued on June 6, 1901, requiring that all "natives," and only "natives," be inoculated before they could travel. Although whites, Asians, and Coloreds could choose to be inoculated, they were under no compulsion. African response to the discriminatory legislation was swift and emphatic. Almost the entire labor force struck work; at the height of the strike their numbers totalled in the thousands.

The strike began on Monday morning June 10, 1901, and continued until Wednesday. Participation on the first day of the strike included Africans employed by the "Harbour Board, the Boating Companies, the Military Army Service Corps, Army Ordinance Departments, together with the Municipality and many of the natives employed in the Main Street stores. . . ." totalling perhaps two thousand. The strike was extremely effective. Reports indicate that the only work done at the ports was by the white crews, supervisors, and Indian calvarymen, all of them exhibiting "true British grit," and that by 9:00 a.m. the wharves had a "Sabbath appearance."[48] In general business came to a standstill. Port Elizabeth was a port town dependent on African labor, so a lengthy strike could prove disasterous. Africans dockworkers loaded and unloaded ships and delivered merchandise to shops and businesses dependent for their operations on receiving these supplies. The railway and military depended on African workers for a variety of deeds, including feeding the soldiers, and the householders were dependent on domestic labor for maintaining a smooth daily routine. Several factors combined to create the atmosphere that ignited the strike.

First, labor was scarce and thus at a high premium. In particular, the war led to an increased demand for labor that generally could not be met.

Work at the port swelled because of increased importation and exportation of military supplies for the war.[49] Similarly, the need for labor rose on the railways and in military employment. Natural disasters in the 1890s, such as the drought in the Cape territories of the Transkei and Ciskei and the rinderpest epidemic in 1896, had already pushed men out to work. The closure of the Transvaal gold mines when the war started in 1899 also forced many men to look for work.[50] But the labor demand exceeded the supply. The result was that wages were up, and African workers were quick to recognize their strong bargaining position. Given these circumstances, it seems that Africans would be more prone to participate in a strike than at other times.

The second factor that influenced Africans to strike were the restrictions on travelling. The problem of discrimination against blacks travelling by rail was legend, and it was practiced against all Africans, whether temporary or permanent residents, working or middle class, Christian or non-Christian, "civilized" or "uncivilized." Consequently, this regulation, especially since it was based on race, must have seemed grossly unfair and extremely frustrating to most Africans, thus providing a basis for unity.

Furthermore, martial law restrictions had already been imposed by the military, requiring that travellers carry a pass.[51] Not surprisingly this regulation was more often enforced against Africans than any other group. Thus, this new inoculation regulation compounded an already unsatisfactory situation. It stipulated that Africans must obtain a plague inoculation certificate before travelling, adding a heavier load to the already burdensome procedure that they had to endure to legally leave Port Elizabeth. The procedure required most Africans to secure an inoculation certificate, and then present it to the military officials at their base office for approval, and then proceed to the Railway Department to buy their train ticket. Undoubtedly, to workers anxious to return home this time-consuming and discriminatory treatment was viewed as unjust government intervention. Moreover, it soon became clear that some of the doctors were trying to illegally charge the black workers for the inoculations when they were already being paid by the government.[52]

But another factor that turned a normally routine problem of racial discrimination into a strike grievance was the effect of the travelling restrictions on the customary practice of work rotation among Harbor Board workers. The new regulations, if observed, threatened to abruptly halt the practice.[53] Work rotation involved one worker replacing another on a weekly rotating basis, thus allowing not only the opportunity for the individual worker to return home more frequently but also to remain there longer. The practice also allowed them to maintain closer kinship and home ties with their families and communities, concomitantly decreasing their dependence and allegiance to life in the urban towns and to wage labor. At this point these workers were closer to the first stage of migrant labor. Consequently there was more access to land and family support and less dependence on wage labor to make a living and thus they were able to exercise more control over their work schedule.

Apparently the rotation practice had evolved over a long period and was viewed by the workers as commonplace. Doubtless to them the government authorities were intentionally trying to deprive them of a basic work right as well as the right to maintain their kinship privileges and obligations in pre-colonial society. Thus, clearly for some workers the strike was viewed as a labor dispute. In a sense the dispute was over their right to limit their dependence on wage labor. Worker rotation was also practiced among members of the aspirant black middle class, such as store clerks.[54] Their underlying reasons for utilizing the system were the same, to remain their own master, but in this case perhaps they viewed the practice as allowing them more time and space to pursue entrepreneurial activities. It is also noteworthy that the work rotation system operated to support kinship ties, since often the rotating workers were bound by blood or marriage. For example, Peter Wauchope worked for a jeweler and his brother, James Wauchope sometimes took his place.

In any case, the restrictions on travel and the inoculation regulation were literally the last straw for the African workers at the Harbor Board, workers who had already been affected by plague regulations issued by their employer. These changes, initiated in May 1901, included restrictions on entry to the Harbor Board grounds and to the location housing compound unless employed and able to show an examination pass.[55] It is worth noting that the Harbor Board was using a popular means among employers to control and discriminate against their workers, by linking work and housing to a discriminatory code. Thus, the employer could force the worker to undergo inoculation in order to work and to secure housing. This type of practice would become even more popular as white supremacy and segregation became widespread and measures to control Africans were implemented.

Furthermore, the Harbor Board declared that the "native" workers were to submit to a doctor's inspection every day. There was to be no lounging during meal hours near the workplace. This restriction, although perhaps innocent sounding from the employer's point of view, meant that the men, who generally ate their meals in groups while sitting on the workplace grounds, were being told to cease this practice. To them this regulation probably represented yet another curb on the routine practice of sharing food together, another customary and obligatory practice, and viewed as a workers' right that helped to create strong bonds of brotherhood, support, and friendship in a foreign environment. This conclusion owes much to Atkins' point that eating in common also held a social and cultural significance often overlooked by European employers primarily interested in regulating labor time.[56] Ignoring such cultural practices could result in resistance from the African workers.

Yet another new work regulation that impinged on African cultural practices was the directive that the workers must wear boots on Harbor Board premises. Wearing boots was a foreign custom to which many Africans probably objected finding little of value in the practice. Especially those African workers who worked at the beach loading and unloading ships would object. Since Port Elizabeth still did not have a proper dock, workers often got their feet wet working so would find little use for boots. Moreover, it is likely that the boots were hard and uncomfortable especially too tender feet not use to wearing them. In this regard, depictions of early African workers often show them with their shoes or boots tied around their neck rather than on their feet. Also, if the workers did not regularly wear boots, they would first have to purchase them, an added expense, unless they were supplied by the Harbor Board; the workers would also have to put them on and take them off each time they entered onto the Harbor Board grounds. The boot regulation took effect in early May. Only a few weeks later thirty men were absent from their work rather than wear boots.[57]

Another significant factor that made this episode of racial discrimination different, one that might be termed cultural distrust based on the concrete reality of differential treatment, was another theory as to why whites were not being inoculated. Rumor held that whites had "sinister motives" and were in fact using compulsory inoculation to try to kill off the African population.[58] Then, too, the colonial authorities themselves feared that the proposed native location would be "looked upon . . . as a Plague Camp," by the Africans at Port Elizabeth.[59] It is notable that the rumors about inoculation and removal to a segregated plague location were associated in the minds of Africans with the whites trying to kill them off. Clearly many Africans did not trust the motives of whites and expected "evil" actions from them. In any case the various cultural and work-related factors discussed provided an explosive mix to which the African workers reacted with concrete action in the form of a strike.

On the first morning of the strike several thousand Africans attended an open-air meeting near Gubbs' location to voice their grievances. Two major grievances were enumerated, the compulsory inoculation and the prohibition against Africans travelling by train unless they showed an inoculation certificate. Several orators, speaking from temporarily erected platforms, decried the fact that only Africans were required to be inoculated, which insinuated that no others could contract the plague.

Further, they said, only Africans had to obtain an inoculation pass before travelling upcountry. The question was raised: Why did the restrictions affect only the Africans and not the whites? This question, the African leaders insisted, must be answered before the strike ceased. Frank Makwena, a well-known Christian and mission educated leader, was one of the speakers. He and the other leaders decided to send a deputation to see the Magistrate to demand that the prohibition on travelling be rescinded or the strike would continue.[60]

Meanwhile, the colonial authorities, anxious to have the workers return to work, took a conciliatory approach. The Magistrate, Mr. Wylde, appeared as a central government respresentative at the next public meeting held in the afternoon. About 3,000 Africans assembled to hear the speeches. Frank Makwena was first to speak but, insisting that he was not a delegate, gave the platform to Mr. Xesi,[61] who had been chosen to represent African grievances to the Magistrate. Xesi reiterated the objections to compulsory inoculation. He stated that: "their grievance was that if they desired to travel up-country, as many of them frequently did, for family or other reasons, they must be inoculated before they had permission to travel. It is not so with the white people. They may travel wherever they desire without restrictions of this sort—why, then, not the Natives?"[62]

In reply, the Magistrate claimed that he had no power to rescind a government order but that he would wire their grievances and the results of the meeting to the Colonial Secretary and return when he received a response. Wylde then denied the rumors that inoculation was causing death, saying that neither "native" or white men had succumbed after being inoculated.

Makwena then spoke briefly saying that:

> It was not that the bulk of the natives were against inoculation—their real grievance was that it was not general—that is to say, compulsory on all classes of the public. Let any impartial person visit some of the shanties in Evatt-street, [near the center of town] and see the condition of some of the white residents. They would then admit that the necessity for inoculation existed as much there as it did in any part of the locations.[63]

The meeting ended on this note.

It is not suprising that inoculation and travel permits were resented. As alluded to previously, the procedure that Africans had to follow to obtain the permits simply to leave the town was quite tedious, requiring a significant amount of time and effort. Each worker had to be inoculated before receiving an inoculation certificate from the Plague Board. The certificate had to be presented to the military authorities before a travel permit was issued. In addition, some African workers, including those at the Harbor Board, were required to obtain a certificate verifying their employment before the military would issue the travel permit. As a result of these various requirements Africans were shuttled from "pillar to post."

Adding insult to injury, it soon came to light that the government-appointed health officials were requesting fees from Africans for the compulsory plague examination and inoculation certificate that was supposed to be free.[64] Thus, not only did the time and irritation involved in obtaining the permits before being allowed to travel anger and frustrate Africans. They must have also been angry and frustrated at being cheated by the government, that is, by being forced to pay an extra charge for an inoculation they did not want and whose effects were thought to be deadly. Moreover, although the issue was not discussed at the public meetings, the system of work rotation was being fundamentally undermined, since it was unlikely that rotation would be allowed unless the work replacement had the proper permits. For the many Africans who used the work rotation system, this would mean double costs for the inoculation certificates.

It should be noted that the Chief Intelligence Officer at Port Elizabeth, Mr. J. P. Hess denied in a letter to the local newspaper that Africans required two or three permits to travel.[65] He stated that Africans travelling to Uitenhage or Grahamstown (and intervening districts) needed only the one inoculation certificate from the plague board. Once they had secured the certificate, Hess emphasized, they were required to present it at the military base office to receive a travel permit, which, regardless of race, every traveller in a martial law area was required to produce. Hess, however, could not deny that the order for inoculation certificates was racially based, since only Africans were compelled to show such a certificate as well as a travel permit before they were allowed to travel.

African Women and the Strike

On Tuesday, the second day of the strike, more railway and military laborers took part, but it was the participation of the African women, the domestic backbone of the town's labor force, that seemed to arouse the most resentment among the whites and to have the greatest impact on bringing the strike to a conclusion. Perhaps this is not surprising, since African female domestic workers were much depended on by European employers for every sundry household activity imaginable.[66] The local newspaper expressed the consternation felt by most white townspeople when it heartily criticized the [male] "natives": "in ordering their women folk to join in the strike, and thereby dislocat[ing] the domestic machinery of unoffending and much to be sympathised with European householders, who found yesterday that "Sanna" had joined "Umjaala" in the protest to Government. . . . The participation of the women added a serious and uncalled for factor and would serve to alienate public sympathy."[67]

The reporters' conclusion that the male "natives ordered their women-folk to join the strike" implies that the African women had no say in the decision to strike but were ordered as subordinate, passive women by the dominant, assertive men. But the reporters' statements may simply re-flect his own racial and sexual biases steming from Victorian notions about partriarchy, race, class, sex, and male/female roles as well as per-ceptions about African culture.[68] For example, the reporter concludes in regard to male workers that the native leaders "called on all boys to refuse to work." On one hand, the "native" leaders ordered the women while on the other, they called on the "boys," seeming to indicate male domination of the women versus an equal relationship between the men. Sexual bias is evident. How much the reporter's conclusions were based on reality is debatable.

In another local newspaper a reporter focusing on the same stated that "natives are calling out the housegirls and boys on strike, and they are threatening those who do not obey the summons."[69] From this report it seems that the leaders of the strike were calling on the workers to strike, regardless of gender, to show worker and racial unity in their disapproval of the inoculation order and the restrictions on travel. Yet whether or not all of the women withdrew their labor voluntarily is at issue, since the local newspapers reported that some women were beaten, if threats alone were unsuccessful, when they attempted to cross the cordrum set up by the strikers to prevent entrance into town.[70] An analysis of African women in general and female domestic workers in particular in Port Eliz-abeth during this period should shed some light on the issue.

To determine what influenced the African women to strike work and how much their participation was voluntary or involuntary, we need to try to answer a number of questions to help us learn about their back-grounds. For instance, how many African women worked as domestics; what other occupations were open to them; what types of social, eco-nomic, religious and political affiliations, in particular the family struc-ture, existed for women?[71] In addition, what was their socioeconomic and class background and what common elements might influence them to strike?

A commonality among African women in Port Elizabeth was that they faced race, gender and class discrimination that limited their access to wage labor outside of domestic work. Domestic work was the major wage employment occupation in the eastern Cape for African females.[72] Although there were some European female and also male domestic workers in Port Elizabeth, sources such as newspapers and committee re-ports indicate that by 1900 the majority of domestic labor was done by

African women. This conclusion is substantiated by the 1891 census, which shows that female Africans in the Cape colony had far surpassed all others in the domestic work category.[73] Nineteenth century Natal and the South African Republic provide a major contrast, where the domestic work force until the 1930s was made up principally of African men.

Drawing from census data including an unofficial census taken in March 1903 of the three municipal locations, Strangers', Cooper's Kloof, and Reservoir, almost two years after the strike, we can put the number of domestic workers at 1,786.[74] From calculating various census figures, I have concluded that the African female population over age 15 was approximately 2,500 to 3,000.[75] If we half this figure, we get 1,500 working at some sort of domestic work, which fits with the 1,786 total. Most of the female domestic workers were women living in a family unit rather than as single individuals. Of a total African population of 10,000, African women described as single only numbered 207, compared to 1,982 single males, while the number for African families was 4,242 [this figure represents about 700 families with an estimated six people in each family]. Presumably the women designated as single denoted an independent economic status and residence, since other single women living with their families were counted as part of a family unit. No matter what the exact number of domestic workers, however, there was a shortage of African female domestic laborers to serve the almost 23,000 whites (15,000 were females over 15).[76]

Compounding the supply and demand problem for the whites was the unwillingness of African women to work for wages. Thus, in 1903 the Civil Commissioner, of Port Elizabeth, J. T. Wylde, reported that: "Many women and girls could be well employed and adequately compensated if they were disposed to engage themselves, but a large number of both men and women do not get employment. This is possibly owing to the amount of money won by their relations who do work, or for the reason that present circumstances permit of their obtaining a living by other means."[77]

Several authors have argued that by the second quarter of the twentieth century black women at the Cape were the most exploitable in terms of wages and work conditions, while white women and African men had other options to domestic wage labor.[78] While this generalization for the most part holds true for a later period, since the overall number of black female domestic workers had risen and they were paid less, still, at the end of the nineteenth century many African women also had other options to domestic service. It is noteworthy that the exploitive domestic labor system, described by Cock's study on maids and madams that had emerged by the mid-twentieth century at the Cape, had yet to take hold in Port Elizabeth.[79] This was because most women were still able to live at home rather than being forced to exist as live-in workers. It is the live-in domestic workers who are said to be the most exploited because they are often powerless against laws and employer demands that force them to leave their families in the black townships or in the countryside. Thus, capitalism was still in its transition stage as far as producing an exploitive domestic labor force in the eastern Cape. Many of the restrictive government laws aimed at establishing white supremacy, such as the 1913 Lands Act, Native Urban Areas Act of 1923, and the pass laws applied to African women had yet to be legislated.

The other means for employment open to African women included working independently rather than for wages, primarily as hawkers (selling produce on the streets) or as beer brewers. In 1901 Port Elizabeth, many African women were less than interested in becoming domestic workers if they had other options, primarily because the work is long and hard, the employer demanding, and the pay and prestige low. The European belief that domestic work (e.g., housework, washing, ironing) was women's work was not necessarily shared by African women in Port Elizabeth. Since most men did not make enough to support a family in the town, it was more often the other means that allowed both men and women to withhold their labor.

Thus, in the growing urban areas many African women, regardless of class, found that beer brewing helped them to meet their economic needs either as single women, widows, or wives. It will be recalled that there were only a few other wage occupations open to African women, and most of these were associated with domestic work including cook, housekeeper, or washerwoman.[80] For Christian and Western-educated African women only jobs as seamstresses or teachers were available to fit their education. Some women probably worked in their family businesses in the bakeries and general dealer stores in the African settlements. However, for the most part race, gender, and class discrimination either drew women of all classes into shared gender exploitation as domestic servants or reduced them to criminals, according to colonial law, as beer brewers. Thus many women found themselves in the position of Shebeen Queen Leah, in *Mine Boy*, of operating a business that included brewing and selling "kafir" beer and running a shebeen.[81] Some women also developed many of Leah's attributes including economic independence; many became housing and property owners and provoked fear and respect among their peers.

Beer brewing was an alternative for women living in the municipal location and also the private locations, including the housing compound administered by the Harbor Board. As we have seen, Africans of all class backgrounds participated in making and selling beer—nee the Hop Beer Church.[82] The attractions of beer brewing were many. For women, brewing and selling liquor allowed more flexibility, since there was no need to leave home to work elsewhere or for someone else, an especially key issue if the women had small children. This occupation also allowed them to acquire a significantly higher income than domestic work could bring. The wages for domestic workers in 1901 were approximately 2–3 shillings per diem while beer brewing could bring in several pounds a week.[83] Of course, the lucrative remuneration held risks, and on numerous occasions African women were arrested and tried before the colonial courts for making and selling beer. In 1894, for example, Nomayeza Bongo was convicted of "kafir" beer brewing and selling and sentenced to pay three pounds or 21 days in *gaol*. Her case is noteworthy because after sentencing, the Magistrate advised Bongo to "do washing."[84] One can imagine his consternation that the woman refused to pursue what he viewed as a more appropriate occupation for an African (working for whites) and for females (domestic work) in general.

By 1903 the fine and *gaol* sentence for unlicensed beer brewing and selling had increased significantly: African women were being sentenced to pay 25 pounds or three months hard labor.[85] For example, Maggie Makwena, the wife of Frank Makwena, one of the negotiators during the strike. She was convicted of making and selling "kafir" beer in 1903 and was probably selling liquor long before this time.[86]

Yet another alternative to domestic work, although admittedly for fewer women, was to become a property owner. By 1900 a small number of African women perhaps forty to fifty, had acquired property, mostly in the municipal locations, where they sometimes rented out rooms or sublet property.[87] Most of the women were probably widows who had inherited the property from their deceased husbands. A few women in Strangers' location held two or three property sites. In pre-colonial African society women were able to use land allocated to their male relatives, so they had land use rights, just as men did [land was not owned individually but communally]; upon their death her children had a preferential right to it.[88]

As noted, many African female domestic workers had in common their living arrangements. That is, most of them lived with their families in African settlements like Strangers' rather than on their employers' premises. This conclusion is supported by the fact that in 1896 concern was voiced about the safety of the great number of "native young girls" who work in the town during the day and "always return home in the evening."[89] Doubtless the "girls" resided with some of the African families who had lived at the municipal locations since the 1850s and 1860s and were into the third generation born in town. Furthermore, the number of female workers residing on their employers' premises must have been minimal or no need would have existed for the strikers to prevent them leaving the location and going into work, since most would have already been at work. (More on this later.)

Among these domestic servants were women from a variety of socioeconomic and class backgrounds, including members of the aspirant black middle class. Although the voices of the African women fail to speak to us through the written and oral sources on this issue, it will be recalled that as early as 1881 the Christian African leader, Isaac Wauchope, in a written report stated that "the wives and daughters [of African men living in the town] were employed as 'washerwomen, cooks, and housekeepers'."[90] Other data on Christian and Western-educated black women by such scholars as Deborah Gaitskell supports this conclusion. She has pointed out in several articles the contradiction of European male and female missionaries educating African women in South Africa for domesticity.

Education for domesticity according to Gaitskell entailed teaching African women that to be good Christians, they had to be good wives, daughters, and mothers and fulfill the nineteenth-century, European, middle class domestic ideal of a "male breadwinner, dependent housekeeping wife and mother, [and] dependent school-going children."[91] According to this ideal, the wife fulfilled the pivotal role of family caretaker for the hearth, home, and children. Associated with industrialization and urbanization, this domestic ideology was applied to women by men, and it was most often focused on the role of the women as wives. Initially promulgated for the middle class during the nineteenth and twentieth century, it became the model for the white working class woman in England.

However, the ideas associated with the European domestic sphere were inapplicable to African women in pre-colonial society, women who were part of a culture quite different from their European counterpart. As Niara Sudarkarsa noted several years ago, the whole European idea of the domestic sphere and the status and roles of men and women as part of a dual level hierarchy is inappropriate and yields inconsistent results.[92]

In fact, it is now being recognized that African women in the African patriarchal society were not defined as inferior nor solely by the domestic sphere. Even though men were dominant in the political realm, this was less true in the socioeconomic institutions. Thus, while most women lacked political authority and were dependent on men for political representation, they also held power among women and in relationship to men.

In Xhosa society, and the majority of the women in Port Elizabeth were Xhosa speakers, much of their power lay in the importance of female fertility and in the fact that African female labor power was the pivotal force of the productive and reproductive cycle, the motor without which the entire society would be transformed.[93] Their position as the agriculturalists and, thus, responsible for providing food for the family enhanced their social prestige and represented limited power.

The homestead family in Xhosa society was the center of life, and there existed among families a strong feeling of interdependence and solidarity.[94] African respect for the homestead family, for which fertile women were necessary for its reproduction, as well as respect for authority and decision-making were key components affecting the society, regardless of gender. Among the Nguni speaking people, which includes the Zulu and the Xhosa (the largest ethnic group in Port Elizabeth), African women were not identified only by their role of wife, which in any case was not limited to a specific domain. Thus, they had privileges, responsibilities and power influenced by their position as wife, mother, daughter and sister.

Isaac Schapera notes that the African family "helped one another in all domestic arrangements and difficulties, freely shared their belongings and consulted together in matters of importance."[95] The male head of the homestead in Nguni patriarchal society was highly respected and "occupied a position of great dignity. He kept order and maintained discipline within the limits of his household . . . and exercised considerable authority." The combination of familial interdependence and male authority did not mean that women were lacking in status, only that their status was different. But the interdependence of men and women rather than hierarchy underlay the societal norms.[96] Consequently, when discussing African societies, we need to take cognizance not only of gender but also of age groups, socioeconomic status, class, rank, marriage and the hierarchies existing among men and women and within families. How did these beliefs and practices change when transferred to the urban areas and how much were they influenced by western education and Christianity?

Many African customs were criticized by the missionaries but were nonetheless retained and reshaped by the African converts in combination with Christian teachings and Victorian morality. Marriage practices, in particular, *lobola* (bridewealth), were railed against by the missionaries yet some black Christians as well as many non-Christian Africans continued the practices or a combination thereof.[97] For example, in 1896 Port Elizabeth a man paid lobola to the father and made plans to marry her in church "but the daughter married someone else by "kafir" custom."[98] Yet respect for the family, and male authority although in a different form, was a key component of missionary teachings. But the missionaries emphasized the separation of the male and female sphere and their gender roles.

The evidence indicates that most Africans including many Christians continued to respect African societal practices in particular the importance of the family and its social organization that dictated customary roles that included rights and obligations. As we have seen, most women, including the domestic workers, still lived with their families, so we can presume that the striking women also had in common a continued respect for the interdependence of the family as well as the authority of the head of the household. Beliefs associated with respect for the elders, parental authority, and decision-making, although altered by Western ideology and capitalism, nonetheless retained their vitality among Christians and non-Christians and were transferred to the urban area.[99] Thus, most Africans continued to respect the family structure in which they remained rooted. Consequently, their status as a family member doubtless influenced their willingness to participate in the strike.

Under these circumstances it seems reasonable to conclude that many of the women struck work as a member of a family that was opposed to racially discriminatory legislation that affected all Africans, regardless of gender. The domestic workers' response was more socio-political than economic because it was a response influenced by the fact that they were being targeted for discriminatory treatment not because of their gender but because of their race. Thus, racial solidarity drew men and women together against the government policy.

Another common grievance of the African women is what I call genderalized anger and frustration about their treatment at the hands of prejudiced whites. They too faced racial discrimination from whites, since regardless of gender, it was common. Some of the treatment was influenced by racial and class stereotypes while some of the treatment was influenced by stereotypes about "non-white" women. Images of black women among whites portrayed them as children, hampered by the same inabilities as the black men. Cock, writing about the Xhosa female domestic servants in the nineteenth century Cape, states that "Black female servants were viewed as lazy, often stupid, lacking in initiative, grasping, careless and ungrateful, by their European employees."[100] The cultural and racial biases exhibited by the white settlers led them to conclude that the African women were products of a barbarous culture that could only slowly be healed by European civilization. Christianity would rescue the women from slavery (agricultural work), polygyny, being sold for *lobola* and such sexually depraved customs as *intonjane* (girl's initiation ceremony).[101] These African practices would be replaced by the work ethic which would, not coincidentally, provide enough labor for the whites.

The imagery of African women as immoral beings, and the disdain with which they were viewed in general is illustrated by the following account of a rape case. An African women brought a case against a black man that she claimed raped her at the rooming house where she lived with her husband. On hearing the case the white Magistrate lectured the court saying that "if these women will constantly pig with the men, they cannot expect the Magistrate to care one penny."[102] Forthwith, he discharged the accused. So the woman who brought the charge was forced to suffer more verbal abuse from a Magistrate, influenced by his ideology about African women as "morally impure." It was these types of actions by the Europeans that could promote gender and race consciousness and become influential when calls were made for racial unity against discriminatory actions.

It also seems clear that women, too, had other grievances that could lead them to strike. One of these grievances was most certainly the innocuous government regulations that discriminated against blacks, regardless of gender. Thus, women had also been involved in the resistance against being removed to a segregated location. They, too, experienced court cases against them for desertion from work, and they suffered through beer raids.[103] Moreover, the inoculation regulation affected not only African men but also African women and children. Thus, they, too, would have to submit to inoculation. In fact, the legislation could affect the women even more, since they were the primary caretakers of the family including caring for family members who became ill either from the plague or from the inoculation. Moreover, the whole question of African women being innoculated by Europeans raises another set of issues about custom and practice and exposure of the body to strangers. So, indeed, the struggle for dignity and the anger against discrimination also affected black female workers and could drive them to strike.[104] The fact that women joined the strike indicates that Africans were well aware of the effect withdrawal of domestic labor would have.

But what of the claim that in the urban areas African women enjoyed a "new freedom?" Especially under christianity African women in the urban areas derived power and authority from their participation in new institutions such as the Christian religion. However, it is worth noting that customarily women in many African societies were also more involved in religious activities, as diviners and sorcerers, in the Xhosa language, *inyanga* or *igqira*.[105]

With their conversion to Christianity, more women became active in the religious life of their family and community. In Port Elizabeth christian church activities included organizing fundraisers, temperance meetings, refugee relief, recitals, and *itimiti* (tea meetings).[106] Women could draw on African customary practices that involved using their organizing and co-operative capabilities such as everyday agricultural work, work-parties, and funerals. It was these women, too, who were also more likely to be organized as part of a church *manyano* (union)[107] active in the aforementioned religious work. Furthermore, it is highly probable they would have been influenced by the ideology of work, unity, self-help, and upliftment from their own societal practices and also from the Christian religion. As we have seen in earlier discussions on christian Africans, in Port Elizabeth *manyanos* existed as early as the 1880s when christian men and women were organized into several self-helf groups such as The True Templar's Lodge, the Band of Hope, The St. Cyprian's Benefit Society and the Native Mutual Improvement Association.[108]

African women were also exposed to the European male and female missionaries transplanting the domestic ideal while simultaneously encouraging them to provide the domestic labor for white families on the mission stations and in the towns.[109] Herein lay the contradiction. The European domestic model was beyond the range of most christian African women because racial discriminination prevented their husbands from attaining the necessary economic class. Given these economic circumstances, to make ends meet, the African women, whether wives, daughters, or mothers, were obliged to provide domestic labor at the hearth and home of the whites while neglecting their own. This meant that African women of all classes, whether christian, or non-christian, literate or illiterate, shared a subordinate position influenced by not only their gender but also their race and class position which sometimes propelled them into domestic wage labor. These factors influencing their subordination probably affected their decision to participate in the strike.

Another issue that deserves comment is the reporter's conclusion in the local town newspaper that the participation of the women in the strike added a "serious and uncalled for factor."[110] The implication in "uncalled for" is that the women had impinged on a personal, one-to-one relationship rather than one between a worker and an employer. Domestic work was an area in the private domain, where relationships between master/mistress and servant were based on a personal rather than impersonal paternalism. Influencing the relationship was the domestic servant working in close physical proximity to the master or mistress. Thus, somehow the personal relationship formed between domestic workers and their employers was viewed by some whites and perhaps by some blacks as one that ought not be subjected to ordinary worker/employee actions when there was a worker's dispute. Otherwise the give and take, the personal closeness that was based more on paternalism, and a dichotomized relationship of deference, subordination, and racial and class superiority vs. inferiority might be jeopardized. Several authors have discussed the relationship between employers and domestic servants where madams (female employers) demanded that domestic servants should be subordinate and deferent and that a certain line should not be crossed while some female employers simultaneously state that the domestic workers are like members of the family.[111] Despite these claims by white employers of familial inclinations towards black domestic workers there were laws regulating the relationship. First, the Kafir labor law and then the Master's and Servant's Law of 1857 made it a criminal offense to break a civil contract.

Similarly, the newspaper editor of the local *Eastern Province Herald* implies that the white householders were the victims of the strike because their domestic workforce was disrupted. Moreover, he implies that these white householders sympathized with the strike prior to the women taking part since their household laborers were not affected. However, when *Sanna* and *Umjaala* (euphemisms used by the newspaper reporter to describe female and male Africans) started messing with the domestic sphere, white support declined and the problem, in his words, became *serious*. It is clear that the participation of the women struck a blow to the weakest spot, the hearth and home, of the many white employers dependent on domestic labor.

In conclusion, the evidence suggests that the women joined the strike for some of the same reasons as the men. These reasons included their continued belief, function, and position in the family structure; respect for and allegiance to familial authority; dislike of racially discriminatory regulations; distrust of the inoculation procedure; frustration and anger at the prejudiced behavior of whites and the ways in which the system operated against blacks and women and treated them with disrespect.

Resolution and Aftermath

Clearly the withdrawal of female domestic labor was a crucial element that profoundly affected the strike and quickly brought the white authorities to their senses. The participation of the women Tuesday morning led to resolution of the strike by Tuesday afternoon at an open-air meeting attended by several thousand Africans. An African deputation was there to meet with E. H. Walton, the MLA for Port Elizabeth. Particularly noteworthy is Walton's speech in which he attempted to cover up the central government's administrative decisions by claiming that there was some controversy surrounding who was responsible for issuing the inoculation regulation. Claims and counterclaims from members of the Plague Board and the Colonial Secretary's office clouded the issue.[112]

Wherever the regulation originated, Walton's explanation meant that the government could pretend that it was unauthorized and, therefore, inapplicable. The denial also allowed the central government under the auspices of the Colonial Secretary's office, to save face by disclaiming the regulation without seeming to bow to the striker's demands. It also to some extent dispelled the notion that the Colonial Secretary had broken his promise to the African population. This is because in April, when the first plague case was discovered, the Colonial Secretary had met with some of the African population in Port Elizabeth and declared that, "government would consider the rights of the native people in a manner which could not help but to create a most favorable and lasting impression on the minds of the natives that whatever grievances they may have had in the past, that with Government administering the Plague Regulations through the local Board, there will be equitable treatment to all entirely regardless of color and race."[113]

Instead of equitable treatment that ignored color and race the Africans at Port Elizabeth had been subjected to inequitable treatment grounded in color and race prejudices. One could argue that the government's failure to keep its promise compounded African grievances and ended in strike action.

In any case, after a two-hour discussion, the Africans agreed to form a committee and to return to work. The Committee would explain their position to the Plague Board and "also explain to the natives the regulation which the Plague Board might find necessary [to issue]."[114] Thus, the strike was over; some workers returned to work immediately, others the next day. The formation of the advisory committee provided some representation for the Africans; the strike had shown that thousands of blacks would challenge racially discriminatory laws to prevent unjust treatment. Thus, while the plague inoculation regulation was being reconsidered, the order against Africans travelling up-country without both a pass and an inoculation certificate was suspended.[115]

The next afternoon a deputation of African leaders from the various locations met with the Plague Board. They emphasized that Africans were quite willing to be inoculated as long as the regulations were applied to all races and generally enforced.[116] A few days later the Plague Board issued new regulations requiring that "all persons [regardless of race] wishing to leave the district must be examined and acquire a pass."[117] Although later grievances were raised related to discriminatory treatment regarding the examination procedure, for the moment at least African demands had been met.

A factor worthy of consideration that the strike spotlighted was the question of the leadership role of Africans drawn from the emergent black middle class and black working class. It seems clear that members of both the African middle and working class acted as the leaders and represented the strikers at meetings with the government officials. However, it appears that many of the western-educated, middle class leaders, generally acknowledged by educated blacks and local white officials as representing the "native" community, were for the most part not directly involved once the strike started.

The evidence suggests that the Africans serving on the two political committees that functioned locally among educated blacks apparently did not take a leading role in the strike. The first committee consisted of Mr. M. D. Foley, chairman; D. C. Lywakadi, secretary; Edward Ngesi; Stephen Katha; and Mr. Masoleng. On the second committee (known as the Location Committee) were Whiley Pikoli, Chairman; E. Tsewu, secretary; Mr. Qaba; John; Kama; Mboti; Bopi; and Tubyi respectively.[118] Not one of these men was mentioned as playing a leading role in the strike. Neither were Reverend Henry Newell, minister of Edward's Memorial Church, and Reverend Kakaza, two of the men generally representing African grievances to the Town Councillors, included. Unfortunately, the sources from the local newspapers are all that is available. Another recognized local leader, Frank Makwena was the only other African mentioned in the reports as taking a leading role.

The reason for Makwena being accepted as one of the main leaders during the strike is, I believe, related to first, his past track record as a community leader, which means that he was already well-known. In this capacity he had been critical of the Town Council, and, it will be recalled, he was also critical of the African and American Working Men's Union and started the Sotho organization in the 1890s. Moreover, he was known as the proprietor of a store and as a housing rental agent. As mentioned in the first chapter, he, like many other members of the aspirant black middle class, moved in and out of the middle class and was recognized and accepted by Africans of different class backgrounds. As we have seen, his wife, Maggie Makwena, was a beer brewer, which could mean that her husband might be more acceptable to some members of the working class. That is, his status as an educated christian who was sometimes in poor economic straits and not a "temperance" man probably influenced how he was viewed and created less distance between him and other economically poor Africans. Fourth his ethnic background as a Sotho-speaker, possibly made a more acceptable leader than a Xhosa or Fingo, since he was outside the emnity between these groups. Finally, there was his role as a defender of the workers against exploitation. It was Makwena who wrote a letter on behalf of the workers in which he complained about their being charged illegally by the Municipal Health Officer for a health examination that was suppose to be free.[119]

To say that many of the recognized leaders of the educated Africans did not take a leading role during the strike is not to say that they were unaware of its possibility and involved behind the scenes, either in promoting or discouraging it. Between the time the inoculation regulation was issued on Thursday, June 6, and the first day of the strike, Monday, June 10, four days elapsed. During this period a group of Africans, perhaps members of the political committee, met with Mr. Searle and Mr. Edgar H. Walton, the MLA's for Port Elizabeth, to protest the regulation. It seems that no agreement was reached, but it was arranged that Mr. Walton would meet with all Africans on Tuesday, June 11.[120] In the interim, over the weekend, perhaps the headmen and/or an element of the western-educated leadership gauged the discontent of the workers and began discussions about a strike. By Monday the stage was set.

It is difficult to determine if the strike was planned or spontaneous; it appears to have been a combination of both. Thus, if the African leaders were working behind the scenes over the weekend, and no decision had been reached about whether or not to strike, this would explain why the Harbor Board workers, who were in the forefront of the strike, arrived at their workplace on Monday morning, milled around for a while, and then returned home. On the other hand, some workers may have gone to the workplace to inform the other laborers of the impending strike. Presumably other workers did the same, since later that morning the public meeting drew thousands of strikers who listened to various speakers test their oratory skills as "a series of rings were formed and the orators took their places on a platform in the center."[121] Intermixed with the meetings were religious services and hymn singing, indicating that the Christian element held some prominence.

One newspaper report mentions that "chiefs and native leaders were imbued with a much more reasonable view,"[122] while another refers to the "headmen."[123] This indicates that both "traditional" and western-educated African leaders were co-operating in coordinating the strike. It is clear that they were also accountable to the workers and strived to obtain majority consensus at the public meetings. For example, on Tuesday morning "some of the natives were for returning to work pending communication with Government, but the majority held that having committed themselves to a policy, they were not inclined to depart from it until the aim was achieved . . . claiming that their grievance would have been ignored if they had not taken the drastic step they had to bring it before the Government. . . ."[124] This drastic step, the local newspaper scornfully stated, was brought about by "agitators" and Africans listening to hotheads rather than their *ordinary leaders and "friends."* (my emphasis)[125] Clearly some of the leaders were questioning the conventional methods of protest, such as consultation with the "friends of the natives" or white liberals before taking action. Other leaders such as Makwena were straddled in the middle between the working class and the liberal alliance.

In this context of particular interest is Makwena's disavowal on the second day of the strike "against the description of their mass meeting as a strike." He declared that "the whole object of the movement, was to hold a mass meeting to enable the natives to have an opportunity of airing their grievances. There was no hall in the town for the purposes, and they could have done nothing unless they had taken the means they did to get the natives together to express their views."[126]

Perhaps we could call this the first stay-a-way campaign to express political dissatisfaction with raciallly discriminatory government policies. In a letter to the editor of the local newspaper signed "native," it was pointed out that the "real" African leaders of the town and those on the two political committees previously mentioned would never call a strike, and the strike had been a mistake.[127] These disclaimers probably represented an attempt to soothe the ruffled feathers of the "friends of the natives" and to assure them that conventional methods of protest were preferable.

The government, apparently alarmed at the failure of the local black western-educated leaders to contain the strike, sent for its own native leader and "friend of the natives." Thus, Reverend E. Mdolomba of Cape Town and R. J. Dick of Kingwilliamstown, were requested to travel to Port Elizabeth in order to aid in ending the strike. Mdolomba was born in the Cape, educated at Healdtown, and worked as a Wesleyan minister. A relative of his lived and worked in Port Elizabeth in the 1890s and was involved in various organizations along with other mission educated Africans.[128] Presumably Mdolomba was bought in because he supported the establishment of the location at Cape Town and occupied a large church there and continued to abet the government in the face of African resistance.

Although undoubtedly Mdolomba was no stranger to Port Elizabeth some African resentment surfaced against him. *Izwi Labantu* (an African newspaper published in the eastern Cape) charged that the government's Native Affairs Department had insulted the intelligence of the natives by bringing in outsiders; that Mdolomba was against location boards and vigilance associations (or local associations formed by blacks) and that he was double-faced. They claimed that if one "ask[ed] the vigilance [associations] at Cape Town, Port Elizabeth, etc., they will say that "Mdolomba is unknown to their association" and that he alone could not be appointed by the government to represent native affairs.[129] In other words, the government could not choose their leaders for them. There was evidently a conflict among Africans as to the intent and the consequences of bringing in an "outsider" rather than negotiating with the local African leaders.

In contrast, *Imvo* declared that Mdolomba was chosen by the authorities as qualified to negotiate because of the good effects of western education and Christianity, which showed the respect whites held for educated Africans.[130] It is not clear exactly what role Mdolomba played, although *Imvo* praised him for contributing to ending the strike. Reports indicate only that he was invited to explain to Africans that the inoculation procedure was harmless and to encourage a return to work. Meanwhile, *Izwi Labantu* ruminated that educated Africans protested on "class" grounds and would always "be at one in protecting their rights from any infringement. . . " a point on which both editors would doubtless agree.[131] The difference of opinion between *Imvo* and *Izwi Labantu*, it should be noted, was not the first. The two newspapers competed against one another, and the editors, John T. Jabavu and Soga were enemies.

The other outside person brought in as a consequence of the strike was R. J. Dick, Special Native Magistrate for Kingwilliamstown, who had worked for the Native Affairs Department for twenty-odd years. He was requested to make a report on the "natives" and the plague, for which he took evidence from Port Elizabeth Africans. Dick recommended that the inoculation regulation not be enforced and that employers be urged to get their servants inoculated.[132] Both Mdolomba and Dick were part of the Cape "liberal tradition," and their input initiated by the government from outside Port Elizabeth, indicates that the western educated African leaders living in Port Eliabeth were unable or unwilling to disagree for the most part with the general strike.

Conclusion

The controversy among Africans and whites regarding black leadership and the role the black western educated christians would and should play was an indication of changes in the liberal alliance and the position of the aspirant black middle class vis-a-vis the working class. Above all, the government wanted to gain control of the African workers to ensure a docile black working class. Yet the significance of the strike as a demonstration of African unity and labor power across ethnic, class, and gender lines could not have been lost on the black nor white population. Such unity could represent a threat to white supremacy.

In particular, the use of organized labor opposition to gain a social and political concession was a new tactic that had profound implications.[133] Such implications had been discussed during the strike in the *Cape Times* which reported that white opinion seemed to fear that by giving in to the strikers the government was allowing too much latitude, and if this were not curtailed, "the blacks will get the upper hand."[134] Along the same lines the *Diamond Fields Advertiser* warned that if the government allowed natives to gain many more such victories, it would add "enormously to the difficulties of solving the native problem."[135] Similarly, the *Cape Daily Telegraph* commented in angry tones that "too much latitude has already been given the nigger and this must be curtailed, or the black man will get the upper hand."[136]

In several letters and editorials the solution suggested was to bring in native labor from Cape Town, Natal, and/or the Transkei so that "natives [at Port Elizabeth would] be taught a severe lesson that they cannot plot to stop the whole trade of the town at their sweet will and pleasure."[137] And some Africans did lose their jobs, primarily store "boys," but the majority of the workers returned to work while supply and demand dictated that those fired were quickly rehired. However, Colonel Garsten, the Military commander, expressed the intention to bring in 300 outside "natives" to work at the port, presumably with the view that as contract laborers they would be more controllable compared to the local black workers.[138]

In order to prevent such an alliance repeating itself, the local and central government would have to convince those African leaders anxious to fit into colonial society that more concessions could be obtained through support of the government than allying with the masses. The more radical African leaders would then have to contend with a conservative black leadership allied with the government. These factors would profoundly influence the upcoming struggle over land and housing and the creation of a segregated African location in Port Elizabeth.

Notes

1. Andrew N. Porter, "British Imperial Policy and South Africa, 1895–1899," in Peter Warwick, ed., *The South African War: The Anglo-Boer War 1899–1902* (London: Longman, 1980), pp. 37–56; G. Blainey, "Lost Causes of the Jameson Raid," *Economic History Review* 18 (1965): 350–366; J. Butler, *The Liberal Party and the Jameson Raid* (London: Oxford University Press, 1968).

2. Byron Farwell, *The Great Anglo-Boer War* (New York: Harper and Row, 1976), pp. 342–343 for Boer commandoes in Cape Colony, indicating that Smuts came as close as 50 miles to Port Elizabeth where British troops and a remount station were located and also a Boer concentration camp; Peter Warwick, *Black People and the South African War, 1899–1902* (Cambridge: Cambridge University Press, 1983), for role of Africans in the "white man's" war.

3. See Elizabeth Van Heyningen, "Cape Town and the Plague of 1901," in *Studies in the History of Cape Town* 4 (1981): 68–74; for an earlier study with a good overview on health and segregation, see Maynard W. Swanson, "The Sanitation Syndrome: Bubonic Plague and Urban Native Policy in the Cape Colony, 1900–1909," *Journal of African History* 18 (1970): 387–410.

4. Christopher Saunders, "The Creation of Ndabeni, Urban Segregation and African Resistance in Cape Town," *Studies in the History of Cape Town* 1 (1984): 4–7; Van Heyningen, "Cape Town and the Plague of 1901," pp. 98–101; I. J. Catanach "Plague and the Tensions of Empire: India 1896–1918," *Imperial Medicine and Indigenous Societies*, ed., David Arnold (Manchester and New York: St. Martin's Press, 1985), p. 153 states that in Hong Kong the British authorities used the army to enforce the hospitalization of the sick and in Bombay, India, the campaign against the plague was handed over to an army general.

5. However, the Mayor, other local officials, and white townspeople in general angrily criticized the central government and charged favoritism toward Cape

Town. For correspondence see *EPH*, "Town Council," 21 February 1901; and "Plague Precautions-The Council's Action," 7 March 1901; "The Plague-Government's Unsatisfactory Attitude," 15 March 1901. The animosity between Port Elizabeth and Cape Town authorities was not new. The eastern Cape colonial territories including Port Elizabeth, Kingwilliamstown, and East London had long engaged in a campaign to establish a government separate from Cape Town. See Basil A. Le Cordeur, *The Politics of Eastern Cape Separatism, 1820–1854* (New York, Cape Town: Oxford University Press, 1981).

6. See *EPH*, "The Plague-The First Case-In Gubb's Location," 17 April 1901; for Dr. Simpson's visit see "The Town's Peril-Professor Simpson's Views," 6 April 1901 and on the same date an editorial on "Dr. Simpson's Report," and further commentary in three letters written to the editor, 1) "If the Plague Came to Port Elizabeth,"; 2) "Fumigation,"; and 3) "About Refuse, & c.," 8 April 1901.

7. "The Plague-The First Case," *EPH*, 17 April 1901; "Town Council," *EPH*, 21 February 1901 for Mayor's comments on the "enormous amount" it would cost for plague administration—too much for the town to pay.

8. "The Plague-The First Case," *EPH*, 17 April 1901.

9. "The Plague Board-A Preliminary Meeting," *EPH*, 24 April 1901. They were Mr. Guthrie representing the Divisional Council, Mr. Walton, MLA for Port Elizabeth, Mr. McIlwraith, Mr. MacIntosh, Mr. Wylde, the RM and the Military Base Commandant, Colonel A. A. Garston.

10. Ibid.

11. See *EPH*, "Plague Board," 2 May 1901; "Plague Board Offices," 14 May 1901; "Plague Board Offices," 21 May 1901. The staff included two medical officers from Cape Town, Dr. Blackmore and Dr. Tebb, who would serve as plague officers for the eastern district. At its first meeting the Board divided the town into seven areas for the purposes of regulation, sanitation, plague inspection, and reports. Each area was to have an official and an office. Two district offices were set up, one at the north end of town and one at the south end.

12. *EPH*, "The Plague Board," 26 April 1901; "The Plague Board," 18 May 1901.

13. Information for this and the following paragraph is from "Insanitary Port Elizabeth—A Deplorable Condition—Dr. Blackmore's Indictment," *EPH*, 25 July 1901.

14. "Town Council," *EPH*, 1 August 1901.

15. According to Plague Board reports the number of cases was 34, fourteen fatal—two Europeans, "Plague Board," *EPH*, 4 August 1901, and for Cape Town see van Heyningen, "Cape Town and the Plague," p. 77.

16. Saunders, "The Creation of Ndabeni," pp. 176–184.

17. "The Plague-Colonial Secretary's Visit," *EPH*, 23 April 1901.

18. See *EPH*, "Town Council," 3 June 1901; And at another meeting, "Town Council," 27 June 1901, according to Councillor Griffin complaints were already being received that [evicted] "natives" and Indians were sleeping out at the Showyard; "Town Council," 4 March 1903, where Dr. Gregory pointed out that the Council had the power to demolish such dwellings under the municipal and health regulations; "Town Council," 13 June 1901. For municipal regulation see Cape of Good Hope, Municipal Amendment Act 27 of 1897, in *Statues of the Cape*

of Good Hope 1652–1905, 5 Vols. ed. E. M. Jackson (Cape Town: Government Printers, 1906), vol. 4, 3782.

19. "Town Council," *EPH,* 1 August 1901. Dr. Simpson made this comment while discussing the necessity for a special Bill to "make the natives live in locations" emphasizing that power would also be needed to prevent "poor whites" occupying the evacuated houses.

20. "Town Council," *EPH,* 22 August 1901; Cape of Good Hope, Municipal Amendment Act 27 of 1897, *Statues of the Cape of Good Hope,* 4, 3782.

21. Lawrence M. Friedman, *Government and Slum Housing* (Chicago: Rand McNally and Co., 1968); Gauldie, *Cruel Habitations;* also see Noreen Kagan, "African Settlements in the Johannesburg Area, 1903–1923" (master's thesis, University of the Witwatersrand, Johannesburg, South Africa, 1978).

22. In Port Elizabeth, Europeans, Africans, Indians, and Coloreds, lived intermixed in areas such as Vlei Post, see Cape of Good Hope, Report of the Select Committee on the Native Reserve Locations Bill, A22-1902, Appendix A.; for similar conditions in living arrangements see on Johannesburg, Riva Krut, "A Quart into a Pint Pot: the white working class and the 'housing shortage' in Johannesburg, 1896–1906" (honors diss., University of the Witwatersrand, Johannesburg, South Africa, 1979); and for Cape Town see Saunders, "The Creation of Ndabeni," pp. 167–169.

23. For a debate on this topic see "Parliament-House of Assembly," *Cape Times,* 11, 15, June 1903, and "Parliament-Legislative Council," 17 June 1903.

24. See *EPH,* various dates between 1901 and 1903 when these men were cited for owning property unfit for human habitation. For example, "Citations," *EPH,* 18 July 1902, J. MacKay, and T. O'Brien-agent cited, 6 June 1901, "Citations," J. H. Gates, 21 June 1901, 19 September 1901, 30 July 1903, "Citations," George Newton 30 July 1903, relative of a Town Councillor.

25. Information in the following paragraph is taken from *EPH,* "Citations," 17 April 1901, 13 May 1903, 19 March 1903, A. C. Reed cited. The Reed Brothers Combination agent said there were three combinations, one of these was certainly A. C. and W. J. Reed. By 1905, it seems that the agent R. Heydenrych was cited, rather than the owners. See *EPH,* "Citations," 23 November 1901; "Citations," 11 July 1903; 26 March 1903; 21 April 1904.

26. "Cleansing the Town-Important Police Proceedings," *EPH,* 25 July 1903. At this time, prostitutes were required to register with the local MOH, and to be examined periodically to ensure they had no veneral disease. Also see Elizabeth Van Heyningen, "Prostitution and the Contagious Diseases Acts; the Social Evil in the Cape Colony, 1868–1902," *Studies in the History of Cape Town* 5 (1984): 79–123.

27. "Cleansing the Town-Important Police Proceedings," *EPH,* 25 July 1903 and "The Reed Judgment," 8 June 1901. The case went to Circuit court on appeal where one conviction was upheld out of four in municipal court for "contravening the municipal regulations by letting houses to tenants for use for ill fame purposes." The case was tried from 25 July 1901 to 31 July 1903; also see 21 July 1901.

28. "Insanitary Dwellings-The Report of the Municipal Office's," *EPH,* 12 February 1902; also see *EPH,* 2,6 February 1902.

29. Four cases of plague were found in one of Reed's houses on Barrack Street, "Plague Board," *EPH,* 18, 19 September 1901, and 12 February 1902.

30. "Insanitary Dwellings," *EPH,* 12 February 1902.

31. "Town Council," *EPH,* 6 February 1902.

32. Ibid.

33. "If the Plague Came to Port Elizabeth!" *EPH,* 8 April 1901.

34. Cape Archives Depot (CAD), NA607, Copy of newspaper clipping from *Port Elizabeth Telegraph* (hereafter PET), 4 March 1901, "The Bay's Insanitary Area."

35. "The Bays Insanitary Area," *PET,* 4 March 1901; "Town Council," *EPH,* 19 March 1901.

36. Even then, a ratepayer wrote a letter of complaint stating that the Sanitary Department had it in for Reed, "Plague Grievance," *EPH,* 10 July 1903.

37. "Plague Reports," *EPH,* 19 April 1901 and "Harbor Board Meeting—the Bubonic Plague," 20 April 1901.

38. "The Plague—The First Case—In Gubbs' Location," *EPH,* 17 April 1901.

39. "The Plague," *EPH,* 17 April 1901, Dr. Galloway the MOH for the municipality reported that the rats were found on Friday—near stacks of mealies and forage that could not be shipped until military orders arrived—this was five days before the Gubbs' case.

40. "The Plague—The First Case," *EPH,* 17 April 1901.

41. "The Plague—The First Case," *EPH,* 17 April 1901, all quotes in this paragraph are from this date.

42. "Plague Reports," *EPH,* 19 April 1901.

43. "The Plague—Important Native Meeting," *EPH,* 10 May 1901. The Plague Board met with the Malays and Indians on 2 May 1901 to encourage inoculation.

44. Van Heyningen, "Cape Town and the Plague of 1901," p. 101.

45. "Inoculation," *Imvo,* 15 July 1901, and "Plague and Rats," *EPH,* 15 July 1901.

46. "The Plague Expert-Dr. Simpson and Dr. Smartt Interviewed," *EPH,* 2 April 1901.

47. See *EPH,* "Plague Board," 27 May 1901 and 1 June 1901.

48. "Port Elizabeth-Natives and Inoculation," *Imvo,* excerpts from the Port Elizabeth Telegraph," 18 June 1901; "The Natives and Inoculation. . . ." *EPH,* 11 June 1901.

49. Warwick, *South African War,* p. 142, and Van der Horst, *Native Labor,* points out that there was a need for an increased labor supply especially at the Ports, p. 16.

50. Charles Van Onselen, "Reactions to Rinderpest in South Africa, 1896–97," *Journal of African History* 13 (1972): 273–288, for rinderpest effects on labor, and Colin Bundy, *The Rise and Fall of the South African Peasantry* (Berkeley: University of California Press, 1979), for economic conditions in the Ciskei and Transkei regions before the South African War.

51. Farwell, *The Great Anglo-Boer War,* states that martial law was extended to the entire Cape colony on 17 January 1901 with the exception of the ports and the African reserve areas. After a long debate and struggle over extension of martial law to the ports, these were included in October 1901, p. 329; For debate see Har-

rison M. Wright ed., *Sir James Rose-Innes Selected Correspondence, 1884–1910*, Series 2, V. 3 (Cape Town: Van Riebeeck Society, 1972), p. 62; "The Natives and Inoculation-Strike Ashore and Afloat," *EPH*, 11 June 1901.

52. (CAD), Port Elizabeth Harbor Board, File 80, Misc. Corresp., No. 3, 1901, Town Clerk to Harbor Board Commissioner, 19 April 1901.

53. "The Natives and Inoculation," *EPH*, 11 June 1901. Many of the workers lived in Grahamstown, or Uitenhage and other areas that were close by so that the rotation system was extremely convenient for them. See *BBNA* for various district reports on labor supply, e.g., 1898, 1899, 1902.

54. "Circuit Court," *EPH*, 11 September 1895. Peter Wauchope worked for a jeweler and his brother James sometimes took his place. Unfortunately, James was accused of stealing two watches. Eventually the latter pleaded guilty to theft. This must have been quite devastating to his well-known christian middle-class family.

55. CAD, Port Elizabeth Harbor Board, File 80, Misc. Corresp., No. 3, 1901, Town Clerk to Port Elizabeth Harbor Board Commissioner, 18 April 1901, for Habor Board regulations.

56. Keletso Atkins, *The Moon is Dead! Give Us Our Money* (Portsmouth, New Hampshire: Heinemann, 1993), p. 122.

57. CAD, Port Elizabeth Harbor Board, File 80, Misc. Corresp. No. 3, 1901, Shore Superintendent to Port Elizabeth Harbor Board, 10 May, 1901.

58. "Inoculation," *Izwi Labantu*, 2 July 1901. This article implies that the "heathen natives" who were superstitious because of ignorance were the ones who held notions of sinister motives while "the educated natives took the more sensible course, objecting to differential treatment on class grounds." However, see *Imvo*, 15 July 1901 where R. J. Dick, the Special Native Magistrate brought in from Kingwilliamstown to assist in ending the strike and also to report on African grievances maintained that "inoculation was believed to be fatal by all races and classes of people,"; Marc Dawson, "Socio-Economic and Epidemiological Change in Kenya: 1880–1925" (Ph.D. diss., University of Wisconsin-Madison, 1983) in discussing Kenya also points out that Africans were fearful of inoculation results, and did not always report the plague and deaths from plague because they were afraid the Medical Officers of Health "wanted the corpses to eat or for medicine," pp. 96–98; also see "Port Elizabeth—Natives and Inoculation," *Imvo*, 18 June 1901 where the R. M. denies reports that those inoculated were dying.

59. Apparently the probability that Africans might refuse to go to New Brighton, the first segregated black location, for fear it was a plague camp, was first raised by Dr. Gregory the MOH for Port Elizabeth, to W. G. Cummings, Secretary of the Native Affairs Department, who then passed the idea on to the Secretary of Public Works. CAD, NA607, 1, 842, W. J. Cummings, SNAD to Secretary Public Works, PE, 5 March 1903 re: probable occupation of Port Elizabeth location.

60. "Port Elizabeth-Natives and Inoculation," *Imvo*, excerpts from the *Port Elizabeth Telegraph*, 18 June 190l; "The Natives and Inoculation. . . ." *EPH*, 11 June 1901.

61. No further information is available on Mr. Xesi.

62. "Port Elizabeth-Natives and Inoculation," *Imvo*, 18 June 1901.

63. Ibid.

64. "Town Council," *EPH*, 27 June 1901, Frank Makwena wrote to the Health Committee questioning why the Health Officer was charging farm worker s5/- to examine them; this was probably not an isolated incident; "Plague Board Meeting," *EPH*, 26 April 1901, where setting up centers for "free" inoculations was discussed.

65. "Town Council," *EPH*, 27 June 1901; "Natives and the Plague," *EPH*, 12 June 1901.

66. "The Native Strike-Second Day's Proceedings," *EPH*, 6 June 1901; Also see Jacklyn Cock, *Maids and Madams* (Johannesburg: Ravan Press, 1980), for dependency of white women on and their relationship with their maids; also see Keletso E. Atkins, "Origins of the Amawasha: The Zulu Washermen's Guild in Natal, 1850–1910," *Journal of African History* 27 (1986): 41–57, on the Zulu Washerman in Natal and their ability to control their labor because of white dependence on them to do the drudgery work of washing clothes.

67. "The Native Strike," *EPH*, 12 June 1901.

68. Cock, *Maids and Madams*, points out that the ideas of European missionaries, colonial officials and upper and middle class white settlers about Africans in general were based on Victorian British ideas. These included notions that males were superior, a belief reinforced by segregation of the sexes in clubs, and schools and the exclusive rights of males in politics and occupations, p. 89.

69. "Intimidation," *Cape Daily Telegraph*, 11 June 1901.

70. "The Natives and Inoculation," *Imvo*, 18 June 1901; "The Native Strike," *EPH*, 12 June 1901; and "A Serious State of Affairs-Girls ordered not to Work," *Cape Times*, 11 June 1901. The African leaders were more successful with the "boys" while intimidation it was reported was used to prevent the "girls" performing their domestic service in town. Similarly, it was also reported in the *Cape Daily Telegraph*, 11 June 1901, that "a number [of women] have broken through the ranks of those "boys" put out to prevent them coming into town."; Saunders, "The Creation of Ndabeni," relates that African resistance at Cape Town against government actions that forced them into the segregated settlement in 1901 included a train boycott enforced by men armed with sticks to prevent Africans from buying tickets or leaving the location to walk to work, p. 183.

71. William Beinart, "Amadelandawonye (the Die-hards): Popular Protest and Women's Movements in Herschel District in the 1920s," in William Beinart and Colin Bundy, eds., *Hidden Struggle in Rural South Africa* (Berkeley, University of California Press, 1987), pp. 222–269.

72. Jacklyn Cock, "Domestic Service and Education for Domesticity: The Incorporation of Xhosa Women into Colonial Society," in Cherryl Walker, ed., *Women and Gender in Southern Africa* (London: James Curry, 1990). Initially, Xhosa women were often arrested for entering the colonial boundaries without a pass and forced by white officials to work for the white settlers. White Cape colonials preferred black female domestic labor and as other options closed more black women were forced into service.

73. Cape of Good Hope Census Report (Cape Town: Government Printers), G6-1892, 316. In 1891, the total European population was 13,939 and the other than

European was 11,469. Both the black and white populations had almost doubled from 1891 to 1903.

74. The census was conducted as part of a government removal scheme to determine the number of Africans needing housing in the categories of single men, single women or families. A separate category was provided for the exempted domestic worker. CAD, NA607: Telegram from Civil Commissioner, Port Elizabeth to Secretary of Native Affairs Department, 10 March 1903. This census placed the total number of Africans at 9,331. The Cape of Good Hope Census (G80-1904), for 1903 puts the total number of Africans in Port Elizabeth at about 15,000, p. 93.

75. Figures are taken from the 1891 census, Census of the Cape of Good Hope (G6-1892) and the 1903 census (G80-1904) and the CAD, NA607 Telegram from CC, P. E. to SNA, 10 March 1903.

76. The total number of females of all races in the Port Elizabeth urban area was 13,152. Of this total 4,780 were under 15 while 10,031 were 15 and over. Also the total number of European females of all ages in the urban area was at 9,881, almost twice as high the total for other than European which was 4,930 (including Africans, Asians and Coloreds). Since we do not know the class background of the white female population it is difficult to determine the number that required domestic servants. For the whole district of Port Elizabeth in 1903, including urban and rural areas the European population was 23,782 and the other than European was 22,844 (including Africans, Coloreds, Asians). Cape of Good Hope census (G80-1904).

77. Blue Book on Native Affairs (BBNA), G12-1904, p. 92.

78. Erica Boddington, "Domestic Service: Changing Relations of Class Domination 1841–1948, A Focus on Cape Town" (masters of social science, University of Cape Town, 1983), pp. 129–130; Cock, *Maids and Madams.*

79. Cock, *Maids and Madams,* esp. Chaps., 6–7.

80. Cape of Good Hope, Medical Officer of Health Report, G5-1897. According to the MOH report on typhoid, in 1896, the Cape Malay population did the bulk of the washing for the whites in Port Elizabeth, Annexures, Table IX.

81. Peter Abrahams, *Mine Boy* (London: Heinemann, 1947).

82. See Chap. 1 on "kafir" beer brewing, *Imvo,* 10 August 1887.

83. The South African Natives Races Committee, *The Natives of South Africa* (London: South African Natives Races Committee, 1901). This figure based on written responses to committee questions. Revd Moffat said colored domestic servants get 2 pounds and more a month in Cape Town. Revd. Rubasana stated 2–3 shillings per month—he might have been discussing farm labor. William Scully, a government official, born in the Cape, said 2 shillings for miscellaneous work, pp. 257–61.

84. "Magistrate's Court," *EPH,* 19 November 1894.

85. "The Town," *EPH,* 5 August 1903.

86. "Ingenious Defense," *EPH,* 1 April 1903; She was again arrested, and fined 100 pounds or six months "Selling Liquor without a license," *EPH,* 8 September 1904, she claimed she did not sell liquor to her three male boarders; another woman Sarah Makwane (sic) convicted of buying brandy illegally was probably

a relative which may indicate that the women ran a *shebeen*, "Liquor Contravention," *EPH*, 9 February 1901, where beer and other liquor was sold.

87. CAD, 3/PEZ, 6/1/1/1/209, Valuation of Huts, Strangers' Location, 1896–1901.

88. Isaac Schapera, The *Bantu-Speaking Tribes of South Africa, an Ethnographical Survey* (London: Routledge and Kegan Paul, Ltd., 1956). Although in theory land was not owned, in practice land continued through generations to be occupied by one family so exclusive claims existed. "It is only in regard to land for residence and cultivation that private rights are universally recognized." Once a man took up or was granted such land, it remained in his possession as long as he lived there; he had a prescriptive right. . . . on his death it was usually inherited by his children. Similarly, men, women and children could possess cattle in their own right, pp. 156–7; Walker, *Women and Gender,* says that among the Sotho also some women acquired property in practice and theory and their ownership was acknowledged by their families and communities. p. 60; Atkins in *The Moon is Dead!,* p. 41, also states that Zulu women possessed land in Natal.

89. 1897 Select Committee Report, p. 68. Testimony of MLA Jones, elected to the Cape Parliament largely by African votes. Jones may have used the term "girls" to refer to unmarried women.

90. BBNA, G8-1883, p. 69.

91. Deborah Gaitskell, "Housewives, Maids or Mothers: Some Contradictions of Domesticity for Christian Women in Johannesburg, 1903–1930," *Journal of African History* 24 (1983): 241.

92. Niara Sudarkasa, "The Status of Women in African Societies," in *Women in Africa and the African Diaspora,* eds., Rosalyn Terborg-Penn, Sharon Harley and Andrea Benton Rushing (Washington: Howard University Press, 1987), p. 26.; Also see Elizabeth Schmidt who states that in pre-colonial Southern Rhodesia, "the distinction between the domestic and the social in African society was more political than economic," in "Race, Sex, and Domestic Labor: The Question of African Female Servants in Southern Rhodesia, 1900–1939," *African Encounters with Domesticity* edited by Karen Hansen (New Brunswick; New Jersey: Rutgers University Press, 1992) p. 222; Some authors argue that it was also inapplicable for European women in Europe, but utilized as an ideal in the colonies by European men, see Joan W. Scott and Louise A. Tilly, "Women's Work and the Family in Nineteenth-Century Europe," *Comparative Studies in Society and History* 17 (1975): 36–64.

93. Jeff Guy, "Gender Oppression in Southern Africa's Precapitalist Societies," in Walker, *Women and Gender,* p. 39.

94. Guy, "Gender Oppression," says that, "The homestead was made up of a man, his cattle and small stock, his wife or wives and their children, grouped in their different houses, each with its own arable land," p. 34.

95. This and the following quote is from Isaac Schapera, "The Old Bantu Culture," in Isaac Schapera, ed., *Western Civilization and the Natives of South Africa* (London: Routledge and Kegan Paul Ltd., 1967), pp. 7–8.

96. Sudarkasa, "The Status of Women in African Societies," pp. 25–26.

97. Africans in 1896 Kimberley debated 'Is *lobola* as practiced at the present time justifiable?' During the debate, W. B. Kawa argued for *lobola* since he was assigned that duty but afterwards called it a relic of barbarism. See Brian Willan, "An African in Kimberley: Sol T. Plaatje, 1884–1898," *Industrialization and Social Change in South Africa*, eds., Shula Marks and Richard Rathbone (London: Longman, 1982), p. 247; Also Schapera, *Western Civilization*, for the custom among educated Africans in the 1930s, pp. 88–89.

98. "Magistrate's Court-Lobola and Christians," *EPH*, 15 January 1896.

99. Scott and Tilly, "Women's Work and the Family," p. 54. Writing about female labor in nineteenth Europe, Tilly states that young women who left home to do domestic work retained their societal values and at least initially sent their wages home to their parents.

100. Cock, "Domestic Service and Education," p. 80.

101. See D. Williams, "The Missionaries on the Eastern Frontier of the Cape Colony 1799–1853" (Ph.D. disser. University of the Witwatersrand, Johannesburg, 1959), for explanation and missionary opinion of *lobola* and *intonjane*.

102. "Magistrate's Court-Rape Case," *EPH*, 26 March 1894; Deborah Gaitskell discusses official white notions about black women in urban areas as morally corrupt in "Christian Compounds for Girls: Church Hostels for African Women in Johannesburg, 1907–1970," *Journal of Southern African Studies* 6 (1979): 45–47.

103. "Magistrate's Court-Masters and Servants Act," *EPH*, 6 April 1900; Van der Horst, *Native Labor* points out that The Masters and Servants Law passed in 1856, amended in 1867, to include native foreigners regulated the contracts between European masters and native servants and was aimed at controlling servants most of whom in the eastern Cape were Africans. The Act attached criminal liability to the breach of certain civil contracts. However, Africans were primarily regulated by the Kafir Employment Act" of 1857, amended in 1858, concerned with the period of service and registration of contracts of "Native Foreigners." Thus, the Masters and Servants Act applied only when the Kafir Act was inapplicable, pp. 35–38; Most of the domestic servants would be excluded because they lived in the African settlements and did not contract with the employer. For a beer raid that resulted in several women being charged, see "Location Raids," *EPH*, 9 April 1902.

104. Beinart, "Amadelandawonye (the Die-hards)," p. 277; Also worth noting are data on African christian women for the 1913 pass campaign in the Orange Free State and the 1920s strikes and boycotts in East London, a town in the eastern Cape, and in Durban, Natal. These respective efforts show the women's willingness to participate and to lead protests. Julie Wells, "Why Women Rebel: A Comparative Study of South African Women's Resistance in Bloemfontein (1913) and Johannesburg (1958)," in *Journal of Southern African Studies* 10 (1983): Helen Bradford "'We are now the men': Women's Beer Protests in the Natal Countryside, 1929," in Belinda Bozzoli, compiler, *Class, Community and Conflict* (Johannesburg: Ravan Press, 1987), pp. 292–323.

105. Schapera, *Bantu Speaking Tribes*, pp. 226, 228; these diviners were primarily women among the Nguni, p. 230; These are combined or merged conceptions among most Bantu, p. 242; Also written in Xhosa *iziyanga* or *abangoma* (diviner) p.

185; Schapera, *Western Civilization*, maintains that "the participation of women in the religious life of the commuity was largely limited to magic." p. 19. He defines magic, as "the belief that by means of spells and the use of material substances the forces of nature could be harnessed for the purposes of man . . . and whose aim was to ensure success and protection," p. 32.

106. The English tea meeting influenced by African culture took on a new meaning when Christian Africans began to hold them in the evening during which dancing and singing were popular. Sometimes tea meetings went on all night and less than Christian activities, at least this is what Europeans claimed. "Magistrate's Court, Tea Meeting," *EPH*, 1,7 September 1893. The tea meeting began to be adopted by working and middle class Africans, christian and non-christian, and variations followed according to David Coplan, "The Emergence of an African Working-Class Culture," in Marks and Rathbone, *Industrialization and Social Change*, pp. 366–367.

107. *Manyano*, a Xhosa word for the Methodist groups, which by the twentieth century were formed in the major cities. Also Godfrey Callaway in *Sketches of Kafir Life* (New York: Negro Universities Press, rpt. 1969, org. pub. 1905) eludes to a *manyano* when he states that "Maria began to tell me . . . of the progress of the Mother's Union at Esiqunqwini," among the Xhosa in the Transkei and this was in the later part of the 1870s, p. 113; Gaitskell notes that *manyanos* did exist in the nineteenth century in D. Gaitskell, "Devout Domesticity? A century of African Women's Christianity in South Africa," Walker, *Women and Gender*, pp. 251–272.

108. BBNA, G8-1883, p. 68.

109. Gaitskell, "Devout Domesticity," p. 241.

110. "The Native Strike," *EPH*, 12 June 1901.

111. Cock, *Maids and Madams*; Hansen, *African Encounters with Domesticity*; Schmidt, *Peasants, Traders and Wives*, Chap. 5.

112. "Mass Meeting of Natives-An Amicable Settlement," *EPH*, 12 June 1901; "Mass Meeting of Natives," *EPH*, "The Natives and Inoculation," *Imvo*, 18 June 1901.

113. "Colonial Secretary's Visit—Some Interesting Interviews," *EPH*, 26 April 1901.

114. "Mass Meeting of Natives," *EPH*, 12 June 1901.

115. "The Natives and Inoculation," *Imvo*, 18 June 1901; also see "Plague," *EPH*, 13 June 1901. The Plague Board decided that no further passes should be issued until they received word from the government.

116. "The Plague Board-Natives and Inoculation," *EPH*, 15 June 1901.

117. "The Plague Board," *EPH*, 19 June 1901.

118. "The Port Elizabeth Native Leaders," *EPH*, 25 June 1901. The location committee probably dealt with location grievances such as water availability, trash disposal, rent and housing. While the problems may have overlapped the other "political" committee conceivably focused on more general grievances related to voting, discriminatory legislation regarding passes, and education. All of the committee members were Christian and presumably western-educated.

119. "The Port Elizabeth Native Leaders," *EPH*, 25 June 1901; for information on Maggie Makwena see "Ingenious Defense," *EPH*, 7 April 1903. The precise role

of headmen in the urban areas and their relationship to the emerging African working class living in the town locations during this period remains unclear. At the municipal locations the headmen were paid by the municipality. However, it seems that the "traditional" headmen held a position of authority, especially among migrant workers while they worked in the town, often acting as their representative to the employers and perhaps to the municipal authorities. For an attempt at unwinding their complex role in Cape Town in the early 1900s during a conflict between the government and African workers see Saul Dubow, "African Labor," *Studies in the History of Cape Town* 4 (1981): 108–134.

120. "The Port Elizabeth Native Leaders," *EPH*, 25 June 1901.

121. "The Natives and Inoculation," *EPH*, 11 June 1901; *Imvo*, 18 June 1901.

122. "The Native Strike-Second," *EPH*, 12 June 1901.

123. "Natives and Inoculation," *Cape Times*, 12 June 1901.

124. "The Native Strike-Second," *EPH*, 12 June 1901.

125. "Natives and Inoculation," *EPH*, 11 June 1901.

126. "Mass meeting of Natives," *EPH*, 12 June 1901.

127. "The Port Elizabeth Native Leaders," *EPH*, 25 June 1901; *Izwi Labantu* also commented that "the Port Elizabeth natives allowed themselves for once to be led away by bad advice . . . " quoted in *EPH*, 25 November 1901.

128. CAD, 3/PEZ, 1/2/1/6, Location Committee minutes, 10 May 1894, see newspaper clipping on "The Location Question" attached to minutes, where Mr. Mdolomba objects to removal of Strangers' location to the North End site.

129. "Inoculation," *Izwi Labantu*, 2 July 1901; On Mdolomba and Cape Town see Saunders, "The Creation of Ndabeni," p. 176.

130. "Native Recognition," *Imvo*, 18 June 1901.

131. "Inoculation," *Izwi Labantu*, 2 July 1901.

132. "Occasional Notes," *Imvo*, 15 July 1901.

133. Alan Cobley, *Class and Consciousness: The Black Petty Bourgeoisie in South Africa, 1924 to 1950* (New York; London and Westport, Connecticut: Greenwood Press, 1990); Helen Bradford, *A Taste of Freedom* (New Haven: Yale University Press, 1987), Chap. 3; Philip Bonner, "The Transvaal Native Congress 1917–1920," in Marks and Rathbone, *Industrialization and Social Change*, pp. 270–313 for a discussion of the black petty bourgeoisie in Johannesburg and the middle of the road position along with the ideological struggle that may occur to radicalize this class; This was by no means the first strike by African workers, especially Harbor Board workers. However, these strikes were for wage increases or for improved working conditions. See Mabin, "The Rise and Decline of Port Elizabeth, 1850–1900," University of the Witwatersrand, *History Workshop* (1984): 9,16.

134. "Natives and Inoculation," *Cape Times*, 13 June 1901.

135. *Diamond Fields Advertiser*, cited in "Inoculation," *Izwi Labantu*, 2 July 1901.

136. "Native Strike," *Cape Daily Telegraph*, 12 June 1901.

137. Ibid.

138. "Town Council," *EPH*, 13 June 1901.

6

Urban Locations, Political Power, and the "Native" Free State at Korsten

Introduction

Between 1902 and 1905 the Africans at Port Elizabeth struggled to maintain their rights to freedom of movement, to choose where they wanted to live, to own property, to vote, to build their own homes, to own businesses in a free enterprise system, in essence, to maintain control of their own lives in the urban areas. Maintaining these rights was becoming more and more difficult for the black residents as the question of segregating all of the Africans at Port Elizabeth in one "location" assumed major proportions for the colonial government. To this end, the Native Reserve [Urban] Locations Act No. 40 of 1902 was passed.[1] On one hand, the legislation aimed to correct the problems at Uitvlugt, the African location created under the Public Health Act at Cape Town, by legalizing it. On the other, it authorized the establishment of a state location at Port Elizabeth and required the black population to live there, except for the exempted.

The Act stipulated that the Cape Governor could proclaim "native" locations in or near urban areas, while Africans were not compelled by law to move into the location, they could no longer legally live within the Municipal boundaries. So non-exempted Africans would have to move into the segregated location or find lodgings beyond the boundaries of municipal jurisdiction. Exempted were domestic servants living on their employer's premises, registered voters, and natives who had been issued special permits by government officials. Significantly, the legislation affected all Africans and the non-exempted included the African property holders, many of them members of those black families who aspired to upward mobility in the colonial society. Many were also members of the African middle class that had begun to emerge in the nineteenth century. Despite owning property they too would have to live in the location or move beyond the municipal boundaries.

Although initiatives toward residential segregation in the disparate parts of South Africa were already administered locally, this was the first time that the colonial or central government had assumed the responsibility of financing and administering location housing for the black workforce. As such, the outcome of this experiment could also influence the government's future involvement in housing schemes. Initially the statute was only proclaimed on an experimental basis in the two towns with the largest "native" populations, Port Elizabeth and Cape Town, but it was anticipated that other towns would eventually also establish labor "townships."

In effect this piece of legislation was an experiment in social control which, it was hoped, would help solve the problem of regulating African labor in the urban centers. Furthermore, it would formalize the living space as well as the economic and social "place" that the black population could occupy in the colonial economy, that is, the racial and class boundaries within which they would be able to develop. The law gave legal authority to the government to formalize segregation away from the workplace, backed by the power of the state apparatus. The entrance of the state into housing was a sign that the living space of urban "native" laborers was viewed principally as a problem of control, one whose solution had eluded the local government.

Clearly as Cooper has noted in discussing the struggle of Africans to retain rights over the use of space, land, and housing in urban areas, how workers are housed has much to do with "how they are integrated into a social order."[2] The Cape government viewed the Native Reserve Locations Bill as a vehicle to establish a structure that would ensure that Africans would be integrated as subordinates.

This objective would be accomplished by requiring that all male Africans carried a pass, while those exempted had to produce a certificate, issued by the Superintendent of Locations; contravention of the Act carried a penalty of no more than £10 or three months imprisonment with or without hard labor. Work, housing and jobs were linked, since Africans had to apply for a pass before a housing site was assigned and present it to their employers before they could be hired. In this way, the government could keep track of the number of Africans entering the town to work (influx control) and curtail their movements by forcing them to reside in the government location. The location would serve as a labor reserve for employers. If the system worked as envisioned by the colonial authorities all Africans would be obliged to report and inform the white officials about their work in order to obtain housing within the municipality. To ensure that the tenants paid rent, the law stipulated that they could be evicted from the very place the government was trying to get them to enter and charged a £5.00 penalty. [This stipulation was probably directed at the Africans at Uitvlugt who had refused to pay rent for several months when they had been forced to move into the location].

But at Port Elizabeth, Africans of all classes, many of whom lived indiscriminately among the white population, refused to co-operate with the legislation. They systematically and for a variety of reasons resisted the law by avoiding "New Brighton," (Map 1.2) the name of the new segregated location newly constructed by the central government at astronomical costs. Instead they moved to various areas outside the municipal boundaries—thousands of black people migrated to Korsten where they purchased land and built dwellings.[3]

Korsten was a freehold village, situated about two miles outside Port Elizabeth. At the turn of the century it was neither racially segregated nor created by government, which meant that its residents were able to enjoy a relative freedom from racially discriminatory and restrictive regulations. From 1901 to 1905, when the settlement experienced unprecedented growth, it became the focus of a political struggle involving the African population, their liberal white allies, and the colonial state. Following the implementation of the Native Reserve [Urban] Locations Act, a concerted struggle ensued over the right of Africans to remain at Korsten. Both blacks and whites realized that the conflict over Korsten and New Brighton was linked to broader issues, including property ownership, the franchise, economic opportunities, and freedom of movement.

In the following pages we will examine four factors that shaped the government's policy on urban segregation. The first three were the growth of a "native" free state at Korsten, the role of the African middle class leaders, and the 1903 Cape parliamentary elections in which blacks who held the franchise provided the "swing" vote for white politicians. The fourth was the reaction of African women to a special government proclamation that would force them out of Korsten and into New Brighton, a proclamation that resulted in the arrest of one woman and, subsequently, a test court case. As is well known, at the Cape the nonracial qualified franchise was limited to males owning property worth £75.00 or earning £50.00 per annum and who were also able to fill out an application form in English or Dutch. A major issue in this local parliamentary campaign in 1903 was the establishment of a Village Management Board for Korsten. An examination of these factors will enable us to gauge the strengths and weaknesses of the liberal alliance, the power of the African voters, the reaction of the African working class to government dispensations toward segregation, and the particular role of African women in challenging discriminatory laws.

The Bubonic Plague and the Growth of Korsten

As we have seen, a drastic change in the housing situation was precipitated by the bubonic plague. Although at Cape Town the colonial government used the 1897 Public Health Act to force Africans living in the town to move into the quickly constructed Uitvlugt, at the segregated native location at Port Elizabeth circumstances were different. When hundreds of Africans were evicted by the Plague Board, primarily from Strangers' and Cooper's Kloof, they could not relocate to New Brighton because it had yet to be constructed. Tents were set up as alternative housing at a temporary camp, but most Africans were unwilling to reside there.

At Cape Town Africans resisted living at Uitvlugt, and many residents refused to pay rent on the grounds that the location was established under the Public Health Act as an emergency measure and therefore to require them to pay rent when they were residing there against their will was illegal. The government responded by passing the 1902 Native Reserve Locations Act to legalize the administration of Uitvlugt and also to avoid similar problems at New Brighton when it was opened. Significantly, this statute, drawn up by the Native Affairs Department was the first legislation in the Cape to allow the government to set aside proscribed areas for compulsory residential segregation in urban areas that would be financed and administered by the colonial government rather than by the Municipality.[4]

Not surprisingly, financing the location was one of the issues of conflict during the Parliamentary debate on the 1902 Native Reserve Locations Bill. The debate centered on whose responsibility it was to pay for housing the African workers. On the one hand, should the local government pay with revenue being raised through taxing the employers of African labor? Or should the central government take over the financing and administration? The Prime Minister, Sir Gordon Sprigg, maintained that Africans were dissatisfied with the Port Elizabeth Town Council and would prefer to be governed by the Cape central government.[5]

Sprigg was correct. Both Frank Makwena and Whiley Pikoli, two of the African representatives chosen to testify before the select committee established to take evidence on the Native Reserve Locations Bill, indicated that Africans were not averse to being administered by the central government.[6] Even before this, when the topic of establishing a "native" location to be administered by the central government was first broached in April 1901, the African leaders had unanimously agreed as long as the 1896 agreement was upheld. African preference for central government administration was neither a fickle or thoughtless judgment; what underlay this opinion were years of struggle between the Municipal Town Council and the African population in Port Elizabeth over what Africans viewed as improper and discriminatory legislation. Africans increasingly distrusted the Municipality's intentions to fulfill the 1896 agreement and hoped that a change in administration would favor their claims. In the end, the central government prevailed, although in the long run the law was never properly implemented because of resistance to the Act.

The creation of New Brighton was an ambitious project, with the state intending to house between 7,000 to 10,000 people at an estimated cost of

£200,000. The plans virtually called for the erection of a complete, self-contained African village, with housing, trading stores, and several churches and schools, all to be located on planned streets. From the government's perspective, New Brighton was a model village for which the Africans should be grateful. But during the time between the passage and implementation of the Act, it became apparent to the government that there were several obstacles to the Act, including the large exempted population, the compensation procedure, and the dissatisfaction with the facilities and proposed administrative policies at New Brighton.

By the end of the century Port Elizabeth's established industries included tanneries, wool washeries, and factories making footwear, soap, explosives, and cigarettes.[7] In 1904 the African population was 20,000 out of a total population of 48,000.[8] As we have seen, the rise in population was a response to South Africa's continuing industrialization and capitalist growth, natural disasters in the 1890s, and the higher wages being paid during the 1899–1902 South African War.

For the most part the wages of the emergent African middle class and African working class were closely aligned, which decreased the distance between them. Working class men filled all levels of occupations such as messengers and building, sanitation, and railway workers, with the majority working at the port. By 1902 the average wage for African men was three to five shillings per day, whether skilled or unskilled. The professional group could earn up to £90 annually, sometimes more.[9] Native teachers, however, were underpaid, earning £5 to £15 a quarter.[10] Among the African women who worked in unskilled jobs, earnings were 20/- shillings to 30/- shillings per month. We do not know the earnings of the African women who by the 1880s were working as food vendors or of the few trained at mission schools, some of whom worked as teachers or seamstresses. Ntame Lukalo was an example of a working mission-educated women; she probably taught at the Wesleyan school in Stranger's location and was a Lovedale alumna, as were her two sisters. She was married to Isaac Wauchope, illustrating the tendency of mission-educated Christians toward ingroup marriage.[11]

Since the Act would apply only to Africans living within the Municipal boundaries perhaps half of the almost 13,000 in the Port Elizabeth district were exempted. Most of these were workers living on their employer's premises registered voters, or people living outside the municipal boundaries.[12] For instance, Africans living at Korsten or in the Walmer Municipality were exempt because these areas were outside the town. With half of the African population exempted, the Act was almost doomed to failure before it was proclaimed. The large number of Africans living outside the municipal boundaries, especially at Korsten, were the greatest obstacle to the Act. Prior to November 1901 Korsten's population was much smaller. But between October, 1901 and April, 1903, the number of residents increased dramatically, due largely to the actions of the Plague Board.

In October 1901 the Plague Board began to condemn African dwellings at the municipal locations of Strangers', Cooper's Kloof, and Reservoir, citing them as health hazards. Eviction notices were served on the residents, and those dwellings declared uninhabitable were burned. In some cases Africans residing at Strangers' were given no more than four days to vacate their homes.[13] While the Plague Board served eviction notices, the Town Council paid the compensation money. Only one alternative housing arrangement was offered to the evicted Africans until the location was built. This was a temporary accommodation camp at the North End of town, set up by the Plague Board in October 1901, where Africans would occupy tents.[14] Several months later the local newspaper, commenting on the fact that Africans did not like the tents, maintained that they were the best made and that "each tent is fitted with a wooden floor and within them the natives and their families will be both comfortable and healthy ... and if the native will look on it as a picnic for a month or two they will be far better off. . . ."[15] Most Africans failed to see their removal to temporary tents as a picnic, and they avoided the accommodation camp. Nonetheless, in a matter of months the Plague Board had partially accomplished what the Port Elizabeth Town Council had been attempting for the past twenty years: move the Africans living at Strangers' out of the town.

Problems between the black population and Plague Board over the evictions surfaced immediately. For instance, an African deputation met with the Town Council in November 1901 to complain that they "were being hustled by the Plague Board and cast out in the street." They asked that the Council influence "the Plague Board to delay action until the people could be properly housed."[16] The Council pointed the finger of responsibility at the central government, maintaining that the "natives" should memorialize [send a letter of protest] to them. Meanwhile, the Council voted to request "that the Plague Board and the Government be asked to stay their hands with evictions until proper provision was made for the housing of the natives."[17] It seems that for a few weeks evictions were suspended, but once the Government purchased the land at Cradock's Place, also called New Brighton, in January 1902 evictions picked up, even though it was understood that a location could not be formally established without a new law being passed by Parliament.

Turned out so abruptly from the municipal locations, many homeless Africans made their own housing arrangements at Korsten. An area privately owned by whites, Korsten was located outside the Port Elizabeth boundaries and thus unaffected by municipal regulations (see Map 1.2). At Korsten, Africans used their compensation money to lease or purchase a plot and to erect new housing; the land was held by freehold—a down-payment could be made on a plot and monthly payments paid toward individual ownership.[18] The plots could be subdivided and space rented out to others. Thus, Africans could become landlords, thereby increasing their income. No government restrictions, such as prohibition against liquor, owning land, owning or grazing livestock, or making building improvements, existed. Although initially, Africans moved to Korsten simply to find shelter, no doubt the relative freedom from official restrictions became an added attraction.

In the interval Africans were caught in the middle of the dispute over when the location would be established, and they continued to go to Korsten. The number of Africans evicted by the Plague Board who relocated at Korsten is uncertain. What is certain is that Korsten's population in October 1901 was approximately 100, and by April 1903 it had reached 3,000.[19] Included in this total were Africans evicted in 1901 and 1902 by the Plague Board from the various municipal and private locations as well as Africans who were being forced to move in 1903 under the Native Reserve Locations Act. As Table 6.1 indicates, at least 4,575 Africans relocated. Some may have been returning home, while others travelled to different areas in search of work.[20] Yet many Africans simply moved outside the municipal boundaries to avoid official restrictions, since neither the 1897 Health Act or the Locations Act was applicable. Africans from all socioeconomic

Table 6.1 **Approximate Number of Africans that Left Port Elizabeth Between November 1901 and March 1903**

Locations	November 1901		March 1903		Population Decrease
	Sites	*Population*	*Sites*	*Population*	
Municipal					
Strangers'	134	1,500	100	405	1,095
Cooper's Kloof	51	520	40	230	290
Reservoir	186	2,000	100	1,563	437
Private					
Gubbs'	500	4,000	500	2,644	1,356
Vlei Post	no estimate	1,400	tents[a]	340	1,074
Town					
Residents	no estimate	2,580	140	2,257	323
Totals	871	12,000	1,280	7,439	4,575

Note: a. Apparently most people lived in tents; only nine houses were listed.

Source: 1901 data from Cape of Good Hope, Report of the Select Committee on the Native Reserve Location Bill, A22-1902, Appendix A; and 1903 data from CAD NA607, Office of the Civil Commissioner of Port Elizabeth to SNAD, Report of Inspector E. C. Allman, Reserve Location, 20 April 1903.

Table 6.2 March 1903 Population of Municipal and Private Locations in Port Elizabeth Compensation Procedure

Locations	Name of Owner	Compensation Paid By[a]	Amount of Compensation	Houses	Approximate Population
Municipal					
Strangers'	Municipality	Municipality	Various	100	405
Cooper's Kloof	Municipality	Municipality	Various	40	230
Reservoir	Municipality	Municipality	Various	500	1,563
Brickmaker's Kloof	Municipality	Municipality	Various	28	140
Mission Buildings	Municipality	Municipality	Various	12	60
Private					
Gubbs'	Syndicate	Government	£3,500	500	2,644
Harbor Bd.	Harbor Bd.	None[a]	None	119	326
Vlei Post	Various	Government	270	9[b]	340
Railway	Cape Govt. RR	Government	49	7	35
Gr'Town	Cape Govt. RR	Government	49	7	35
Hills' Slaughter House	Mr. Kemp, Mr. Wells, and others	Government	Various	600	3,000[c]
Korsten	—	—	—	—	—
Dassie's Kraal	—	—	—	—	—
Klein School	London Missionary Society	Government	420	60	300
Bethelsdorp	London Missionary Society	Government	105	15	75
Town					
"Native" houses	Various	Government	None	140	2,257

Walmer Municipality[d]

Emslie's	Mr. Emslie	None	None[e]	140 rooms, 9 cottages, 1 shop	912
Duffy's Kraal	Mrs. Duffy	None	None[e]	6	30
Municipal Camp	Walmer Municipality	None	None[e]	50 municipality tents	300
Findlay	Mr. Findlay	None	None[e]	2	27
Willet	Mr. Willet	None	None[e]	4	30
	Total		£4,393	2,340	12,712

Notes: a. Compensation was paid only for dwellings, not for property.

b. There were about nine wood and iron houses, average value £30.

c. A decision was made to leave the Korsten area "for further inquiry, because Africans who had moved to Korsten were entitled to a freehold under the 1896 agreement.

d. The Municipality of Walmer adjacent to Port Elizabeth was included as part of the District of Port Elizabeth. However, the Native Reserve [Urban] Locations Act of 1902 was inapplicable at Walmer.

e. Unauthorized location. The Municipal Inspector reported that the place was overcrowded and in an unsanitary condition.

Source: CAD NA607, B1673 Office of the Civil Commisioner of Port Elizabeth to SNAD, Report of Inspector E. C. Allman, Reserve Location, 20 April 1903.

classes migrated to Korsten during this period, and it was the Plague Board evictions that initiated the exodus. Thus, although the Plague Board helped to rid the town of at least half of the African population, they also contributed to the rise of Korsten, an unrestricted area, which provided Africans with an alternative to New Brighton and thus undermined the Act. Another obstacle to implementation of the Act resulted from the insensitive treatment meted out to Africans during the compensation procedure which left many of them bitter toward both the local and central government (see Table 6.2).[21] Not surprisingly, the Africans involved in the 1896 agreement were incensed at their predicament, which placed them in such a vulnerable position that the Town Council could deprive them of their right to freehold title. It will be recalled that under this agreement they were entitled to compensation for their dwelling and freehold title to a plot whenever they were removed to a new site.

The Town Council claimed, however, that, unfortunately, the new location Act nullified the 1896 local agreement and, as a result, they could pay compensation for only the dwellings. Since New Brighton would be administered by the central government, the question of freehold titles would have to be taken up with them. Meanwhile, once Africans accepted compensation payment, both the land at the Racecourse site, allocated in the 1896 agreement, and the land at Stranger's and Cooper's Kloof locations reverted to the Council. The Council held the winning hand, and the Africans ended up suffering a significant financial loss, especially because the land at Strangers' location, situated as it was in the center of town, was of considerable value. The value stood at about £10,000; this figure would increase considerably once the location was removed. In contrast, the land at New Brighton was valued at £20,000, but the area was three times the size of Strangers' and the site was five miles from town.[22] The tradeoff was inequitable, to say the least.

Even though the residents at Strangers' and Cooper's Kloof were paid compensation for their dwellings in the amount of £4,008 and £1,528, respectively, this was unsatisfactory in comparison to their right to freehold property ownership under the 1896 agreement, a right that was lost to them. Indeed, even if Africans moved to New Brighton, the probability of receiving freehold title was slim. Most Africans involved in the 1896 agreement probably believed that more pressure could be exerted from outside New Brighton than by moving there. Thus, as they received compensation they moved to Korsten or other areas, avoiding New Brighton. The compensation procedure was also causing problems at Gubbs' location. The central government had agreed to pay compensation to the African owners of the dwellings (see Table 6.2).[23] The Mill Park Estate Syndicate, owners of the Gubbs' site, wanted the government to pay them compensation for the loss of revenue, a proposition the government refused to consider. Despite the government's refusal, the Syndicate, perhaps anticipating reconsideration, held off closing Gubbs' until the last minute. As a result, two weeks after the Native Reserve Location Act was proclaimed, the Syndicate issued notices to the tenants that they must vacate the premises within 48 hours. Caught in the middle and hoping for a reprieve, the tenants requested two months' exemption from the Resident Magistrate.

Not only did the Magistrate refuse the exemption, but he also threatened to prosecute them if they did not "remove without delay. . . ."[24] Thus, almost 3,000 people had only two days to gather their belongings and find accommodations. Because notice was so short, many residents were unable to collect their compensation until after they had moved. At New Brighton one month's rent was required upon occupation. No doubt some Africans avoided the location simply because they had no funds to pay the rent. Many others, assuredly, must have resented and viewed with frustration and anger the callous treatment meted out by the Syndicate as well as the government and avoided New Brighton as a signal of their discontent. Still others chose areas that were not controlled by the government, where they could avoid restrictive regulations, build their own dwellings out of inexpensive materials, and pay a nominal rent for a site. In particular, self-built housing was an issue on which all classes could agree, because it cost much less for Africans to build their own houses than to pay rent for both dwellings and site.

As the proclamation date approached, the dissatisfaction of the African population with the discriminatory legislation and the government officials became increasing apparent. It seemed that Africans would rather live anywhere but New Brighton. June 1, the deadline date, came and went, and by the second week in June only about 400 Africans had relocated to New Brighton.[25] In July 1903 the Mayor reported that New Brighton's population was 800, whereas the Inspector of Native Locations, Mr. T. Dent, estimated two weeks later, a population of 1,200. Whatever the correct number, it was significantly below the projected population of 5,000. In contrast, Korsten's population ironically rose in July to approximately 5,000.[26]

From the point of view of the central government the refusal of most Africans to enter New Brighton created a financial and administrative disaster. Not only had the government expended a substantial amount of funds, about £98,000 thus far, to establish a location that was virtually empty, but also the possibility of exerting control over the African population had become even more remote.[27]

The large expenditure to establish the location was justified to the white ratepayers by such arguments as the following, stated to the House of Assembly by the Prime Minister, Sir Gordon Sprigg: "The Natives paid a rent for the use of the buildings so that the locations would not be any burden upon the colonial taxpayer, and the inhabitants would pay the interest upon the cost of establishing the locations."[28] Thus, it seemed that an immediate return on the investment was expected by the government, but this was not forthcoming, since Africans opted to enter Korsten.

Korsten was privately owned by whites and from 1854 had been laid out as a village.[29] Residing in the settlement were Africans, Europeans, Malays, Coloreds, and Chinese. By July 1903 the population had reached about 5,000; a year later it had risen to 7,000. It fell to 6,300 by 1905 because of prosecutions and voluntary outmigration.[30]

Most dwellings at Korsten were in poor condition, having been quickly constructed from corrugated iron and tin or other easily attainable materials and without spatial planning. The more "respectable" houses included doors and windows and brick and mortar fireplaces, but the majority of the 1,680 dwellings were declared unfit by the plague board. Water and sanitation facilities were virtually nonexistent. Many residents relied on rainwater, while others purchased water taken from the municipal waterpipes, and sold on the streets of Korsten by the barrel.[31] Notwithstanding these problems, most Africans did not see the need to relocate to New Brighton after the implementation of the Native Reserve [Urban] Locations Act in June 1903.

And the law did not stipulate that once the Africans left the town locations they had to enter New Brighton, since during the parliamentary debates and the select committee review the compulsory clause had been challenged by white liberals and leading Africans, which had prompted its withdrawal. Consequently, although non-exempted Africans continuing to live in town were subject to arrest and fine, they could choose not to enter New Brighton. Thus, the exempted population included not only domestics, voters, and employees living on their employer's premises but also thousands of other Africans who had moved to nearby settlements outside the municipal boundaries. Moreover, aside from the 5,000 blacks living at Korsten, there were about 600 people whose property had not been condemned remaining at Stranger's, while over 1,500 were still at Reservoir location because of a dispute between the residents and the Town Council regarding compensation for property and land rights.[32] Thus, almost half of the black population, many of them voting against the law with their feet, were exempt.

The government was well aware of African grievances against the establishment of the state "township" as a repressive, racist structure. Prior to the passage of Act 40 of the Native Reserve Locations Bill several black representatives testifying before the select committee expressed common grievances. Frank Makwena was opposed to the passes, the criminal penalty for non-payment of rent, the limits on businesses, the use and sale of alcohol, and the district-wide application of the bill. Whiley Pikoli, who was a general laborer and chairman of the Strangers' Location committee, stated that if the "oppressive clauses in the Bill, which will mean hard treatment to the natives," were not changed, the Africans would prefer to stay where they were. Moreover, at the regional level Africans had vigorously opposed the legislation. For example, the South African Native Congress, a regional organization made up mostly of Christian and Western-educated Africans, sent a resolution in October, 1902 emphasizing that it: "Considers [the Native Reserve Locations Bill] extreme, harsh, oppressive, seriously interfering with liberties of his Majesty's subjects and calculated to create widespread discontents. Approves principle of Government control of Municipal locations, but would limit powers of inspectors. *Fixity of tenure absolutely necessary.*"[33] Like Makwena and Pikoli, the Congress may have been primarily representing the interests of the property holders, yet clearly the above complaints touched on sentiments held by most blacks.

Leaders such as Makwena and Pikoli saw themselves as communicating African grievances to the Town Council, to the colonial government in negotiations and petitions and in testimony to committees. The objections against living at New Brighton provided the basis for a cross-class unity, since the leaders' opinions were shared by thousands of other Africans residing at Korsten.

Advantages at Korsten

There were specific restrictions under the Native Reserve Locations Act that influenced Africans to avoid New Brighton and to live at Korsten. Understandably, some regulations at New Brighton were unanimously disliked, such as the passes; others had a different degree of importance for the black Korstenites depending on their class background. For example, at New Brighton property ownership and self-built housing were not allowed. Housing and land ownership could provide the basis for an independent livelihood as well as for meeting the voting qualifications, which were major issues for middle and aspirant middle class Africans. In contrast, at Korsten the possibility of property ownership and house building was a perquisite enjoyed by all, and many had used their compensation money to buy land. As for those renting, it was often cheaper to pay a stand rent and erect their own dwellings.

Business opportunities at New Brighton were extremely limited, especially since the government tended to favor whites. Out of the fourteen trading stands there, only one was operated by an African.[34] Even renting rooms, an enterprise available in the old locations, was prohibited at New Brighton. At Korsten occupations (both legal and illegal) were more ubiquitous, despite competition among the various ethnic groups. Several Africans including William Wauchope and Moses Foley, both recognized as African leaders and both members of well-known Christian families, operated general stores. There were butchers, bakers, and other black shopkeepers who owned property at Korsten.[35] Further, numerous residents either added to their income or, like the father of Mr. A. Sangu, made a living renting out rooms.[36]

Africans living at New Brighton could not become landlords, nor could they offer their friends and relatives hospitality because the government wanted to discourage the settlement of the unemployed. By controlling the social and economic aspects of life outside the workplace, the state sought to create a dependent and compliant labor force. This was the role of the compounds and urban locations in the other colonies at the time.[37] However, Korstenites were free to operate businesses and to offer room and board to relatives and friends who had migrated to town for reasons of work, school, and health.

The most problematic and most lucrative business at Korsten that was forbidden at New Brighton was the liquor trade. Brewing and selling liquor had always been an important urban enterprise that the government had sought to control, and it remained a sphere of struggle between Africans and government authorities.[38] Newspaper accounts of court trials and police reports emphasize that the liquor home brewing problem that had plagued the municipal locations had been transferred to Korsten. Africans living in New Brighton, Reservoir and other areas now travelled to Korsten to obtain alcohol and to socialize often at a *shebeen* (a place where illegal liquor is sold and dancing often occurs) which was a popular pastime.

While the liquor trade could have ill effects on the work force, it could also supplement incomes, and it was a major activity for women, who were responsible in "traditional" society for brewing beer. It was an economic enterprise that required little special training or capital, that could be done at home by both women and men, and that produced a quick return. Thus it is not surprising that the trade drew in Christian and non-Christian, middle and working class, and illustrated the fluidity that existed between classes. Although many middle-class Christian Africans advocated temperance and liquor prohibition, as we have seen, others in this group were active in the brewing profession.[39] In any case, the independent livelihood derived from the liquor trade and other businesses by Africans played havoc with the government's plan to promote a black labor force dependent on wages.

Undoubtedly the greater independence, freedom of choice, and liberty from restrictions were clear advantages at Korsten and were of crucial importance to the residents. Thus, Mr. Sangu, who remembered growing up in Korsten in the early 1900s, answered with a distinct air of pride to the question "who controlled Korsten?" that "there was no such thing in those days as a headman or superintendent [appointed by the government], the people were property owners and paid rates at the Town Hall." Similar opinions were expressed by ex-Korstenites in the 1980s when recalling their residence in the freehold village, indicating that the issues of liberty and owning property were indeed potent ones.[40]

Black independence at Korsten was, however, viewed in a different light by the colonial officials. For example, Dr. John G. Uppleby, the District Surgeon for Port Elizabeth, thought it unfortunate that "a native free state has grown up outside the municipal boundaries at Korsten . . . [which] is practically under no supervision."[41] Given the several advantages in the socioeconomic and political realm of living at Korsten, it was unlikely that most Africans would voluntarily move to New Brighton if changes were not made. To this end, a government select committee was appointed in July 1903 to review the operation of the Act. Included among their recommendations was that the rent and railway fare at New Brighton be reduced and that an area be set aside where heads of "better-class" families would be allowed to rent a site and to erect their own dwellings.[42]

Anxious to gain tenants at New Brighton, the government offered its first "concession" by reducing the rent but not at the rates suggested by the select committee. The rate had been 30 shillings at the Class B and 25 shillings at the Class C housing for married couples (for a family of four). It was reduced to 25 shillings and 20 shillings, respectively. There was no rent reduction for single housing, which was 8 shillings for each person (in a wood-and-iron room built for five people), nor was the 6 shillings railway fare altered.[43] Given the relatively low wages of the black population, these scales were still prohibitive, consuming over one-third of their wages. By 1902, for instance, wages for the unskilled averaged between £39 to £72 per annum while some of the aspirant middle class were slightly better off, with their income ranging from £60 to £90 per annum. Thus, in 1904 African location police, messengers, and wardsmen were paid £60, interpreters at the Magistrate's Court £72, and assistant clerks, £81–90.[44] The average wage for married Africans was "18 shillings a week out of which food and clothing have to be purchased in addition to the payment of rents and railway fares."[45]

The government refused to lower the rental rates further because they had been set to ensure recovery of the government investment and not according to what the tenants could afford to pay. Criticism of the high rent had been rife, even drawing the observation from the Mayor of Port Elizabeth that a considerable profit would be made. Although he denied calling the government a rack-renter clearly this seemed to be the implication. Furthermore, neither the municipalities nor the colonial government wanted to tax the white ratepayers, so the decision was made to administer the location entirely through rent income.[46] In any case, the general opinion among whites was probably characterized by that of Dr. A. J. Gregory, Medical Officer of Health for Cape Colony, whose reports and statements strongly influenced many of the government's decisions. He believed that Africans could afford to pay the rent, and, as he explained to the Secretary of Native Affairs:

> The contention of Natives, so often put forward, that the rents charged . . . are unfairly high, is unsound, for, quite apart from all the other points, the health and Sanitary standard of the accommodation necessary to be provided must cost considerably more than the filthy accommodation which they are content to provide for themselves . . . it is difficult to understand why a native earning good wages should expect to be relieved of expenditure for Sanitary and Health needs anymore than a white man.[47]

Another government concession was aimed at the "better-class" Africans. It was agreed that Africans could apply to lease landsites at New Brighton where occupants could erect their own dwellings as long as they met official specifications. But the rental rate for the sites was significantly higher than in the old locations. As Reverend William Bottoman, the African minister at Edwards' Memorial Church in Korsten sardonically remarked: "It was proposed to charge a ground rental of £4.00 per annum. The natives had the same privilege in Port Elizabeth from the Town Council at £1.7s.6p. per annum."[48]

Especially influencing black middle-class reaction to the "concessions" was the complete omission of any reference to freehold title, the major objective of over 300 Christian heads of families representing about 1,800 people (based on an estimate of six people per family) who had been entitled to property under the 1896 agreement with the Port Elizabeth Town Council. As it stood, if they agreed to build on the government sites at New Brighton, they would simply be tenants, not landowners, and could be arbitrarily relocated. They also believed that the Cape government had reneged on a promise to provide freehold sites in New Brighton. Their belief was based on the fact that even before the Native Reserve Locations Act was passed, the colonial secretary, T. C. Graham, and other government officials, met with African representatives in Port Elizabeth in 1902 to discuss the removal. A verbal contract was struck that the central state should administer the "native" population, build a location, and fulfill the 1896 land agreement between the Town Council and the property holders.[49]

However, by the time the Act was passed, the basis for the 1901 verbal agreement had been completely altered by the government's decision to establish a "native" policy that would not only control the African working class but also limit opportunities for the middle class. The new statute created a location where all occupants would be tenants and denied property ownership, including land rights. Moreover, the administrators of the location churches and schools who in the past had been issued titles were also denied this privilege. By restricting these rights, the government would be able to use the law as a vehicle for disfranchisement, since Africans living at New Brighton would be unable to fulfil the property qualification either through buying on their own or purchasing missionary land. Undoubtedly, the authorities also wanted to withhold land rights to accommodate future removals whenever necessary. Then too if the status of the black population was to be redefined to facilitate segregation, it was particularly impolitic to continue to provide land, which was one of the major avenues through which Africans could avoid wage labor.

But the government had underestimated the groundswell of black popular opposition against moving to New Brighton. By ignoring African grievances, the State had to contend not only with general black hostility but also specifically with the Christian families who were adamantly opposed to entering New Brighton without land and house building rights. Although these families were now scattered—many evictees lived at Korsten while others remained at Stranger's and Reservoir—they were unified in opposition to resettlement. John McKay, a town councillor and former member of the legislative assembly, wrote to the Prime Minister warning that "there was a great deal of unrest among the natives [and that] unless there was a modification in the[ir] treatment . . . there will be trouble." McKay emphasized that those Africans with whom he was in daily contact taunted him with such words as, "Oh you preach goodwill to men, but if your doings are the outcome of Christianity, save us from it for we are treated as animals, not as human beings."[50] Although no disturbance erupted, disenchantment with the government was illustrated by the fact that between August 1903 and April 1904 not one African left Korsten to rent a leasehold site for £4.00 at New Brighton.[51]

After both the Town Council and colonial government had reneged on their promise to provide land, many Africans recognized that they would be able to protect their rights only if they could apply pressure to force government concessions. This was not only because they were denied comparable sites at New Brighton but also because they had a new agenda.

The Struggle for a Korsten Village Management Board

In any conflict the timing of repression and concession is crucial. Between 1901–1903, before the implementation of the Native Locations Act, there were occasions when Korsten Africans in general, and property owners in particular, might have moved readily into New Brighton. However, by mid-1903 many Africans had developed a new agenda. They had settled at Korsten; established churches, schools, and businesses, and were engaged in buying, leasing, and renting property. Moreover, middle class Africans wanted to fulfill their political, social, and economic ambitions. through the establishment of a Village Management Board (VMB). The VMB would set stand rents and taxes, provide sanitation and security, and in general represent the interests of the residents and serve as an "autonomous local authority and neither the Divisional nor the City Council could interfere in any way."[52] No longer would the current situation prevail whereby Korsten was supervised by the Divisional Council, which had limited powers. For instance, the Divisional Council had no authority to enforce sanitary or building regulations nor subdivision of land.

In the context of the period the issue of establishing a VMB was a radical one because it directly opposed the aims of the government. Such a structure held several advantages for the African residents, including self-governing status with a local board elected by the voters; security for property owners; stability for residents fearful of being removed to New Brighton; and the opportunity for Africans to administer, and thus to some extent control, their living space. These boards usually consisted of three elected members whose duties included framing regulations and administering roads and works and sanitation; property rates were paid to the Divisional Council. VMBs' operated in several areas of the Transkei and by the 1890s at Hackney and Kamastone in the eastern Cape where the chairmen were Africans.[53] However, the Korsten Board would be the first in an urban area where African could potentially gain some semblance of power.

Support for the VMB came from the mixed voting population at Korsten, and probably many white employers, dissatisfied with the workings of the Native Locations Act, were not averse to the notion. White employers were faced with African workers who showed their discontent by withholding their labor, arriving late, or, once having arrived, displaying a belligerent attitude. This was because prior to the Act most Africans walked to work and paid no transportation costs. But since New Brighton was further from their homes, in order to arrive at work on time, the residents were forced to rise earlier to take a train, and pay the added transportation costs, or walk the greater distance. The regular starting time was 6:30 a.m. Some white employers, anxious to ensure that their employees arrived before 8:00 a.m., began to pay their train fares. In effect, they were subsidizing their workers' wages to avoid losing even more money. As one official explained, "The merchants have got to pay their fares in order to carry on their business, because it is impossible to take delivery of goods delivered by the Harbor Board if you have no boys there to receive them. The Harbor Board insists that goods have to be taken delivery of before eight o'clock in the morning, in order to cope with the trade of the Port."[54] There had even been talk of a wage increase to accommodate the higher rents and train fare. The discussion emphasized the controversy over who would pay for segregation—the municipalities, the colonial government, or the employer.

Such talk promoted dissension among the whites, and many turned a blind eye to their employees settling at Korsten, which was within walking distance, thus eliminating the need for wage increases, train fares, and higher rents. In fact, many employers reacted by applying for exemptions to allow their workers to live on their premises, which also undermined the Act. A major culprit in undermining the law was the municipal Harbor Board; to exempt their employees, they set up a compound to house over 400 port workers shortly after the law was passed.[55]

Another group supporting the VMB were the landlords at Korsten who benefitted from sub-dividing their property for sale and lease to Africans. A few of these landlords were prosecuted under the private Native Reserve Locations Act of 1899, but the cases were difficult to prove, since those charged argued that they had entered into legal purchase agreements with the tenants. Also, some of the owners were Town Councillors such as Mr. Fox-Smith, a slum landlord who grasped the opportunity to provide housing for the evicted Africans by purchasing land in Korsten. Slum landlords had been a nuisance for many years, but as some were government officials and owned property in various areas where they accrued rack-renting profits, it was difficult to eliminate the problem.[56]

Opposition to the formation of the VMB came primarily from government officials anxious to bring Korsten under the control of the central government. For example, Dr. A. J. Gregory, the Medical Officer of Health for Cape Colony, a staunch proponent of the 1903 Native Reserve Location Act, argued that Korsten was unsanitary, the buildings dilapidated and it "should be permanently and promptly wiped out."[57] He further explained that the residents, both black and white were ill-equipped to form a board that could properly control sanitation and that its power would be insufficient to clean the area. Yet, Gregory's perspective about Africans serving on the board also reflected his racist beliefs about the ability and the right of Africans to administer, as well as the unacceptable race and class behavior of the whites. Thus, in correspondence to the Port Elizabeth Resident Magistrate, Dr. E. Walton, Gregory declared that there were only twenty-five Europeans at Korsten and many of these were irresponsible, implying that only whites could be considered as prospective board members despite the thousands of Africans at Korsten, many of them Western-educated.

Some officials wanted Korsten to be incorporated by the municipality or an amended Native Reserve Location Act passed to bring it under state jurisdiction. However, many of them vacillated, much like the Port Elizabeth Mayor, first supporting the incorporation of Korsten and then, after realizing the financial costs, supporting the VMB. Meanwhile, the postwar Parliamentary election in 1903, gave Africans an opportunity to use their votes to lobby for a VMB.

The 1903–1904 Election

The timing of the movement for this particular VMB was fortuitous for the black voters, since both political parties needed their vote and because the formation of a Board at Korsten became a key campaign issue. In 1903 the voters had a clear choice between the Progressive Party (PP) and the South African Party (SAP). The former was made up primarily of Englishmen, many of whom were part of the commercial class at the Cape with financial interests in Kimberley and the Transvaal. Led by Leander Starr Jameson, the Progressive Party issued a platform manifest favoring the growth of the colonies in close co-operation with Britain; support for Sir Alfred Milner, the British High Commissioner and Governor of the Cape and Transvaal; and Rhodes' policy of equal rights for all civilized men (although initially the statement was "equal rights for all civilized white men") and elevation of the "native" races. The definition of elevating "natives" was synonymous with "civilizing natives" and, as Cope has recently discussed, "civilizing natives" was closely associated with the European institution of wage labor,[58] which in practice meant finding ways to compel Africans to work for whites, a goal with which whites in both parties agreed. All Progressive Party candidates had to pledge their allegiance, which took the form of a promise "that he would resign if he should differ from the majority of the caucus."[59]

The South African Party, controlled by the Afrikaner Bond, included English moderates and liberals; they desired federation and growth of the colonies without British interference. On the native question a few well-known "friends of the natives," including J. W. Sauer and J. X. Merriman (head of the South African Party), both had allied with the Bond after the 1896 Jameson Raid, continued to support limited privileges for Africans. But both Merriman and Sauer were defeated, at least partially, because of remarks made by Transvaal Prime Minister Louis Botha on the importation of Chinese labor to work in the Transvaal gold mines, which was a major issue of the day and one which African voters opposed.

Both parties claimed to be opposed to the importation of Chinese labor. The South African Party argued that the Progressives, who had financial interests in the mines and who wholeheartedly supported Milner, favored the introduction of Chinese labor. They "told the Bantu [Africans] that the introduction of Asiatics would deprive them of work on the Rand and that these Asiatics would soon compete with them in other fields of labor."[60] Merriman and others denied this, and they were supported by John Tengo Jabavu, editor of *Imvo*. Jabavu was a long-time Merriman advocate and he advised African voters to cast their ballot for liberal individuals who worked in their interest rather than simply Progressive Party politicians who were campaigning along "race" lines as the English party against the Dutch South African Party. However, when Botha "proposed as an alternative to Chinese importation, that the Bantu reserves . . . be broken up and the natives forced on to the labor market," his remarks struck a death blow to much of the African support for the South African Party. Jameson declared to a colleague about Botha's comments that "you may be sure we shall use [it] for all it is worth," and they did, by claiming that Botha's remarks represented the Bond's native policy and conjointly the South African Party.[61]

Although the Progressives claimed to oppose Chinese importation, in fact many of them, because of their financial interests in the Transvaal, favored it but were fearful of open support lest Africans withhold their votes. The Progressives in the Cape and the Transvaal wanted a South Africa firmly tied to Britain and industrially strong through the development of the deep level goldmines. The reconstruction of the Transvaal mining industry, a pivotal point in the development of a future South Africa, required cheap labor.

Following the war, black workers had withheld their labor primarily because the Transvaal Chamber of Mines had cut their wages. As a short-term remedy, Milner, the architect of post-war reconstruction, had submitted a proposal for the importation of Chinese labor to work the gold mines.[62] In the long run the colonial government intended to create a migrant labor system to facilitate the exploitation of cheap African labor. Viewed within the context of building a national infrastructure for capitalist growth, the experiment in Port Elizabeth and Cape Town takes on heightened importance. The right of blacks to own land in the urban areas was clearly undesirable if a new policy were to emerge to replace the liberal idea of incorporation.

Although the number of enfranchised blacks was small compared to the number of Europeans, Africans tended to vote *en bloc*, increasing their effectiveness. Thus, African grievances had to be seriously considered. In particular, the Progressive Party needed African support if they were to win since the English were the minority white group and it was normally the Bond that controlled the Parliament. It is also noteworthy that much of the black population that was not on the voter roll attended meetings and voiced their grievances, and the politicians had to take this into account. In Port Elizabeth out of a total registered voting population of 10,952 at least 1,114 were African, and perhaps more since some Africans were listed as Colored. The white voters numbered 8,486, while the Colored totalled 1,041. About 338 Korstenites were listed.[63]

Although Port Elizabeth was a Progressive Party stronghold, the election was not guaranteed, and here the Progressives proved their shrewdness, because it was they who supported the burning local issue affecting the black voters—the establishment of a Korsten VMB.[64] At the election meetings a major topic of discussion was the repeated attempts by the Korsten Committee, made up of residents of all races, and the Legislative Council members, to gain approval from Prime Minister Sprigg for the VMB. But when Sprigg visited Port Elizabeth on a campaign stop in early October 1903, he conceded that the government might approve building rights and freehold title at New Brighton to the Korsten land holders and voters, but he refused to discuss the question of establishing a VMB, which is exactly the reason why much of the audience had attended.[65]

Several Africans spoke in support of a VMB, including the well-known African leader, Moses Foley, the owner of a general dealer's shop at Korsten, who exclaimed that: "Sir Gordon [Sprigg] had said they should progress, and the natives would be thankful if . . . [he] would sanction a Village Management Board, so that they could manage their affairs like civilized people."[66] Supportive comments came from Frank Makwena:

> He wanted the Government to give them an opportunity of showing that they could govern themselves. If they were always to be governed by other people and shifted into another location, their children would say they were incompetent to manage their own affairs . . . it was only recently they had to carry their things from other locations, and they did not know where to have worship, and as soon as they were again settled there came a movement to shift them to another site.[67]

A week later a big meeting was held at Korsten for the Progressive Legislative Assembly candidates Messrs. Wilmot, John Pyott, and Hurndall. Sprigg and the South African Party were bitterly criticized but more importantly the candidates, the Mayor, and some of the Town Councillors and merchants pledged to support the formation of a Korsten VMB.

The Progressive Party won the 1903 Legislative Council elections by a majority of one, and in 1904 they carried the Assembly elections by six seats. Soon after, the government approved the establishment of a Korsten VMB, which was elected on July 6 1904. Most residents took a holiday, and enthusiasm was high. Altogether about one hundred fifty votes were cast at the Congregational Church at Korsten for the six candidates. The three elected were Moses D. Foley, a member of several organizations including the *Iliso Lomzi,* and the African and American Working Men's Union; William J. Kemp, a white businessmen who owned the Korsten brickyards and several plots; and Matthew Johnstone, on whom information is lacking although it is likely that he was Colored which means that the VMB was representative of most of the "races" at Korsten.[68] But the Board was given little opportunity to administer the village. In December 1904, after functioning for approximately four months, it was unceremoniously dissolved by the Prime Minister.[69]

This startling development leads one to raise a number of questions. Were there other motives behind Progressive support for the formation of a Korsten VMB? Was their support a response to African and white demands? A fulfillment of the election promise? A realization that the amended Native Locations Bill required further changes? A rejection of the task of administering Korsten? Certainly all these issues were influential. The evidence suggests, however, that most important was the Progressives' need for the African vote in order to put through the Additional Representation Bill shortly after the election.

For quite some time the question of additional representation had been debated. It is noteworthy that at the beginning of the 1904 Parliament the Additional Representation Bill promoted by the Progressives came up for vote. The legislation called for the creation of three Legislative Council seats and twelve Legislative Assembly seats. Because most of the seats would represent urban areas, where the Progressives were favored and where the English were stronger, the Bill promised to increase representation especially in the southeastern circle, which included Port Elizabeth.[70] While the Progressives hoped to gain a larger majority in Parliament through passage of this bill, the South African Party was bitterly opposed, declaring that it was meant to crush the Bond. For the most part African voters supported the bill, which became law on April 22, 1904. A few months later, after a lively campaign, three more Progressives were elected for Port Elizabeth. It is significant that at the campaign meetings these candidates cited their track record in bringing about the formation of a Korsten VMB.[71]

Undoubtedly the Progressive party realized that it would need the African vote to elect additional representatives in 1904, and to ensure black support they agreed to promote the formation of a VMB. But once these elections were over, Progressive support began to evaporate. In an attempt to bind the candidates to their word, prior to the 1903 election enfranchised Africans had required them to sign a document "promising to do all in their power to get a VMB appointed."[72] The Progressives kept their promise and then rapidly found justification for recanting.

For example, a few months after the Board was elected, Colonel Crewe, the Cape Colonial Secretary, visited Port Elizabeth as part of a general fact-finding tour of eastern Cape towns and also in response to complaints about the unsanitary state of Korsten. Crewe met with local officials, who wanted to know how the state intended to alleviate the plague and whether or not the Native Locations Act would be enforced. He also met with New Brighton traders who complained that their businesses were failing because the consumers the government had promised had not materialized.[73] Both the officials and traders would benefit from a dissolved board and an amended Native Locations Act, since the Council would no longer have to contemplate the expense of absorbing Korsten, while an increased population at New Brighton could save the traders' businesses.

Next Colonel Crewe inspected New Brighton and Korsten. Afterwards he heartily praised the former, especially its sanitation facilities while the latter was harshly criticized for unsanitation. On meeting the Korsten residents, Crewe threatened to dissolve the Board if improvements were not made in three months, stating that his decision would be based on a report from the Acting Resident Magistrate at Port Elizabeth, H. C. Becker. He was a well-known critic, and, not surprisingly, he unhesitantly recommended in November 1904 that the Board be withdrawn.[74]

The government's willingness to abolish the VMB was not extraordinary, since aside from the sanitation problem, Korsten as an entity was steep competition with New Brighton. Other methods to compel Africans to enter the "township" had already been tried, with limited effect. For example, New Brighton's population had risen from 800 in July 1903 to 2,125 in December 1904 as a result of prosecutions and evictions; all the married housing was full, but over a thousand single units were vacant. However, complaints from the opposition had led to a cessation in prosecutions, and Africans had moved back to their old dwellings; New Brighton's numbers fell in March 1904 to 1,000.[75]

Yet it is noteworthy that most of the evictions affected the Reservoir location, and some of the families forced out in December 1903 were apparently persuaded by Whiley Pikoli to enter New Brighton. His change of mind represented a crack in the leadership, since he had been opposed to accepting government "concessions." Unquestionably the opportunity to become the only black trader at New Brighton in October 1903 influenced his decision. Pikoli's collaboration with the government broke the unity among the property owners as well as lowered his esteem, and he admitted that "my friends at the Reservoir location and at Korsten are cross with me for coming to open a shop here."[76] Nonetheless, for the most part the African property owners continued to avoid New Brighton, and the government began to prepare plans to use the Health Act and to amend the Native Locations Act to compel Korstenites to move. In December 1904, the same month that the VMB was disbanded, the Colonial

Secretary authorized the use of the Public Health Act at Korsten. This was done on the advice of the MOH who had suggested that the Public Health Act be used to evict non-exempted Africans at Korsten, and that once this was accomplished, the amended Native Locations Act due to be submitted to Parliament in 1905 should be implemented.[77] The amended law would extend the boundaries ten miles so that non-exempted Africans living in Korsten would have to move elsewhere, although again it would not be mandatory that they enter New Brighton. Thus, the Health statute could be used to force non-exempted Africans out of Korsten and the amended Native Locations Act to keep them out.

But almost four months elapsed while Port Elizabeth Town Council members and colonial government officials debated the legality of applying the Health Act to Korsten and tried to draw up a suitable regulation that would pre-empt and neutralize black and white opposition. The problem was the need to meet the stipulation under Section 15 of the Health Act that an "urgent necessity" to prevent the spread of disease must exist for the Act to be applied. But five months had passed since the last reported plague case at Korsten. As Dr. Gregory pointed out, "the persons affected by its operation would seize upon the fact that Plague is not now greatly in evidence to protest against the promulgation of the regulation."[78]

During the delay the colonial government tried to arrange an agreement with the Korsten property owners to ensure a voluntary move to New Brighton. If their co-operation could be gained, it would be much easier to apply the legislation to the other Africans, since much of the organized resistance would be nullified. Consequently, in early 1905 Becker was authorized to meet with an African deputation to offer freehold title at New Brighton. However, the deputation refused the offer, demanding that the VMB be re-established. Only if there was to be no VMB would they consider moving to New Brighton, and if so, they wanted full compensation for their property at Korsten and a right to a freehold plot in the "township."[79]

Unable to negotiate with Becker, the opposition sent a four-man deputation to Cape Town to meet with the Prime Minister on March 24, 1905. This was prior to implementation of the Health Act and passage of the amended Native Locations Bill. Among the delegates were Reverend William Bottomon, Tobias Mvula, and William Wauchope. Also present was Mr. F.Z.S. Peregrino, an immigrant to Cape Town in 1900 from Accra, Ghana, and editor of the *South African Spectator,* a newspaper of opinion about Coloreds and Africans. The delegation repeated the demand made to Becker and stated that "The people who owned land and had vested interests at Korsten were anxious to assist the Government; and that they would be in a better position to do so if they had the Board and further that they were fully determined to give their aid in removing the "float-ing population" and the undesirables to whose presence the difficulties that had occurred were mainly attributable."[80] However, they continued, if the government refused to re-establish the VMB, then black property owners should receive land and compensation if they moved into New Brighton.

At the meeting Prime Minister Jameson agreed to pay £5,000 in com-pensation and to consider reforming the Board when Korsten was clean and sanitary and the non-exempted Africans were removed. Jameson in-sisted that it was not intended to use the legislation to move the "landed proprietors," only the "floating population," a catch-all term that in-cluded black migrant and permanent workers, the unemployed, crimi-nals, and the non-Christian, all of whom were considered "uncivilized." The deputation agreed.[81]

These government concessions persuaded the black leaders to co-oper-ate, since the interests of the middle class would be served. In return for their co-operation the deputation apparently expected the government to re-establish the VMB in Korsten and to exempt the property owners and voters from the amended Act. The agreement between the government and the deputation to collaborate in removing the "floating population" from Korsten denoted their acceptance that the policy of segregation would differentiate between Africans based on race and class. At this point the leaders were preoccupied with protecting the rights of the prop-erty owners, and the issues that affected all Africans at Korsten became secondary to securing the right to own land in the urban area. Although it seems that the deputation was not authorized to make a final decision until it had reported back to the Korsten residents, there seemed to be lit-tle doubt that the agreement would be supported. As the meeting con-cluded, it was agreed at Jameson's suggestion that a Korsten Advisory Committee would be formed "to advise the government as to the best manner of carrying out the measures now in progress." However, when the deputation returned to Port Elizabeth, it found that in its absence the government had implemented the Health Act and an explosive situation had developed.

The Korsten Test Case and African Women

On April 1, 1905, over three hundred eviction notices had been served by the police on Korstenites. They were authorized by the Civil Commis-sioner and Acting Resident Magistrate of Port Elizabeth, Mr. H. C. Becker. Becker was also chairman of the Plague Board. As they served the notices the police told the people to go to New Brighton. Members of the Plague Board, the coordinating government body that would cleanse Korsten, designated specific blocks of areas as unsanitary and ordered them closed permanently or temporarily for repairs. Once these blocks were selected, then individuals had been issued eviction notices. The area at Korsten called "Hills Location" was the first *en bloc* area targeted. Of the three hundred notices sent out, only thirty met with compliance. Meanwhile, many of the Korsten residents informed the authorities that they did not intend to move. Among those also issued notices were property owners and law-abiding Christians, which seemed to belie Jameson's promise to evict only the "floating population."[82]

One determined Christian African woman named Mrs. Tsotsole who refused to obey the order evicting her family became the focus of a court trial when she was arrested at Korsten. African and white alike realized that the court case would be a barometer by which to gauge government enforcement and also to gauge how Christians would be treated. The background of this case deserves analysis because what occurred prior to, during, and after the arrest indicates that the woman's actions were part of a specific strategy of African resistance that pitted the men and women against the government and pushed the women to the forefront.

Apparently shortly after the eviction notices were served, the deputation returned from Cape Town and finding the people in an uproar, had to respond quickly to a deteriorating situation. Thereafter the African men and women began to meet to decide on a protest strategy. By this time not only were Africans adamantly against obeying the eviction notices, they were also probably less than pleased with their primary African leaders who had consented to the removal of the "floating population." But the leaders had not intended for the government to evict Korstenites like Mrs. Tsotsole who were Christians and "better-class" permanent dwellers. The problem was that the property of these residents was in poor condition, and so they were treated by government as part of the "floating population." Yet once they were ousted from Korsten and the amended Native Locations Act was passed and implemented, they might not be able to return. The government promised the titleholders they could return once their property was sanitary. But if they obeyed the special health regulation, they could be forced into New Brighton unless they could afford to go elsewhere.

Moreover, if they relented and moved voluntarily to New Brighton, their property, land, housing and voting rights would be lost. In many cases Africans had made a downpayment on the land to the white owners on the "easy-payment plan" and built a house; this, too, would be sacrificed.[83] Also lost would be their civil and human rights to move about freely and make their own decisions. This was true for both the men and the women, except for the voting rights held only by men.

The land factor cannot be overemphasized, since it allowed economic freedoms at Korsten unattainable at New Brighton. One of these freedoms was the decision not to work for the whites, which owning land at Korsten could facilitate. It has been noted by other authors that African mothers and fathers worried about their daughters' virtue and the corrupting influences of the town on their male and female children. On this account one official stated that "some African parents would not allow their daughters to go to town to work unless special arrangements were made and even then the daughters were often compromised. Town service has become abhorrent to the best class of parents."[84] Doubtless many parents at Port Elizabeth worried about their daughter's exposure to corrupting influences as the girls worked as servants to whites in the town. Thus, the opportunities owning land at Korsten offered for Africans to supplement their income, for example through subletting, opening a business, or using family labor rather than sending them out to work for whites was a significant issue.

It will be recalled that some of the Christian women who held prescriptive rights to land at the Municipal locations had moved to Korsten and purchased land or rented sites. Thus, besides having already been subjected to eviction by the plague board they also would lose their land rights as individuals or as family members. In addition, since Mrs. Tsotsole was not the owner of the house, if she were convicted, the government would establish a precedent of arresting and charging anyone residing on the premises.

A point worth mentioning that probably influenced the decision to resist this particular regulation is that many African men and women had past experiences with police and native affairs officials who abused the laws by illegally entering and searching their homes. Evidently as early as the 1890s, it was a routine practice for the Superintendent of Locations to peek into the homes of residents and to use his master key to enter when they were out. The government defended these actions in court as necessary to curtail crime, in particular "kafir" beer brewing.[85] Obviously this was a practice that was open to abuse, with many Africans growing resentful of indiscriminate entry into their homes.

Although eventually the Superintendent of Locations was reprimanded by the town council and Africans were informed that these entries were illegal, they continued.[86] In fact, responding to information that the Superintendent's actions were illegal, in 1892 several African women refused to allow him to enter their homes to search for liquor. For this they were charged with breaking a colonial law, arrested, and convicted.[87]

Similar actions that Africans doubtless construed as illegal entry were carried out by colonial authorities in 1904, such as early morning police raids to enforce the Native Reserve Locations Act. As mentioned, the raids took place at odd hours of the morning to catch more non-exempted people in the net. Many Africans were arrested and convicted of violating the law and then advised to go to New Brighton. Under these circumstances it was not unusual for Africans of all classes to exhibit community solidarity in resisting police attempts to enforce colonial laws.[88] At Korsten, for example, Detective Quirk complained of a code of silence when "two native storebreakers escaped from the local *gaol* and were last heard of in Korsten . . . I cannot trace them as their friends refuse to assist me or give any information." Similarly, at Reservoir location when the police tried to arrest a man for receiving stolen property, "his house was quickly surrounded by at least 150 drunken natives who threatened them." To avoid conflict, the man was not handcuffed, and when the police arrived at the station, the stolen articles had disappeared and the case could not be proved. The point is that based on their collective experiences Africans had good reason to be wary of government officials entering their territorial boundaries to enforce the colonial laws.

Meanwhile, the decision to challenge the regulation was made and Mrs. Tsotsole became the main player. The sequence of events regarding the eviction notice were as follows. The first notice was served on Mrs. Tsotsole on the 5th of April by the police, "telling her to leave by the 8th."[89] Bad weather on the weekend extended the removal day to Monday. Mr. H. C. Becker, Civil Commissioner and Acting Resident Magistrate, had been authorized by the Colonial Secretary to use any force necessary for compliance with the order. It was Becker who personally told the accused woman to leave by 3:00 p.m. on Monday afternoon, the 10th of April, but that was again extended to Wednesday. Back again on Tuesday, Becker, in the presence of Mrs. Tsotsole, instructed Sergeant Strang, "if she had not removed by then to use force to remove her from the premises and to put her things outside."[90] Some of the Korsten residents were holding a religious ceremony, and one wonders if Becker threatened Mrs. Tsotsole in front of this crowd. In any case, this is how Strang came to be at house #33 in a section of Korsten called Hill's Location [much of the adjacent land was owned by town councillor, Mr. Fox-Smith], on Wednesday at 3:15 p.m. trying to force the woman to give him the keys.

Apparently it was agreed that the men would stay away from the area, either going to work or elsewhere and the women would refuse to co-operate. So when Strang asked her name three times, Mrs. Tsotsole quietly but firmly refused to co-operate in her own eviction. She declined to give it to him. She did tell him, however, when he requested the keys and indicated that he "was going to carry out the orders of the Magistrate" that "he could carry out the orders of the Magistrate, but that they never gave keys to strangers. She further told him that if he brought back her husband the police could get the key." Clearly this was a ploy, since her husband was well aware of the eviction notices, and they were expecting Sergeant Strang that day. Indeed, only that morning the R. M., Mr. Becker, had told Mr. Tsotsole "to go out and prevent a scene, but he said he would not."[91] The officer refused to wait for her husband, especially since this was the third eviction notice. Instead, he arrested Mrs. Tsotsole and took her to the police station.

Mrs. Tsotsole did not face the police alone—it was reported that over 300 people, mostly women and children but also a few men, crowded the yard where they were holding a religious service. It may be coincidence that there were reports of three hundred eviction notices and three hundred people at the prayer vigil in anticipation of the evictions. Also present were Tobias Umvola, [Mvula] and William Wauchope, both members of the deputation to Cape Town and second generation members of the emergent black middle class.

Prior to travelling to Cape Town, Mvula was advising "natives" not to go to New Brighton.[92] As a result, the Resident Magistrate at Port Elizabeth had warned the Secretary of Native Affairs that Mvula would possibly be the chief stumbling block to a settlement. Mvula knew perhaps more than others how important the Korsten VMB was to the emergent African middle class in gaining a foothold to pull up the "race" in the urban colonial society. He was probably especially bitter at the VMB having been abolished in December 1904, since he had been elected sanitary inspector for the Korsten VMB, resigned his job and was due to begin work on January 1, 1905.[93]

It is clear that many Africans being evicted viewed the government's actions, represented by the police and the Resident Magistrate, as illegally using the law to enforce an unpopular colonial regulation. An underlying issue in the minds of many was the abolishment of the Korsten VMB which represented Africans and their interest, and the belief that if it were reappointed, it would have resolved the sanitation problems. This issue was alluded to at the court trial, but the RM refused to allow it to be brought into the case. Many Africans felt that the VMB was not given a chance because, neither the local nor the central government wanted Africans to administer Korsten, since this would serve to draw other Africans to the area and also support the growth of a freehold black community with voting rights. Furthermore, Africans said that the VMB was abolished to get rid of a legitimate local authority that could protest against the application of the Health Act. Certainly this fact was in the minds of the African leadership and their followers as they attended the trial.

In the court case, brought on April 12, 1905, the African woman was accused of "wrongfully and unlawfully and willfully refusing entrance to one John Strang, a sergeant in the Cape police.[94] The police were attempting to enforce the special health regulation authorizing them to close unsanitary dwellings. It required "that all persons who were not exempted were to remove from or cease to reside within the area."[95] In effect, the woman had refused to allow Strang admission to her house and was charged with hindering police officers in the execution of their duty. She pleaded not guilty. Reminiscent of the bubonic plague proclamation of 1901 in its discrimination against Africans as well as in the reaction of the women, this special health regulation was applicable only to Africans residing in Korsten and the women combined in protest against racial and gender exploitation. The fact that the police arrived to evict the woman in the afternoon when the men were away at work may indicate that the officials viewed the women as the weaker element and less able to defend themselves. As we have seen, the authorities were in for a surprise.

The courtroom was jammed for the trial. Several newspapers reported on the large number of Africans, both male and female but predominantly women, in the courtroom and also about those who waited outside during the proceedings which lasted all day. Mr. Brown, hired by the Korsten VMB, defended Mrs. Tsotsole. Having had only a short time to prepare the defense he argued that the authority vested in the police by the special regulation was illegal. And even if the police intended to enforce the eviction notice, they had no right to enter the house with the intention of taking away goods. In essence, Brown was arguing that the police wanted to stretch the law to cover illegal entry into the defendant's home and try to force her to go to New Brighton. Of course, this was the aim of the trooper in evicting the resident although legally he could not force Africans to go to New Brighton. However, Sergeant Sprang as he tried to evict Mrs. Tsotsole "asked the woman to go to the New Brighton location."[96]

Then Brown used the gender card, in stating that "the law laid down that the wife was under the control of the husband. Therefore why had the husband not been brought forward. He was the proper person." Brown continued that the whole case was full of difficulties and anyway "everybody knew that New Brighton was a white elephant, and the government wanted to blacken it with natives."[97]

Although the reports do not indicate that Mrs. Tsotsole testified in her own behalf (she could speak English quite well), Mvula and Wauchope did testify about what they saw the day of the arrest. At the trial Mvula stated that he had acted as an interpreter between Sergeant Strang and Mrs. Tsotsole. He called her a model of Christianity and said that he had known her since childhood, indicating that she was probably born, raised, and married in Port Elizabeth. Both Wauchope and Mvula stated that Mrs. Tsotsole would never use filthy language, disputing a claim made by the police.[98] Their testimony paints a picture of a model female citizen of good character, just the type of person that would be needed to challenge an unjust law if such a strategy were agreed upon.

But the Acting RM Barry rejected Attorney Brown's argument and the good character testimony and pronounced Mrs. Tsotsole guilty. The disappointment of the Africans who filled the courtroom at the guilty verdict must have been audibly impressive. However, the verdict was no surprise, since, as Chief Constable Hingle of the Cape police stated at the beginning of the trial "if the case was not resolved it would be too difficult to enforce the regulation . . . and would interfere with the removal."[99] Clearly, the primary objective of the colonial authorities was to evict Africans from Korsten and to rule in favor of Mrs. Tsotsole would undermine their aims. Barry fined Mrs. Tsotsole £6 pounds or five weeks *gaol.* The fine was paid and an appeal lodged.[100] The case adjourned at 5:15 p.m., and "the scene as a large number of "Kafir" women left the Court attracted great attention."[101]

Despite the verdict, more Africans refused to move and were prosecuted. This was the state of affairs a few days later when the deputation met with the Korstenites to report back from Cape Town. At the meeting tension was high, and it was apparent that the whites were fearful that Africans would react with violence. D. M. Brown, a white lawyer, who had defended Mrs. Tsotsole, cautioned the crowd not to use force and not to resist the law. He also stated that, "Help would be given them as long as they kept with the law, and he advised them to keep their hot-headed wives at home. He called upon the men to fight the battle, and hoped the police would arrest no more women, let the men go to prison, and not the women—but when they did go to prison let them see that they had justice on their side."[102]

Brown advised the men to remain non-violent and to control their wives. But the men were not totally ignorant of what the women intended to do. For that matter, neither was Brown, since he had been working with the Korsten VMB prior to the deputation travelling to Cape Town. It appears that the men probably believed that the officials would not arrest the females. Once Mrs. Tsotsole was arrested, she had the support of the community, and Brown insisted at the trial that she had every right to refuse to allow the police to enter her home. Nonetheless, Brown's comments imply that it was expected that the women's rightful place was to maintain a more tranquil and domestic role rather than challenging government edicts.

The large number of women attending the religious service and waiting for the police on the day of the arrest is clear evidence of the organizational power of the women; it emphasizes that at an early date they relied on the Christian religion and their beliefs to challenge what they viewed as unjust laws. The quick response of the women and their unity and co-operation points to the existence of *manyanos,* or prayer unions, that could be drawn upon when needed. One wonders how involved the ministers were and if they were at the religious meetings on Tuesday and Wednesday. It seems likely that Reverend William Bottoman, the African minister mentioned earlier who was a member of the deputation to Cape Town, and also a long-time leader among Africans in Port Elizabeth, was probably among the few men. A number of churches were situated at Korsten, including the old Wesleyan Methodist Edward's Memorial Church and several African independent churches. One also wonders why the police focused on the Tsotsole family. Mrs. Tsotsole and/or her husband were probably recognized leaders in the Christian African community. We know that Mvula had known the woman since childhood, so she was more than likely born and raised in Port Elizabeth, and the Resident Magistrate knew her husband. These are questions that for now must remain largely unanswered. However, in later years other women in other places would go to prison rather than obey unjust and racially discriminatory laws, for example in the women's anti-pass campaigns.[103]

Meanwhile, the guilty verdict opened the way for the Port Elizabeth Municipality to proceed with evicting Africans from Korsten. Colonel Stanford, the newly appointed Secretary to the Native Affairs Department, was sent to Port Elizabeth to mediate and oversee the removals, since there was a real fear among whites that violence would erupt. As one official had emphasized, the exact method of application would require careful consideration because, "the Port Elizabeth natives are adepts at engineering strikes and disturbances and unless great care and tact is exercised forcible resistance may be experienced and even bloodshed may result."[104] This may explain why, on meeting with the Korsten Committee, Stanford thought it necessary to have a forty-man armed police detachment on standby in clear view. When the leaders complained about the troops, Stanford replied that "there was no good reason why it should destroy the comfort of any well intentioned man."[105] Clearly he wanted it understood that coercion was at hand if the leaders did not co-operate.

Stanford assured the representatives consisting of whites, coloreds, and blacks that only the "floating population" would be removed. Any "respectable" individuals evicted would be relocated temporarily, and when repairs were complete, they could move back into their houses. Stanford's emphasis on the exemption of the "respectable" was a response to complaints from blacks and whites that property owners and voters alike should be exempted. It was also a deliberate ploy to gain the support of the black middle class and to split the opposition, which he frankly admitted in correspondence to another official: "I regard this concession as being educative in its nature, in that it is intended to accustom the minds of the Natives to the distinctions which are to be observed in determining what classes will eventually be permitted to remain at Korsten to the exclusion of all others quite apart from the Public Health Act now being enforced."[106]

Apparently the role of the Korsten committee was to identify the exempted, which was determined by their "civilized" status, as the police went block by block "picking out" the people who would have to move.[107] Some of the African leaders were understandably suspicious of government promises regarding the fate of "civilized" Africans who were only supposed to be moved temporarily. Moreover, they questioned the motives for using the Health Act. Thus, a group of Africans, many of them members of the deputation that had travelled to Cape Town, charged that the government had opportunistically fabricated the plague case at Korsten in March 1905 to justify using the Health Act to remove Africans, whereas other areas where plague existed were not condemned. The accusation was supported by the fact that over a period of several months only the one "questionable" plague case was reported at Korsten compared to at least four in the same period at New Brighton.[108] Moreover, the government was aware that the source of the plague was the merchant general stores, and these were allowed to continue operating.

The amended Native Locations Act was applied in May 1905 at Korsten and other areas to remove the non-exempted. Significantly, the Act had been amended to exempt the owners of property valued at £75. Both blacks and whites had protested that this figure was too high; the Korsten siteholders of all races had petitioned the Town Council requesting a £50 exemption, since more Africans, including those who used land for agricultural purposes, could meet this qualification.[109] By placing the exemption at £75 (the same as the voting requirement), the Parliament was able to split off those who leased or owned less valuable property, many of them members of the aspirant middle class, and force a larger number of Africans into New Brighton. Also, those already evicted would not be exempted. Thus, blacks buying property on the installment plan were not exempted, and the Parliament voted against paying them compensation despite protests from liberal members of both political parties.[110] Yet the inability of the government to enforce the legislation was clear—in spite of the early morning raids and subsequent prosecutions—so that Africans evicted from Korsten continued to move back or to other areas to avoid New Brighton.[111]

Following the evictions the government re-established the Korsten VMB in October 1905. One reason was to avoid the financial burden of administering Korsten once the government had used the legislation to force Africans into New Brighton. Another was to salvage the liberal alliance by fulfilling the agreement made with the Korsten Africans. But the control the African middle class had hoped for was elusive, since when the VMB was re-established, the black voters were forced to agree to the stipulation that during the first year only whites would serve as board members.[112] Given the choice of no VMB or one with only whites, these Africans chose what they felt was the lesser evil. This stipulation was doubtless fostered by some of the white slum landlords at Korsten, who had resented the composition of the first board. But the VMB became an autocratic board one with virtually the same members until its disband-ment in 1931 when Korsten was incorporated into the Municipality.[113]

In the 1930s the government used the Slums Act, citing ironically, a breakout of bubonic plague, to force Africans to move out of Korsten. As had been the case at the turn of the century, this legislation was only par-tially successful, and Africans remained in Korsten despite continued ef-forts to remove them into the 1950s.[114]

Conclusion

The Cape colonial government was never able to translate the 1902 Na-tive Reserve Locations Act into effective policy because of opposition from both whites and Africans. Several options remained that allowed the black population to avoid these prescribed areas, including that of re-siding in settlements such as Korsten, where the colonial law was inap-plicable or unenforceable. On the one hand, Korsten's continued exis-tence testified to the resilience of African opposition to the state's attempt to tighten control as envisaged and served as an example of an alterna-tive solution to segregated "townships." On the other, although the es-tablishment of New Brighton did not supply the hoped-for solution to controlling Africans, as one of the first state "townships" it did establish a precedent under colonial law and helped to redefine the relationship between blacks and whites.

The deliberate attempt by the Cape government to insulate the black middle class from the rest of the black population by using property val-ues as a criteria for exemption was a tactic that most of them resisted, re-alizing that their number and strength would be reduced. However, in the end they had little recourse when the amended legislation was passed by the Progressive Parliament that they had helped to elect. By recruiting the support of the landowners at Korsten in removing the "floating pop-ulation," the government shifted the direction of the resistance away from a cross-class, popular unity to a focus on the specific interests of the landholders.

Clearly this conflict emphasized that the liberal alliance was too weak to withstand segregationist legislation and that it held few rewards and represented limited power for Africans. While some white liberals continued to support privileges for "civilized" Africans, it was increasingly acceptable that segregation rather than incorporation was the key to continued white dominance. Thus, the black middle class would have to be contained and co-opted. With the exclusion of blacks from the Korsten VMB, it became evident that their aspiration for some control in local government would be blocked by the racist sentiments of whites and Coloreds. Nonetheless, the space the Africans carved out for themselves at Korsten helped to slow the process of segregation, maintain the principle of freehold in the urban areas, and sustain some aspect of self-respect and independence after the Union of South Africa in 1910. Meanwhile, the establishment of New Brighton created a new site that called for Africans to develop different tactics in the struggle over urban segregation.

Notes

1. *Statues of the Cape of Good Hope, 1652–1905* (Cape Town, 1906), p. 4511.

2. Frederick Cooper, ed., *Struggle for the City: Migrant Labor, Capital, and the State in Urban Africa* (Beverley Hills and London: Sage Publications, 1983), p. 25.

3. Joyce F. Kirk, "A 'Native' Free State at Korsten: Challenge to Segregation in Port Elizabeth, South Africa, 1901–1905," *Journal of Southern African Studies* 17 (1991): 309–336.

4. Although the other colonies passed legislation to force Africans to live in segregated urban compounds or locations these were under municipal control. See T.R.H. Davenport, "African Townsmen? South African Native (Urban Areas) Legislation Through the Years," *African Affairs* 68 (1969): 95–109.

5. "Notes in the House," *Cape Times,* 9 September 1902; for opinions supporting local government administration of African locations see "Parliament-Legislative Council," *Cape Times,* 1 September 1902, and "Parliament-House of Assembly," 30 September 1902, for Merriman's full comments.

6. Cape of Good Hope, Report of the Select Committee on the Native Reserve Locations Bill (Cape of Good Hope, Government Printers), A22-1902 (hereafter 1902 Select Committee Bill Report) 34.

7. Alan Mabin, "The Rise and Decline of Port Elizabeth, 1850–1900," *International Journal of African Historical Studies* 19 (1986): 275–303.

8. Cape of Good Hope, Results of a Census of the Colony (G6-1892); and the 1903 census (G80-1904).

9. £1.00 = 20 shillings, calculated on a six day a week thirty day a month daily average, CAD, NA734, Port Elizabeth Native Location, est. of expenditure for the year ending, 30 June 1906.

10. "The Location Question," *EPH,* 23 January 1902; CAD, NA734, Port Elizabeth Native Reserve Location, 30 June 1896.

11. Sheila Van der Horst, *Native Labor in South Africa* (London: Oxford University Press, 1942), p. 94; R. Hunt Davis, Jr., "School vs. Blanket and Settler: Elijah

Makiwane and the leadership of the Cape School Community," *African Affairs* 78 (1979): 12–31.

12. CAD, NA607, Office of the CC of PE to SNAD, Report of E. C. Allman, Inspector (New Brighton) Reserve Location, 20 April 1903.

13. CAD, NA608, Native Locations, Port Elizabeth, Memo by Town Clerk, 30 June 1903.

14. "Plague Board," *EPH*, 2 October 1901.

15. "Tent Life," *EPH*, 29 May 1902.

16. "Town Council," *EPH*, 14 November 1901.

17. Ibid.

18. CAD, NA608, Native Locations, Port Elizabeth, Memo by Town Clerk, 30 June 1903, and NA597, Mayor J. C. Kemsley, Port Elizabeth to NA office, 12 May 1904.

19. CAD, NA607, CC to SNAD, Report of E. C. Allman, 20 April 1903.

20. The figures for Table 6.1 were estimated by comparing population data contained in 1902 Select Committee Report, Appendix A. Report by R. J. Dick, Special Magistrate, and the data in CAD, NA607, Report of E. C. Allman, included in the correspondence between the office of the CC, PE to SNAD, 20 April 1903.

21. See Table 6.2, for population and compensation; CAD, NA607, Telegram from the Mayor of PE to SNAD, 3 June 1903.

22. See Map 1.2; CAD, NA597, J. C. Kemsley-Mayor, PE to SNAD, 12 May 1904; Report on the Select Committee on the Native Reserve Locations Act of 1902, A15-1903 (hereafter 1903 Report of the Select Committee Act), p. 38, for testimony of Revd. Newell, Minister at Edward's Memorial Church on value of Strangers' and p. 113, for building costs at New Brighton; Select Committee Bill Report, A22-1902, Appendix A, letter from Thos., Stevenson, Mgr. of the South African Association for the Administration and Settlement of Estates, to R. J. Dick, regarding Cradock Place and Deal party (New Brighton), describing the size and buildings on the site, 19 November 1901.

23. Table 6.2 for population and compensation; CAD, NA607, Telegram from the Mayor of Port Elizabeth to SNAD, 3 June 1903, regarding the Gubbs' Syndicate request for money from the central government to compensate for loss of hut revenue; also see CAD, NA607, CC, PE to SNAD, Report of E. C. Allman, 20 April 1903.

24. CAD, NA607, Telegram from Mayor to SNAD, 3 June 1903, for central government's failure to reply to Syndicate's request; CAD, NA607, Telegram from the CC, Port Elizabeth to the SNAD, 12 June 1903.

25. CAD, NA607, weekly report for week ended 6 June 1903, PE Native Location Inspector to the Chief Inspector, Public Works Department, Cape Town, 8 June 1903.

26. 1903 Report of the Select Committee Act, pp. 56–7.

27. Ibid., p. 133.

28. "Parliament," *Cape Times*, 11 June 1903.

29. J. W. Redgrave, *Port Elizabeth in Bygone Days* (Cape Town: Rustica Press Ltd., 1947), pp. 43–48; CAD NA597, B154, W. C. Becker, Acting Resident Magistrate (ARM) to Secretary of Native Affairs, 15 November 1904, and Report from W. H. Quirk, Detective to ARM, 31 October 1904.

30. "Plague Board," *EPH*, 11 February 1905 for comparative figures for 1904 population and ethnic breakdown at Korsten see table 'Population According to the Census on 3 April 1904', in CAD, NA608, 10, 1085, MOH, report to SNA, 12 January 1904.

31. CAD, NA597, D. C. Rees, Senior Government Plague MOH to MOH, Cape Town, 25 September, 1902, re: Village of Korsten.

32. The Reservoir site was established under the 1883 Native Strangers Location Act but only a few Africans moved there from the town locations. CAD, NA607, Office of the CC of PE to SNAD, 14 March 1904, and NA607, Report of E. C. Allman, Inspector, New Brighton Reserve Location to CC, 20 April 1903. However, many residents claimed the right to titles under the 1896 agreement by virtue of the three year occupation clause. Their predicament will be discussed in the next chapter.

33. 1902 Select Committee Bill Report, pp. 2–44; "Editor's Corner," *Izwi La-Bantu*, 7 October 1902.

34. The trader was Whiley Pikoli, "Colonial Secretary's Visit," *EPH*, 30 September 1904.

35. CAD, Registration of Voters, List of Persons residing in the Electoral Division of Port Elizabeth (Cape Colony: 1903, and 1907), e.g., James Dlwati and James Gobe at Korsten and James Funani at Dassie's Kraal; "Fire at Korsten," *EPH*, 12 June 1906; Joyce F. Kirk, "The African Middle Class, Cape Liberalism and Resistance to Residential Segregation at Port Elizabeth, South Africa, 1880–1910" (Ph.D. diss., University of Wisconsin, Madison, 1987). Appendix 1, Africans Leaders in Port Elizabeth, 1880–1910.

36. Interview with A. Sangu at New Brighton, 19 July 1981.

37. J. Rex, "The compound, reserve and urban locations, essential institutions of Southern African Labor Exploitation," *South African Labor Bulletin* 1 (1974): 4–17.

38. For beer trade in Port Elizabeth see Chap. 1.; for recent focus on politics of liquor in South Africa see Paul la Hausse, *Brewers, Beerhalls and Boycotts* (Johannesburg: Ravan Press, 1988).

39. "Ingenious Defense," *EPH*, 7 March 1903 and "A Public Danger," 10 July 1904; CAD, NA608, Native Locations, Port Elizabeth, Memo by Town Clerk dated 30 June 1903.

40. All Interviews at New Brighton with A. Sangu, July 1981, G. Pemba, and H. Nyati, August, 1988; also see Janet Cherry, "Blot on the Landscape and Center of Resistance: A social and economic history of Korsten" (honors thesis, University of Cape Town, March 1988); and Bozzoli, *Class, Community and Conflict*.

41. Report of the MOH for the Colony on the Public Health (Cape Town, G35-1904), p. 113.

42. 1903 Report on the Select Committee Act, p. 113.

43. Blue Book on Native Affairs (hereafter BBNA) (G12-1904), p. 93.

44. CAD, NA734, Part 1, Port Elizabeth Native Reserve Location, Estimates of Expenditure for Year Ending 30 June 1906.

45. 1903 Report of the Select Committee Act, p. 36.

46. Ibid., pp. 12,17.

47. CAD, NA608, MOH to SNAD, 1 December 1904.

48. "The Election Contest," *EPH*, 13 October 1903.

49. "Colonial Secretary's Visit," 23 April 1901 and "Native Locations," *EPH*, 27 February 1902.

50. CAD, NA608, John McKay to Sir Gordon Sprigg, 22 September 1903.

51. "Korsten Affairs," *EPH*, 5 October 1903.

52. "Editor's Corner," *Izwi LaBantu*, 7 October 1902.

53. The Village Management Act, No. 29 of 1881 amended No. 35, 1905, *Statutes of the Cape of Good Hope*, p. 1797; Andre Odendaal, "African Political Mobilization in the Eastern Cape, 1880–1910" (Ph.D. diss. University of Cambridge, 1983), p. 149.

54. "Native Servant Question," *EPH*, 8 July 1903.

55. The Town Council's protest to the government against a permit being issued to the Harbor Board fell on deaf ears, CAD, NA598, 1525, R.M., P.E., to Deputy Assistant Treasurer, Cape Town, 15 May 1903.

56. "Town Council," *EPH*, 11 February 1905, Mr. Fox-Smith became a Councillor in 1904.

57. CAD, NA608, Native Locations, Port Elizabeth, Report from MOH to SNAD, 1 December 1904.

58. R. L. Cope, "C. W. de Kiewiet, the Imperial Factor, and South African 'Native' Policy," *Journal of Southern African Studies* 15 (1989): 486–487.

59. M. S. Grundleigh, "The Parliament of the Cape of Good Hope, with Special Reference to Party Politics, 1872–1910," Ph.D. diss., University of Stellenbosch, 1945 pub. in *Archives Year-book for South Africa* (1969): 289; "The Progressive Manifesto," *EPH*, 30 October 1903.

60. Grundleigh, "The Parliament," p. 285.

61. J. Tengo Jabavu to J. X. Merriman, 4 April 1903, promised to support Merriman because the Progressives were only willing to sponsor liberal candidates in their party, and J.A.G. Sishuba to J. X. Merriman, 19 October 1903, wrote that the Progressives fought the election almost along "race" lines, in Phyllis Lewsen, *Selections from the Correspondence of J. X. Merriman, 1899–1905* (Cape Town: Van Riebeek Society, 1966), pp. 381, 400.

62. S. E. Katzenellenbogen, "Reconstruction in the Transvaal," in P. Warwick (ed.), *The South African War* (Essex: Longman, 1980), 341–361; S. Marks and S. Trapido, "Lord Milner and the South African State," *History Workshop* 9 (1979): 50–80.

63. "A Korsten Meeting," *EPH*, 28 September 1903. For total number of voters see *South African Native Affairs Commission, 1903–05*, Minutes, 1903, V. 5, p. 8, "List of Persons residing in the electoral division of Port Elizabeth"; for Korsten voters see CAD, NA608, Village of Korsten and Dassie's Kraal: Proposed Action under Plague Regulations, from MOH to SNAD, 8 December 1903.

64. For a stimulating and important discussion which touches on the significance of issues with local resonance see N. Gwala, "Political Violence and the Struggle for Control in Pietermaritzburg," *Journal of Southern African Studies* 15 (1989): 506–524.

65. "A Korsten Meeting," *EPH*, 28 September 1903.

66. "Korsten Affairs," *EPH*, 5 October 1903.

67. "Korsten Affairs," *EPH*, 5 October 1903; "Editor's Corner," *Izwi LaBantu*, 7 October 1902.

68. "Korsten-Village Management Board," *EPH*, 7 July 1904.

69. "Divisional Council," *EPH*, 18 March 1905.

70. "Parliament-Legislative Council," *EPH*, 22 April 1904.

71. "The Legislative Council," *EPH*, 27 June 1904 and "Mr. Brookes at Korsten," 28 June 1904.

72. "Town Council," *EPH*, 17 March 1904.

73. "Colonial Secretary's Visit," *EPH*, 1 October 1904.

74. "Colonial Secretary's Visit," *EPH*, 1 October 1904; CAD, NA608, Report from MOH to Under Colonial Secretary, 10 December 1904.

75. CAD, NA607, CC and ARM to SNAD, 14 March 1904 and NA597, W. C. Becker ARM to SNAD, 15 November 1904; BBNA (G12-1904), p. 96.

76. "New Brighton Location," *Imvo*, 1 December 1903.

77. CAD, NA507, ARM to SNAD, 15 November 1904.

78. CAD, NA608, MOH for the Colony to SNAD, 1 December 1904.

79. Ibid.

80. CAD, NA607, B1677, Report on Deputation to Cape Town, April 1905.

81. Ibid.

82. CAD, NA734, Part 1, David C. Rees, Senior Government Plague Medical Officer, to MOH for the Colony, 17 May 1905. W. C. Becker received authorization on March 24, 1905, from the Colonial Secretary to issue the Health regulation; *EPH*, "Plague Board," 11 February 1905 and "The Plague Board," 30 March 1905.

83. CAD, NA607, J. Wells, Port Elizabeth to M.L.A. J. Pyott, Cape Town, 8 March 1905.

84. CAD, NA598 B1525, N. Janisch, Colonial Secretary's office, Cape Town to Colonel W. E. Stanford, C.M.G. Department of Native Affairs, 16 January 1905; Also see Deborah Gaitskell, "Christian Compounds for Girls: Church Hostels for African Women in Johannesburg, 1907–1970," *Journal of Southern African Studies* 6 (1979): 44–69.

85. CAD, NA734, Part 1, F348, T.N.B. Miles, Acting RM, Port Elizabeth to SNAD, 21 August 1908.

86. Declared illegal by the town council, *EPH*, "Town Council," 20 May 1892; but the practice continued, "Magistrate's Court," 6 April 1894.

87. "Magistrate's Court," *EPH*, 24 June 1892 and 23 September 1892.

88. The next two quotes are from CAD, NA597, Report from W. C. Becker, Acting RM to SNAD, 15 November 1904, Enclosure, report by Detective W. H. Quirk.

89. "Korsten-a test case," *Cape Daily Telegraph*, 14 April 1905, and "Korsten Case," same date for all references in this paragraph.

90. "A Korsten Case," *EPH*, 14 April 1905.

91. Ibid.

92. CAD, NA607 B1766, Telegram from RM, PE, to SNAD, Cape Town, 23 March 1905.

93. "Divisional Council," *EPH*, 18 March 1905. In March, the divisional council recommended that he receive a month's salary at 180 pounds per annum.

94. "A Korsten Case-the right of entry," *EPH*, 14 April 1905.

95. Ibid.

96. The regulation was implemented by the Resident Magistrate who conferred to the police the powers to evict and set furniture out which is what Brown was challenging. He maintained that a special order had to come from the Colonial Secretary authorizing the police with such powers. "Korsten Case," *Cape Daily Telegraph*, 14 April 1905.

97. Ibid.

98. "Korsten Case," *Cape Daily Telegraph*, 14 April 1905.

99. "A Korsten Case," *EPH*, 14 April 1905.

100. The conviction was upheld. "Korsten Appeal," *EPH*, 31 May 1905.

101. "A Korsten Case," *EPH*, 14 April 1905; "Korsten Case," *Cape Daily Telegraph*, 14 April 1905.

102. "Korsten," *EPH*, 17 April 1905.

103. Julia Walker, "Women's Resistance to Passes in Bloemfontein during the inter-war period," *Africa Perspective* 15 (1980): 16–35.

104. CAD, NA608, Dr. Mitchell to W. G. Cummings, SNA, n.d.

105. CAD, NA607, B1677, W. E. Stanford to SNAD, 24 April 1905.

106. Ibid.

107. CAD, NA734, Part 1, D. C. Rees, Senior Government Plague MOH to MOH for the Colony, 17 May 1905.

108. "The Native Persecution at Port Elizabeth," *Imvo*, 2 May 1905, among them were William Wauchope, Tobias Mvula, Richard Fila, James Mama, John Mangena, J. Dlaumbuie, William Mapela and Esekiel Lesutho.

109. *Statutes of the Cape of Good Hope, 1652–1905*, The Native Locations Amendment Act (no. 8 of 1905); CAD NA597, B1524, Korsten petition attached to letter from Dave Walker, Town Clerk to Premier Jameson, 18 May 1904.

110. "Cape Parliament," *EPH*, 11 April 1905.

111. CAD, NA734, Part 1, David C. Rees, Senior Government Plague MOH to MOH for the Colony, 17 May 1905, said that unexempt Africans were returning to unoccupied premises at Korsten at night and sleeping there; CAD, NA734, Part 1,F348, ARM, P. E. to Assistant RM, New Brighton, 21 August 1908 on Africans hiding out in Korsten to avoid paying rent owed at New Brighton; As a result of the evictions at Korsten, New January, 1905 to 4,516 in August 1905, BBNA (G46-1906); For police actions see "Korsten Raid," *EPH*, 25 August 1905.

112. "Korsten," *EPH*, 1 October 1905; CAD, NA607, Telegram from W. E. Stanford to SNA, 1 October 1905.

113. CAD, NA607, B1677, E. Dower to Dr. Gregory, 15 September 1905; CAD, 4/PEZ, 4/1/271, "Control of Korsten Area," May 1946.

114. Information on 1930s removals from interviews in New Brighton with A. Sangu, July 1981, H. Hyati and G. Pemba, August 1988,; for the 1950s see Cherry, "Blot on the Landscape," p. 106.

7

New Brighton, African Protest, and the Evolution of Residential Segregation

It is in the towns that the native question of the future will in an ever-increasing complexity have to be faced.[1]

Introduction

In 1919 E. Barrett was the Acting Secretary of Native Affairs when he made the above prediction from the perspective of his personal observations and his long career as a colonial civil servant. His prediction has proven to be accurate. As we have seen, by the turn of the century government officials and Africans in places like Port Elizabeth were already facing the complexity of the "native question" in the towns. For the Cape Colony the answer to the "native question" was the experiment of creating the African "townships": Ndabeni at Cape Town and New Brighton at Port Elizabeth. Government-imposed institutions like segregated black "townships" were aimed at repressing, exploiting, and disfranchising black people in order to create a cheap labor force and a reserve labor pool for whites to draw from and to prevent blacks from competing in the labor market with whites. In addition, from the viewpoint of the colonial government the separation of blacks from whites was necessary to establish the essential social living conditions to promote white supremacy. As mentioned in other chapters, the specter of poor whites living alongside poor blacks and "coloreds" was becoming a problem to which the colonial authorities were directing their attention more and more.

Yet institutions are shaped by struggle rather than simply created. This is, of course, what makes situations like these so complex. The 1902 Native [Urban] Reserve Locations Act, amended in 1905, failed to solve the problem—as perceived by the colonial government—of containing the African population at new Brighton and controlling what blacks could and could not do in the town. For a time, however, the Cape government used the Act to establish formal administrative structures intended to relegate increasing numbers of Africans to New Brighton. Yet even though these actions added to the African population of the location, and more Africans were now restricted to a specific geographical space (about half of the total black population) the struggle against residential segregation and racial discrimination continued. Thus, although for many Africans the site of the struggle shifted to New Brighton, the question remained for the black residents of how much control the government would exercise over their social, economic, and political lives. Clearly, whether they were segregated at New Brighton or lived outside the location, Africans faced a common fate as objects of the racially discriminatory social engineering of the government.

Of course, Port Elizabeth was not the only area to establish a segregated black location. For example, East London, in the eastern Cape, established Duncansville in 1904; Johannesburg, in the Transvaal region, created its first formally segregated "native" location, called Klipspruit, in 1904 in response to an outbreak of bubonic plague. And near Bloemfontein, in the Orange Free State, a 1903 municipal ordinance authorized the administration of separate African locations.[2] In contrast to the situation in Port Elizabeth and at Cape Town, however, the local white municipality administered these locations. Nevertheless, strong similarities existed in these disparate geographical regions with regard to government administration, living conditions, lack of freehold rights, and the African resistance to segregation that was emerging.[3]

Significantly, the 1902 Native [Urban] Reserve Locations Act, amended in 1905, made Port Elizabeth a pilot project for the future segregation of urban South Africa. It raised issues relating to influx/efflux control (government restrictions on the movement of Africans into and out of the towns), residential segregation, passes (identification documents) tied to residence and labor, the right to freehold property, land ownership, the right to self-built housing, liquor control, criminality and rent, and advisory boards (local township committees made up of Africans who were partially elected by qualified Africans and partially appointed by the Superintendent of Native Locations).[4] Indeed, the Union government included most of these locally instituted segregationist policies in the 1923 Native Urban Areas Act as part of its goal to establish a national policy of compulsory segregation for urban Africans.

At this time in Port Elizabeth, however, Africans' energies were absorbed in five immediate questions that will be addressed in this chapter. These were (1) Would Africans be allowed to own land and property at New Brighton and could relatives inherit? (2) How would residential segregation affect the size of the family household and structure? (3) Would the living conditions be better than or comparable to their old residences outside New Brighton, and would residents be able to erect their own housing? (4) With regard to individual and civil liberties, e.g., free movement and use of alcohol, what restrictions would residents face? and (5) Who would pay for segregation?

Between 1903 and 1910, when formal residential segregation was in its early stages, it is noteworthy that for Western-educated Christians and members of the aspirant black middle class the conflict at New Brighton continued to be rooted in African demands for land, property ownership, and civil rights. The aspirant black middle class coalition also tried to protect the right of families to occupy housing and to include young and old members, regardless of their abilities to provide labor for the whites, within the residential sphere. This resistance to the break-up of the family was a clear contradiction and challenge to government's principles of influx control, and that Africans were objects of labor, and that labor must be regulated for the benefit of whites. At this juncture the protest tactics of the Christian and liberal African leaders—petitions to the government, meetings with government officials—remained much the same, but their effectiveness was at an all-time low.

Nonetheless, Africans were able to undermine the segregation process and slow it considerably by exerting the tried-and-true protest method of voting with their feet, many escaped from New Brighton to return to the countryside or to live elsewhere in Port Elizabeth. The government called it "absconding," which is defined as escaping hastily or secretly, especially from the law. While "absconding" in and of itself may seem of small significance, when we realize that Africans were leaving New Brighton without paying the house rent, it becomes clear that this was a momentous problem, because the house rent was the very method the government had planned to use to pay for the construction and administration of New Brighton. Consequently, a good deal more leverage occurred than what conventional theorists have assumed. So although African men and women in the urban areas were increasingly forced into segregated government "townships" and their political and economic disadvantages increased, they continued to resist government statutes and proclamations. By examining how Africans and their supporters attempted to resolve these questions under conditions of a changing political economy, including the balance of power, we can gain insight into and observe emerging patterns of protest and resistance.[5]

In these struggles by Africans for land and residence rights at Port Elizabeth in general and New Brighton in particular, the "Ethiopian," that is, the African independent church movement that affected black Christians during the last quarter of the nineteenth century, became an active player for a while under the leadership of Reverend James Dwane.[6] Although Dwane was distrusted by many whites, he used his knowledge of the divisions among Western-educated European Christian leaders to gain important concessions for his followers at New Brighton.

Other problems at New Brighton emerged over the rental rates and criminality, for the Native Reserve Act stipulated that residents unable to pay their rent could be convicted and jailed. In opposition to this insensitive government policy, Africans, regardless of class, ethnicity, or gender, stood together on this issue. This was particularly true because an economic downturn between 1906 and 1908 led to a retrenchment that affected the income of African workers (as well as some business people) and the ability of the workers to pay rent. Also, the rent controversy affected the struggle over residential segregation by underscoring the old question of who would pay for segregation, the African population or the government. Patterns of class formation and conflict become evident as we examine the methods Africans used to protest against the rents charged at new Brighton and the government tactics to ensure that Africans paid for residential segregation. In later years rent strikes would become part of the pattern of African protest against segregation and apartheid in the urban townships.

A contributing factor to the government's financial problems at New Brighton was its failure to fulfill its promise that in comparison to the old locations, this new location would be a better place for Africans to live in terms of sanitation, housing, and living conditions. Moreover, the government paid less attention to the needs and wants of the potential African residents; this contributed to their dissatisfaction with residing at New Brighton and fostered a willingness to relocate if the opportunity arose. These factors undermined residential segregation as envisioned by the government. Before we move to examine these factors, it is necessary to explain the administration at New Brighton.

Administration at New Brighton

New Brighton consisted of seven wards, each intended to house about four hundred residents. Within each ward houses—"huts" really since the structures were shells provided with walls and a roof and the occupant supplied the rest, including doors, ceiling, and floors—were divided into three categories. These included: two-room Class A houses for married, "better-class" families; one-room Class B houses for lower-class or average families; and Class C barracks primarily for single men, although a few single women occupied them as well.

Even before the residents moved in, however, the government decided that the Class A houses were too costly, so not many of these were built. By August 1903 only a total of 88 houses were complete and functional; the remaining 44 were still under construction. Also, four of the Class A houses were being used for official buildings, including one for the office of the Superintendent of Locations. The total number of Class B houses was eight (four partitioned units), with 72 dwellings for 72 families or a total of 288 persons. There were 48 Class C houses, 432 dwellings, with eight men in each, totalling 2,160.[7] In the end fewer Class A houses were built, and eventually African families were temporarily placed in altered Class B and Class C houses. Not surprisingly, these uncomfortable circumstances brought major complaints about the cramped spaces and overcrowding.

Although the government contemplated building more dwellings at New Brighton, census discrepancies as to the number of people from other areas, such as Korsten and Vlei Post, who would occupy the housing led to the decision to convert the already-built Class B and Class C houses into living space for families and to build no more "expensive" Class A houses. In fact, Class C houses—but very basic—had no kitchen and were converted to family housing by inserting a partition. The government's decision not to build more housing also was influenced by two factors: the lack of financial resources because of the depression that followed the end of the war in 1902 and the failure of the New Brighton residents to pay rent, a major area of conflict between the residents and the New Brighton officials, to which we will shortly return.

New Brighton fell under the dual authority of the Native Affairs Department and the Department of Justice. Between 1903 and 1908 the principal official appointed by the Native Affairs Department (NAD) was the European inspector, also called the Superintendent of Locations, who supervised the daily running of the location. Other staff members assisting the Location Superintendent (as he was more commonly known) included an interpreter, two inspectors, two native assistant clerks, and a hospital staff, including a Medical Officer of Health, two nurses, several African wardsmen (some worked as policemen and some worked as headmen) and a maintenance and sanitation crew.[8] For matters of criminal justice a Department of Justice official, the Resident Magistrate (RM) and/or the Assistant Resident Magistrate (ARM), presided over a weekly court. Here residents charged with disobeying the location regulations and engaging in petty criminal activity were tried.

Although the Superintendent of Locations was charged to administer the location, he was obliged to defer to the RM in matters of law. The Superintendent and the other staff members, white and black, all lived in New Brighton, making them more accessible and able to stay in touch with the residents. Nonetheless, the evidence suggests that the Department of Justice officials were primary in administering and overseeing New Brighton between 1903 and 1908. Not until 1908 was a permanent

Location Superintendent hired at New Brighton who stayed long enough to establish some consistency in administration. Until that time J. A. Verschuur, the Assistant Resident Magistrate from 1903–1908, seems to have appointed most of the staff at New Brighton.

Although the administration of a "native" location in an urban area was uncharted territory for the central government—in a sense a "new frontier"—some experiential knowledge existed. The Cape colonial government had already imposed a similar system of reserve locations among Africans in the rural territories that were administered by a resident magistrate and an African headman. To this model was added the Superintendent of Location. Perhaps this is why the Superintendents between 1903–1908 at New Brighton seem to have held less power than the Assistant Resident Magistrate. But location inspectors had functioned in the municipal locations so Africans were familiar with dealing with this officer. However, many times the location inspector was generally viewed in the capacity of a policemen whose objective was to harass the African residents. It seems that the Superintendent of Locations acted more as a law officer of the NAD. As such, Africans might avoid the Superintendent of New Brighton and prefer interacting with the Resident Magistrate, the government agent who had primary judicial authority and thus represented the law.

In the process of abstract colonial rule evolving into actual rule, it is noteworthy that opposition from rural Africans shaped the outcome just as it did in the urban areas.[9] The rural model was applied to the urban locations at New Brighton and Ndabeni, with differences in the authority and power of the headmen. At New Brighton, however, the Superintendent of Locations appointed the headmen and apparently few held traditional or legitimate authority recognized by the residents. Yet because of their varied role, they probably settled disputes between the residents according to custom. This was in contrast to the role of the headmen in the rural locations, whose authority more often emanated from a combination of heredity rule and government appointment. As Beinart and Bundy illustrate in *Hidden Struggles in Rural South Africa*,[10] the role of the headmen depended on several factors, including the degree of intervention by the state.

The main officials with whom New Brighton residents interacted most frequently, however, were the African headmen from the NAD appointed by the Superintendent. The headmen in each ward had several administrative duties. These included ensuring that all residents possessed a registration card (the same as a pass); recording residents and visitors; reporting on residents' illness, health, and death; conducting daily inspections; and collecting rents.[11] It is likely that the role of the headman in the rural areas was the model for the urban "native" location.

Perhaps a less frequent visitor than the headmen but still a constant authority figure were the location police. Although they were also known locally as wardsmen or special constables, they were used primarily as policemen.[12] Their numbers fluctuated according to economic changes and the size of the population at New Brighton. For example, in June 1904 two policemen were dismissed because their services were no longer needed when New Brighton experienced a population decrease of over one thousand. Following passage of the 1905 amendment about a year later, the ARM, J. A. Verschuur, instructed the Location Superintendent at New Brighton to appoint three additional men for the increased population and also so that, "Two wardsmen can now be made use of in following absconders to the neighboring locations."[13] The police were required to maintain law and order, including making arrests. Often the duties of the police and headmen overlapped, since the wardsmen/headmen were expected to report illegal occurrences and act much like a plainclothes policeman.

From 1903 to 1918 the Superintendent and his wardsmen (African headmen and police) conducted all administrative and police duties. However, between 1903 and 1908 several different men held the position of Location Superintendent, which contributed to a lack of consistency and tended to destabilize efficient administrative control. Evelyn Grattan, the Superintendent appointed in 1908, brought a measure of stability and efficiency to the office, which he held until 1923 when New Brighton was transferred to the Port Elizabeth City Council (PECC). When the assistant magistrate's office was abolished in 1909 for financial reasons, the Superintendent took complete control. Until that year the Magistrate's court and the *gaol* were at New Brighton under the control of the Superintendent. Then the magistrate and periodical court were removed, probably because of lack of finances, in 1909. The Superintendent became a Justice of the Peace (JP) and heard simple cases. The residents greatly resented this action and viewed it as a betrayal because they had been promised their own Magistrate and court.[14]

Although the duties of the police were primarily to patrol the wards and maintain law and order at New Brighton, it seems that some of them spent more time breaking the laws than they did enforcing them. For quite some time the police were notoriously unreliable. In fact, several policemen were fired for harassing female residents, extorting sex from them, being intoxicated while on duty, and exhibiting lax behavior. Some also deserted the police force. An example in July 1905 was one Charles Mitshabo, dismissed for extorting sex from a female renter, and in July 1906 James Didiza was fired for enticing girls to his room.[15]

While we do not know the specific social and psychological effects upon the young women who were accosted, it must have been considerable in a culture where customarily premarital sexual intercourse was forbidden. As to the effects upon the policemen, the mother of one of Wardman Didiza's victims prosecuted him for enticing the girl to his room to have sexual intercourse several times. Doubtless, these types of activities did little to create a positive image of the police in the location.

Although many of the duties of the location police resembled those of the Cape police, the location police were regulated by different rules under the NAD. Thus, the local authority, in the guise of either the Superintendent of Locations or the Assistant Resident Magistrate, regulated the New Brighton constables. In practice it was very difficult to control the location police, since no formal regulations existed to carry out disciplinary measures. Often firing the location police was the only recourse. At least that was one of the complaints of the ARM, J. A. Veschuur.

Verschuur, who was ARM from 1903 to 1908, rather than the Location Superintendent of New Brighton appointed most of the staff at New Brighton. Almost from the beginning it was evident that he was dissatisfied with the wardsmen's unreliability and lack of moral qualities. And because there was a rapid turnover of wardsmen/policemen, we know it is likely that initially the staff was quite unreliable. Apparently at least for the first two years the New Brighton Superintendent found it difficult to hire satisfactory men. In 1905 job turnover was so rapid that Verschuur suggested that married men be employed as wardsmen and be paid a higher wage, with the possibility of progressive increases serving as inducements. Undoubtedly the prior sexual behavior of the policemen affected Verschuur's recommendation to retain only married men, as Verschuur was probably hoping that taking on married men would curb the exploitation of female residents. He maintained that signing on married men and paying a higher wage was necessary if they wanted to engage responsible, intelligent men with a fair education to police New Brighton, in contrast to employing ordinary men who "tend to accept bribes and shield friends carrying on illicit liquor dealings."[16]

It seems that for the wardsmen who accepted bribes the salary of £60 per annum plus living quarters, maximum £80, were insufficient. Yet they were among the higher-salaried civil servants and in the economic category of the middle class of that time. The corrupt wardsmen, both the headmen and police, probably contributed to the problem of collecting the rent as well.[17]

Escape from New Brighton—Rents, "Absconders," and Revenue

Once Africans were forced into New Brighton beginning in 1903, financing the location became a major hurdle as the township's population grew. As Davenport pointed out several years ago, colonial administration in the different settler societies of Africa shared common thinking about urban policy that "led to the establishment of similar kinds of machinery for the running of urban African government."[18] Colonial government also shared the notion that black populations should be segregated without cost to the white taxpayers or to the white-run businesses for whom most Africans labored. In eastern and southern Africa the locations were financed by a separate native revenue account, with a portion commonly derived from the sale of traditional liquor. Although this was true in the African urban "townships" in Natal,[19] at Port Elizabeth the government opted to allow African voters to engage in controlled domestic brewing. So residential rents were New Brighton's primary source of revenue to administer the location. This was a problem, since the residents, for several reasons, failed to pay rent.

Almost from the establishment of New Brighton in 1903 Verschuur, the ARM, complained about nonpayment of house rents. Hundreds and sometimes thousands of pounds were owed in rent. For example, in February 1905 the irrecoverable rents, as the government called the unpaid rent, implying that government officials believed that expecting the rent to be paid was a lost cause, were £435.10.0; for the same period, arrears rent was £445.2.0.[20] By June 1905 the irrecoverable rent was £1692.16/-, with £447.0.9 of this amount collected during July.[21] By 1909 the arrears rent was £2,450, the majority of which, according to the RM report on New Brighton, was irrecoverable.[22] A more optimistic report from the Location Superintendent at New Brighton in 1910 stated that arrears rates were £995 17s 6d, with many more residents paying their rent promptly—that is, in the month that it was due—while irrecoverable rates were £124 11s 6d.[23]

One of the reasons for the 1905 amendment to the 1902 Native [Urban] Areas Act was to extend its boundaries so as to authorize the government to evict from Korsten and Dassie's Kraal the Africans who were not exempted from the law, as well as those who owed rent arrears at New Brighton. (see Chapter 6) The government called the people who owed rent at New Brighton "absconders" and vagrants.[24] It is clear, however, that many Africans viewed their actions as an escape, a bid for freedom from an unjust law that imposed numerous restrictions.

In 1905 Verschuur, blamed the inefficient administration of the Inspector at New Brighton for the large number of rent "absconders." He stated, "The laxity of control by a former inspector, his failure to grasp the functions of his office, and want of tact in dealing with natives is . . . why natives have left this location before meeting their liabilities to government. An efficient officer has now been appointed to the office of inspector."[25] Already in September 1904 Verschuur had claimed that a considerable number of Africans absconded because of the previous Inspector's lack of

tact in dealing with them. He cited the Inspector's "refusal to accept arrear rates and his unfriendly conduct generally towards residents in the
discharge of his official duties." Verschuur included figures to prove that
both the Location Superintendent and the wardsmen had inflated the
numbers to show a larger total of residents at New Brighton and that the
number of "absconding natives has been considerably understated."[26]

Thus, the inflated figure listed by the Inspector was 1,821; the wardsmen had listed a total of 1,310, much closer to the correct figure, counted
by the ARM, of 1,276. The number of Africans who did not pay rent by
August 1904 should have been 649. This is an astounding figure, almost
half the correct total number of residents at New Brighton. The Inspector
may have inflated the population figures or simply been an horrendous
bookkeeper, or both; the wardsmen were not supervised in bookkeeping,
resulting in no record of the dates that Africans left. In addition, both
wardsmen and the Inspector listed as absconders Africans who were actually rent-paying residents at New Brighton.

Other Africans listed as resident in New Brighton had long since escaped, but no dates were given. Verschuur noted that "several hundreds
of natives appear to have been marked off as having absconded just
about the time when I decided to take the census of the location in order
to ascertain whether the figures submitted to me by the Inspector from
time to time were substantially correct. I nevertheless found his population 495 was in excess of my total."[27] Nonetheless, the amount of rental
arrears indicates that whatever the population total, the rent was not
being paid as the colonial authorities had anticipated. As Table 7.1 illustrates the fluctuation in New Brighton's population was considerable.

Although the ARM, J. Verschuur blamed the Inspector at New Brighton
for the rent arrears and the Inspector's actions were probably of some importance, obviously there were several other reasons why so many
Africans chose to leave the location to avoid paying rent. These reasons
were related to both the high rental rates and other socioeconomic and
political issues. Among these issues were: (1) high rent, (2) lack of resources to pay the rent, (3) prosecutions for failure to pay rent, (4) resentment at being forced into and being segregated at New Brighton, (5) poor
housing conditions, (6) restrictions on movement and social activities, (7)
sexual harassment, (8) poor administration, and (9) no land and property
rights. From the beginning, and even before New Brighton opened,
Africans complained about the high rents and these related issues. In response to these complaints by Africans and also because of a downturn
in the economy after the war ended in 1902, the government lowered
rents several times between 1903 and 1909 as shown in Table 7.2.

The rents remained at the 1909 level until 1918. Although the rents were
progressively lowered, eventually amounting to one-half to three-fourths

Table 7.1   New Brighton Population Returns, 1903–1910

Month	1903	1904	1905	1906	1907	1908	1909	1910
January	—	3,007	1,791	4,363	3,735	3,794	2,150	3,156
February	—	3,487	2,350	4,395	3,694	3,807	2,214	3,187
March	—	2,554	2,602	4,357	3,710	3,747	2,253	3,187
April	—	2,612	3,313	4,376	3,657	3,776	2,333	3,182
May	254	2,081	3,805	4,294	3,603	3,771	2,479	3,193
June	965	1,960	4,198	4,163	3,614	3,681	2,570	—
July	1,239	1,925	4,232	4,047	3,574	3,598	2,721	—
August	1,387	1,807	4,067	3,948	3,591	3,462	2,836	—
September	1,434	1,283	4,133	3,903	3,539	3,367	2,972	—
October	1,517	1,310	4,222	3,850	3,551	1,994	3,080	—
November	1,573	1,309	4,441	3,849	3,724	2,002	3,106	—
December	2,125	1,411	4,516	3,812	3,773	2,099	3,105	—

Source: Blue Book on Native Affairs, Cape of Good Hope, Compiled from reports on New Brighton, Location Population Figures for Years, 1903–1910.

Table 7.2   New Brighton Rent Reductions, 1903–1909

Rent Reduction	Original	1903	1905	1907	1909
Class A two-roomed	30/–	25/–	20/–	15/–	8/–
Class B one-roomed	25/–	20/–	15/–	12/6	6/–
Class C converted SMQ single men's quarters [and women]		17/6	12/6	10/–	5/–
Class C dormitory room	8/–	8/–	6/–	6/–	3/–

Source: Blue Book on Native Affairs, Cape of Good Hope, Compiled from reports on New Brighton for years 1903–1910.

of the original amount, many residents still found it difficult to pay. Part of the problem was that the rents were payable in advance, and at the beginning of the month. However, many African workers were paid at the end of the month, received lower wages than white workers, and found it difficult to make ends meet. Unfortunately, the informal color bar directed blacks toward unskilled jobs that paid less so that the government could promote a cheap labor force to white employers. These low wages made it doubly difficult for the Africans to pay for their own segregated housing. Moreover, work was scarce because of the depression from 1904 to 1909, and so the unemployment rate among Africans was high. Thus, for the many Africans unable to pay their rent, the easiest solution was to escape from New Brighton.

But this is not the whole story. For aside from the high rents and the economic depression, indications are that many Africans left New Brighton without paying their rent because they resented being *forced* to live there. Clearly, some Africans were reacting to the government decisions that left them in segregated and cramped spaces by refusing to pay rent and/or absconding on rent arrears.[28] In fact, many had been forced into New Brighton because the plague board (see Chapter 5) had evicted them from municipal locations or because the police considered them to be among the non-exempted, and so they had nowhere else to go. Thus, in 1903 W. H. Quirk, the Location Superintendent at New Brighton, declared that most rent absconders were natives who had been ejected from the town locations by the municipality or Plague Board. He stated as follows: "They simply came out here until they could obtain accommodation elsewhere and then absconded. It is presumed that the majority of them went to Korsten and the other unauthorized locations in P. E., whilst the single men left for other towns. When threatened with ejection natives treat the matter with contempt knowing there are several unauthorized locations in the District to which they can go."[29] Once they escaped, "all trace of them was lost afterwards."

Among the unauthorized locations Africans migrated to were Vlei Post, near the middle of town; Emslie's at Walmer, which was a village settlement beyond the municipal boundaries; Kleinschool and Bethelsdorp, near the edge of town and administered by the London Missionary Society. A few also went to Reservoir which was the last remaining municipal location. (See Map 1.2.)

It is clear that many non-exempted Africans avoided New Brighton because of the numerous restrictions compared to living elsewhere. In fact, outside of the government location, Africans could own property, build their own houses, drink and sell alcohol, operate businesses, rent out their property, and move about town and into and out of their living areas without restrictions. So even the rent reductions failed to persuade many Africans to reside at New Brighton.

On this subject, in 1903 the Resident Magistrate at Port Elizabeth stated, "The reduction [in rent] may prove tempting though there is a great objection, apart from [the] question of rent—to reside in a location at all, and so, if rent was entirely wiped off, so long as government regulations were enforced as to intoxicants, trading and sanitation, the general body of natives would prefer to reside beyond the location."[30] As we have seen, intoxicants (alcohol), trading, and sanitation as well as restrictions on movement and social behavior inside and outside New Brighton were the object of conflict between Africans and the government.

The African workers, especially the single temporary or "target" workers resented living at New Brighton for several reasons, not the least of
which was the high rent that caused their wages to be eaten up by the
colonial system in which they had no vested interest. Many African
workers preferred to live frugally so they could save the money to pay
their taxes or to offer *lobola* (bridewealth). It will be recalled that during
the 1901 general strike a major concern of the black workers was how the
restrictions on Africans travelling without a plague certificate and other
passes interfered with the system of work rotation whereby "relatives"
worked the same job so they could return home frequently, in essence enabling them to chose and better control their work routine. Similarly, several aspects of the Native [Urban] Reserve Location Act, including the
identification passes, monthly rent payment, and restricted occupation,
could also destroy the work rotation system. (See Chapter 6 on the 1901
strike and work rotation.)

Supporting this supposition are remarks in 1903 from R. J. Dick, the
Special Magistrate at Kingwilliamstown. Although referring to Kingwilliamstown, similar working conditions existed at Port Elizabeth. With
regard to labor time, he said as follows:

> The bulk of the laborers are weekly laborers. . . . The engagement here as a
> rule is weekly . . . there is a decided preference for the weekly system as
> compared with the monthly, the principle reason given by the Natives being
> that they are enabled by the weekly system to terminate their engagements
> if their employer is not in favor with them, and secondly, because it gives
> them the chance of handling their money every week instead of having to
> wait for a month. This is not done by domestic servants . . . rather, it applies
> to laborers employed by the Municipality and by those large employers of
> labor, the stores, factories, workshops, and so on.[31]

Being paid weekly also meant that the laborers could leave without paying the monthly rent or rent arrears either they or their "brothers" owed.
This would explain why the workers usually absconded on the week-
ends, according to the Resident Magistrate (RM) at New Brighton. In 1905
this weekend traffic prompted the RM to suggest that some of the
wardsmen be detailed to watch the evening trains that left Port Elizabeth
on Saturdays, Sundays, and Monday nights, since this was the time that
the Africans normally escaped.[32]

Once the workers received their pay, it was probably quite logical to
them to leave New Brighton, an area in which they had been forced to
live because of race. After all, they had already been obliged to work a
long distance from home by the new economic system that was controlled more and more by whites. It is likely that they resented govern-

ment attempts to take away their right to choose their living quarters as well as their right to travel from one place to another. From an economic standpoint, the rent at New Brighton was higher than rent in other places, and the restrictions on the number of occupants in a dwelling also meant their resources were eaten up by room and board.

Special Magistrate R. J. Dick's description of the housing that Africans preferred at Kingwilliamstown are similar for Port Elizabeth.[33] Dick declared that these [housing frequented by African workers] were "sleeping dens, which may be hired by eight or ten natives." The housing could be cottages or rooms; this type of shelter was sufficient especially for those involved in the work rotation system who were concerned less with comfortable, spacious lodging, than with returning home often with their wages. Dick claimed that perhaps one-half of the population was living in such places.[34]

Many Africans at Port Elizabeth preferred to reside in this type of housing. For example, at Vlei Post in Port Elizabeth one Samuel Molaba, a registered voter, was arrested and fined for holding a "tea" party or meeting that included men and women who were illegally residing in Port Elizabeth. Molaba rented out rooms in his house; one night the police found 10 people in one room and 13 in another, all sleeping. In the other two rooms a tea party was going on that included men and women.[35]

These alternative housing options were affected by the ability or inability of the police to enforce the Native Reserve Locations Act. Indeed, it is apparent that enforcement remained problematic, since by 1910 one-half of the black population continued to live outside of New Brighton. The police raided the unauthorized locations for the non-exempted and "absconders" and to control liquor brewing, so periodically New Brighton's population would rise temporarily. However, in enforcing these various colonial laws against Africans, the police often met resistance from the residents in the African settlements. For example, on October 28, 1905, Saturday evening around 11:00 p.m., Detective Charles Henry Gibble, two other white officers, and four African "traps" (see Chapter 3), went to Emslie's Location with the intention of arresting the proprietor for illegally making and selling honey beer. However, when the police tried to destroy the large caches of liquor made for the Saturday night revelry, the crowd of men from many different housing areas, including the Harbor Board Compound, turned from a jovial crowd into an angry one intent on chasing down the police. Apparently a week before the conflict the police had arrested a woman for selling liquor. "On that occasion some of the accused threatened Garner Mbotskelwa, the African "trap," and the Detectives, telling them that they would never come there again and arrest a person for selling liquor." In the ensuing chase two officers were injured and Detective Gibble was seriously wounded; among his injuries were ten scalp wounds. Gibble lingered overnight and died Monday morning. The white townspeople were outraged. Eventually thirty-two African men were charged with Gibble's murder. In January 1906, the case was sent to the Attorney-General and thus far the results have not come to light.[36]

As a result of the implementation of the 1903, amended 1905, Native [Urban] Areas Act, some of the cheaper and more overcrowded dwellings were eliminated, forcing Africans to move into other areas including New Brighton. As we have seen, many went to the unauthorized settlements, but eventually single migrant laborers found cheap rooms in one of the most unlikeliest places—New Brighton. This occurred amidst African refusal to move into New Brighton, complaints about the rent and the conditions there, lack of revenue from rents, and the economic downturn, which apparently convinced the administrators to change direction. Consequently, most of the Class A,B, and C huts were converted into family housing to meet the demand, single workers were housed in larger numbers in family housing, and single workers and sometimes even whole families became lodgers of renters.[37] As a result, New Brighton residents rented out portions of their dwelling to increase their capital, a practice that had been frowned upon by government administration. Moreover, single workers were housed in kitchen quarters where they paid less rent, perhaps 3 to 5 shillings instead of 8 shillings. Sometimes 5 families could be accommodated or 25 single persons in a dwelling. These living situations added to the overcrowding, exactly what the government hoped to avoid in establishing New Brighton. Nonetheless, some African landlords could increase their capital while tenants overall paid less rent to the New Brighton administration. Also, class divisions could be eroded by this living style, making racial combinations in times of strife more likely. Thus, as more families needed housing and fewer funds became available to administer New Brighton, the policy of separating the Africans into classes was not diligently followed.

Pass Laws

As if there were not already enough restrictions on the movement of Africans, Mr. Quirk, the Location Superintendent, recommended early in 1905 that government impose a pass law, combined with a penalty for not paying the rent, to reduce the rate of arrears. Under the Native Reserve Locations Act of 1902 both a penalty and pass law already existed that made failure to pay rent at New Brighton a crime. Thus, the Act stipulated that before a resident left the location to go upcountry or move elsewhere (aside from going to work), the resident must take out a pass. It also stipulated that Africans leaving New Brighton for long-distance travel by train—and presumably headed for the countryside or rural areas—needed a pass from the Superintendent (Inspector) of Locations. However, "In practice such passes were not granted until rent was paid up-to-date."[38] But the law, it seems, was not being enforced, thus Quirk's suggestion that it be applied to try to ensure that more Africans would not escape paying the rent owed. In any case, Africans frequently left New Brighton without paying the amount due or securing a pass. Still others received a pass based on the pretext that they were looking for work and used it to leave town. In other cases, as we have seen, the Inspector and the wardsmen kept an erratic count of the residents, making it easier for the Africans who left New Brighton without paying their rent to get away without being traced. Thus, the pass law remained unenforceable. Even when some who had escaped were traced, the rent was not paid. For example, the ARM at New Brighton, J. A. Verschuur, related to the SNAD in 1904 that "those absconders who can be traced to Korsten and Dassie Kraal have no means . . . [to pay the rent owed]."[39]

It is clear that many Africans consciously left Port Elizabeth in order to avoid paying the rent at New Brighton. Some of them would give fictitious names, avoid "hot" railway stations where they knew the police would be waiting to arrest "absconders," leave at the height of the weekend rush, and so on. Although some departed on foot, most purchased train tickets for a longer journey. In order to prevent Africans who owed rent from leaving by train, the government installed several mechanisms. First, Africans could only purchase so-called "cheap" tickets, the lowest-priced tickets, at the New Brighton station. Second, the authorities tried to prevent "absconders" from leaving New Brighton by requiring them to show a pass or an exemption certificate prior to being allowed to purchase a ticket.

Meanwhile, the police were instructed to arrest any natives from New Brighton whose rent was in arrears and who did not have a pass from the Inspector to leave the location. But soon after some "absconders" had been arrested at the New Brighton station, most Africans switched to taking trains at Port Elizabeth, North End, and Zwaartkops. Consequently, enforcement of the Act was almost impossible, because most Africans left by train from other sites, thus eluding the police who watched the New Brighton railway station. Once this occurred, the escapees were virtually untraceable, especially if they returned to their homes in the countryside.

In an attempt to enlist further help from the railway department to make it more difficult for the Africans who owed rent to elude the police, Colonel Stanford, the Secretary of Native Affairs, authorized the implementation of a new pass regulation in August 1905. It stipulated that *all* Africans, regardless of their residence, were required to show a pass signed by the New Brighton Location Inspector before they could purchase a train ticket to leave the district of Port Elizabeth.

It is important to note that the plague regulations at Port Elizabeth remained in place until December 1905. Consequently, all newcomers had to undergo a "medical examination . . . while those desirous of leaving the location are obliged to undergo a similar examination before a pass of good health is granted."[40] Having said this, it remains unclear to what extent the plague regulation was being enforced. But we do know that African complaints against the plague board did not cease after the 1901 general strike. Despite the concessions promised during that strike (see Chapter 5), the enforcement efforts against the plague were racially discriminatory and in some cases quite violent, e.g.,the Zwartkops incident. In this case an African man was killed in 1901 as he tried to leave town by the Zwartkops pathway adjacent to the town near New Brighton. (See Map 1.2.) Armed men authorized by the Plague Board to man a guardpost to prevent Africans leaving town shot and killed him. This apparently was not an isolated incident and surely angered many Africans.[41]

But a plethora of problems resulted from the 1905 pass regulations being applied to all Africans simply on the basis of race which led to complaints from whites as well as Africans. For example, since over one-half of the African population resided outside of New Brighton, it was difficult for them to obtain a pass from the inspector, whose office was at New Brighton, and they had to make other arrangements. The other arrangements included Africans having to request passes from their employers or from some other government agent, such as the Resident Magistrate.

Many Africans lived on their employers' premises, but no provision for exempting them had been included in the regulation. In practice this meant that each employer had to issue each employee a pass before the worker could travel. The employers complained that it was inconvenient to issue passes to employees before they could purchase a railway ticket to go beyond a certain point. Added to these complaints were those of the Resident Magistrate who said that his staff was too small to issue the passes to all non-exempted Africans, which is what would happen if the regulation were enforced, especially since some masters [employers] were unwilling to issue them.[42] Africans were also being issued alternative passes at Korsten by the Vigilance Committee, but the Port Elizabeth Resident Magistrate suggested that the staff at New Brighton take over this task, since he feared the Korsten Committee would request payment for their services.

Those Africans who were exempted and lived in other areas (only those without a voter's certificate) also complained about being inconvenienced in having to secure a document proving their exemption because of a "few people in New Brighton evading their rents or rates."[43] It was also inconvenient for "natives" coming from the country who would not have a pass. It was generally known that Africans resented carrying passes and that they avoided destinations that required them to do so. Not surprisingly, a Port Elizabeth official pointed out that "... it is inadvisable to place too many restrictions on the movement of natives, the majority of whom would be made to suffer for the sins of a few."[44] Clearly, this official realized that enforcement of the regulation could lead prospective African workers to avoid Port Elizabeth. With all of these complaints it is not surprising that the Secretary of Native Affairs advised the general manager of railways at Cape Town on 29 December 1905, a period of four months after the new pass regulation was issued, to stop enforcing the regulation.

The problem with rent "absconders" continued, and in 1908 the Assistant RM at New Brighton, Mr. B. Whitfield, suggested that the African headmen in the rural areas be enlisted to help trace and collect the rent arrears from the non-rentpayers in the urban locations. Whitfield declared that the reason the Africans were untraceable "is that the natives register under false or fictitious names and addresses but primarily because of the apathy of the Headmen of Locations upon whom Magistrates and the Police must rely for assistance and information in matters of this nature." Then Whitfield related a story to illustrate how one Headman regarded his duty to turn in "absconders" to the government.

> When I . . . was stationed at Kentani, the Headmen, at first, worked very well indeed and the majority of absconders were at first traced and the amounts due by those found were recovered by the headmen, but in each case the headman applied for a share of the rent collected by him, and upon their being informed that no portion of the sums collected could be awarded to them for the services they had rendered, they appeared to be greatly disappointed, and thereafter they reported invariably that they could not trace the man in their location, that he was unknown or had not returned home. From these facts I concluded that they no longer interested themselves in the matter.[45]

Whitfield went on to suggest that headmen be offered about 25 percent of the rents recovered and be put on a diligent search for the "absconders" so that "by methods and means of their own a large amount of the rents would be collected."[46] Apparently Whitfield's suggestion was ignored, since the problems with nonpayment of rent continued.

Eventually Inspector Grattan of New Brighton, who was appointed in 1908, initiated a new method of collection. He began to send out late notices around the fifteenth of each month. Sometimes these numbered three to four hundred per month. "Those who paid and those who interviewed the inspector before the date of hearing, had their summons withdrawn. The date of hearing was always fixed for the last Friday of each month."[47] By 1911 the Inspector was threatening to take to Court everyone who was not responding to the late summons; he also stated that he would not withdraw a summons once it was issued and that each person would have to appear in court. It seems that most of the people who owed rent were unmarried, so it is likely that many of them were relatives of the registered occupants. It is obvious from the aforementioned that collecting rents and arrears was extremely difficult and financing the location through rents remained problematic.

Land, Housing, and the Clash of Cultures

Paradoxically, while some Africans were anxious to escape from New Brighton, others had been willing to voluntarily enter the segregated township for the right concessions. These concessions included owning land and property, acquiring sanitary and attractive housing, and establishing a Native Advisory Board to represent the residents. Among this group were many aspirant middle class blacks who were permanent long-time residents; some had already moved into New Brighton, while others remained at the old Reservoir municipal location, at Korsten Village, or elsewhere. As we have seen in Chapter 6, some Africans believed this new "urban frontier" might allow them to exercise more socioeconomic and political options.[48] This was especially true of those Africans who had been part of the 1896 land grant agreement with the Town Council and continued to share an ideological base; they hoped that the central government would honor the promise of titled land grants made first in 1896 by the Town Council and then intimated by several officials representing the central government. Thus, despite their different residences they felt compelled to continue negotiating with the government to obtain land rights in the segregated New Brighton "township."

Their belief that moving to New Brighton could be beneficial if they received the concessions was influenced by the promises made by the Cape Prime Minister, Gordon Sprigg, to concerned Africans and Europeans at Port Elizabeth in October 1903. At a public meeting held at the Independent Church at Korsten, Sprigg promised that the Africans already owning land at Korsten, and who were therefore exempt from moving into New Brighton, would receive freehold title landrights at New Brighton if they moved there voluntarily. Africans already residing at New Brighton could also apply for a land site and to build their own houses, but they would not receive freehold but rather leasehold rights. Also, Sprigg gave support to the idea of establishing a Native Advisory Board. In later correspondence Sprigg reiterated the right of Africans to apply for a land site and to build houses at New Brighton, and he authorized the Resident Magistrate at Port Elizabeth to take applications. Within the context of the debate over rights to land and property for Africans in the urban area, this was a major concession and a victory for proponents. A variety of pressures had led to this concession; doubtless a primary one had been continued resistance to residential segregation among working and middle-class Africans and their liberal white supporters through legal means—court cases, avoidance of New Brighton, and the political struggle over the Korsten Village Management Board. In any case, members of the aspirant black middle class who resided in areas outside of New Brighton, such as Korsten Village and Reservoir location, welcomed the promise of land and property rights at New Brighton if they voluntarily moved there.

But when it came to implementing the concessions, disagreements between the aspirant black middle class and the Cape central government officials on the terms of occupation of the leasehold and freehold sites created new obstacles to Africans acquiring land and property rights at New Brighton. The disagreements hinged on two issues. First, who would be allowed to occupy the housing sites? Second, who would pay for building the housing structures? The answers to these questions were affected by the views of blacks and whites about the role of the location and the black labor force.

When it came to an opinion about Africans living in the towns, many Europeans visualized an available, productive, controlled, able-bodied black work force, living under temporary or migrant conditions without land and property rights, so the workers could be relocated and even forced to move more easily if it became necessary. Theoretically, the government maintained that the requirements of migrant (temporary) workers and permanent workers were different in the areas of housing, wages, and lifestyles. The migrant workers did not have their families with them, so they could be supplied lower standard housing and paid lower wages than would support one person.

Some Europeans, although agreeing that the town was a white preserve, were in the liberal camp and believed that the "civilized" permanent black population living in the town and the "uncivilized" temporary or migrant population should be treated differently. The aspirant black middle class should have privileges such as property and land rights and some say in the running of the location. As we have seen, from the point of view of an important colonial government official like Colonel Stanford, concessions to the aspirant black middle class would help to maintain the wedge between the two emerging classes, called by white officials the permanent and floating "native" population.

However, the promise of land and property rights to Africans threatened the idea that blacks were only in the urban areas to serve the needs of the whites as implied in the Native [Urban] Areas Amended Act of 1905. Moreover, many whites, even those who favored property ownership for some blacks, wondered how to maintain control of *all* Africans without giving too many concessions and without paying any more than necessary for segregating Africans from Europeans?

This concern was reflected in the comments of one official in a letter to the Office of the Secretary for Public Works in July 1902, about the list of proposals from a committee of Africans at Uitvlugt location in Cape Town regarding plots of land on which to build their cottages. He stated that "The project is fraught with considerable risk as to questions that might arise in future respecting ownership or tenancy of both land and buildings, so government should erect dwellings as proposed by the natives, retain them as its property, and let them to the natives on leases extending over say one, two or three years, subject to certain terms and conditions restricting the number of persons in occupation, and imposing sanitary and other regulations." He concluded that he suspected the "natives," chief aim is "probably the acquisition, on terms absurdly generous on the part of the Government of Buildings, which they desire to secure, by tacit if not expressed arrangement, irrevocable rights of possession or tenancy—a point in their scheme which commends itself to very careful consideration and treatment. Moreover, the proposal [of the natives] is *"WRONG IN PRINCIPLE."*[49] Cummings, the SNAD, agreed with the official, but as we have seen, leasehold, freehold, and house building rights had been promised to Africans who moved from Korsten into New Brighton and to those already living at New Brighton.

In contrast to the opinions of many of the whites, the aspirant black middle class visualized decent living conditions, freehold land rights, permanent housing for their families, educational and church institutions, business opportunities and a viable Native Advisory Board to represent them in local government matters—in effect, an "urban frontier" that would provide chances for upward mobility in the colonial society. However, when the central administration framed regulations under the Native Reserve [Urban] Locations Act 1902, amended 1905, regarding the conditions of sale of surveyed plots that were to be leasehold or freehold at New Brighton, disagreements on two conditions surfaced. They read as follows: "1) that the plots are liable to confiscation in the event of intoxicating liquor being found on the premises and 2) that the owner of a plot is not allowed to keep his aged parents, who are unable to work and provide for themselves, on his premises."[50] Although space does not allow a lengthy discussion on the first clause to do with "kafir beer," it is noteworthy that in 1908 the central government offered another "concession" to New Brighton residents by establishing a rotation system of limited domestic beer brewing. The Location Superintendent issued the one-week permits only to "registered occupants of houses whose rent payments were up to date and not to *lodgers.*" Doubtless, although it was illegal to sell the liquor, it is highly probable that there was abuse, as the right to brew rotated from the "wet" areas to the "dry" areas.[51] Moreover, as mentioned earlier, some residents rented living space to *lodgers* at New Brighton, and this, too, would lend to selling liquor to other residents who were non-voters.

The second clause that Africans objected to dealt with the right of occupation in New Brighton on leasehold and freehold property and *aged parents*. Perhaps this problem was most illustrative of the different viewpoints held by blacks and whites about the role of the location and family and kinship ties. This problem also influenced the answer of who would occupy the sites, which would seem to be easily answered. After all, most of the potential property holders, many of them members of the aspirant black middle class, lived in a family setting and were party to the 1896 agreement. Therefore, we would expect that their families would live in whatever housing was erected at New Brighton as had been the practice. So what was the occupation debate really about?

The disagreement about the interpretation of the clause with regard to the occupation of the houses at New Brighton and whether or not the *aged parents* were able-bodied is worth closer examination. To many Africans this clause was an attack on their practices of kinship and family welfare. This was because with the removal of Africans to New Brighton, government regulations required that the residents be productive, able-bodied, and rent-paying. In fact, it probably seemed to many Africans that the white government and white employers were desirous of abandoning so-called nonproductive workers, along with reducing the number of people who could occupy a house and, concomitantly, the family size. Was this an indirect attack on the extended family practices that continued to be important to many Africans of this period. Could it be that the "nuclear" family model often associated with the growth of industrial capitalism, and which many times scholars implicitly take as representative as a unit of analysis, is what the colonial government had in mind when it talked about "occupation" and "the family" compared to the meaning and operation of the extended family for Africans?

The predominant African family form was the lineage family—extended clans (families) tracing their ancestry in common. The government's aim was to exclude unproductive black labor, which included the young and aged. Many Africans probably viewed this requirement as an indirect attack on African family kinship, which provided for the welfare of all age groups, including the young and elders. From the 1890s on, the demands and complaints of Africans living in the municipal housing settlements and later New Brighton touched on the issue of the number of people who could occupy the house, which influenced the size of the family, as well as inheritance rights if the head of the household died. In addition, Africans were very apprehensive about the welfare of aged black men and women.

In this respect in 1903 William Yokwe, one of the African leaders at New Brighton, asked the following in a petition to the Acting Inspector: "What government intended doing in the case of *aged* men and women who have no friends and who are compelled to earn a living by doing odd jobs in Port Elizabeth. He said they are barely able to earn enough to live on and that they would starve if they had to pay 8/- per mensen rent and 6/- per mensen railway fare. He hoped that some distinction would be made between these people and ablebodied men and women."[52]

Similar concerns were expressed about family welfare in April 1904 in the petition of an African deputation from Korsten. It requested that to protect family members from being separated, the terms of exemption from the 1903 Act be broadened to include "registered voters with their wives, children and *aged parents*, also the widows and *blood relations* of those who were registered voters" and "visitors who hold a residential permit from the Clerk of the Board to live with relatives for a period of three months." (my emphasis)[53] Among the southern Nguni (including the Xhosa, Zulu) the extended family or corporate kin group could include not only the consanguinity or relatives by birth (blood) but also the conjugality or relatives by marriage.[54] So Africans were trying to protect the rights of the extended kin group or corporate family including not only relatives by marriage, which Europeans were more familiar with, as well as relatives with whom they had blood ties. Also, when the Native Reserve Locations Bill was first proposed in 1902, Africans complained about the government's failure to exempt widows and families of registered voters from the Act, and they were supported in their demands by local officials.

African leaders argued for the protection of the aged and for them to be treated with respect and accorded certain privileges. Certainly they wanted the government to explain how the clause about the able-bodied would affect the aged. This concern for the aged was related to several concepts exhibited through kinship relations in the extended family and also the larger society among many African groups, including the southern Nguni. Thus, respect for the extended family, generally discussed as an African kinship practice, is also related to age and includes a hierarchy where one is accorded certain privileges and obligations by age. Schapera relates that "the eldest members of a family demand and obtained the greatest respect. . . . The hierarchy of age was rigidly maintained. Children were taught subservience to their elders as the fount of all wisdom and experience. . . . This regard for one's elders was extended beyond the family toward the community as a whole."

In many African societies, kinship terminology places "whole groups of relatives, sometimes of different categories or generations . . . under the same relationship term." Thus, people senior in age to oneself were universally to be addressed as *baba* (father) or (mother) and had to be treated with deference and respect. "Any insolence or disobedience was strictly punished." Schapera states that, "the same general type of behavior [was observed] toward all the relatives," who were called by one term; and they "reciprocated by observing a certain prescribed line of conduct, the nature of which varied with the relationship."[55]

Although in the urban towns we find altered kinship and family practices influenced by Christianity, Western culture, free trade, capitalism, and individualism, the reciprocity terminology and kinship practices according to age and rank continued to be observed. In essence, the social networks, especially the extended family, survived and operated among all classes of Africans in the urban areas, including the practices of offering lodging and hospitality.[56] Clearly the transference of the respect for the aged continued to operate among these Africans, since they recognized that in the social hierarchy the elders had made their contribution to the family "community" and deserved to be taken care of, or at least have their interests protected as the new segregationist laws were applied to Africans.

This communal practice was sometimes criticized by European officials, who believed that the "communistic" habits of Africans provided an economic safety net and allowed them to refuse to go out to work. Some officials feared that the unemployed, often called "vagrants," would become a "menace to life and property." But these fears were often groundless and based upon racial and class prejudice. In fact, according to the comments made in 1908 by the Acting R.M., "in spite of the general poverty existing amongst Natives at present and the artificially high price of foodstuffs, their communistic habits of life have so far enabled them to live without any apparent tendency to become a 'menace to life and property.'"[57] Keeping in mind this societal tendency to provide "hospitality" and the continuation of kinship networks, we can better understand the general concern for the young and the aged. Influencing this concern must have been the fact that failure to pay rent at New Brighton was a criminal offense that could lead to fines and eviction. Unfortunately, it was exactly those who were unable to provide for themselves, such as the elders, who would be arrested, imprisoned, and possibly evicted. Even then, the rent was still due.

Concern for the welfare of the elders was also voiced during the continued debate over land and property rights at New Brighton. For many

Africans it became a thorny issue that demanded a solution. For instance, Whiley Pikoli, leader of a deputation from New Brighton in 1905, was the first to discuss the linkage of the welfare of aged parents, the sale or lease of plots, and the self-built housing option. Pikoli, the only African with a trading stand at New Brighton, maintained that Africans were refusing to take up freehold plots because they objected to two clauses in the conditions of sale. One was that "the owner of a plot is not allowed to keep his *aged parents,* who are unable to work and provide for themselves, on his premises." (emphasis mine)[58]

In response, Dower, the Secretary of the Native Affairs Department, explained that "the determining question was whether the aged parents were able or not to earn a livelihood and thus provide for themselves; if they were, they would not really be dependent upon their son and should at least contribute their fair quota toward the expenses of the location in respect of sanitary, water supply and other services, while if they were not, they were clearly exempted from the requirement of the regulation as regards payment."[59]

Apparently Dower thought that the matter had been settled satisfactorily. But in 1906, at another meeting between Africans at New Brighton and J. A. Verschuur, the ARM, at New Brighton, the same issue was raised, and the deputation complained that nothing had been done since the first discussion. In fact, the stipulation had not been altered, which meant that the Africans would have to trust to official interpretation and enforcement. It seems that the Africans believed that aged parents who were not able-bodied would not be allowed to remain in the location. The confusion may have emanated from the regulations that limited the number of people who occupied a house and allowed for those who had defaulted on their rent to be evicted from the location. At some point apparently the matter was resolved satisfactorily, since in later meetings between Africans and the officials the question was not raised. Also, further problems prevented many Africans with these concerns from taking up freehold or leasehold sites at New Brighton.

Another obstacle to Africans acquiring land and property rights at New Brighton revolved around the question of who would pay for building the houses. The government had promised that Africans who moved into New Brighton from Korsten could exchange a plot for a plot and that those who already lived there could apply for a site. So during this period why were Africans unable to acquire these rights in New Brighton? The answer was related to the economic depression following the war, racial discrimination that limited occupational and business opportunities for blacks, and misunderstandings between the government and potential siteholders about the terms of occupation and inheritance. But all were linked to financing the New Brighton location and controlling the black population. So while most white interest groups agreed that Africans should be segregated but allocated certain rights and privileges no substantive action was taken.

Obviously the central government was ambivalent about supplying land and housing for Africans. While in the liberal spirit many thought that it was a good idea, no group wanted the responsibility for paying for it or the possible repercussions of struggling over removing an entrenched, black, landowning population. For example, at a meeting in 1902 Mr. Wylde, the RM at Port Elizabeth, declared that the government would most likely be against land titles being issued to individuals; he said he believed that if titles were issued to location residents, it would result in numerous problems, especially if removals became necessary. Nevertheless, Wylde continued, natives could build their own houses from their private funds and according to government building specifications and then acquire a long-term lease to the property. This lease would allow for transfer of the building to a subsequent applicant and/or for the government to purchase or take over the building at an agreed-upon price if the owner wanted to sell.

It is clear that African leaders and their white supporters were willing to compromise with government officials in order to work out an agreement to ensure land and property rights at New Brighton. Even before passage of the 1902 Native Reserve Locations Act a deputation made up of African leaders and their supporters met with the Port Elizabeth Resident Magistrate in July of that year. Residents at Cooper's Kloof and Strangers' appointed Ben Simuka and Edward Ngesi to discuss whether or not the government would agree to allocate land titles at Cradock Place or Deal Party [the land where New Brighton was situated] to those who could build houses from their own funds or who "might raise money to build on the lands" at New Brighton.[60]

Wylde said he thought the government would object, that titles would undermine proper control and maintenance, and that inconveniences would arise, especially in trying to transfer the land. Wylde continued that the government might be willing to issue a long-term lease for a ground rental that could be transferred to an individual or sold to the government. In cases of death the lease could be formally transferred to the appointed successor. Both Ngesi and Simuka thought this [the lease] would remove some doubt among the people who wanted to erect buildings. Also, the Mayor and Reverend Henry Newell of Edward's Memorial Church, the largest church in Port Elizabeth serving an African congregation, thought that the proposal was one the natives could "readily understand and appreciate."[61]

But Africans clearly wanted freehold land tenure, not leasehold. Therefore, one year later another deputation led by Frank Makwena and Moses

Foley, representing Reservoir, Strangers', and Cooper's Kloof, met with the Town Council and requested that they fulfill the 1896 agreement.[62] Still, nothing was done until so few people moved into New Brighton that the Cape Prime Minister Sprigg visiting Port Elizabeth in October 1903 conceded the right of Africans at Korsten to exchange titled plots for similar freehold plots at New Brighton. Also, other Africans were awarded the right to claim a long-term leasehold rather than a freehold plot and were allowed to build their own houses. Presumably many of the potential leaseholders would be Africans already living at New Brighton.

But W. G. Cummings, the Secretary of Native Affairs for the Cape colony, expressed the fears of many government officials with regard to land rights at New Brighton, stating that the "natives" would view the leases as title. Cummings said, "Experience has shown that once a Native enters into occupation of a piece of land, he is very unwilling to relax his hold on it. No matter what the circumstances may be which require him to give it up, he will be sure to feel aggrieved."[63] Although Cummings was not ready to recommend that the applications for leasehold be refused, he suggested that a "definite reply be deferred" and that the "natives" be told that they should move in first and then decide if they wanted to retain residence under a restricted title.

In September 1903 the government offered leasehold plots to Africans whereby they could construct their own houses on land they would occupy on a long-term lease, but they would not own the land. Although the leases could be transferred and/or inherited, the government would have the right to remove the leaseholders. Despite there being at least two hundred potential applicants, months passed and no applications were submitted until January 1904.[64] Even then only a mere sixteen people applied. Because a building had to meet government standards and have government approval before it was erected, most of the applications were submitted along with building plans for the typical 70 by 62-1/2-foot house. Also, the sites could not be sold or sublet without government consent. Moreover, other "suggestions" were attached to the leasehold scheme, including a limitation on occupancy (no more than four to a sleeping room, regardless of size) and the requirement that the building had to be completed in four months. In addition, Africans would also have to pay a survey and title fee, which was calculated to be £3,17/-.

Many of the applicants were long-time residents of Port Elizabeth who already lived at New Brighton. Among them were Isaac Wauchope, Whiley Pikoli, and Edward Tsewu.[65] Three women, Mary Dlififa, Sarah Samson, and Dinah Bobby, applied for sites, but they did not submit building plans. Most of the house plans were modest but distinctly designed, having at least two bedrooms, a dining room, and a kitchen. All were larger than the ready-made location government houses that all looked alike. At least eight of these applicants requested that the central government agree to loan the funds for building the housing and that the loan be repaid on the installment plan.

The Civil Commissioner considered eleven applications to be bona fide or valid. "Bona fide" referred to the ability of the applicant to pay for the construction of the house as well to pay the £4 that was annual site rent.[66] The applicants were quickly informed that the government was unwilling to pay for constructing the houses. When notified of this situation, several of the applicants agreed to erect their own buildings; none of the women was in this category. Nevertheless, it soon became clear that most Africans could not afford building materials. Moreover, builders would not assist the Africans unless they could make payment and pledge their sites as security for further payment.[67] Of course, this was impossible, since the sites would be leased from the government and not owned by the individual applicant. The refusal of the government to assist the Africans to build at New Brighton must have been discouraging to the prospective Korsten residents who had been promised freehold and the exchange of a site at New Brighton for their site at Korsten. It is probable that many Korstenites were in dire straits and needed assistance to build housing at New Brighton.

The only applicant for building at New Brighton whom the government flat out refused a site was Isaac S. Wauchope. Wauchope was a relative of Reverend Isaac Wauchope, a pillar of the African community until he took up a ministerial post at Ft. Beaufort. The Wauchope family had long provided African leadership in Port Elizabeth. Issac S. Wauchope was the leader of a group of men applying for a site to erect a building "to be known as New Brighton Hall," to be used for social gatherings. He requested that the government finance the building, in effect issuing a loan to the group. The other members of the syndicate were J. S. Wauchope, L. T. Mvabaza, G. K. Npengesi, C. Mji, B. H. Buhlunga, and J. W. Gallana.[68] But the government denied the application, primarily because the men had no funding. Instead, the men were offered the use of the New Brighton courthouse to hold meetings, which they accepted.

In essence, the stipulation that Africans had to pay for building their own houses rendered moribund the government concession that Africans could lease land at New Brighton and build their own houses. To break the deadlock with regard to building the houses, Mr. Pyott, Member for the Legislative Assembly (MLA) and one of the progressive members that Africans had helped to elect in 1903, suggested in June 1905 that the government lend money to Africans who wanted their own houses at New Brighton. He stated that "The Natives have little spare cash and the title they will receive for buying plots right out is a conditional one, that they can only sell to Natives (also a stipulation in the 1913 Lands Act). No private person or institution would lend money on those conditions for building purposes unless the government would guarantee them.... Monthly payments could be arranged like a Building Society ... with 8 percent interest per month on a £2 per month payment."[69]

In response to Pyott, E. E. Dower of the Native Affairs Department stated that the Prime Minister had read the proposal with interest, but "he regrets that your proposals involve a charge against public funds." So the proposal could not be approved without a parliamentary act, and in any case Dower felt the scheme was impractical. Using Pyott's plan, Verschuur, the Assistant Resident Magistrate at Port Elizabeth, calculated it would cost £30,000 to build 320 plots. But Dower said that Dr. Jameson, the Prime Minister, had suggested that the government could provide, in the conditions of the title deeds to grants of allotments made at New Brighton, that the right to mortgage might be exercised subject to the approval of government. In this way if a native borrowed from his employer to build a house and could not repay the loan, he [the native] could sell or lease [the dwelling] to another native. But the government could not support a building scheme, especially given the money it had already lost in the New Brighton location scheme.[70]

The Role of the African Churches

Apparently, Pyott the MLA, had discussed the idea for the Building Society with the Reverend James Mata Dwane. Dwane is best known for his role in linking in 1896 the "Ethiopian" or African independent church movement with the African-American church based in the United States the African Methodist Episcopal Church (AMEC). This led to the AMEC establishing roots in South Africa. Pyott first broached the idea of subsidizing Africans in May 1905. Since Dwane travelled to Cape Town in June 1905 while the Parliament was in session, it is likely that the two met and shared the idea of the building society.

As we know, by 1905 several groups of Africans that made up the emergent black middle class were trying to negotiate land and property rights at New Brighton. Correspondence between the Superintendent of Locations, the SNAD, and African leaders of churches indicates that the "Ethiopian" (as all churches headed by Africans that separated from the founding white mission body were called by whites) movement was a new force in the ongoing struggle. The "Ethiopian" (usually termed separatist or independent) African churches, often described as representing a nascent form of African nationalism, were viewed with suspicion by many whites, who feared a challenge to their authority in the church and a lose of white sovereignty in general. Hitherto studies on the "Ethiopian" church movement seldom analyzed its workings in relationship to the permanent black population and their local struggles. From an analysis of this influence we gain a deeper understanding of the emergence of black intraclass and interclass conflict and its impact on black resistance to segregation in urban areas. As in the past some issues promoted black unity; others served as a wedge that the government could use to demobilize unified protest. Clearly the complexity of the struggle over land and housing at New Brighton increased because of the Ethiopian or independent church movement among Africans. Before proceeding to the analysis, it is necessary to provide a background to the African independent church movement.

The Ethiopian Movement and Conflict Over Land at New Brighton

Reverend James M. Dwane was initially a Wesleyan deacon on the Port Elizabeth circuit, beginning shortly after his ordination in 1881. He was drawn into the Ethiopian church by Reverend Mangena Mokone, founder of the Ethiopian church which Dwane joined and represented on his visits to the United States of America. Mokone, who was based at Kilnerton, the Methodist school near Pretoria, in the South African Republic, resigned from the Wesleyan church in October 1892. In a Declaration of Independence document, he listed his grievances, including charges of separate district meetings according to race, positions of authority such as chairman and secretary held by whites, differential pay scale and fringe benefits awarded according to race, and disrespect for blacks in general by white officials. Mokone went on to establish his own independent congregation at Pretoria, which he called the "Ethiopian Church." Meanwhile, James Dwane resigned from the Wesleyans and joined Mokone's church in 1894. In 1896 the Ethiopian Church sent Dwane to the U.S. to form a union with the AMEC. Upon his return he successfully proselytized, thus rapidly increasing the number of adherents.

The reasons for the attraction to the separatist church movement in general and the AMEC in particular were the promise that the African ministers and churches would be more independent, and hold positions of authority as they directed their congregations. As we have seen from the analysis of the AAWMU in Chapter 4, the common experience of racial discrimination faced by blacks in both the United States or in South Africa also drew these groups together.[71] The black Christians demanded the right of self-determination, including handling church funds and holding the chief ministerial positions of power and authority. As the independent church movement expanded to the Cape colony in the 1890s, whites began to complain against the purposes of the AMEC.

Not surprisingly, much of the criticism against the "Ethiopian" churches emanated from the large number of established European missionaries spreading the gospel in the Cape colony, including the Presbyterians, Congregationalists, Methodists, Baptists and Episcopalians. As a result, when the Ethiopian churches, including the AMEC, entered the arena they were often viewed as "missionary raiders." But not until Bishop Henry M. Turner of the AMEC visited the Cape Colony from the United States in 1898 did concerted criticism erupt against the black Americans and their church.[72] Moreover, Bishop Turner and the *Voice of Missions,* the AMEC newspaper, were seen as leading a movement, both religious and political, to oust the Europeans. There was some truth to the idea that the AMEC wanted to convert Africans to Christianity and believed that it was especially equipped to do so because of divine providence.[73]

In broad terms the independent churches were viewed as a menace because their independence spoke of self-determination and challenged white supremacy and control. In this regard the fears and the prejudices of the white missionaries were often transmitted to the government, resulting in a refusal of concessions normally accorded the white mission churches. This had a significant effect, since in order to exert their independence, the newly formed black independent churches needed the recognition of the state to offer their congregations many of the benefits associated with Christian conversion. These included a land site on which to erect a church, church buildings, and church schools as well as the right to conduct marriage ceremonies. So although colonial authorities may have disagreed with the European missionaries and believed that the AMEC or the other independently established denominations were no threat, they still decided to placate the white missionaries. Thus, in some cases the government denied recognition of the independent churches as "legitimate" and therefore refused to recognize the right of the ministers to operate church and school sites and to conduct marriage rites.[74] A factor that influenced the reception of the independent black churches was whether or not they continued to adhere to the same constitution or church laws as the mission churches. Perhaps this explains why there was less white resistance to the black church in Port Elizabeth.[75]

In Port Elizabeth prior to the Ethiopian movement the largest African denomination was the Edwards Memorial Church, a Congregational Church established by the Wesleyan Methodists, with a white minister at its head. Other denominations that served the African population included the London Missionary Society, the Basotho Church, and St. Stephens' Catholic Church. Most of these congregations, but not all, were headed by white ministers with African ministers in the secondary slot. Apparently many of the ideas and attitudes of the European missionaries at Port Elizabeth were grounded in racial beliefs of the times about the superiority of whites vis-a-vis blacks, trusteeship, and Africans as children. For black ministers this resulted in lack of advancement in the church, in particular being excluded from holding important positions that would allow them power, authority, and control of church funds. In essence a color bar blocked black advancement in the church because white missionaries refused to give up positions of authority as the "first" ministers. Many missionaries believed that Africans were ill-equipped and even inherently inferior and "so did not have the qualities needed for pastors and bishops and that African churches must be ruled by Europeans backed by colonial governments."[76]

Fortunately, not all European denominations shared this view; it will be recalled that both black and white ministers of the Wesleyan and Congregational denomination had brokered the 1896 agreement between the Port Elizabeth town council and the Africans who would be affected. Also, some African and European ministers were involved in the more recent deputations to gain land rights at New Brighton. Until the breakup of the African settlements in 1903 and the creation of Korsten and New Brighton, some of the black ministers provided consistent leadership and representation for their congregations in negotiations through deputations and petitions with local and central government. Among these ministers, all of them Wesleyan Methodists, were Isaac Wauchope, Benjamin Dlepu, and Gavan Kakaza.[77]

Nonetheless, some African ministers aspired to more opportunities and independence from the mission churches, so that the independent church movement had also spawned other sects in Port Elizabeth. By September 1902 the total number of independent church adherents was estimated at seven hundred. Apparently the seven hundred figure referred to several African congregations called independent or Ethiopian, including the AMEC, the African Presbyterian, and the Ethiopian. The Ethiopian church had two church sites at Reservoir and one at Korsten. Also, there were meeting places in Reservoir, Cooper's Kloof, Gubbs', and Vlei Post. The African Presbyterians had a chapel at Cooper's Kloof, with two hundred followers, headed by Reverend William Bottomon, a long-time African leader and previously minister at one of the Wesleyan Methodist churches serving a black congregation. Bottoman later moved his flock to Korsten where he continued to challenge the government's racially discriminatory initiatives. The AMEC minister also had two hundred followers at Cooper's Kloof.

The Resident Magistrate reported that although these sects were "working principally amongst recognized religious bodies," he did not have reliable information about the character and tendency of their teachings.[78] Still, it is clear that in 1902 the independent African churches in Port Elizabeth were not viewed as a threat. For example, in February 1901 the Ethiopian church headed by S. T. Mdliva requested a land site to build their church at Reservoir location, and the Town Council consented. From the point of view of the Town Councillors who supported segregating Africans at New Brighton, the independent churches were perhaps controversial but favored religion and education for blacks and were unopposed to separation of whites and blacks.

But with regard to Port Elizabeth, how did the Ethiopian movement affect the local struggle over land, housing, and residential segregation? The answer brings us back to Reverend Dwane. When he joined the AMEC, many of his circuit followers also converted. To acquire a church and school site for the AMEC in Port Elizabeth, Dwane applied to the Town Council in March 1899 for a plot in the Reservoir Municipal Location. The Council's Location Committee, a local government body appointed by the Town Council to handle native affairs, approved the application; however, before the site was occupied, Dwane left the AMEC in 1899 and formed the Order of Ethiopia. Much has been written on the reasons for his departure, including disagreements over the use of church funds, objections from the AMEC officers to his appointment as the Vicar Bishop, the failure of the government to recognize the AMEC, and the government's subsequent refusal to authorize marriage officers.[79] In any case, the result was that some of the AMEC followers stayed with Dwane and supported the new church, while another section supported Bishop Mokone and remained with the AMEC.[80]

Despite Dwane's departure from the AMEC, the Port Elizabeth church members were allocated a church site and apparently took up residence at Reservoir in 1901. Although it is unclear who was minister at that church, it is noteworthy that an African-American AMEC missionary was stationed at Port Elizabeth in 1899 and that his opinions on land and economic prospects were published in the *Voice of Missions*.[81] Meanwhile, Dwane arranged to be accepted with his followers as a separate order into the English Anglican (Catholic) church. In the long run Dwane's hopes for independence were limited by the fact that the Order of Ethiopia was governed by the Anglican constitution.

Between 1903 and 1905, during the time the government refused loans or assistance to Africans to build houses at New Brighton and Korsten residents were still refusing to move into the location, Dwane's Order of Ethiopia became entangled in the struggle to acquire land and property rights at New Brighton. As we know, Africans had protested against moving into New Brighton, especially those who were Christian and Western-educated, unless they were awarded land and property rights. Also, the various church denominations had continually requested title to church plots at New Brighton. For example, some of the established churches, such as Edwards' Memorial and St. Stephen's, applied to the central government, and requests emanated from individual Africans and from the church congregations. Although the government agreed to allocate church sites, it refused to issue freehold title, since if it became necessary to remove Africans from the land, it might prove too difficult, and the government might have to pay compensation. Thus, the risk of more financial obligations was too great.

By this time Dwane's Order of Ethiopia church congregation was affiliated with the Catholic Church. Also, other churches were applying for freehold, including the AMEC and the African Presbyterian at new Brighton. As we have seen, all church applicants were granted church sites at the Reservoir municipal location, but the government refused to grant them titles. It seems that the government decided to follow this policy at New Brighton as well. Eventually, however, the Order of Ethiopia was granted a freehold title to a church site at New Brighton, but this privilege was withheld from both the old established churches and the newly founded independent denominations. This was a startling development and so deserves further comment.

Several factors should be kept in mind: first, Dwane's withdrawal from the AME and consequent establishment of the Order of Ethiopia and affiliation with the Catholic order; second, the resentment and fear of the white missionaries with regard to losing their congregations to African independent churches; third, the infighting among the white missionaries and the independent black ministers over church property and church members; and, finally, the government's desire to promote occupation of New Brighton by members of the aspirant black middle class.

Dwane was granted a freehold church site for the Order of Ethiopia in 1905 primarily because of church politics and his willingness to capitalize on the fears of white missionaries and white officials. As mentioned, Dwane had affiliated with the Anglican Church, that is, the Church of the Province of South Africa. Many of the AME members followed Dwane, and several thousand were among his own Xhosa people in the Grahamstown (the town adjacent to Port Elizabeth) diocese. Dwane, a Xhosa, was originally from Middledrift in the Ciskei. By February 1901 the Order of Ethiopia had established a church site at Reservoir Location, and by June 1903 it had occupied two wood-and-iron churches and rented a third. Dwane had about six hundred followers throughout the town. In effect, this meant that an African minister who had deserted the Wesleyans because of racial discrimination had now returned to the church controlled by whites in denunciation of the church controlled by blacks (American Negroes and Africans). In fact, according to the Reverend Cox of the local St. Stephen's Anglican Church, the Order of Ethiopia "has already proved the most formidable opponent of their former co-religionists, and the order has been eminently successful in reaching the heathen and the lapsed Christians and is growing rapidly. From a political point of view it is the organization best fitted to counteract any disloyal tendency there may be in the American Methodists. . . . "[82] Thus, to many whites, Dwane must have represented vindication of their church practices and organization and their belief that it was too soon for the natives to be in control of their own churches.

It is noteworthy that a few years later, in October 1905, the Reverend Cox was involved in a dispute with two African men over school property at Korsten. Apparently these men had withdrawn from St. Stephen's and taken some of the property with them to start a church and school. After finding the property at a private mission school a few yards away from St. Stephens, Cox sued them for theft. During the court proceedings Cox admitted that there was a church dispute; subsequently, the case was dismissed.[83] The *Imvo* newspaper related that "much to the joy of the accused the case was dismissed by the Solicitor-General. Thus, bigotry, autocracy and priestcraft which 'boss the show' in the church have received a rude awakening at the hands of an ever watchful Nemesis. How are the mighty fallen!"[84]

To the white ministers Dwane represented a bridge and even a compromise between the independent African churches and the European congregations that would counteract losing their members to the African independent churches. Clearly they viewed Dwane as a church loyalist, and, as in the past, loyalists were to be rewarded. Still, when he initially applied for a church site at New Brighton in 1903, his application was refused. Then the Reverend Cox intervened and vouched for Dwane's loyalty. Cox wrote to the Secretary of the Native Affairs Department stating that the Order of Ethiopia, which was affiliated with St. Stephen's mission church under the Church of England, had a strong claim and that it "would combat the AME who were becoming a danger to the state."[85] Dwane was immediately allocated title to a church and school site, and in 1904 the Order of Ethiopia moved their building from Reservoir location to New Brighton. However, even Dwane was unable to secure freehold, since the land agreement stipulated that when no longer being used, the land would revert back to the state.[86]

Meanwhile, in May 1905, shortly after the passage of the amended Native Locations Act, Dwane wrote to the ARM that he "was not only in thorough sympathy with the government scheme of locating the natives at New Brighton, but I have worked hard to make the thing a success."[87] Dwane went on to apply for 102 building sites at New Brighton, two for churches, one for a school, and 99 for members of his church congregation. Also, he applied for a trading stand (a site to open a business for trade) on behalf of his congregation. Dwane's application for the trading stand at New Brighton was forwarded to the office of the SNAD by the Acting Civil Commissioner for Port Elizabeth, H. C. Becker. In his letter Becker stated "[I] strongly recommend that this site be granted to the Revd. Dwane who has now gone over to New Brighton with all his men. . . . "[88] Not surprisingly, Dwane's application for the stand was approved. He was obviously being rewarded for agreeing to move into New Brighton, since he and his members would be the first ones to take up the leasehold sites and break the deadlock against moving there.

But having moved into New Brighton, Dwane's people were soon in dire financial straits, because many of them were unemployed and unable to pay for building the houses they had envisioned. As a solution Dwane suggested that the government support the establishment of a Mutual Building Society to assist the African plot holders to build houses. According to Dwane, after a public meeting at New Brighton he determined that "about two to three hundred natives . . . will be benefitted [sic] by such a society."[89] Meanwhile, since the government had not issued building regulations or provided for a water supply, the stipulation that the houses had to be constructed in three months could not be enforced. The building society scheme was potentially beneficial to aspirant property holders if the government would agree to it. The value of the fully paid shares would be £100 each, whereas payments would be 10/- a month. Dwane pointed out that the society would be able to sell the property (to the natives, of course) in case "anyone failed to fulfil conditions on which his house was built for him."[90]

J. Verschurr, the ARM for New Brighton, when passing along Dwane's request to H. C. Becker, the Acting Civil Commissioner for Port Elizabeth, explained that the Africans who would be allocated plots at New Brighton would be those who were Building Society members, and that the Society would be under government control. Contractors would be invited to submit bids for construction and each:

> plot holder [would be] debited with the cost of his building. He will be at liberty to pay off as much as he is in a position to, but not less than a certain fixed sum per month, the object . . . to provide each Native plot holder with house which will in due course become his property. Mr. Dwane has reason to believe that on this basis the contractors will act, provided the Government agree to the scheme and guarantees the payment of a certain fixed sum per month, in the event of there being a shortfall.[91]

But there were also other problems, which were discussed at a public meeting in New Brighton. There it was pointed out that before New Brighton was built, Prime Minister Sprigg promised that the land plots would be the same size as those at Grahamstown. In fact, the plots at Grahamstown were three times the size of those offered at New Brighton, and in September 1905 Dwane told the RM, "The work of building houses cannot be started without its being settled."[92] After further consultation, Dwane wrote that in lieu of larger sites at New Brighton, Africans preferred two sites and that one of these should serve as a garden to be attached to the residential site. Obviously, some of Dwane's members had previously been involved in land negotiations with the government, and they were still hoping to gain control of land and property in Port Elizabeth. In the end neither Dwane's group nor any other

Africans were able to acquire individual freehold or leasehold title at New Brighton, primarily because no one could afford to build a house without assistance. Eventually the churches at New Brighton—and there were at least seven, including Church of the Apostolic Holiness League, St. Stephen's Mission, and Congregational Union—were granted title but with the same stipulation that applied to Dwane's Order of Ethiopia.

By 1908 B. Whitfield, the ARM at New Brighton, wrote that Africans did not move into New Brighton because there was no provision for lease or land rights and none for moving their property there. Africans have indicated that "as soon as the regulation for the sale and lease of residence and garden plots in the location are promulgated, many respectable natives will move into the location."[93] Similarly, in that same year, William Scully, the RM at Port Elizabeth, proposed a land scheme to get Africans to move into New Brighton. The plan included freehold and gardens, but this idea also was never brought to fruition. Thus, one major obstacle to Africans gaining land and houses at New Brighton remained who would pay for segregation. Meanwhile, New Brighton's population fluctuated, but by 1910 it began to stabilize at around 3,100, which was almost twice what the population had been prior to the passage of the 1905 amended act.

Of the total population figure at New Brighton, 3,100, perhaps a third did not pay rent. So although the central government had implemented the Native Locations Act and forced one-half of the total African population of approximately 10,000[94] to move from the town, many did not pay rent. As Table 7.3 indicates, blacks continued to live in the town, in Korsten, and elsewhere.

Table 7.3   1911 Port Elizabeth Population

Area	Blacks	Coloreds[a]	Whites	Total
Urban and suburbs	1,730	11,191	18,579	31,500
Korsten	2,352	1,660	510	4,522
New Brighton	3,414	184	52	3,650
Walmer	221	285	1,086	1,592
Total	7,717	13,320	20,227	41,264

Note: a. Some Africans were listed as Coloreds. See the voters' registration list for 1903 where the people listed as Colored obviously belong to the African group. As discussed in a previous chapter, this was not unusual since racial discrimination was influenced by color, culture, class, and physical features but the number that preferred to be listed as Colored remains uncertain.[95]

Source: Pretoria Archives, STK 077-081, Population Census, 1911.

Census figures indicate that the total urban African population of Port Elizabeth increased in 1904 from 7,418 to a total of 7,717 in 1911. For Coloreds the figures are 10,332 in 1904 to a total of 13,320 in 1911, approximately 300 for each group. Of this total, at New Brighton in 1904 there were 1,310, and by 1910 there were 3,414. According to Christopher, in measuring segregation this amounted to an increase in the black population of 26 percent in 1904 at New Brighton; by 1911 the percent of the black population had risen to 44.2, and all other municipal locations had been closed. Two other locations, those run by the Harbor Board and the Walmer municipality, housed an additional 4.8 percent of the black population.[96]

These figures indicate that by 1911 almost one-half the black population resided in segregated housing, either at New Brighton or the Harbor Board. Part of the increase occurred in 1909, when Reservoir, the last of the municipal locations established in the nineteenth century by local government, was closed. The dispute between the Reservoir residents and Town Council, a remnant from the 1896 agreement, led the exempted Africans in 1903 to refuse to go to New Brighton until properly compensated, and they had also stopped paying rent. The Town Council finally agreed to pay compensation for the dwellings and pay for the move to New Brighton, and it promised the resisters that they could occupy leased housing sites.[97] At least 229 standholders and their relatives relocated, including 21 women.[98] Nevertheless, many of these families were exempt from the Native Locations Act and chose to go to Korsten and elsewhere. Thus, only a small increase occurred between October 1909 and May 1910, when the population rose from 3,080 to 3,193, an increase of 113, which would indicate that many Reservoir residents chose to enter Korsten rather than New Brighton. (see Table 7.1)

Despite some possible discrepancies in total figures for the African non-exempted population residing outside of New Brighton, by 1910 spatial segregation had increased, and most Africans lived in segregated housing, whether in the town or at other settlements outside New Brighton.[99] Although many Africans may not have viewed segregation as a social barrier, it tended to cut off Africans from political and economic opportunities that would occur through integration and to impede them from competing with the wider society. For example, one avenue to enfranchisement, the property qualification, could not be fulfilled at New Brighton. The New Brighton Advisory Board established at New Brighton through the 1905 Native Location Act was apparently to replace the enfranchisement rights that were lost. However, Africans could only vote to elect Advisory Board members if their rent was paid up. New Brighton residents voted for four and the other two members were appointed by the Superintendent of Locations. Moreover, as Christopher points out, "The mere fact that people were assigned to groups was of significance for the politicians, bureaucrats and others who came to accept the groups so created as immutable, and framed laws and regulations on this basis."[100]

Conclusion

It is apparent that by 1910 the New Brighton experiment in the segregation of Africans was well underway, but it had not emerged as the government or the Africans had envisioned it. It was, however, the beginning of a segregationist housing and land policy that the government was pursuing in other areas of South Africa. Although the configuration was different, the government's intent was the same: to segregate and to control and exploit African labor. Exempted Africans in Port Elizabeth retained the right to live elsewhere, but theoretically the nonexempted Africans could be forced into New Brighton. Both exempt and nonexempted Africans, however, avoided New Brighton, continuing to live illegally in town and in other settlements.

Several of the influences that had prevented the government's implementation and/or enforcement of segregationist legislation remained important, including lack of government funding, which could also be translated as lack of interest or "will." Moreover, disputes continued between the government and the emergent African middle class over compensation, freehold land titles, and property rights. There was also conflict over rent, restrictive regulations, train services, liquor and beer brewing rights, and free movement in and out of the Port Elizabeth district. Between 1903 and 1910 it became clear that forcing Africans into New Brighton was very different from creating and controlling a docile, passive labor force that would pay for its own segregation "away in the locations." For several years New Brighton operated at a financial loss, and administration was a constant struggle. In addition, unsanitary and overcrowded conditions at New Brighton led to a deterioration in health for its residents.[101]

The influence of the liberal alliance continued to decline as evidenced by the inability of its supporters to gain freehold for their churches and for members of their congregations who resided at New Brighton. Nor could the liberals convince the government to finance the housing scheme. Moreover, the government broke its promises, and challenges by Africans through legitimate channels, such as appealing to Parliamentary representatives, proved to be unproductive. The liberal alliance was aimed at protecting the rights of Christian Africans and members of the aspirant black middle class. This was accomplished to a limited extent by the 1905 amendment to the Native Reserve [Urban] Locations Act, since some Africans and their *blood relations* were exempted if they were registered voters or if they could show that they owned property valued at £75 or more.

Furthermore, Africans found several ways to avoid the location regulations or to so vehemently oppose the government's new restrictive initiatives that they were able to prevent implementation. Although as several writers have pointed out one-half of the African population at Port Elizabeth was segregated by 1910, one-half was not. Moreover, the one-half that was segregated had managed to maintain some dignity by refusing to carry passes; establishing an advisory board, independent churches and schools; and creating a home for themselves and their families even though titles remained unobtainable. Also, Africans in family housing were subletting rooms to single men and women, another illegal activity now conceded by government to New Brighton residents.

The name of the first formal segregated African township in Port Elizabeth, New Brighton was suppose to reflect a new and bright beginning. After all, the white officials argued, residential segregation was the best thing for the Africans in the town. They promised that segregation would benefit Africans by providing decent housing, sanitation, water, and schools—in essence, an African urban village. Somehow, the name did not seem to impress much of the African population in Port Elizabeth, nor did Africans accept the message that it was for their well-being to move there. Thus, many Africans, regardless of their class background, refused to move voluntarily to New Brighton.

Notes

1. E. Barrett, Acting Secretary for Native Affairs, 8 January 1919. Report of the Department of Native Affairs for the years 1913–1918, U.G. 7-1919.

2. Noreen Kagan, "African Settlements in the Johannesburg Area, 1903–1923" (master's thesis, University of the Witwatersrand, Johannesburg, 1978), 25; T. R. H. Davenport, "The Beginnings of Urban Segregation in South Africa: The Natives (Urban Areas) Act of 1923 and Its Background," *Institute of Social and Economic Research*, Rhodes University, Grahamstown, 1971, pp. 5–6. This authorization was extended to other municipalities in 1904 and to the villages in 1906.

3. By 1914 there were marked similarities in the extraordinarily poor sanitary conditions at native locations, and tuberculosis was widespread, *Tuberculosis Commission Report*, Cape of Good Hope, U.G. 34-1914. pp. 6–7. Also see Kagan, "African Settlements," Chap. 3,4,5; for African resistance in the twentieth century, see Hilary Sapire, "African Settlement and Segregation in Brakpan, 1900–1927," *Holding Their Ground* edited by Philip Bonner, et al. (Johannesburg: Ravan Press, 1989), pp. 141–176; Davenport, "The Beginnings of Urban Segregation," discusses the laws affecting the rights of Africans to buy property in town. He notes that only in the Cape was there a stipulation in the amended 1905 act that allowed the

local authority to make regulations providing for the lease or grant of building lots for natives who desired to erect self-built housing in the location, p. 9.

4. Native Reserve Locations Act 40 of 1902, *Statues of the Cape of Good Hope*, amended 1905. (1) Influx/efflux control into the town and the location: Authorization from the Inspector of Locations was needed to reside in the location. (2) Residential segregation. (3) Mandatory passes or badges that were tied to residence and employment: Employers were prohibited from hiring laborers not carrying a pass. (4) Prohibition on freehold property ownership—amended to allow leasehold. (5) Prohibition on self-built housing: All housing was provided by the government; amended to allow the erection of buildings by special permission from the Governor. (6) Prohibition on liquor—amended to allow regulated domestic brewing of kafir beer by voters. (7) A criminal penalty for nonpayment of rent. (8) Establishment of advisory boards.

5. During later periods in other areas of South Africa, especially after the passage of the 1923 Native Locations Act, similar types of protest and resistance would be repeated. By this time several organizations had been formed: South African Native National Congress, in 1912; Industrial and Commercial Workers' Union (ICU), in 1919; and the Socialist Party, in 1918 (later the Communist Party). Also, Africans held a general anti-pass campaign in Johannesburg in 1919. The aforementioned protest was related to earlier protests that we saw at Port Elizabeth, where Africans had already conducted labor strikes in 1855 and during the 1880s. Analyses of the ICU point out that it, too, was rooted in economic and socioideological complaints because racial discrimination was a factor that influenced the African protest. Moreover, the pass campaign was tied to social and economic issues—much like the 1901 general strike—partly related to economics and wage labor and partly connected to ideological and social or civil rights. See Helen Bradford, *A Taste of Freedom: The ICU in Rural South Africa 1924–1930* (New Haven and London: Yale University Press, 1987); Shula Marks and Richard Rathbone, eds., *Industrialization and Social Change in South Africa: African class formation, culture and consciousness 1870–1930* (New York: Longman, 1982).

6. T. D. Verryn, "A History of the Order of Ethiopia" (unpub. mimeo, Johannesburg, 1962), AB484f, in the Church of the Province of South Africa Archive (CPSA) Cullen Library, University of the Witwatersrand, Braamfontein, South Africa; Walton R. Johnson, "The AME Church and Ethiopianism in South Africa," *Journal of Southern African Affairs* 3 (January 1978): 211–224; Chirenje, *Ethiopianism and Afro-Americans in Southern Africa, 1883–1916* (Baton Rouge: Louisiana State University, 1987); B.G.M. Sunkler, *Bantu Prophets in South Africa* (London: Oxford University Press, 1961, 2nd ed.).

7. Cape of Good Hope, Blue Book on Native Affairs (hereafter BBNA) 19 August 1903.

8. Cape Archives Depot (CAD), NA734, Part 1, estimates of expenditure for Native Reserve Location, year ending 30 June 1906. The formal title under the 1902 Act was Inspector; officials under the jurisdiction of two central government agencies administered the government in New Brighton. The Native Affairs Department appointed the Superintendent.

9. William Beinart and Colin Bundy, *Hidden Struggles in Rural South Africa* (London: James Currey, 1987)), Chap. 2 says that making use of African customs of

government and terminology but shaping them to fit their interests, the Cape colonial government established "indirect rule." In pre-colonial Nguni society, the smallest effective political unit was "the subdistrict or ward, under the control of a local headman." He was "usually appointed by the Chief, or at least confirmed by the chief, with the latter being the more usual since the office tended to be hereditary." Also, a similar system implemented in the rural areas, in such districts as Glen Grey, were now being transported to the urban areas. In the rural areas the power of the headman was more substantial, since there were fewer Europeans and the environment often promoted a peasant economy rather than a settler dominion. Nevertheless, headmen had the power to allocate land, to regulate religion, and to regulate the entry of strangers, states Isaac Schapera, The Bantu-Speaking Tribes of South Africa (London: Routledge and Kegan Paul, Ltd., 1937), p. 185.

10. Beinart and Bundy, Hidden Struggles, Chap. 2.

11. CAD, NA 635, Part I, B2196, J. A. Verschuur, ARM New Brighton location to SNA, Cape Town via C.C. 26 January 1904.

12. CAD, NTS178, 1177/14F435, Inquiry into Policing at New Brighton, 9,10 December 1919.

13. CAD, NA614, Part II, B1824 Verschuur, ARM, New Brighton to SNA, 16 June 1904. Also see same file Verschuur, ARM, Population return, September 1905 to 14 November 1905.

14. CAD, NTS178 1177/14F435, Police Inquiry, 9,10 December 1919.

15. CAD, NA614 Part II, B1824,F1, Verschuur, ARM to SNA, 16 July 1906; other information in the same file on wardsmen and native clerks at New Brighton for various dates covering 2 September 1903 to 26 July 1906. Also see Robin Hallett, "Policemen, Pimps and Prostitutes—and Police Corruption," Center for African Studies, University of Cape Town, Studies in the History of Cape Town, Christopher Saunders, ed., 1 (1984): 1–41.

16. CAD, NA614, Part II, B1824, ARM Verschuur, New Brighton to SNAD, E. Dower, 29 December 1905.

17. CAD, NA734, Part 1, 30 June 1906.

18. Davenport, "African Townsmen?," pp. 96, 100.

19. M. W. Swanson, "The 'Durban System': Roots of urban apartheid in colonial Natal," African Studies (1976): 159–176.

20. CAD, NA648,B2338, 30 June 1904. Return of outstanding, arrear, and irrecoverable revenue in the Port Elizabeth Native Location. Also unpaid were business stand rents of £27 and water rates of £11.6, for a sum of £908.3.6 covering the period June 1903 to June 1904.

21. CAD, NA607, Part II, B1678, ARM Verschuur, New Brighton to Asst. Treasurer, Cape Town, 31 July 1905.

22. BBNA, G28-1910.

23. BBNA, U17-1911.

24. CAD, NA607, B1677, ARM J. A. Verschuur, to SNAD, New Brighton Location, Irrecoverable Hut Rent, re. 12 August 1904.

25. CAD, NA649,B2338, 4 February 1905, ARM J. A. Verschuur, to SNAD, New Brighton Location. Inspector Dent testified before the Select Committee on the

Locations Act in 1903. See *1903 Select Committee Report*, 36–37. Also see letter, 9 January 1904, Inspector Dent, to ARM, CAD, NA614, Part II, B1824.

26. CAD, NA656, Part 1, ARM Verschuur, Return of population New Brighton Location, 21 September 1904.

27. CAD, NA607, B1678 Verschuur to SNAD, 19 Oct. 1904.

28. Similarly, at Cape Town Africans conscientiously refused to pay rent as a resistance tactic Christopher Saunders, "The Creation of Ndabeni, Urban Segregation and African Resistance in Cape Town," *Studies in the History of Cape Town*, University of Cape Town, Center of African Studies, 1 (1984): 165–193, see esp. 178–184.

29. CAD, NA597, B1524 Letter from Inspector W. H. Quirk to ARM New Brighton, 1 February 1905.

30. CAD, NA734, Part 1, F348, 11 August 1903, RM, Port Elizabeth to SNA Cape Town.

31. SANAC, V. 2, p. 482 #6266.

32. CAD, NA597,B1524, 27 July 1905, ARM Verschuur to RM to SNAD.

33. For example, Mayor Kemsley of Port Elizabeth stated that at Korsten "private [land] speculators have erected a number of tenement buildings in which natives herd together in an overcrowded and insanitary condition." CAD, NA597, Mayor J. C. Kemsley to SNAD, Compensation to Native Owners of Houses in the Municipal Locations, 4 May 1904.

34. South African Native Affairs Commission, 1903–1905, Report and Proceedings, V. 2, R. J. Dick testimony, #6267, p. 482.

35. "Vlei Post Tea Party," *EPH*, 21 November 1905. In another case at Vlei Post twenty-five Africans were charged; all but five were found guilty of residing illegally.

36. "Emslie's Location Outrage," *EPH*, 9, 25 November 1905; "Emslie's Location," *EPH*, 16 January 1906.

37. Gary Baines, "New Brighton, Port Elizabeth c. 1903–1953: A History of an Urban African Community" (Ph.D. diss., University of Cape Town, Cape Town, South Africa, 1994), p. 53; Central Archives—Pretoria (CAP) NTS 2442 1/291, SNA to Prime Minister, 14 February and Memo to Minister of Native Affairs, December 1910.

38. For Inspector W. H. Quirk's suggestion see CAD, NA597, B1524 Letter from Inspector W. H. Quirk to ARM, New Brighton, 1 February 1905; CAD, NA734, Part 1, F348, Edward Dower, SNA, Circular to all CC and RM and Detached ARM in the Colony Proper and to all RM in the Transkeian Territories—Absconders from Ndabeni and New Brighton Locations, 15 January 1908.

39. CAD, NA607 B1677, ARM J. A. Verschuur to SNAD, 12 August 1904.

40. MOH Report, G35-1904, p. 3.

41. "Zwartkops Shooting Fatality," *EPH*, 4 August 1901.

42. CAD, NAD, CC, PE to SNAD, Cape Town, 5 December 1905.

43. CAD, NA597, B1524, CC, P.E. to SNAD, 5 December 1905.

44. CAD, NA597, B1524, Acting General Mgr., of RR to SNAD, 21 July 1905.

45. CAD, NA734, Part 1, ARM B. Whitfield, NB to SNA, 1 October 1908, Part I, on Absconders from Native Reserve Location.

46. Ibid.

47. CAD, NA734, Part 1, F348, Report of a Public Meeting held in the Court Room at the New Brighton Location on 27 February 1911; NTS156, 6224/F348, Minutes of New Brighton Native Location Advisory Board, 12 October 1911. The conclusion that single people were adults raises a whole other set of questions with regard to cultural practices and beliefs about age, marriage, work, and the role of family members and African customs that cannot be addressed here. Nevertheless, it can be said that in many African societies a person was not considered an adult until he or she was married. Responsibilities to the family differed, and if someone were a family member, the administration may have expected that person to pay rent. But the families may have had other expectations about what the person's role should be, such as attending school. Also, it could be that the single men and women did not pay their rent if they resided with married people. That is because single individuals often sent their wages home to their families, where they intended to return.

48. Igor Kopytoff, ed., *The African Frontier: The Reproduction of Traditional African Societies* (Bloomington, Indiana: Indiana University Press, 1987), p. 27.

49. CAD, NA546, A802, Letter from Sgd. Joseph Newey, Chief Inspector of Public Works to Office of the Secretary for Public Works, 18 July 1902.

50. CAD, NA734, Part 1, B1677, J. A. Verschuur, ARM to SNAD, 13 November 1906. The actual draft regulations with regard to the aged parents declared that "no persons other than the wife of the registered holder of any lot held either under title or lease, or any of his children or any person dependent upon him for support shall be allowed to occupy any buildings on such lot without the permission of the Magistrate who may grant such permission in respect of any *bona fide* visitor free of charge, or in respect of any other person upon the payment of the rate for sanitary and other services."

51. Report of the Department of Native Affairs for the years 1913–1918, U.G. 7-1919. p. 18; Baines, "New Brighton, Port Elizabeth," p. 122. It is noteworthy that the practice of renting to lodgers at New Brighton was a violation of the original regulation, an indication that the law was unenforceable.

52. CAD, NA607, B1678, A. C. Allman, Acting Inspector of Native Locations at New Brighton to ARM New Brighton, 22 June 1903. The inspector also indicated that Africans complained about the partitions between the rooms in the Class C huts that do not extend to the roof and that the rooms are not sealed, so Class C huts were drafty.

53. CAD, NA597, B1524, petition dated 27 April 1904 and attached to letter from Town Clerk, Port Elizabeth to Dr. Jameson MLA, Premier, Cape Town. Also see, 3/PEZ, 1/2/1/14, petition dated 27 April 1904; Minutes of meeting re Korsten and Native Reserve Location amendment Act, 17 May 1904.

54. For discussion of family social relations see Schapera, *Bantu-Speaking Tribes*, pp. 70–82.

55. Isaac Schapera, *Western Civilization and the Natives of South Africa* (London: Routledge and Kegan Paul Ltd., 1967), pp. 15, 21.

56. D. H. Reader, *The Black Man's Portion* (Cape Town: Oxford University Press, 1961), pp. 140–141. Also see Alan Cobley, *Class and Consciousness: The Black Petty*

Bourgeoisie in South Africa, 1924–1950 (London; New York; and Westport, Connecticut, 1990), for a discussion of the extended family among the African middle class. p. 70. My own personal experiences in South Africa from 1981–1983 during my first fieldwork trip verify this hospitality. In fact, it was extremely difficult for me to find lodging because of the apartheid laws governing residence, such as the Group Areas Act. Because I judiciously avoided "international" hotels, I had to find room and board in the African townships. Many Africans opened their homes to me as an act of hospitality.

57. CAD, NA734, Part 1, F348 T.N.B. Miles to ARM New Brighton, 21 August 1908.

58. The other clause stipulated that "the plots are liable to confiscation in the event of intoxicating liquor being found on the premises." CAD, NA734, Part 1, ARM Verschuur to SNAD, 13 November 1906.

59. CAD, NA734, Part 1, F348, W. E. Stanford, SNA to ARM New Brighton, 19 December 1906. The stipulation with regard to aged parents was contained in Section 8 of the regulations.

60. CAD, NA734, Part 2, Memo of Conference held in CC office, PE, 28 July 1902. Whiley Pikoli had also been selected, but he was unable to attend.

61. Ibid.

62. "A Native Grievance-Deputation to the Council," *EPH*, 25 June 1903.

63. CAD, NA611, B1780 Letter from W. G. Cummings, SNAD, to Civil Commissioner, Port Elizabeth, 15 May 1903.

64. CAD, NA734, RM to SNAD 18 September 1902 (200) married couples. The sites would be alongside the location, and Africans could lease them for £4 per year and build their own houses The £4 would cover water supply, sanitation, medical treatment at the location hospital, and other miscellaneous services. NA611, 16 March 1904, Memo, SNA, Cummings to NAD.

65. Subsequently, in 1906 the same or another Tsewu moved to Johannesburg and in pursuit of freehold land ownership, that same year he sued the government and won.

66. CAD, NA611, W. J. Cummings, SNAD, Memo, 14 March 1904. For application and house plans, see CAD, NA611, B789 29 February 1904 and attachments.

67. CAD, NA734, Part 1, ARM to SNAD, 28 June 1905.

68. CAD, NA611, B780 1904, Memo, Cummings to NAD, 16 March 1904.

69. CAD, NA734, Part 1, Mr. Pyott, MLA, to Dower, and reply to Pyott from Dower dated 29 June 1905.

70. CAD, NA734,Part 1,F348, E. Dower to Pyott, MLA, 29 June 1905.

71. Michael O. West, "Pan-Africanism, Capitalism and Racial Uplift: The Rhetoric of African Business Formation in Colonial Zimbabwe," *African Affairs* 92 (April 1993): 263–283.

72. CAD, NA498, A96, *Christian Express*, 1 July 1898; During his visit in March 1898 to Capetown, Johannesburg, Pretoria, Queenstown and Bloemfontein, Turner ordained 31 elders and 29 deacons according to Walton R. Johnson, "The AME Church and Ethiopianism in South Africa," 212; For more on Turner see Josephus R. Coan "The Expansion of the Missions of the African Methodist Episcopal Church in South Africa, 1896–1908" (Ph.D. diss. Hartford Seminary Foundation, 1961).

73. Sylvia Jacobs, ed., *Black Americans and the Missionary Movement in Africa* (Westport, Connecticut: Greenwood Press, 1982). The providential design argument declared that Africans were enslaved and brought to the Americas so as to be converted to Christianity and rescued from their "heathenism." Then they were to return to Africa to Christianize their "heathen" brothers and sisters. Thus, many viewed slavery as a blessing in disguise and that in particular, African Americans were better equipped than Europeans to conduct missionary activities in Africa.

74. CAD, NA497,96, J. G. Sprigg, Prime Minister, 1 December 1901.

75. Some African congregations were independent from the old European denominations while others were not. That is, they retained the same church laws as the mission churches but were headed by an African minister. Carol Page in "Black Americans and the Missionary Movement in South Africa," pp. 177–195, points out that the AMEC and most of the black congregations supported British imperialism. See Jacobs, *Black Americans and the Missionary Movement*.

76. Jacobs, *Black Americans and the Missionary Movement*, p. 21.

77. Although Isaac Wauchope moved on to minister at Ft. Beaufort, Cape Colony, in the 1890s, several members of his family remained in Port Elizabeth.

78. CAD, 3/PEZ, 1/2/1/11, Report of Location Committee, 18 October 1901 and NA498,A96, Telegram from RM, PE to SNA, Cape Town 1 September 1902.

79. CAD, NA497,96, Sprigg Report, 2 December 1901; *South African Native Affairs Commission*, Testimony of Revd. James M. Dwane, November 12, 1903. (Cape Town: Government Printers 1904), v.2. pp. 708–716; Johnson, "The AME Church and Ethiopianism in South Africa," 211–224.

80. CAD, NA754, F243, A.F.F.S. Registrar, Department of Public Health, 28 January 1909. Yet another sect under I. G. Sishuba and H. R. Ngcayiya eventually left the AMEC to form the Ethiopian Church, reverting back to the 1893 position; Verryn, "A History of the Order of Ethiopia."

81. CAD, 3/PEZ 1/2/1/10, 17, Report of the Locations Committee, January 1901. His letter appeared in the 1 June 1899, *Voice of Missions;* cited in Cell, *The Highest Stage of White Supremacy* (Cambridge: Cambridge University Press), p. 45.

82. CAD, NA 527, Revd. Cox to CC Port Elizabeth, 18 June 1903.

83. "A Case that Failed," *Imvo*, 3 October 1905.

84. Ibid.

85. CAD, NA527, F516, Revd. S. W. Cox to C.C., Port Elizabeth, 23 June 1903; Dwane's church was subject to the constitution and canon of the English Anglican church, and the alliance proved less than beneficial to the Order of Ethiopia. At one point the Order of Ethiopia threatened to withdraw, particularly because Dwane was deprived of his headship. Eventually an agreement was reached, but the African clergy were unable to exercise the independence they had hoped for in allying with the Catholic church. See Church of the Province of South Africa (CPSA), AB652, Order of Ethiopia Records, 1902–10, Cullen Library, University of the Witwatersrand, Braamfontein, South Africa.

86. BBNA, G46-1906, p. 76.

87. CAD, NA734 Part 1, F348, B1677 James M. Dwane to J. H. Verschuur, ARM, New Brighton, 10 August 1905.

88. CAD, NA587, 1435, Acting CC, H. C. Becker to SNAD, Cape Town, 13 May 1905.

89. CAD, NA734, Part 1, James M. Dwane to ARM J. Verschuur, 10 August 1905. Dwane's idea for the Building Society fits the cooperative ideas associated with Booker T. Washington's self-help schemes, which we saw in Chapter 4 influence the establishment of the African and American Working Men's Union. In the United States African Americans had worked co-operatively in the 1870s to purchase and to construct housing. Similarly, land buying schemes in the Cape among Africans also occurred, e.g., in East London. See Cape of Good Hope, Report of a Departmental Commission on Occupation of Land by Natives in Unreserved Areas, G46-1908 (Cape Town: Government Printers, 1908).

90. CAD, Letter from James Dwane, New Brighton to J. Verschuur, Assistant R.M., 1 August 1905.

91. CAD, NA734, Part 1, B1677, Verschuur to the SNAD via the Acting CC, H. C. Becker, 16 August 1905.

92. CAD, NA734, Part 1, B1677, James M. Dwane, to RM, to Verschuur, 26 September 1905.

93. CAD, NA734, Part 1, B. Whitfield ARM, New Brighton to SNAD, Cape Town, 7 September 1908.

94. The total African population in 1903 was almost 13,000, but part of this number were Colored. This calculation is derived from comparing the 1903 census done by government officials to determine where Africans resided and how many would be moving into New Brighton and 1910, BBNA, Population of Port Elizabeth, 1911. (Also see Table 1.1 for total population of P.E. 1855–1911)

95. CAD, CCP11/1/44. Cape of Good Hope, List of Persons Residing in the Electoral Division of Port Elizabeth whose names have been registered in the Year 1903.

96. A. J. Christopher, "Race and Residence in Colonial Port Elizabeth," *South African Geographical Journal* 69 (1987): p. 16.

97. CAD, 3/PEZ 1/2/1/15 Minutes of the Meeting of the Reservoir Location Committee, 8 March 1909.

98. CAD, 3/PEZ, 6/1/1/1/269 List of Siteholders, Reservoir Location, 31 October 1909.

99. It is quite possible that there may be some discrepancy in the total figures for Africans and "Coloreds," given that some Africans were listed as "Coloreds" and various racial and social restraints influenced the census count. These included blacks who refused to be counted or who distorted the actual number of people occupying the houses, and white officials who distorted figures in an attempt to fulfill governmental expectations for segregation.

100. Christopher, "Race and Residence," p. 4.

101. Report of the Department of Native Affairs for the Years 1913–1918, U.G. 7–1919, p. 17; R. Packard, *White Plague, Black Labor: Tuberculosis and the Political Economy of Health and Disease in South Africa* (Berkeley; Los Angeles: University of California Press: 1989).

8

Conclusion

Since my arrival in Port Elizabeth a few weeks ago, I have heard a great deal of the question of the aboriginal natives residing within the urban district of Port Elizabeth and the dangers surrounding the condition of affairs. Of course, I have also noticed the abundance of these people promenading the streets . . . at night. In the report of the proceedings of the Town Council on Wednesday, I noticed several strong remarks were made in this connection. I do not know if the town council has any regulation which makes it necessary for the owner of a house to make sure that his tenant or prospective tenant is a person who is qualified to live in town, but if there is none, I should think that the making or passing of such a regulation would go far to limit the evil. The present state of affairs is undoubtedly not a pleasant one, and in fact, one that might end in causing trouble of some sort.[1]

As so often happens, a visitor's observations tell us much about the state of affairs, at least on the surface. The comments of this anonymous visitor in 1910, which appeared in the *Eastern Province Herald*, could have been made in 1855, the same year the Port Elizabeth local government established Strangers' location to house the African workers in a segregated settlement. Apparently from this visitor's point of view both the local and central government had been unsuccessful in ridding the town of the "dangerous natives." From his point of view this visitor was, of course, quite correct. The transition from African "strangers'"—a reference to Africans entering the colonial borders—to African workers who lived away in a segregated township was far from complete. So Africans still thronged the passageways and lived in several areas of the town, some of them alongside whites, but to a lesser extent. This was because segregationist legislation had not only reduced the housing and property options of Blacks but also their related political, economic, and social options. Consequently, it was a lot more hazardous for nonexempted Africans to live in the town, since by colonial law it was illegal and they could be fined and imprisoned. Nonetheless, Africans continued to avoid New Brighton housing at the risk of prosecution. In fact, on the same day that the visitor's letter appeared in the local newspaper, three African men were convicted of residing illegally in the town. Because they were not registered voters and thus not exempt from the Locations Act, they were sentenced to pay a fine of £3 or to spend one month in jail.[2]

The criminal convictions of the African men tell us not only that Africans contrived to avoid New Brighton but also that two other consistent obstacles to segregation continued to exist. The first obstacle was the slum landlords, white, black, or Asian, all of whom recklessly disregarded the Locations Act and continued to rent housing to nonexempted Africans. Africans wanting to avoid residing in segregated, controlled areas that curtailed their social and economic choices, to live closer to work, and to pay less rent found housing made available by landlords in several areas of the town.

From an economic standpoint these landlords fulfilled a housing need that the government seemed unable to meet, which brings us to the second obstacle. The second consistent obstacle was the government's inability to offer enough housing at New Brighton or other segregated areas to accommodate the nonexempted African population, which often led to temporary nonenforcement of the law. The criminal prosecutions would cease periodically until more housing was built at New Brighton and the Africans would "abscond" to restricted areas. Since there was a consistent lack of government-controlled, segregated housing available for African workers, the establishment of New Brighton, the erection of additional housing there, and even the formation of other townships in Port Elizabeth in the 1920s still failed to meet housing needs.

However, it was not only the lack of housing that affected the failure of the segregation initiative, it was also that many Africans preferred not to live in government-controlled, segregated locations, so that even when the housing was available, boycotts of especially ill-constructed single men's housing occurred.[3] Consequently, there were ongoing obstacles to the government's attempts to enforce residential segregation, not the least of these was the lack of available housing. So as numerous government officials pursued residential segregation, they were plagued by the same old problems: How to convince Africans to reside in the locations, how to control the landlord class, and what to do about the lack of financial allocation to enforce segregation. As we have seen, by 1910 about one-third of the New Brighton population was in arrears in paying their rent. Thus, the government's goal for the location to pay for itself was still unfulfilled.

Of course, some whites were simply not convinced that segregation was the way to solve the "native" problem. In particular, the European employers failed to obey the laws that forced their African laborers to reside far away from them. Many European employers, unable to comprehend giving up the comforts associated with live-in domestic service, preferred to have their domestic servants live on their private premises, so they applied for exemptions. These employers increased the number of Africans who were exempted from segregationist legislation. As we have seen, even large businesses preferred to establish their own housing compounds for their workers, for example, the Harbor Board, and this, too, undermined enforcement of the government regulations. Support for segregation came from a number of quarters: Local and central government health officials, some ministers who believed that segregation would protect the Africans from the less desirable white lifestyle, some town council members, some private homeowners, some merchants who wanted to better control their workforce, and land investors desirous of obtaining the land on which the municipal locations were situated.

Two related obstacles were the lack of police power to enforce the segregationist legislation and the lack of government willingness to foot the expensive segregation bill. Segregation costs were a lot higher than expected, and once this was realized and periodic economic recessions set in, and once the crisis that often precipitated government actions toward segregation had abated, there was a tendency to drift along without enforcing segregationist laws. For example, as the bubonic plague scare receded in Port Elizabeth in 1905 and Africans resisted entering New Brighton, the urgency to enforce segregation declined. Because Port Elizabeth's commercial capitalist economy did not expand rapidly compared to the fast-growing gold mining areas like Johannesburg, the urgency and support for segregation failed to sustain itself. Even when the auto and tire industry established American companies at Port Elizabeth and the African population increased rapidly in the mid-1920 and 1930s, strict segregationist enforcement failed to materialize for many of the reasons already discussed. These include the resistance of the African population to high rents and unfair laws and the unwillingness of government to invest the funds or effort to enforce the laws.

Meanwhile, the black middle class—those who were voters and property owners and their blood relatives—continued to be exempted from the Location Acts. So although it was clear that segregation had become the government policy, legal options to prescribed residential segregation still existed for a small number of Africans. But the political rights of the black middle class became increasingly restricted. In Port Elizabeth the 1908 elections, which were the last before Union, did little to enhance the position of Africans. In 1910 the establishment of the Union of South Africa increased the move toward segregation and white supremacist ideology. This was evident in the constitutional agreement before Union to exclude Africans from full participation in the political arena and the passage following Union of several discriminatory laws aimed at establishing white dominance and control.[4] In 1936 the small number of Cape Africans who retained the vote were struck off the rolls, effectively eliminating the right of Africans to vote until 1994.

Even though the 1902 (extended 1905) legislation was partially successful, was there still a major problem with controlling the natives? Doubtless, because almost from the beginning the African population, led by the aspirant black middle class, had resisted racially discriminatory legislation and the erosion of their civil rights. From Strangers' Location in 1855 to Korsten and New Brighton in 1903, and up to 1910, the Europeans created in their minds the mythology of white superiority and black superiority upon which they built the terminology of segregation. The colonial government passed and imposed racially discriminatory legislation. This legislation included residential segregation based on the assumption that residing in closer proximity to Africans would contaminate whites—economically, morally, physically, socially and psychologically. Many Africans, recognizing the segregationist aims of the government or "class" legislation, continually challenged those laws, because they were quite aware that their supposed inferiority was a falsehood. Therefore they saw no need to obey unjust laws despite the possibility of criminal prosecution.

The responses of the Africans to residential segregation initiatives varied according to class, gender, age, ethnicity, race, and geographical location. Members of the aspirant African middle class used petitions, voting, strikes, desertion, letters, meetings, organizations, and alliances with African Americans. Even the formation of independent African churches can be viewed as a response to white racism, since African ministers were being denied equality because many of the European missionaries who believed that the African clergy were not appropriately "civilized." Racial consciousness and community or family consciousness was personified in the 1901 general worker's strike that transcended class, ethnic, and gender background. At issue were rights that most people took for granted: the right to move about freely, the right to return home, and the work rotation system which was an important ingredient that had developed to assist African workers in slowing the process of becoming dependent on wage labor. Similarly, the participation of women in the 1901 strike exhibited family and race solidarity against racist legislation.

The government repeatedly attempted to develop a "native" policy of residential segregation while creating mechanisms to co-opt the emergent black middle class. Still, the vision of the black middle class of becoming land and property owners at New Brighton remained elusive. By 1910 the steady erosion of the Cape liberal alliance, which at one time counseled social upliftment through hard work and supported individual land ownership and the vote for "civilized" men, had adapted to the policies

tions before they are civilized," and he described the customs as devilish. Mvula's response was that "Mr. Thompson's seven years have taught him little or nothing of the native tribes and customs. Yet, like many others of his type, he poses as an authority." Mvula explained the significance of *intonjane,* the rite or ceremony which girls undergo before they can be chosen as wives. The rite is to wish the girls prosperity on entering into the state of womanhood. After further defending the African customs, Mvula concluded, "I boldly say there is no white man in the whole world who is an authority on the native question and who knows the real meaning of our rites, nor is there any who knows by reasons of his official knowledge of the (Act of Union), native races unless the man becomes a native, act like a native, think as a native, bear the burden as a native and then be born of European descent."[13]

Meanwhile, the 1923 Native Urban Areas Act, modeled on earlier colonial laws to prevent Africans from legally residing in urban areas was passed. It is significant that, with few exceptions, the Union government included all of these locally instituted segregationist practices in the 1923 Native Urban Areas Act, which aimed to establish a national policy of compulsory segregation for urban Africans. These included (1) influx/efflux control into the town and the location, (2) residential segregation, enforced through mandatory passes or badges that were tied to residence and employment (3) a prohibition on liquor, (4) criminal penalty for nonpayment of rent, and (5) establishment of advisory boards (to advise on local issues rather than voting in Parliamentary elections; Cape Africans retained the right to elect only white representatives to Parliament). Robin Bloch argues that the 1923 Act instituted five "principles" for urban native policy at a national level but these were evident in local laws long before 1923, as I argue in Chapter 7.[14] Another important change in the 1923 legislation was the provision for the establishment of a separate Native Revenue Account to finance the locations. As we have seen, prior to the passage of the Cape 1902 Act financing the state locations had provoked hot debate, since neither the municipalities nor the colonial government wanted to foot the bill. One other change worth noting is the exclusion of Europeans from owning land in the locations, thus opening the way for more Africans to run businesses. In fact, Africans in Port Elizabeth had long requested exclusive trading rights, but their requests had been ignored.

Perhaps the most significant change in the 1923 Act, at least from the standpoint of the African middle class and some white liberals was the decision by the national government to eliminate the freehold option in the segregated settlements. As we have seen, Cape liberalism was under attack from its opponents beginning in the 1880s, but there was still the belief among some whites that white supremacy could coexist alongside freehold rights among the "civilized," or advanced, Africans. On this issue of freehold continued ambivalence (because of the contradiction) is discernable as well in the extended debate about urban freehold for "advanced" Africans in the segregated locations envisioned by the government under the 1923 Urban Areas Act. It is noteworthy that the Act (initially proposed and drafted in 1918) was passed in response to a terrible influenza epidemic in 1918 that took thousands of lives nationwide.[15]

In any case, as Davenport illustrates with regard to the debate about freehold for Africans in urban areas, on one hand there were members of the Native Affairs Commission who in 1918 intended to "give Africans a stake in their locations ... by providing for the establishment of native villages where fixity of tenure can be secured and the Native may build his own house subject to the health and sanitary requirements of the local authority." On the other hand, the Transvaal Local Government Commission "was wedded to the dogma that 'the native should only be allowed to enter urban areas, which are essentially the White man's creation, when he is willing to enter and to minister to the needs of the White man, and should depart therefrom when he ceases to minister'."[16]

The same disagreements that split the emergent African middle class at Port Elizabeth and the local and central government with regard to freehold and segregation in the urban area now in 1923 drew the lines among the Committee members appointed to review the Bill. On the Native Affairs Commission to review the Bill was Dr. A. W. Roberts of Lovedale; General L. A. S. Lemmer from the Transvaal, previously Receiver of Revenue, and member of the Transvaal Legislative Assembly; and Dr. C. T. Loram, who had been Chief Inspector of Education in Natal. Both Roberts and Loram were known as "friends of the natives," in the Cape liberal tradition. And although they equivocated much like the Cape liberals, they were trying to balance between segregation and white supremacy while also protecting the rights of the "civilized" Africans to freehold landrights in urban areas. It is also significant that the Commissioners mentioned favorably what they called the "native" townships apart from the European city, where Africans held fixity of tenure (freehold land rights), including the one at Korsten. The Commissioners discussed and debated the issue for several months at official and unofficial meetings with whites and Africans. For example, a conference was held in May 1922 at Bloemfontein, Orange Free State that included members of the SANNC. Not surprisingly, they supported freehold in the segregated townships.[17]

When the Bill went to a Select Committee on February 14, the prospect for "native" villages and freehold tenure was still viable. By the time the clause emerged from the Select Committee on Native Affairs, the principle of "native" villages and individual title was rejected. Many people spoke in favor of land ownership in the urban areas for Africans, including H. Selby Msimang, representing the Johannesburg Joint Council, Dr. A. W. Roberts, and Dr. C. T. Loram.[18] The result was that after the 1923 Act was passed, freehold tenure was available to exempted Africans only in areas like Korsten, where they had been able to acquire land rights before Union.

Still, the history of African resistance to residential segregation influenced the way in which the local and central governments applied segregationist legislation. Thus, although New Brighton was incorporated into the Port Elizabeth Municipality (PEM) in 1923, the Urban Areas Act was not applied until ten years later. Until then New Brighton continued to be administered under the old system established by the 1902, amended 1905 legislation. The transfer from the Cape central government to the PEM was enabled by Act 49 of 1918. Among the reasons for the ten-year delay were financial concerns having to do with building further housing and improving some of the old, how to handle the freehold property owners and the system of beer-brewing (the administration feared protest, especially from the women), and in general the low priority accorded "native affairs." The association with women and beer-brewing is because this was continually a source of livelihood in the urban areas, as we have seen in earlier chapters.[19] It is clear, however, that not all African men and women at New Brighton or Korsten favored beer brewing or the use of hard alcohol, since there was always a Christian contingent that petitioned against the use of alcohol for both religious and social reasons. On the other hand, African women sent deputations to protest against the curbing and inappropriate application of the restrictions against beer-brewing in New Brighton. In any case, in 1933, when the Port Elizabeth city government took over administration and control of New Brighton, as other scholars have noted recently, even then the law was unenforceable until the 1950s. Domestic beer-brewing remained an option in contrast to the Durban system of a municipal monopoly that was more compatible with a migrant labor force rather than a permanent one as existed at Port Elizabeth.[20] Thus, although the laws mirrored the intentions of the local government at Port Elizabeth and in South Africa in general, the administration was not always able to make them stick.

As noted earlier, although by 1910 the Strangers' Location, Cooper's Kloof, and Reservoir municipal locations were destroyed and whites had taken over the land, residential segregation remained incomplete. Even with the application of the 1923 Native Urban Areas Act to New Brighton, Africans continued to "abscond" to Korsten, which was a constant reminder of the results of African resistance to and nonco-operation with government. Moreover, as an alternative residential site, Korsten still allowed more freedom than did New Brighton. This was true at Korsten despite the fact that portions of the settlement were overcrowded and unsanitary and the fact that Africans had failed to be elected to the board to manage their own affairs. Korsten, and other settlements where Africans lived outside of New Brighton, were concrete evidence of the ability of the African population to resist the government's discriminatory practices and to maintain their living space outside of the governmental sphere. Also, Korsten and the similar housing settlements served as evidence of the government's continued inability or unwillingness to provide adequate housing for African workers, the lack of strong police enforcement, and the weakness of administration.

Given these circumstances, it is not surprising that following the passage of the 1923 Act, Korsten drew closer scrutiny from the Port Elizabeth City Council and the central government. Official discussions about incorporating both New Brighton and Korsten into the city's boundaries led to indecision and subsequently postponement. When the idea of incorporating Korsten was first suggested in 1926 by the Port Elizabeth City Council, "the Secretary of the Port Elizabeth and District Vigilance Committee in Korsten wrote to the newspaper stating emphatically that their inclusion in Port Elizabeth would only be disadvantageous for them." F.H.M. Zwide stated in the letter that "The ignominious removal of the old locations—Russell, Strangers, Coopers' Kloof and Reservoir—is still fresh in the minds of the survivors of that gruelling time. The torturing methods for their removal will never be forgotten. . . . In plain words the people of Korsten do not in the light of past experience trust the Municipality."[21] Zwide's words exhibit the importance of memories of unjust treatment, and remind us why many Africans moved to Korsten in 1901 in the first place: because they had been forcefully evicted under the Public Health Act. Clearly those affected as well as their families and friends had not forgotten or forgiven how they been treated by the Port Elizabeth government. Such memories often provide the kernels that contribute to a tradition of resistance among an oppressed people and influence later actions.

The incorporation was delayed until 1931, seemingly until after some mutual agreement was reached between the Korsten Village Management Board or the residents and the local government. At this time its population was 21,300, 26 percent Colored, 64 percent Africans. Apparently about one thousand Korsten Africans owned their homes while thousands more rented. But again the government proved untrustworthy, and exactly what F. W. Zwide had feared if Korsten was incorporated into the city of Port Elizabeth occurred, the forced removal of Africans from Korsten to New Brighton. In 1936, using the Slums Act of 1934, which accorded the Port Elizabeth City Council enhanced powers to remove dwellings unfit for human habitation, nonexempted African residents of Korsten were forced to move to a segregated area, called Mc-

Namee Village, named for Mr. James Percival ('Paddy') McNamee, the Superintendent at New Brighton from 1926 to 1945.[22] One elderly black resident of New Brighton remembered that the government evicted Africans from Korsten on the grounds that it was unsanitary and that the bubonic plague had taken root. He stated that although the residents were removed, they were not paid for the value of their property, which left bitter feelings against the government.[23]

The removal experience of the Korsten Africans in 1936 was similar to that of their predecessors in the old municipal locations in the early 1900s, who also faced evictions and false promises. It was ironic that Korsten's population had initially become a burgeoning one as a consequence of the bubonic plague scare of 1901. Now that same health reason was being used to force many of the Korsten residents to live in McNamee Village. Bubonic plague did exist, and nineteen people died from it, but on this basis thousands of people were evicted and their homes and belongings destroyed. Despite this removal the Korsten population grew rapidly during and after World War II, back to over 21,000, partially because many Africans preferred to avoid the segregated areas controlled by the government and also because of the government's failure to enforce the separatist residential housing laws.[24]

The protests generating first from the municipal settlements for Africans in the 1880s, then from the townships, including New Brighton and from Korsten, represented the birth of a tradition of resistance to segregation. Vestiges of the tradition of resistance established in the early years of African settlement in Port Elizabeth were clearly evident in subsequent struggles as Africans challenged segregation and apartheid. The successive African leaders at Port Elizabeth, both men and women, who challenged segregation and apartheid through rent strikes, bus boycotts, school boycotts, and the trade union movement built on the groundwork already laid.[25] The highly politicized working class and middle class at Port Elizabeth doubtless owed something to the earlier generations who had fought against racial exploitation and residential segregation.

Notes

1. "Natives in the Town," *EPH*, 29 April 1910.

2. Ibid.

3. This was true for New Brighton and also in 1929 when new housing built for single black men was left empty because the rent was too high and the housing was uncomfortable.

4. For African opinion on the Act see "Resolution against the Natives Land Act of 1913 and the Report of the Natives Land Commission" by the South African

Native Congress, 2 October 1916, in *From Protest to Challenge*, 2 vols., edited by Thomas Karis and Gwendolen Carter (Stanford: Hoover Institution Press), vol. 1, p. 86.

5. A. Sangu, Interview, 1981, New Brighton; Cherry, "Blot on the Landscape and Center of Resistance" (honors thesis, University of Cape Town, 1988), p. 75.

6. "Labor Day Treat in Sport World," *Buffalo American*, 25 August 1921, for Kakaza; for the Garvey movement in South Africa see "Africa for the Africans: The Garvey Movement in South Africa, 1920–1940," by Robert A. Hill and Gregory A. Pirio, in *The Politics of Race, Class and Nationalism in Twentieth Century South Africa*, eds. Shula Marks and Stanley Trapido (London and New York: Longman, 1987): pp. 209–253. Hill and Pirio indicate that Kakaza was the President of the Buffalo division of the UNIA rather than only a member, but my source is unclear on this issue.

7. "Mr. T. Masiza Kakaza," *Imvo*, 27 May 1903. Translated by Peter Huna.

8. R. Hunt-Davis, Jr. "Black American Education Component in African Response to Colonialism in South Africa: c. 1890–1914," *Journal of Southern African Affairs* 3 (January 1978) 71–73 and Clements Keto, "Pre-Industrial Education Policies and Practices in South Africa," ed. Mokubung Nokomo, *Pedagogy of Domination* (Trenton: Africa World Press, 1990), p. 38, on AMEC missionaries in Cape Town promise to raise funds for higher education.

9. Gary Baines, "The Contradictions of Community Politics: The African Petty Bourgeoisie and the New Brighton Advisory Board, c. 1937–1952," *Journal of African History* 35 (1994): 79–97.

10. Andre Odendaal, *Black Protest Politics in South Africa to 1912* (New Jersey: Barnes and Noble, 1984), p. 82. Similarly, Dr. A. B. Xuma, a leading AMEC layman and president of the ANC in the 1940s, was married to an African American woman; T. D. Mweli Skota, *The African Yearly Register: Being an Illustrated Biographical Dictionary (Who's Who) of Black Folks in Africa* (Johannesburg: R. L. Eddon and Co., Ltd., 1931).

11. Cherry, "Blot on the Landscape," p. 23, for women's resistance at Korsten 86–87; CAD, 3/PEZ 1/724 Minutes of PECC, 3 December 1924, for women's temperance union.

12. Robin Bloch, "The High Cost of Living: The Port Elizabeth Disturbances of October 1920," *Africa Perspective* 19 (1982): 2–40; Gary Baines, "From Populism to Unionism: The Emergence and Nature of Port Elizabeth's Industrial and Commercial Workers' Union, 1918–1920," *Journal of Southern African Studies* 17 (1991): 679–716.

13. "Native Customs," *EPH*, Letter to Editor from Tobias Cekiso Mvula, 29 April 1910, written from Korsten.

14. *Statues of the Union of South Africa*, Native (Urban Areas) Act 21 of 1923 replaced by Act 25 of 1945; Robin Bloch and Peter Wilkinson, "Urban Control and Popular Struggle: A Survey of State Urban Policy, 1920–1930," *Africa Perspective* 20 (1982): 2–40; Rodney Davenport, "African Townsmen? South African Native (Urban Areas) Legislation Through the Years," *African Affairs* 68 (1969): 99. Davenport relates that although included in the 1902 legislation, influx/efflux control was enhanced "with the aid of strengthened pass machinery," p. 99. Also, unem-

ployed Africans could be deported from urban areas. For comparison with the Native Reserve Locations Act of 1902 see Chap. 7, note 4.

15. See Howard Phillips, "Black October: Cape Town and the Spanish Influenza Epidemic," *Studies in the History of Cape Town*, 1 (1984): 88–106 for an indication of its ravages.

16. T.R.H. Davenport, "The Beginnings of Urban Segregation in South Africa: The Native (Urban Areas) Act of 1923 and Its Background," *Institute of Social and Economic Research*, Rhodes University, Grahamstown, 1971," p. 13.

17. Davenport, "Beginnings of Urban Segregation," pp. 14–15; For evidence of C. T. Loram's liberal position towards education for Africans in South Africa see "Charles T. Loram and the American Model for African Education in South Africa," pp. 108–126, in *Apartheid and Education: The Education of Black South Africans* edited by Peter Kallaway (Johannesburg: Ravan Press, 1984).

18. Ibid., p. 18.

19. Report of the Native Affairs Department for the years 1913 to 1918, UG 7-1919, p. 18; CAD, 3/PEZ 1/724, Minutes of PECC, 3 December 1924.

20. CAD, 3/PEZ 1/724, Minutes of PECC, 3 December 1924. See Mayor's Minute, 1928, Annual Report of the Superintendent, New Brighton, pp. 93–94 for women and beer-brewing. Also Gary Baines, "New Brighton, Port Elizabeth c. 1903–1953: A History of An Urban African Community" (Ph.D. diss., University of Cape Town, 1994), pp. 124–146.

21. Jennifer Robinson, "The Power of Apartheid: Territoriality and State Power in South African Cities, Port Elizabeth 1923–1972" (Ph.D. diss., University of Cambridge, 1990), p. 203

22. Baines, "New Brighton, Port Elizabeth, c. 1903–1953," p. 84.

23. Mr. Sangu, Interview, 1981. Similar responses were offered by other Korsten residents. See Cherry, "Blot on the Landscape," pp. 52–56.

24. Cherry, "Blot on the Landscape," pp. 70–71.

25. Tom Lodge, *Black Politics in South Africa Since 1945* (Johannesburg, Ravan: 1983); Cherry, "Blot on the Landscape"; Janet Cherry, "The Making of An African Working Class: Port Elizabeth 1925 to 1963" (master's thesis, University of Cape Town, 1992); Baines, "New Brighton, Port Elizabeth," esp. Chap. 8; Jennifer Robinson, "The Power of Apartheid," esp. Chap. 7.

Selected Bibliography

Archival Sources

Cape Archives Depot, Cape Town
Official Records

Colonial Secretary Office (CO)
Native Affairs Department (NA)
Civil Commissioners and Resident Magistrates in the Colony: Miscellaneous letters received and other documents.
Civil Commissioners and Resident Magistrates Correspondence Files
Secretary for Native Affairs (SNA)
Medical Officer of Health (MOH)

Municipal Files

Town Clerk East London
Town Clerk Kingwilliamstown
Town Clerk Port Elizabeth
Miscellaneous Correspondence Files re Locations
Periodical Publication
Blue Book on Native Affairs
Cape Provincial Government Gazette
Justice Department files
Port Elizabeth Voters' List for the House of Assembly 1913
Port Elizabeth Town/City Council Publications
Mayor's Minutes
Municipal Commissions
Report on the Census
Report on Public Health
Yearbooks and Directories

Central Archives Depot, Pretoria

Native Affairs (NTS)

Other Archival Sources

Church of the Province of South Africa (CPSA) Department of Historical Papers, University of the Witwatersrand, Braamfontein

Order of Ethiopia Records, 1907–1912, AB652

Verryn, Trevor David, "A History of the Order of Ethiopia" (mimeo, 1962) AB484f

African Studies Institute (now Institute for Social and Economic Studies), Oral Collection and Miscellaneous Manuscripts, University of the Witwatersrand, Senate House

Union Government

Blue Book on Native Affairs for 1910 (Cape Colony)

Report of the 1911 Census

Report of the Native Affairs Department for 1911

Report of the Native Affairs Department for 1912

Report of the Native Affairs Department for the years 1913 to 1918

Report of the Native Affairs Department for the years 1919 to 1921

Report of the Economic and Wage Commission of 1932

Tuberculosis Commission Report, U.G. 34-1914

Cape Province

Select Committee Reports

G4–1883 Report and Proceedings with appendices of the Government Commission on Native Laws and Customs, Cape of Good Hope Blue Book, rpt. (Cape Town, C. Struik), 1968).

A28-1883 Report of the Select Committee on the Port Elizabeth Strangers' Location Bill

A9-1897 Report of the Select Committee on the Port Elizabeth Act Amendment Bill

A22-1902 Report of the Select Committee on the Native Reserve Locations Bill

A15-1903 Report of the Select Committee on the Native Reserve Locations Act 40 of 1902

A10-1906 Select Committee on the Poor White Question

G8-1898 Report on Redistribution of Seats Commission 1897–98

G48-1908 Report of a Departmental Commission on Occupation of Land by Natives in Unreserved Areas

Intercolonial

Report of the South African Native Affairs Commission, 1903–1905

Newspapers

Cape Times

Eastern Province Herald

Cape Daily Telegraph (later the Port Elizabeth Weekly Telegraph)

Imvo Zabantsundu

Izwi Labantu

Published Sources

Selected Articles and Books

Atkins, K.E. "Origins of the Amawasha: The Zulu Washermen's Guild in Natal, 1850–1910." *Journal of African History* 27 (1988): 41–57.

_____. "'Kafir Time': Preindustrial Temporal Concepts and Labor Discipline in Nineteenth Century Colonial Natal." *Journal of African History* 29 (1988): 229–244.

_____. *The Moon is Dead! Give Us Our Money!: The Cultural Origins of an African Work Ethic, Natal, South Africa, 1843–1900.* Portsmouth, New Hampshire: Heinemann, 1993.

Baines, G. "The Administration and Control of Port Elizabeth's African Population, c. 1834–1923." *Contree* 26 (1989): 13–21.

_____. "The Origins of Urban Segregation: Local Government and the Residence of Africans in Port Elizabeth, c. 1835–1865," *South African Historical Journal* 22 (1990): 61–81.

_____. "From Populism to Unionism: The Emergence and Nature of Port Elizabeth's Industrial and Commercial Workers' Union, 1918–1920." *Journal of Southern African Studies* 17 (1991): 679–716.

_____. "The Contradictions of Community Politics: The African Petty Bourgeoisie and the New Brighton Advisory Board, c. 1937–1952." *Journal of African History* 35 (1994): 79–97.

Beinart, W. & C. Bundy. *Hidden Struggles in Rural South Africa.* Johannesburg: Ravan Press, 1987.

Biddiss, M D. ed., *Images of Race.* New York: Holmes and Meier Publishers, Inc., 1979.

Bloch, R. and P. Wilkinson. "Urban Control and Popular Struggle: A Survey of state urban policy, 1920–1970." *Africa Perspective* 19 (1981): 39–59.

Bonner, P. *Holding Their Ground: Class, Locality and Culture in 19th and 29th Century South Africa.* Johannesburg: Ravan Press, 1989.

Bonner, P. "The Transvaal Native Congress 1917–1920." in Marks, S. and R. Rathbone, eds., *Industrialization and Social Change Essays on African Class Formation, Culture and Consciousness, 1870–1930.* New York: Longman, 1982. pp. 270–313.

Bozzoli, B. compiler. *Labor, Townships and Protest: Studies in the Social History of the Witwatersrand.* Johannesburg: Ravan Press, 1979.

Bradford, Helen. *A Taste of Freedom: The ICU in Rural South Africa, 1924–1930.* New Haven: Yale University Press, 1987.

Bundy, C. *The Rise and Fall of the South African Peasantry.* Berkeley: University of California Press, 1979.

Butler, J. and R. Elphick and D. Welsh, eds., *Democratic Liberalism in South Africa.* Claremont, South Africa: David Philip, distributed by Harper and Row: Scranton, 1987.

Cell, John. *The Highest Stage of White Supremacy: the Origins of Segregation in South Africa and the American South.* Cambridge: Cambridge University Press, 1982.

Chirenje, J.M. *Ethiopianism and Afro-Americans in Southern Africa, 1883–1916.* Baton Rouge: Louisiana State University Press, 1987.

Christopher, A.J. "Race and Residence in Colonial Port Elizabeth." *South African Geographical Journal* 69 (1987): 3–20.

_____. "Formal Segregation and population distribution in Port Elizabeth." *Contree* 24 (September 1988): 5–12.

Cobley, A. *Class and Consciousness: The Black Petty Bourgeoisie in South Africa, 1924–1950.* New York; London: Greenwood Press, 1990.

Cooper, Frederick. *Struggle for the City: Migrant Labor, Capital, and the State in Urban Africa.* Beverley Hills and London: Sage Publications, 1983.

Crais, C. *White Supremacy and Black Resistance in Pre-industrial South Africa*. New York: Cambridge, 1992.

Curtin, P. *Images of Africa*. Madison: University of Wisconsin Press, 1964.

Davenport, T.R.H. "African Townsmen? South African Natives (Urban Areas) Legislation through the Years." *African Affairs* 68 (1969): 95–109.

_____. and K.S. Hunt, eds. *The Right to the Land*. Cape Town: David Philip, 1974.

Dean, H. *The Pedro Gorino: The Adventures of a Negro Sea Captain in Africa and on the Seven Seas in his Attempt to found an Ethiopian Empire*. New York: Houghton and Mifflin, 1929.

Dubow, S. *Scientific Racism in Modern South Africa*. Cambridge: Cambridge University Press, 1995.

Elphick, R. and Hermann Giliomee, eds. *The Shaping of South African Society, 1652–1840*. Middletown, Connecticut: Wesleyan University Press, 1989.

Erlmann, Veit. "A Feeling of Prejudice: Orpheus M. McAdoo and the Virginia Jubilee Singers in South Africa, 1890–1898," *Journal of Southern African Studies* 14 (1988): 331–350.

Esedebe, P. *Pan-Africanism: The Idea and Movement, 1776–1963*. Washington: Howard University Press, 1982.

Gaitskell, Deborah. "Housewives, Maids or Mothers: Some Contradictions of Domesticity for Christian Women in Johannesburg, 1903–1930." *Journal of African History* 24 (1983): 241–256.

Harlan, L.R. *Booker T. Washington: The Making of a Black Leader, 1856–1901*. New York: Oxford University Press, 1972.

Hunt-Davis, R. "The Black American Education Component in African Responses to Colonialism in South: (ca. 1890–1914)." *Journal of Southern African Affairs* 3 (1978): 65–83.

Inggs, E.J. "Mfengu Beach Labor and Port Elizabeth Harbor Development, 1835–1870." *Contree* 21 (1987) 5–12.

Jacobs, S. *Black Americans and the Missionaries in Africa*. New York and Westport, Connecticut: Greenwood Press, 1982.

Jones, G. *Social Darwinism and English Thought: The Interaction between Biological and Social Theory*. New Jersey: Humanities Press, 1980.

Jordan, W. *White Over Black: American Attitudes Toward the Negro 1550–1812*. Baltimore: Penguin Books, 1969.

Keto, C. "Black Americans and South Africa, 1890–1910." *A Current Bibliography on African Affairs* 5 (1972): 383-406.

Kirk, J. "A 'Native' Free State at Korsten: Challenges to Segregation in Port Elizabeth, 1901–1905." *Journal of Southern African Studies* 17 (1991): 309–336.

_____. "Race, Class, Liberalism and Segregation: The 1883 Native Strangers' Location Bill in Port Elizabeth, South Africa." *International Journal of African Historical Studies* 24 (1991): 293–321.

_____. "Black Americans, Pan-Africanism and Economic Uplift in South Africa in the Nineteenth Century." *Paths Toward the Past: African Historical Essays in Honor of Jan Vansina*. Edited by Robert W. Harms, Joseph C. Miller, David S. Newbury and Michele D. Wagner. Atlanta, GA. African Studies Association Press, 1994, pp. 325–344.

Kopytoff, I. ed., *The African Frontier: The Reproduction of Traditional African Societies*. Bloomington, Indiana: Indiana University Press, 1987.

Lauren, P.G. *The Politics and Diplomacy of Racial Discrimination.* Boulder: Westview Press, 1995.

Lewsen, P. "The Cape Liberal Tradition—Myth or Reality?" University of London *Institute of Commonwealth Studies,* Collected Seminar Papers on the Societies of Southern Africa in the 19th and 20th Centuries, 1 (1969-1970): pp. 71–84.

Lodge, T. *Black Politics in South Africa since 1945.* New York: Longman, 1983.

Mabin, A. "The Rise and Decline of Port Elizabeth, 1850–1900." *International Journal of African Historical Studies.* 19 (1986): 275–301.

_____. "Labor, Capital, Class Struggle and the Origins of Residential Segregation in Kimberley, 1880—1920." *Journal of Historical Geography* 12 (1986): 4–26.

Marable, M. "Booker T. Washington and African Nationalism." *Phylon* 35 (1974): 398–406.

Marks, S. and A. Atmore, eds., *Economy and Society in Pre-Industrial South Africa.* London: Longman, 1980.

_____. and R. Rathbone, eds., *Industrialization and Social Change in South Africa: Essays on African Class Formation, Culture and Consciousness, 1870–1930.* Longman: London and New York, 1963.

_____. and S. Trapido, eds., *The Politics of Race, Class and Nationalism in Twentieth Century South Africa.* London and New York: Longman, 1987.

Martin, Tony. *The Pan-African Connection: From Slavery to Garvey and Beyond.* Dover, Massachusetts: The Majority Press, 1983.

Massey, D. and N. Denton, eds., *American Apartheid: Segregation and the Making of the Underclass.* Cambridge: Harvard University Press, 1993.

Mayer, P. *Townsmen or Tribesmen.* Cape Town: Oxford University Press, 1961.

Morrison, Toni. "Unspeakable Things Unspoken: The Afro-American Presence in American Literature." *Michigan Quarterly Review* (Winter, 1989): 1–34.

Odendaal, A. *Black Protest Politics in South to 1912.* New Jersey: Barnes and Noble, 1984.

Pauw, B.A. *The Second Generation.* Cape Town: Oxford University Press, 1963.

Peires, J. *The Dead Will Arise: Nongqawuse and the Great Xhosa Cattle-Killing Movement of 1856–7.* Johannesburg: Ravan Press; Bloomington, Indiana University Press, 1989.

Reader, D.H. *The Black Man's Portion.* Cape Town: Oxford University Press, 1961.

Redgrave, J.J. *Port Elizabeth in Bygone Days.* Wynberg, Cape: Rustica Press, 1947.

Richards, D. "The Ideology of European Dominance." *Western Journal of Black Studies* 3 (1979): 244–250.

Rich, P. "Ministering to the White Man's Needs: the Development of Urban Segregation in South Africa, 1913-1920." *African Studies* 37 (1978): 177–191.

Saunders, C. "The Creation of Ndabeni and African Resistance in Cape Town." *Studies in the History of Cape Town.* 1 (1984 rpt): 165–193.

Schapera, I. *The Bantu-Speaking Tribes of South Africa, an Ethnographical Survey.* London: Routledge and Kegan Paul Ltd., 5th Impression, 1956.

_____. ed., *Western Civilization and the Natives of South Africa: Studies in Culture Contact.* London: Routledge & Kegan Paul Ltd. 1967.

Schmidt, E. "Race, Sex, and Domestic Labor: The Question of African Female Servants in Southern Rhodesia, 1900–1939." *African Encounters with Domesticity* edited by Karen Hansen, New Brunswick, New Jersey: Rutgers University Press, 1992.

Skota, T.D. Mweli. *The African Yearly Register: Being an Illustrated Biographical Dictionary (Who's Who) of Black Folks in Africa.* Johannesburg: R.L. Eddon and Co., Ltd., 1931.

Stephan, N. *The Idea of Race in Science.* Ithaca: Cornell University Press, 1991.

Sudarkasa, Niara. "The Status of Women in African Societies." in *Women in Africa and the African Diaspora,* eds. R. Terborg-Penn, et al. Washington: Howard University Press, 1987, pp. 24–35.

Swanson, M. "The Durban System: Roots of Urban Apartheid in the Cape Colony, 1900–1909." *African Affairs* 35 (1976): 159–176.

_____. "The Sanitation Syndrome: Bubonic Plague and Urban Native Policy in the Cape Colony: 1900–1908." *Journal of African History* 18 (1977): 387–410.

_____. "The Asiatic Menace, Creating Segregation in Durban, 1870–1900." *International Journal of African Historical Studies* 16 (1983): 181–205.

Switzer, L. *Power and Resistance in an African Society: The Ciskei Xhosa and the Making of South Africa.* Madison: University of Wisconsin Press, 1993.

Terborg-Penn, R. and S. Harley and A. Benton Rushings, eds., *Women in Africa and the African Diaspora.* Washington: Howard University Press, 1987.

Trapido, S. "The Friends of the 'Natives': Merchants, Peasants, and the Political and Ideological Structure of Liberalism in the Cape, 1854–1910," 247–274 in S. Marks and A. Atmore, eds., *Economy and Society* in Pre-Industrial South Africa. London: Longman, 1980.

Van der Horst, S. *Native Labor in South Africa.* London: Oxford University Press, 1942.

Van Heningen, E. "Cape Town and the Plague of 1901." *Studies in the History of Cape Town* 4 (1981): 68–74.

Walker, C. *Women and Gender in Southern Africa to 1945.* Cape Town: David Philip, 1990.

Walters, R. W. *Pan Africanism in the African Diaspora: An Analysis of Modern Afrocentric Political Movements.* Detroit: Wayne State University Press, 1993.

Wells, J. "Why Women Rebel: A Comparative Study of South African Women's Resistance in Bloemfontein (1913) and Johannesburg (1958)." *Journal of Southern African Studies* 10 (1983): 55–70.

West, M. "Pan-Africanism, Capitalism and Racial Uplift: The Rhetoric of African Business Formation in Colonial Zimbabwe." *African Affairs* 92 (1993): 263–283.

Williams, G.W. The *History of the Negro Race in America from 1619–1880.* New York: G.P. Putnam's Sons, 1882.

Unpublished Theses

Baines, G. "New Brighton, Port Elizabeth c. 1903–1953: A History of an Urban African Community." Ph.D. diss., University of Cape Town, 1994.

Boddington, E. "Domestic Service: Changing Relations of Class Domination 1841–1948, A Focus on Cape Town." masters of social science, University of Cape Town, 1983.

Cherry, J. "Blot on the Landscape and Center of Resistance." honor's thesis, University of Cape Town, 1988.

Cherry, J. "The Making of an African Working Class: Port Elizabeth 1925 to 1963." master's thesis, University of Cape Town, 1992.

Kagan, N. "African Settlements in the Johannesburg Area, 1902–1923." master's thesis, University of the Witwatersrand, 1978.

Kirk, J. "The African Middle Class, Cape Liberalism and Resistance to Residential Segregation at Port Elizabeth, 1880–1910." Ph.D. diss., University of Wisconsin-Madison, 1987.

Mabin, A. "The Making of Colonial Capitalism: Intensification and expansion in the economic geographpy of the Cape Colony, 1854–1899." Ph.D. diss., Simon Fraser University, 1976.

Odendaal, A. "African Political Mobilization in the Eastern Cape, 1880–1910." Ph.D. University of Cambridge, 1983.

Robinson, J. "The Power of Apartheid: Territoriality and State Power in South African Cities, Port Elizabeth 1923-1972." Ph.D. diss., Cambridge University, 1990.

Interview

Interviews in English and Xhosa by the author and Interpreter: Nosipho
A. Sangu. New Brighton, 1981
G. Pemba, New Brighton, 1988
H. Nyati, New Brighton, 1988

Newspaper Translations

Imvo Zabantsundu from Xhosa to English by:
C.B. Bosiki
Peter Huna
Z.K. Kwinana
T. Mda
M. Ntwasa

Index

321